CONTENTS

DIRECTORY OF WORLD CINEMA
AUSTRALIA & NEW ZEALAND

Volume 3

DIRECTORY OF WORLD CINEMA AUSTRALIA & NEW ZEALAND

Edited by Ben Goldsmith and Geoff Lealand

intellect Bristol, UK / Chicago, USA

First Published in the UK in 2010 by Intellect Books, The Mill, Parnall Road, Fishponds, Bristol, BS16 3JG, UK

First published in the USA in 2010 by Intellect Books, The University of Chicago Press, 1427 E. 60th Street, Chicago, IL 60637, USA

A catalogue record for this book is available from the British Library.

Publisher: May Yao
Publishing Assistant: Melanie Marshall

Cover photo: Keisha Castle-Hughes in *Whale Rider*, 2000, New Zealand Film Comm.

Cover Design: Holly Rose
Copy Editor: Heather Owen
Typesetting: Mac Style, Beverley, E. Yorkshire

Directory of World Cinema ISSN 2040-7971
Directory of World Cinema eISSN 2040-798X

Directory of World Cinema: Australia & New Zealand ISBN 978-1-84150-373-8
Directory of World Cinema: Australia & New Zealand eISBN 978-1-84150-342-4

Printed and bound by Gutenberg Press, Malta.

ACKNOWLEDGEMENTS

This book would not have ɔeen possible without the assistance and support of a large number of people Our sincere thanks go to the editorial staff at Intellect and in particular May Yao, Jennifer Schivas and Melanie Marshall. We would also like to thank John Berra for his advice at the outset of this project. Thanks to John Hughes and Melinda Robertson for help in sourcing the image of Cecil Holmes. Ben Goldsmith would like to express his profound love and gratitude to his long-suffering famil⋏ Elizabeth, Eloise and Sam. Geoff Lealand would like to especially thank Ben Goldsmith for his help in navigating a way through the early stages of this joint project, as well as thanking all the New Zealand and Australian authcrs who ccntributed to this first important volume.

Ben Goldsmith and Geoff Lealand

Next page: *Caterpillar Wish*, Beat Fx.

AUSTRALIA

INTRODUCTION: AUSTRALIAN CINEMA BEN GOLDSMITH

Film-making in Australia has a long and distinguished history, dating back to October 1896 when a French chemist, agent of Lumière et Compagnie, and trained operator of the Lumière cinematographe, Marius Sestier, filmed passengers alighting from a ferry at Manly, Sydney. The following month, Sestier shot thirteen films at Flemington racecourse, including the first footage of the 'race that stops the nation', the Melbourne Cup horse race. The interest in this event and the fabled Australian love of sport prompted four different teams of film-makers to film the Cup the following year. Despite this early interest in documenting Australian sporting life – other early films included footage of the touring English cricket team – with only a few notable exceptions, sports films have not achieved a prominent place in the Australian film pantheon. Short films, by contrast, have remained an important component of film-making in Australia, even during the long fallow period in feature film production from the end of the Second World War to the early 1970s when short films produced by avant-garde and experimental film-makers like the Cantrills and the Ubu Films group were virtually the only forms of local film production. The short form has grown in importance since the introduction of state support for film-making in the late 1960s and early 1970s, and especially since the creation of the Australian Film and Television School (now the Australian Film, Television and Radio School) in 1973. Short films have been the principal mode of production at the national film school since its foundation, as they were at the Swinburne Film School, at Swinburne's successor the Victorian College of the Arts and most of the other training institutions that have been set up over the last four decades, with many of the most prominent Australian film-makers learning and honing their craft in the short form. Today, several hundred short documentaries and fiction films, both live-action and animated, are made in Australia each year, most of which are screened at one or more of the 60 film festivals devoted to shorts that run here annually. As Lisa French observes in her essay on short films in this volume, short film-making is a fertile and diverse form of Australian production, with practitioners winning awards and acclaim at all major festivals and ceremonies around the world in recent years. Like the other genres and groups of films high-lighted in this volume, Australian short films are often hybrids and do not always fit neatly into a single genre category.

For the next decade and more after Marius Sestier's first films were screened, 'going to the pictures' in Australia meant, as it did in the United States and in Europe, going to see a programme of short films, typically a mixture of actualities and 'trick' films. Within a few years, various cycles or groups of films sharing themes, settings, and eventually narrative and dramatic arcs, began to appear. The Salvation Army, the most important institution in film production in Australia at the turn of the twentieth century, produced a series of short religious-themed films for their touring illustrated lecture shows. For these multimedia extravaganzas – *Social Salvation* (1899), and *Soldiers of the Cross* (1900) – the Army's film-making branch, the Limelight Department under the direction of Joseph Perry, restaged events such as the burning of Christian martyrs and the drowning of Bishop Calepodius in a glass-walled studio in the centre of Melbourne and in a local swimming pool (Long & Sowry 1994: 65). In 1902 the Department made *Under Southern Skies*, a dramatization of Australian history from Captain Cook's voyages of discovery in the 1770s to Federation which contained filmed segments amounting to an astonishing 100 minutes (Long,1995a: 54). The Limelight Department also produced the first Australian long-form documentary films, including the official record of the ceremonies of national foundation, *The Inauguration of the Commonwealth of Australia* (1901). Australian film-makers have been both burdened and empowered by the national frame through which their work has been viewed ever since. More than any other art form or media, film in Australia has been the site of vigorous contest over the representation of national and colonial history, over Australia's international cultural and industrial relations, and over the constitution of national identity. The idea of the 'national type' was explored and created by film-makers from an early date, and films featuring local settings, subjects and stories found a ready audience, whose enthusiasm inflated Australian cinema's first boom in the years before the World War I.

Perhaps the first Australian film (sub)genre, meaning a type and group of films which originated in Australia rather than drawing on international precedents and examples, was the group of historical films made between 1906 and 1914 about the fictional and documented exploits of Australian bushrangers or outlaws. These films are, as Ramon Lobato notes in his essay in this volume on Australian crime films, a subset of the broader crime genre. They merit a distinct entry because of their numerical significance in the early years of the twentieth century, and because of the importance of one film in particular: the Tait brothers' *The Story of the Kelly Gang* (1906). Although this was not the first Australian film with a bush-ranger theme (that honour probably goes to the Limelight Department's Joseph Perry who made *Bushranging in North Queensland* in 1904), *The Story of the Kelly Gang* is universally acknowledged as the most significant bushranger film, and the most important Australian film of this early period. It '[set] the pattern for the bushranger films to follow', and was by no means simply an imitation of the early American western (Bertrand and Routt 2007: 61). The *Story of the Kelly Gang* is an extraordinary enigma, a landmark film and a remarkable piece of the international jigsaw that is the early history of cinema. In 2007, 101 years after it was made, the film was put on UNESCO's Memory of the World register of internationally-significant documents alongside the Bayeux Tapestry, the Rigveda, and the archive of Ingmar Bergman. The film was not quite 'the world's first feature length film,' as inscribed in the register, since longer, multi-reel films of boxing matches running up to 100 minutes, passion plays, and films of important national events like the 1901 royal visit were not uncommon at this time. Rather, its importance lies principally in the fact that, at 67 minutes, it was the longest narrative film made anywhere in the world to that date. Although popular, narrative cinema was still very much in its infancy in 1906, and virtually all story films produced anywhere in the world at this time were less than ten minutes long (Bertrand & Routt 2007: 15). It would be another ten years before narrative films the length of *The Story of the Kelly Gang* became standard cinematic fare in the larger American and European film industries. In addition to its length, the film is significant for its use of the pan – the sideways turn of the camera now commonplace, but previously difficult to perform steadily with cameras of the time. And it is hugely significant because fragments of the film still exist. As with 90 per cent of Australia's silent film heritage, much of the film is now lost, although the discovery of footage in the British Film Institute archive in 2006 means that 17 minutes of the film have now survived the ravages of time. The film clearly influenced contemporary film-makers, and not only in subject matter as multi-reel films became more common in the years after 1906.

While the bushranger films featured themes and iconography similar to the American 'western', which was also emerging at this time, the bushranger film and the western developed separately and should be considered as distinct tendencies. William D Routt (2001) makes this argument powerfully, observing that despite parallels in historical setting and the shared frontier location, and notwithstanding the 'rough coincidence between the heyday of the bushranger film (1906–1911) and what Ed Buscombe (1988: 25) has called 'the crucial formative years' of the American Western (1903–1913)', it is difficult to sustain the proposition that one form had a direct influence on the other. Approximately a quarter of films made in Australia between 1906 and 1912 featured the exploits of infamous bushrangers like Ned Kelly, Ben Hall, John Vane and 'Captain Thunderbolt', and several films were based on Rolf Boldrewood's 1888 bushranger novel *Robbery Under Arms* (Routt 2001). *The Story of the Kelly Gang* was remade in 1910, while police in Victoria prevented another version from going into production two years later. Throughout this period, politicians, police and moral crusaders worried over the effects of such films, which not only often depicted successful criminal activity but also usually portrayed the police negatively: the *Bulletin* magazine reported in May 1907 that the Victorian government had moved to ban screenings of the 1906 film in 'Kelly country' (the area of Victoria where the gang had been active), and eventually all screenings of films about bushranging were banned in New South Wales and Victoria in 1912.

As Stephen Gaunson describes in his essay in this volume on the bushranger film, while some film-makers tried to circumvent the intervention of state censors, producers' enthusiasm for the bushranger film waned after 1912. While the bans remained in place until the 1940s, some films with bushranging themes were passed by the censors if they portrayed the bushrangers as criminals and the police and judicial system in a positive light. Over the years, various film-makers have revisited the genre with varying degrees of success. British director Tony Richardson's 1970 version of the Ned Kelly story, which starred Mick

Jagger, was critically derided and largely ignored by audiences, while Philippe Mora's 1974 film *Mad Dog Morgan* is notorious for the extraordinary behaviour of lead actor Dennis Hopper during production. More recently, comedian Yahoo Serious's first film *Reckless Kelly* (1993) achieved some success by updating the Kelly gang mythology to the present day.

The censorship of the bushranger cycle of films was an expression of rising concerns from a diverse range of community groups and organizations about the social and cultural impact of film. Censorship also presented an opportunity to shape the popular image of Australia on screen – a task which was undertaken with gusto following the outbreak of the First World War. Film scenarios had to be passed by state censorship boards, while new federal agencies were established during the War to censor imported films. The War provided the inspiration for a new cycle of Australian films; thirteen war-themed films met the censors' expectations and were released between November 1914 and May 1916. The films, known as 'patriotics', have been credited with boosting enlistment in the armed forces. They were modelled, at least initially, on war films produced in Britain, with storylines featuring 'spies, rapacious Huns and upper-class Britons', as Daniel Reynaud describes in his essay in this volume on Australian war films. Other films depicted key campaigns or engagements involving Australians, including *The Hero of the Dardanelles* (Alfred Rolfe, 1915) and *Within Our Gates, or Deeds that Won Gallipoli* (Frank Harvey, 1915) about the Australian 'baptism of fire' at Gallipoli, and *How We Beat the Emden* (Alfred Rolfe, 1915) about the sea battle between HMAS *Sydney* and the German warship SMS *Emden* near the Cocos Islands in November 1914. Other films sought to exploit popular fears about German spy rings operating in Australia (*For Australia*, Monte Luke, 1915) and paranoia about a potential German invasion of Australia (*If the Huns Came to Melbourne*, George Coates, 1916). In part because of a public campaign during the war which characterized cinema-going as frivolous and unnecessarily extravagant, and in part because attitudes to the war effort and to the style of film which borrowed heavily from British war narratives and which 'typically also copied the intense patriotism of the British Empire and the current Social Darwinist beliefs about the superiority of the British race' were changing, their popularity declined for the remainder of the war (Reynaud 2005: 4). After the war, the figure of the Anzac became a contested symbol, particularly in the 1920s and 1930s:

> officialdom and Empire loyalists wished to celebrate the war in conservative terms as a great national-imperial success championing the loyal Anzac; many returned soldiers were disillusioned with Empire and politicians and turned to radical politics, mobilising the image of the larrikin digger; while others who had not gone to war were tired of the whole thing. (Reynaud 2005: 6)

Between the two world wars, Australian films featuring Anzacs, or with storylines about the conduct or aftermath of the First World War, often played for comedy. And, as Daniel Reynaud observes, the tendency in these films to portray the war positively was in marked contrast to war-themed films produced in Europe in this period. This approach was manifest in one of the most successful Australian films of the first half of the twentieth century, Charles Chauvel's *Forty Thousand Horsemen*, which was released in 1940 and intended as a self-described 'message of inspiration for a new generation of soldiers'. The film portrayed the heroic exploits of the Australian Light Horse cavalry regiment, commanded by Chauvel's uncle General Sir Harry Chauvel, in the Sinai Desert campaign during the First World War. Events in the Great War, specifically the Gallipoli landings, were the subject of the most prominent war film made after the revival in feature production in the 1970s. Peter Weir's *Gallipoli* was released to great public and critical acclaim in 1981. This homage to the spirit and sacrifice of the Anzacs followed the line of Australian war historians from C E W Bean (who had witnessed the Gallipoli landings first-hand) and onwards in placing the blame for this bloody and ultimately ill-fated campaign squarely at the feet of aloof and incompetent British generals. By contrast, the film venerated the qualities of the Australian troops – mateship, camaraderie, loyalty and simple bravery – and chimed with a contemporary, assertive nationalist mood and with the cinematic treatments of Australians at war in two earlier films, Tom Jeffery's *The Odd Angry Shot* (1979, about Australians in the Vietnam War), and Bruce Beresford's *Breaker Morant* (1980, set in the Boer War). While several other films have subsequently covered aspects of Australia's Second World War history (*Blood Oath*, Stephen Wallace, 1990, about the post-war trial of Japanese troops over a massacre of Australian troops at a prisoner of war camp; *Paradise Road*, Bruce Beresford's 1997 film about women prisoners of war in Sumatra; *Kokoda*, Alister Grierson's 2006 film about the battles between Australian and Japanese troops along the Kokoda Track in New Guinea; *Australia*, Baz Luhrmann's musical epic from 2008 featuring the bombing of Darwin), stories featuring other Australian wars and engagements, like those in Korea, Iraq, Afghanistan and East Timor, have yet to be made.

Historical films have been a staple component since the earliest days of film production in Australia. Stories of Australian bushrangers jostled for public attention with tales of hardship and fortune-hunting on the goldfields, and historical dramas adapted from Australian and international plays and novels. Among the latter were several versions of Marcus Clarke's convict-era novel *For the Term of His Natural Life*, originally published in 1870. The most notorious adaptation was directed by the American special-effects master Norman Dawn. Upon release in 1927, the film was the most expensive Australian production to that date, and one of the most controversial. Celebrated Australian director Raymond Longford had spent a year working on the script and preparing the production before he was dismissed in 1926 and replaced by Dawn. This action became something of a *cause célèbre* at the 1927 Royal Commission into the Moving Picture Industry, and it was seized upon by those arguing for government intervention to reinvigorate feature film production in the 1960s as an example of the scandalous treatment of Australian film-makers and a contributing factor both to Longford's decline into obscurity and to the slow demise of feature production. The film is now particularly notorious for a spectacular and enormously costly scene depicting a fire on a ship; two tonnes of old nitrate film stock, including many early Australian films, were used as fuel for the fire, which was described by historian Eric Reade as 'the final flicker of what has been called 'the bright flame' of early film productivity in Australia' (in Verhoeven 1995: 135).

Australian crime cinema, into which category *For the Term of His Natural Life* could be placed (although like many Australian films it straddles a number of categories from literary adaptation, and special effects spectacular, to epic blockbuster), is a broad-ranging category. The genre includes such different Australian films as the McDonagh sisters' *The Cheaters* (1930), a melodrama about a family-run criminal empire Bruce Beresford's 'inside-job' heist film *The Money Movers* (1978), Jon Hewitt's police drama *Redball* (1998) and Dee McLachlan's *The Jammed* (2007), about one woman's efforts to save a group of women who have been forcibly brought to Australia to work as prostitutes. Ramon Lobato observes that while crime films have not been especially numerous in Australian cinema, they have been a consistent feature of Australian film production over the last hundred years. Several subgenres or subsets of the crime film can be identified. The bushranger film is clearly the earliest, but there are others, most obviously prison films, which Ben Goldsmith argues includes films about convict life along with contemporary films about life inside prisons. In retrospect, it may be a little surprising that so few films about the convict era have been made in Australia, especially since in the very early period, and again in the years after the revival, film-makers sought distinctively and uniquely Australian subjects and stories. In the early years, there was considerable ambivalence about Australia's convict history and some shame attached to those whose ancestors had been forcibly transported. More recently, this heritage has been more proudly remembered, especially since the publication in 1986 of Robert Hughes' *The Fatal Shore*. And yet there have been relatively few convict films made over the last hundred years. Italian producer Dino DeLaurentiis did announce an intention to adapt *The Fatal Shore* to the screen as one of the first of the slate of films he proposed to produce at the new film studio on the Gold Coast in the late 1980s, but this project fell through when DeLaurentiis's American company was forced into bankruptcy and he had to withdraw from Australia. And, in recent years, three films have been based on the story of escaped convict and alleged cannibal Alexander Pearce but, in part because of ambivalence about the past and in part because of the expense of making historical films, convict-era films have been relatively few and far between. In the recent golden age of historical film production from the mid-1970s to the early 1980s, film-makers, and more importantly the government agencies that controlled film financing at the time, preferred films set in rural Australia in the late nineteenth century. As Bonnie Elliott notes in her essay on the period films (or 'AFC genre', as they became known), the key historical references for these films were late nineteenth- and early twentieth-century novels and, in particular, the paintings of the Heidelberg School of artists from the 1890s that played on a sense of nostalgia, which gives perhaps another reason for the lack of films set in the convict era.

The emergence of the AFC genre in the mid-1970s has been linked to a desire within the funding agencies to shift the popular image of Australian cinema away from the knockabout larrikin characters and scatological humour of the 'ocker' cycle of comedies that had proven so commercially successful in the early 1970s. These films – *The Adventures of Barry McKenzie* (Bruce Beresford, 1972), *Stork* (Tim Burstall, 1971), *Alvin Purple* (Tim Burstall, 1973), and the various sequels, spinoffs and other titles they inspired – unashamedly celebrated the Australian vernacular, and spoke directly to the Australian audience with little concession made to the possibility of international circulation. They were enormously popular, not least because they tapped into a strain of Australian nationalism that prided itself on its distinctiveness and, in particular, on its difference from Britain. The commercial success of the ocker films in the first years of the revival proved the viability and value of Australian cinema to private investors and to potential film-makers and, as Tom O'Regan has noted, these films 'paved the way for the more respected 'revival' films that followed' (O'Regan 1989: 78). The films demonstrated once again the popularity of comedies with distinctively Australian subject matter. As Lesley Speed notes in her essay in this volume, the popularity of Australian-themed comedies dates back at least to the seven Hayseeds films of Beaumont Smith (beginning with *Our Friends, the Hayseeds*, 1917) and to Raymond Longford's *The Sentimental Bloke* (1919) and *On Our Selection* (1920), the latter two adapted from popular literary works. In the 1930s, vaudeville comedian George

Muriel's Wedding, Ciby 2000.

Wallace starred in a series of hit films, while remakes of *The Sentimental Bloke* (FW Thring, 1932) and *On Our Selection* (Ken G Hall, 1932) also proved popular with local audiences. In recent years, several cycles or groups of comedies have continued to prove the resilience of the genre and residual affection local audiences have for films which display an Australian sense of humour, from the 'quirky comedies' of the 1990s (*Strictly Ballroom*, Baz Luhrmann, 1992; *Muriel's Wedding*, P J Hogan, 1994; *Priscilla Queen of the Desert*, Stephan Elliott, 1994, *Love Serenade*, Shirley Barrett, 1996), and the group of films made by the diverse collection of comedians who first worked together on the television sketch comedy series *The D-Generation* in the late 1980s (*The Castle*, Rob Sitch, 1997; *The Dish*, Rob Sitch, 2000; *Crackerjack*, Paul Moloney, 2002; *Bad Eggs*, Tony Martin, 2003; *BoyTown*, Kevin Carlin, 2006), to the 'wogsploitation' (Speed 2005) or 'wogboy' (Collins 2009) comedies like Aleks Vellis's *The Wog Boy* (2000) and Paul Fenech's *Fat Pizza* (2003), and the 'bogsploitation' mockumentary *Kenny* (Clayton Jacobson, 2006). The success of all of these films pales before the real monster of Australian comedy, *Crocodile Dundee* (Peter Faiman, 1986), which is still by some distance the highest-grossing Australian film in Australia, and the most successful Australian film internationally.

In numerical terms, the coming-of-age film has been possibly the most prominent genre of Australian cinema. It is also, perhaps, the most written about, with many critics seeing in the numerous Australian films about rites-of-passage metaphors for both the film industry and the Australian nation. In her essay in this volume, Kristina Gottschall identifies a variety of films which deal with the transition between childhood and adulthood, or feature characters growing up and discovering the world around them and finding their own identity. One important subset is films set in schools. In the first decade of the revival, the trials and tribulations of young women in Victorian boarding schools provided the drama in *Picnic at Hanging Rock* and *The Getting of Wisdom* (Bruce Beresford, 1977), while an oppressive Catholic boys' school in the 1950s was the setting for Fred Schepisi's directorial debut *The Devil's Playground* (1976). Another group of films depicts the growing pains of Indigenous Australians, with tragic outcomes in Beresford's *The Fringe Dwellers* (1986) and Stephen Johnson's *Yolngu Boy* (2000). Gottschall also highlights a number of films about adolescent girls leaving home to search for their absent fathers; this figure, the failed or departed father is a vital 'presence' in a whole string of recent Australian films.

Two recent coming-of-age films – Elissa Down's *The Black Balloon* and Cherie Nowlan's *Clubland* (both 2007) – feature lead characters negotiating their path to adulthood in a domestic environment that is shaped by the needs of their mentally-disabled brothers. In her essay on Disability in Australian Cinema, Katie Ellis charts the changing representation of disability in Australian cinema, and describes a shift – represented by these two films – from the use of disabled characters to illuminate or highlight aspects of the national character (as in Ken G Hall's *On Our Selection*, 1932, and *The Squatter's Daughter*, 1933), and the 'triumph over disability' (as depicted most prominently in Scott Hicks' Oscar-winning story about the pianist David Helfgott, *Shine*, 1996) to stories in which 'disability is … recognized in terms of social restriction rather than physical ailment'.

By contrast with the popularity and acclaim accorded to Australian comedies, Australian horror films have historically been marginalized in discourse and scholarship around Australian cinema. Today, though, as Mark David Ryan makes clear in his essay in this volume, horror movies are perhaps the most popular genre of films for Australian film-makers, especially those working with low budgets. While there are several examples of what Ryan calls 'horror-infused thrillers' in the early Australian cinema, the recent popularity of Australian horror films and film-makers both here and in international markets is due principally to the commercial success of James Wan and Leigh Whannell's *Saw* franchise (which only became possible when the film-makers relocated from Australia to the United States due to the lack of support they received for their concept from Australian funding agencies and investors), and in particular Greg Mclean's *Wolf Creek* (2005).

A significant number of Australian horror films play with the themes of the 'monstrous landscape' and the idea that Australia, and in particular the Australian outback, is a dangerous place. To differing and often less horrifying extents, these themes animate two other genres of Australian cinema: the road movie, and science fiction/fantasy films. As Fiona Trigg notes in her essay on Australian road movies, a group of films she terms the 'road movie/ *amour fou* hybrid' involve extended chases across an inhospitable landscape, often ending with the death of the protagonists. In his essay on science fiction/fantasy films, Sean McMullen discusses the violence and lawlessness of *Mad Max*'s Australia. Both of these essays make the point, as do others in this volume, that the films we might label as 'road movies' or 'science fiction/ fantasy' are extraordinarily diverse in their styles and subject matter, and often better understood as hybrids rather than clear-cut examples of any single genre. To this end, Fiona Trigg includes the documentary travelogues of Keith Adams, the Leyland brothers, and Alby Mangels in her essay on road movies, while Sean McMullen draws together such different films as *The Matrix* (Andy & Larry Wachowski, 1999), the Oscar-nominated short animation *The Mysterious*

Geographical Adventures of Jasper Morello (Anthony Lucas, 2005) and *Picnic at Hanging Rock* (Peter Weir, 1975).

Picnic at Hanging Rock, as Martyna Olszowska notes in her essay on Peter Weir, is for many Europeans and other non-Australians the first film that comes to mind when thinking of Australian cinema. Weir is undoubtedly one of the best known and most highly-acclaimed Australian directors. Although he has not made a film in Australia since *The Year of Living Dangerously* in 1982, and while his subsequent films that have been produced around the world (parts of *The Year of Living Dangerously* were shot in the Philippines, parts of *The Mosquito Coast*, 1986, in Belize; *Master and Commander*, 2003, in Mexico and the Galapagos Islands; and his current film, *The Way Back* in India, in Morocco and at the former Bulgarian national film studio now known as Nu Boyana), he has returned to Australia on several occasions for post-production. Weir began his career in television and in documentary film-making at the Commonwealth Film Unit (which became Film Australia in 1973, and which was absorbed into the mega-agency Screen Australia in 2008). His first feature film, the gothic horror *The Cars That Ate Paris* (1974), was a bold and imaginative black comedy and one of the first Australian films to screen at the Cannes film festival, where its memorable prop, a Volkswagen Beetle festooned with spikes, created enormous media attention. Two years later, the acclaim that greeted his next film *Picnic at Hanging Rock* when it screened at Cannes announced the arrival of the revived Australian cinema on the international scene. *Picnic* also validated and compounded the Australian Film Commission's preference for European-style art films as the acceptable face of Australian cinema. In subsequent years, Weir has time and again proved his versatility and consummate ability to work within the Hollywood system while retaining his individualism and personal style with the production of films like *Witness* (1985), *Dead Poets Society* (1989), *The Truman Show* (1998) and *Master and Commander* (2003). While far from being a prolific director – he has made only ten films over the last thirty years, and just five since 1990 – Peter Weir remains an enormously important and influential figure in Australian cinema.

The two other directors profiled in the Australian section of the Intellect Directory of Australian and New Zealand Cinema began their careers outside Australia and produced their most significant Australian films during the long fallow period in feature production between the end of the World War II and the early 1970s known as 'the interval'. Cecil Holmes, a communist and celebrated documentary film-maker who started his career in the National Film Unit of New Zealand, only directed two feature films in a long career, but is rightly described by Adrian Danks in his essay in this volume as 'one of the most significant and ambitious film-makers to work in Australia during the 1950s, 60s and 70s'. Holmes' feature films, *Captain Thunderbolt* (1953) and *Three in One* (1957), were among only 25 made in Australia during the 1950s. Stylistically innovative and highly idiosyncratic, both films clearly display Holmes's cineliteracy and knowledge of international aesthetics and techniques. Danks identifies the influence of Soviet montage and Italian neo-realism which complemented Holmes's documentary sensibility. As Danks notes, Holmes's career is most notable for his work on documentaries which revealed to mainstream Australian audiences the lives and cultures of Indigenous Australians. Michael Powell, the British director and subject of Danks' second profile, like Holmes, only made two feature films in Australia, *They're a Weird Mob* (1966) and *Age of Consent* (1969). Danks observes that Powell's career in Australia 'is a tale of extreme tenacity, pragmatism and, ultimately, missed opportunities'. The work that he did manage to produce here is quite remarkable, and quite distinct from the films he made in Britain and Europe in the 1940s and 1950s, often in partnership with his long-term collaborator Emeric Pressburger. In Australia, *They're a Weird Mob* is now considered an insightful and influential comedy about migrant life and the difficulties of assimilating into Australian society in the 1960s. *Age of Consent* paired the young Helen Mirren with James Mason in the story of an ageing artist who travels to a tropical island in an effort to rediscover his creativity and finds inspiration in the form of a beautiful young woman. Both films were adaptations: *They're a Weird Mob* from a novel by John O'Grady writing under the pen-name Nino Culotta, and *Age of Consent* from a 1938 novel by Australian artist and writer Norman Lindsay, and, while neither has received the acknowledgement they deserve outside Australia, they are both important and visionary films that deserve wider acclaim.

Forty years ago, around the time that Powell was active in Australia, film critic Sylvia Lawson lamented that '[i]n other countries, locally-oriented film comment is about actual films; here it is always about the industry, or rather the non-industry, because until the industry properly exists, there will be virtually no Australian films for discussion' (Lawson [1969]1985: 175). Twenty years later, and almost twenty years after the revival in local production, academics and film historians Susan Dermody and Elizabeth Jacka echoed this sentiment in a criticism of film agencies' neglect of film culture when they noted that 'there is a professional discourse to talk about the economics of films and a popular one to *promote* them; but ways of discussing our cinema in its aesthetic and political aspects are severely underdeveloped' (Dermody & Jacka 1987: 106). Today, the aesthetic (if not political) aspects of Australian films are widely discussed, although the travails of the production industry and local audience indifference about Australian films still tend to be the dominant topics of conversation. And yet, despite the widespread discussion of Australian cinema in print, online and on the airwaves, and despite the regular division by critics and scholars of Australian films by kind, type or common theme, genre film-making and genre analysis have, until recently, tended to be seen as beyond the boundaries of Australian cinema. This perception was tackled head-on in a set of articles in the first issue of a new journal, *Limina*, published by the Australian Film, Television and Radio School. The School's Head of Screen Studies, Karen Pearlman, introduced the section, entitled 'Genre is not a Dirty Word', by asserting that collectively the four articles represent 'a provocation to move beyond the notion that genre is somehow beneath us' (Pearlman 2009: 83). While the authors, and the School, are to be applauded for continuing an emphasis on genre film-making that has been developed over a number of years, and that was kicked along significantly by a short course on Horror cinema convened by Teresa Rizzo in 2006 and 2007, the section unfortunately reinforces the misguided idea that genre film-making is something that exists outside Australian cinema, or as something 'other'. All four articles – on horror films, musicals, westerns and a new category, the 'self-help' genre – take as their principal points of reference films from the American cinema. In so doing, the authors both deny the contributions Australian film-makers have made to all of these genres, and ignore the history and new vibrancy of genre film-making in Australia.

There are a number of reasons for this continuing tendency in critical writing on Australian cinema to marginalize genre films. Dermody and Jacka both describe and promote a tendency within the critical establishment, among some film-makers, and within funding agencies from the 1970s until the present day, to consider 'traditional' genre films, by which Dermody and Jacka meant genres typically associated with Hollywood cinema: 'thrillers, exploitation, splatter movies and action pictures (Dermody & Jacka 1987: 147), as antithetical to the core mission of the film industry, which, for many, is to represent national identity and to tell distinctively Australian stories. Genre films have been seen as part of an international or transnational rather than locally-oriented cinema, commercially rather than culturally minded, less 'aesthetically interesting' than those films which expressly set out to represent and explore Australia onscreen, and, worst of all, prone to 'erasing all signs of their local production' (Dermody & Jacka 1988a: 24). This has been their ultimate failing: to be an authentic contribution to Australian cinema and screen culture, a film made in Australia, by Australians, must foreground its local specificity and its geographic and cultural origins and maintain an ethereal originality. Those that did not and, instead, took their cues from films made here or elsewhere, or had the temerity to consider audiences beyond Australia, were damned by Dermody and Jacka as 'culturally stupid … emblematic of a 'carpetbagger mentality' (1988a: 49), and 'chilled by commercial or exploitationist motives' (1988a: 43). These attitudes have pre-vailed for many years. Those Australian films that used generic templates with a local inflection were branded 'eccentrics' and 'limbo-like' by Dermody and Jacka (1988a: 47). Succeeding generations of critics and scholars, and succes-sive funding agencies, have accepted this line, and have tended to view films that display the codes and conventions of recognizable film genres as somehow beyond the acceptable boundaries of the national cinema. Genre films, or even consideration of Australian films in terms of genre, have not sat easily with the 'underlying notion that film served the identification and refinement of essential Australianness [that] was the confident starting point for everybody' involved in arguing the film industry into existence from the 1960s onwards (Dermody & Jacka 1987: 27). So, even though the study of film genres was becoming an established practice in Britain and the United States from the late 1960s, the dominant critical paradigm in Australia in the 1970s and 1980s, and even to some extent to the present day, has been the nation and the national cinema. In this framework, Hollywood is routinely cast as the 'other', with 'cultural exac-titude' measured, in part, by difference and distance from Hollywood forms, themes, concerns and commercialism. The emphasis on 'cultural exactitude' has valorized and lauded difference and distinction, and relegated genre films for their unthinking similarity and derivativeness.

As Dermody and Jacka document, the introduction of tax concessions under Division 10BA of the Income Tax Assessment Act in 1981 led to an influx of private investment in film production and boosted the number of genre films made in Australia. And yet they argue that, on the evidence of films produced between 1970 and 1988, Australian cinema was 'not genre-based nor nearly prolific enough to be so' (Dermody & Jacka 1988a: 47). That is, genre film-making was constructed as the preserve of a film industry of a certain size and output, though what this size and output might be was not specified. But, curiously, Dermody and Jacka, like so many writers and critics before and after them, could not resist describing and discussing the films by grouping them into particular types or kinds. 'Type' or 'kind', as Steve Neale helpfully reminds, is the literal translation of the French term 'genre' (Neale 2000: 9), so, at some level, it seems odd that Australian cinema is both considered to be *not* genre-based, and yet still divisible into types of films.

Several recent events and developments have encouraged a re-evaluation of Australian genre film-making, and of the place of genre in Australian cinema. The first was the runaway success of Greg Mclean's horror film *Wolf Creek*, released in 2005. This low-budget film was by no means the first horror film produced in Australia, as Mark David Ryan outlines in his contribution to this volume. *Wolf Creek* did however open the eyes of funding agencies and other investors to the potential of horror films, and shone a spotlight on the thriving but critically-marginalized genre. In 2008, the release of Mark Hartley's feature length documentary *Not Quite Hollywood* presented an opportunity to re-evaluate the diversity of genre films made in Australia in the 1970s and 1980s that were often popular either in Australia or overseas, influential in their genres, but critically derided in Australia and marginalized from the project of construct-ing an Australian cinema the nation could be proud of. Hartley coins the term 'Ozploitation' as a label for the variety of films covered in his documentary, although, as Deborah Thomas points out in her essay on Ozploitation in this volume, the term covers a diverse variety of genre films including soft-core por-nography, ocker comedy, horror and 'creature features', and action films. In the 1970s, Ozploitation film-makers like John Lamond (*Australia After Dark*, 1974; *The ABC of Love and Sex: Australian Style*, 1978; and *Felicity*, 1979), Tim Burstall (*Alvin Purple*, 1973), and Anthony Ginnane (*Fantasm*, 1976; *Fantasm Comes Again*, 1977; *Patrick*, 1978) explored the new freedom in production afforded not only by government subsidy but also by the relaxation of censorship laws and the introduction of the 'R' or 18+ rating in 1971.

Many of the Ozploitation films and the core group of directors and producers involved in their production – Brian Trenchard-Smith, Richard Franklin, Anthony Ginnane, and Colin Eggleston – also benefited from the introduction of the 10BA tax concessions in the early 1980s, with most of the horror and action films produced in this decade. As Hartley notes in his film, and as Deborah Thomas outlines in more detail in her essay, the marginalization of these genre films was a consequence of the official preference for 'quality' films. The subsequent neglect of these films by scholars (although not, it should be noted, by audi-ences, both in Australia and overseas) is due, in part at least, to the critical orthodoxy established by Dermody and Jacka that denied the cultural value and even the very existence of genre film-making in Australian cinema. As Hartley's film reveals, the sheer number of films produced in the 1970s and 1980s that fall broadly into the Ozploitation category, and the influence they have had not only on Australian audiences and film-makers but also, as Quentin Tarantino and other contributors to *Not Quite Hollywood* make clear, to film-makers and audi-ences around the world, makes their marginal status much harder to maintain. And, as Deborah Thomas notes, the 'positive cultural values now assigned to exploitation cinema', due in no small part to the evangelism of Tarantino and his fans, have aided the revisionary approach to the variety of genre film-making in Australia in the 1970s and 1980s.

A further boost to the reconsideration of genre film-making in Australia came with the publication in 2006 of Albert Moran and Errol Vieth's book *Film in Aus-tralia: An Introduction*. The book opens with a statement of its aim to 'promote the study of Australian feature films in terms of genre' (Moran & Vieth 2006: 1), which, as the authors note, is a departure from usual approaches to Australian cinema. The authors group Australian films into thirteen broad genre categories: adventure, art film, biopic, comedy, crime, detective, horror, musical, science fiction, social realism, suspense thriller, teenpic and women's film. This Direc-tory builds on Moran and Vieth's approach. While the groupings of films in this volume differ somewhat from those in *Film in Australia*, the motivation and senti-ment behind this volume is the same as Moran and Vieth's: that is, to encour-age new considerations of Australian films and to provide new perspectives on Australian cinema. The contributions to this volume come from a variety of writ-ers, many of whom are at early stages in their careers as academics, critics, and contributors to Australian screen culture. It is hoped that future editions of the Directory will feature the work of other writers, perhaps drawn from contributors to the worldcinemadirectory.org website, which is open to public submissions.

Identifying and grouping genres of Australian films are, of course, principally critical and scholarly exercises, and it is to be expected that some film-makers, scholars and commentators will disagree with the classifications outlined here. The important point is that this process of revision, of looking at Australian cinema in terms of genres or types of films rather than seeing the entire output of Australia's film-makers as a single genre, as some bizarrely continue to do, provides a means to think about the things that films share in common; to consider their relations with other films both Australian and international; to explore what these films share and what makes them distinct; and, crucially, to connect with audiences. Genre films resonate with other films, with audiences, and with film-makers. Genre, as Rick Altman (1999) reminds us, is useful as a blueprint and guide for film-makers, as a label for distributors and exhibitors to sell a film and for audiences to make decisions about what to see. And the description of a film in terms of a particular genre, with distinct stylistic and narrative features, represents a contract between audiences and film-makers that sets up certain expectations on which audiences will judge the value of the film and of the experience of viewing.

In marked contrast with the situation even five years ago, genre films are now much more prominent in Australian cinema and scholarship, although the state of the industry and the Australian audience's apparent dislike of Australian films remain the core topics of conversation. If the recent crop of Australian productions and the range of writing about Australian film is any guide, the institutions of Australian cinema – industrial, critical, bureaucratic – appear to be sloughing off their previous hostility or ambivalence towards genre films. The synopses of films at various stages of production in Australia in September 2009 give some flavour of Australian film-makers embrace of genre, and of the diversity of films currently being made here: An environmental disaster creates a killer fog that destroys everything in its path; Australian soldiers tunnel beneath the trenches of the Western Front during the First World War; a rape victim embarks on a revenge mission against her attackers; a young man fights his way from the suburbs of Melbourne to a boxing world title; a group of friends are marooned on a remote reef surrounded by sharks after their pleasure cruiser sinks; eight teenagers work together to fight an invading army. These film-makers understand that, while 'Australian film' may not on its own be a selling point for local audiences, tagging films with genre labels and embracing the codes and conventions of established genres may just be the best way to make their film stand out and, most importantly, to enable them to find an audience. In the process it may just be that the historical ambivalence that Australian audiences display towards Australian films, and which the industry and commentariat endlessly worry over, might just be surmounted

Ben Goldsmith

Gentle Strangers, 1972. Writer and director, Cecil Holmes. Copyright Screen Australia.

DIRECTORS
CECIL HOLMES (1921–1994)

Although born in New Zealand, Cecil Holmes is nevertheless one of the most significant and ambitious film-makers to work in Australia during the 1950s, 1960s and 1970s. A dedicated leftist, in fact a communist, his work consistently demonstrated a humanist commitment to the socially disenfranchised, ranging from the underlying capitalist conditions that force decent citizens into bushranging and stealing, to the social and economic conditions confronting indigenous communities in contemporary Australia. In the 1950s, Holmes briefly moved from his background in documentary to feature film production, but all of his work demonstrates a keen eye and ear for the 'actuality' of the moment being captured. Although he is often regarded as a maverick director who struggled hard to make films – and he did produce only two features in a relatively long career – he nevertheless consistently produced work in the 1950s, 1960s and early 1970s for a variety of governmental, corporate and philanthropic organizations, as well as at the behest of such individuals as Australian leftist author, Frank Hardy.

Holmes is most well known to contemporary commentators on Australian cinema for his two highly-idiosyncratic features, *Captain Thunderbolt* (1953) and *Three in One* (1957), two of only a very small number of truly local features made in Australia during the 1950s. *Three in One*, in particular, represents one of the highpoints of post-war Australian cinema, reframing the common or characteristic theme of 'mateship' within more explicitly leftist contexts. But what is most remarkable about the film – which is uneven, possibly inevitably so considering its tripartite form – is its visual style, both reaffirming and transforming the common preoccupations of Australian landscape cinema. Also significant are the international models of film-making aesthetics that it openly draws upon, ranging from Soviet montage (seen clearly in the opening story's use of low-angle framing and expressive caricature or typage) to Italian neo-realism. These visible influences also betray Holmes' cinephilia; he was a key figure in the New Zealand film society movement of the 1940s, and ran a company, New Dawn Films, that distributed European cinema later in the 1950s. It is nevertheless the middle section of *Three in One*, based on Frank Hardy's short story 'A Load of Wood', that remains a classic expression of Australian colloquial understatement, a minimally-worded, visually high contrast and largely location-shot paean to worker unity set during the 1930s' Depression.

These two features tend to somewhat skew understandings of Holmes' broader career, especially considering the fact that he mainly worked within the realm of documentary. Although several of his works in this field do deal with worker and union issues – such as *Words for Freedom* (1956) about the union press, made between the two features – his career is most remarkable for its commitment to indigenous causes and issues (many of his documentaries in this mode were shot in the Northern Territory). But this genuine and empathetic concern has also made much of his work difficult to see, often being restricted in its subsequent distribution and visibility. Made for a range of organizations, including the Australian Broadcasting Commission, Film Australia, and the Institute for Aboriginal Studies, these documentaries move from the more conventionally ethnographic to committed and troubling works concerned with Aboriginal rights and the conflict between modern and traditional ways of life. Two of his most remarkable documentaries remain *I, the Aboriginal* (1961), made for the ABC and based on Douglas Lockwood's bestselling book, and the more troubling *Faces in the Sun* (1965), focusing on a range of Aboriginal characters living varied but conflicted lives in Arnhem Land and Darwin. Each of these films is a fascinating artefact of its period, attempting to 'accurately' depict Aboriginal life while caught between

an understanding of tradition and the 'needs' of assimilation. Containing numerous images, sounds and ideas that are discomforting for contemporary audiences
from any background – let alone specifically indigenous ones – both films (and
later more positivist films like *The Islanders* 1968, and *Return to the Dreaming,*
1971) are nevertheless important, committed and often potent contributions to
Australian cinema and television in the 1960s.

After starting his career with New Zealand's National Film Unit – where he
made the Grierson-like short, *The Coaster* (1947) – Holmes instigated the first
public service strike in New Zealand, and not long after fled to Australia. His
initial work in Australia was completed under John Heyer at the Shell Film
Unit, hardly the most apt or nurturing environment for a film-maker of Holmes'
overriding political and social allegiances. Moving out from under such corporate and governmental patronage was certainly the making of Holmes as a
film-maker, even if he often struggled to get his subsequent films of the 1950s
into the marketplace. Thus, both *Captain Thunderbolt* and *Three in One* were
funded independently by companies or figures sympathetic to Holmes' leftist
views. *Three in One*, for example, was initially conceived as a stand-alone short
funded from the European royalties earned by Hardy's *Power Without Glory*.
But neither film has ever been widely seen locally, and *Three in One* – which
in aesthetic terms easily competes with many comparative international films
of its time – has never been released in Australia. Both films were more widely
seen overseas before limited showings on Australian television at the end of the
decade.

Thus, despite being critically lauded in some circles, Holmes remains a
relatively unknown or uncelebrated figure of postwar Australian cultural life.
Nevertheless, the breadth and innovation of his work in the areas of both the
fiction feature and documentary remains remarkable. Holmes is inevitably one
of the truly singular figures in Australian film history, a committed, vital and often
rebellious director whose approach and idiosyncratic career is neatly summed up
by the title of his episodic 1986 'autobiography', *One Man's Way*.

Adrian Danks

Captain Thunderbolt

Country of Origin:
Australia

Production Company:
Associated T.V.

Producer:
John Wiltshire

Director:
Cecil Holmes

Screenwriter:
Creswick Jenkinson

Cinematographer:
Ross Wood

Editor:
Margaret Cardin

Art Director:
Keith Christie

Music:
Sydney John

Duration:
69 minutes

Genre:
Bushranger

Cast:
Grant Taylor
Charles Tingwell
Rosemary Miller
Harp McGuire
John Fegan
Jean Blue

Year:
1953

Synopsis

Inspired by Frank Clune's 1948 book about nineteenth century bushrangers. *Wild Colonial Boys*, *Captain Thunderbolt* is an idiosyncratic, if at times predictable, story of downtrodden individuals driven to lives of crime. Fred Ward and Alan Blake are sentenced to hard labour on Cockatoo Island after being found guilty of horse stealing by the repressive colonial authorities. While working on a chain gang breaking rocks in a quarry they break free and escape to the Mainland and take up the life of bushranging (Regan adopts the epithet of 'Captain Thunderbolt' not long after). Enjoying their cavalier lifestyle, they mostly steal from the decadent capitalist class and gain the sympathy of many in the community. After the pursuit of Ward and Blake is 'abandoned' by Dalton – a sympathetic policeman with allegiances to the fugitives' families – it is taken up by the sadistic Sergeant Mannix. He relentlessly pursues them to a final shoot-out. Blake is killed and wilfully mistaken for Ward, while rumours persist that Captain Thunderbolt continues to ride throughout the countryside.

Critique

Captain Thunderbolt is one of the most bracing and visually adventurous of bushranger films, a truly indigenous genre somewhat blighted and stunted in its growth by the New South Wales ban on the form in the silent era. Not surprisingly for a film directed by communist Cecil Holmes. it emphasizes the social, political and cultural circumstances that led Fred Ward (Captain Thunderbolt) to a life of crime. The film also draws upon Holmes' experience in documentary – particularly visually – and his own tastes and background as a cinephile. For example. his exaggerated portrayal of the capitalist squatocracy and the higher echelons of the legal system and, at times, highly expressive and self-conscious visual style – most famously evidenced in the shot where the camera peers up through a glass table – are plainly indebted to his sympathetic knowledge of the Soviet Montage School and Eisenstein's theories of character typology. The very real limits of characterization found in the film are also partly a result of this key influence.

Like Holmes' subsequent feature, *Three in One* (1957), *Captain Thunderbolt* met with little success or sympathetic distribution in Australia. Financed and produced independently of the local distribution and exhibition system – which was largely controlled by American and British interests – it struggled for several years to gain a very limited Australian release. A relatively low budget film costing £15,000. it was produced by a company attempting to break into and pre-empt the market for television drama (a medium that was not launched in Australia until late 1956). Ultimately gaining a release in Europe and America, and more than returning its budget from these sales, *Captain Thunderbolt* was a significant departure for Holmes, who had made his name producing documentaries in New Zealand and for the Shell Film Unit (and for leading the first public service strike in New Zealand).

Shot mostly on location in the rural area of New England in early 1951, *Captain Thunderbolt* is less impressive as a whole – there are numerous clumsy scenes and performances – than it is for individual moments and points of emphasis. For example, it contains a very sympathetic representation of a female Aboriginal character, an aspect that perhaps reveals and points towards Holmes' more sustained interest in Aboriginal issues in his documentaries of the 1960s and 1970s (such as *I, the Aboriginal*, 1961, and *Faces in the Sun*,1965). But equally striking is the form of the film itself. Although some of the gaps of narrative and continuity can probably be accounted for by the shorter television version that now survives in the archives, the film's mode of address and point of view are consistently innovative, if not always totally successful in delivery. Therefore, although the most sympathetic, iconic and appropriately-dashing character in the film is obviously Captain Thunderbolt, the film's voiceover is actually given to the policemen – one of whom tells the story through a very self-conscious voiceover flashback. Although this could be explained away in terms of the film's perspective being aligned with the forces of law, the odd, arch and often harsh tone of the voiceover routinely underplays this possibility. Although the film's largely positive view of bushranger life is hardly unique, it does reflect a key shift in the leftist understanding and use of folk culture in this period – the soundtrack features various folk ballads including 'The Wild Colonial Boy' – and the kinds of stories it can tell about class inequity and social injustice. *Captain Thunderbolt* is both a curious anomaly in Holmes' career – his only real attempt at genre film-making – and totally in keeping with his broader preoccupations and values.

Adrian Danks

Three in One

Country of Origin:
Australia

Production Company:
Australian Tradition Films

Producer:
Cecil Holmes

Director:
Cecil Holmes

Cinematographer:
Ross Wood

Editor:
A. William Copeland

Music:
Raymond Hanson

Synopsis

Three in One comprises three separate stories surveying the distinctively Australian theme of 'mateship', introduced by the plummy tones of John McCallum who is seemingly 'captured' relaxing between performances in his theatre dressing room. This trilogy of ostensibly stand-alone short films moves in time from the 1890s through the early Great Depression of the 1930s to the hustle and bustle of modern mid-1950s' Sydney. Though thematically related, each of the three stories takes a different tone and approach, ranging from the initial, often comic, sun-scorched adaptation of Henry Lawson's 'The Union Buries its Dead', through the atmospheric, isolated, low-key night-time Jindabyne setting of Frank Hardy's wonderful 'A Load of Wood', to the more anonymous – though distinctly Sydney-set – treatment of Ralph Peterson's original story and script, 'The City'. The first two stories of *Three in One*, in particular, highlight the relation of figures to the iconic Australian landscape, though each is equally preoccupied by what might constitute community in each of these isolated environments and situations. The closer the film gets to the present

Voiceover:
John McCallum

Duration:
89 minutes

Genre:
Drama

Year:
1957

Joe Wilson's Mates

Screenwriter:
Rex Rienits, from the short story 'The Union Bury its Dead' by Henry Lawson

Cast:
Edmund Allison
Reg Lye
Alexander Archdale
Charles Tasman
Don McNiven
Jerold Wells
The Bushwackers Band

The Load of Wood

Screenwriter:
Rex Rienits, from the story by Frank Hardy

Cast:
Jock Levy
Leonard Thiele
Ossie Wenban
John Armstrong

The City

Screenwriter:
Ralph Peterson

Cast:
Joan Landor
Brian Vicary Betty Lucas
Gordon Glenwright
Ken Wayne
Styewart Ginn

day the more it moves away from such conceptions of community, the final part focusing predominantly on the more conventional cinematic and narratological framework of the romantic couple. But even in this final section – which presents an uncommonly gritty view of Australian life – the couple is characteristically assisted by their workmates and the communal possibilities of modern life are subtly indicated.

Critique

Although rarely screened, Cecil Holmes' *Three in One* is one of the most singular, significant and impressive features made in Australian between World War II and the film revival of the 1970s. The only truly local feature film made in 1957, it is a profoundly-independent work that robustly demonstrates Holmes' idiosyncratic film-making capabilities. A significant aesthetic advance on the more piecemeal triumphs of *Captain Thunderbolt*, *Three in One* nevertheless failed to attain a proper Australian release on its completion, individual episodes ultimately being screened as supporting shorts by a local exhibitor. This sits in contrast to the film's international distribution which, although hardly lucrative, saw it being released in numerous European countries *and* New Zealand, and garnering awards and strong critical notices at the Edinburgh and Karlovy Vary film festivals in 1956.

The strongest section of *Three in One* is definitely the middle one. Initially designed as a short film in its own right, and financed by the European earnings of Hardy's novel *Power Without Glory*, 'A Load of Wood' is a brilliantly shot – by the great Ross Wood – and acted two-hander that evokes a palpably-chilly atmosphere and tension. In many respects, the opening story of the film is the weakest, and is certainly the most leisurely and digressive entry in the trilogy. It does feature some striking exterior shots with low-angle framing, creating vistas that are reminiscent of late 1920s' Soviet cinema, a key point of reference for both Holmes' visual style and his politics. But despite its pro-union stance, and display of game leftist sympathies in the context of the Cold War and a broader anti-communism, the film is more concerned with creating a jovial atmosphere around the two songs contributed by the pub folk band (The Bushwackers) than any truly-potent political or social message. The final section of the film, 'The City', is both more conventional and somewhat bleaker than the two that precede it. It is also the section the film that moves farthest away from the broader concept of 'mateship'. This section is less remarkable for the somewhat-mundane domestic drama that unfolds – involving a young couple despairing about the cost of housing and stalling their marriage as a result – than its portrait of night-time Sydney as a hive of activity and forbidding shadows. Although far from film noir in its broader sensibility, the visual stamp of this imposing style certainly makes its mark. But Holmes' model is equally that of neo-realism: a key stylistic, thematic and ethical benchmark throughout his fiction and documentary work. *Three in One* stands, for all its inconsistency, as Holmes' greatest and most iconic contribution to Australian cinema.

Adrian Danks

DIRECTORS
MICHAEL POWELL
(1905–1990)

English film-maker Michael Powell's career in Australia is a tale of extreme tenacity, pragmatism and, ultimately, missed opportunities (amongst his other mooted projects was a film based on Arthur Upfields 'Bony' novels). The two films that he made 'down under' in the 1960s – *They're a Weird Mob* (1966) and *Age of Consent* (1969) – are amongst a small number of features produced in Australia during that lean decade. They are also amongst the highest-profile and biggest-budgeted Australian films of the era. Though they are, in some ways, studies in contrast – *They're a Weird Mob* working to embrace the Australian idiom and character; *Age of Consent* to escape the pressures and changes of 'present day' Australia on the idyll of Dunk Island – they are, equally, accounts of outsiders or exiles learning (or relearning) the rhythms and nuances of Australian life. In this respect, as well as in terms of their interest in themes of community and creativity (less the case in *They're a Weird Mob*, inevitably), they are less departures from Powell's visionary, highly European and often romantic British work (much of which he made in collaboration with Emeric Pressburger for their production company, The Archers) than somewhat benign revisitations of the more emotionally-engaged and tortured terrains of such masterpieces of the 1940s as '*I Know Where I'm Going!*' (1945), *Black Narcissus* (1947) and *The Red Shoes* (1948) films largely set outside England and equally responsive to the specificity of place (even when filmed in the confines of the studio).

Although they were never intended as final works – Powell continued to dream of and plan further features up until the 1980s – both of his Australian films nevertheless display a more relaxed and accepting tone than many of Powell and Pressburger's celebrated works. As a result of this lack of intensity, as well as the relative invisibility of these two Australian co-productions on the world stage, both *They're a Weird Mob* and *Age of Consent* have been critically-undervalued films, routinely regarded as directorial afterthoughts in the career of one of the greatest film-makers of the mid-twentieth century. Thus, despite the consistently rising reputation of Powell – he is now commonly regarded as Britain's greatest film-maker, alongside Alfred Hitchcock – these two Australian films have mostly met with either silence or faint embarrassment. Nevertheless, in the last decade or so, this position has started to change, with both Australian and international critics and film-makers starting to become aware of some of the pleasures and achievements that these two films offer. Although *Age of Consent* is never going to be regarded as more than an amiable curiosity of Australian cinema, or as a highpoint in Powell's career (it is a disappointing final feature, ultimately), *They're a Weird Mob* has emerged as something else: a classic time-capsule of Australian culture, a prescient model for local film production, and a surprisingly-nuanced portrait of migrant life and how such migrants might negotiate the transition from the governmental and social policies of assimilationism to multiculturalism.

The key difficulty of Powell's Australian films is that they represent and belong to a pragmatic model for making commercial films in Australia: a logical and powerful 'starting point' for a country without a viable feature film industry. The

Age of Consent. Columbia/Nautilus.

films' reputations have suffered mightily from their rejection by both those in Australia pushing for a government-supported film industry and those expecting a clear reaffirmation or even rejuvenation of Powell's film-making powers and points of obsession. *They're a Weird Mob* was made at a particularly low point in Powell's British career. It follows the critical and commercial disaster of *Peeping Tom* (1960), the supremely underwhelming *The Queen's Guards* (1961), and the piecemeal work Powell had started to undertake in British television. Thus, *They're a Weird Mob* represents both a retreat and an embrace of new challenges – core ideas that are coincidentally at the centre of *Age of Consent* – the tale of an expatriate Australian painter burnt-out by the New York art scene. The problem is that the ambition of *They're a Weird Mob*, and the extraordinary work and effort Powell and his collaborators put into securing production funds and wide Australian release, was not visible or evident to international critics or audiences.

Powell himself appeared to be quite pleased with *They're a Weird Mob*, as indicated in the second volume of his magisterial autobiography, *Million-Dollar Movie*, and he was very aware of his own achievements in successfully negotiating deals with notoriously-fickle local exhibitors (who in the 1960s were loathe to show or commit to anything Australian). In this light, Powell's decision to adapt an extremely popular and picaresque novel by Nino Culotta (pseudonym of John O'Grady), a comedy of acculturation and assimilation, should be viewed less as a case of artistic affinity (though he plainly enjoyed it as romp and saw some affinity in its 'outsider's view' of a community) than creative pragmatism – he rightly saw more ambitious and risky films as something to be attempted only after the (re)establishment of a viable feature film industry. In this regard, his approach to film production in Australia is not so far removed from that of his countrymen Harry Watt and Ralph Smart who worked for Ealing in the 1940s and early 1950s. Although *Age of Consent* is based on a 1938 novel by Norman Lindsay which seems somewhat closer to Powell's existing preoccupations – essentially the life of the artist and his attempts to shape the world around him – it is equally broad and stereotyped in its view of character and situation. Powell himself was very dismissive of Lindsay's novel, considering the main attractions of his film to be the picturesque and isolated surroundings of Dunk Island, the star power of James Mason, and the corporeal beauty of a young Helen Mirren. Both films were successful on their Australian release – *They're a Weird Mob* massively so – but both failed to achieve significant overseas exposure.

Ultimately, Powell can be seen as the embodiment of the figure of the 'sympathetic outsider': an overseas film-maker who committed the time and effort to make two popular features in Australia during one of the most difficult periods for local film production. Although there is some continuing disappointment that these films never reached (or even tried to) the level of Powell's work of the 1940s and early 1950s, they should now be regarded, and possibly celebrated, in terms more appropriate to their production conditions and circumstances, as pragmatically visionary and commercially ambitious films for a country just starting to really make films again.

Adrian Danks

They're a Weird Mob

Country of Origin:
Australia

Prod Co:
Williamson-Powell International Films

Producer:
Michael Powell

Director:
Michael Powell

Screenwriter:
Richard Imrie [Emeric Pressburger], from the novel by Nino Culotta (John O'Grady)

Cinematographer:
Arthur Grant

Editor:
G. Turney-Smith

Art Director:
Dennis Gentle

Music:
Lawrence Leonard

Duration:
112 minutes

Genre:
Comedy

Cast:
Walter Chiari
Clare Dunne
Chips Rafferty
Ed Devereaux
Alida Chelli
Slim de Grey
John Meillon
Charles Little

Year:
1966

Synopsis

An Italian sports journalist Nino Culotta is summoned to Australia to work on an Italian-language magazine called *La Seconda Madre*. On arrival, he discovers that the magazine has gone into liquidation and so finds himself stuck in a foreign country he knows little about and with few points of contact. Eventually finding employment as a builder's labourer, he is acculturated into the Australian way of life and its distinctive idiom.

Critique

Throughout this laconic, though often quite genteel picaresque tale, Nino is introduced to a wide array of Australian types, rituals (including that of courtship, and the pub 'shout') and iconic situations, ranging from swimming at Bondi Beach to arranging for the purchase of his own block of land. *They're a Weird Mob* can be seen as an important precursor of the 1970s' 'ocker' film, though its view of masculinity, the Australian character, urban life and cultural difference is considerably less chauvinistic and far more gentle and whimsical than that of such later films as *Stork* (Tim Burstall, 1971) and *The Adventures of Barry McKenzie* (Bruce Beresford, 1972).

The source novel *They're a Weird Mob* was a huge bestseller when it was first published in 1957. It was reprinted many times, serialized for radio, at one point mooted as a television series, and was followed by a string of further novels featuring its central character, Nino Culotta. The film – the only Australian feature released in 1966 – was a local success that made approximately A$2,000,000 in Australia on its initial release from a A$600,000 outlay. Despite also being a hit in New Zealand, it received very limited release or success elsewhere in the world. Though often dismissed or disregarded in discussions of the film revival of the 1970s, it is nevertheless now regarded as a central work of Australian National Cinema – a significant pointer towards particular possibilities for film production in this country. It is now more commonly discussed in relation to the broader work and life of its director Michael Powell. Powell's work in Australia, often regarded as a significant downturn after such visionary films as *A Matter of Life and Death* (1946) and *The Red Shoes* (1948), should actually be considered in more pragmatic terms, providing hard-fought expressions of popular Australian forms made in the context of a country without an established film industry. In this regard, Powell's tireless ability to get films made and seen by large audiences within a climate notoriously hostile to Australian content is equally visionary.

They're a Weird Mob is a film with a curiously hybrid pedigree. It is based on a novel written by a Celtic Australian (John O'Grady) posing as an Italian author, Nino Culotta (it is a mock autobiography), directed and produced by a romantic, almost European Englishman, from a final script adapted by a Hungarian using an Anglo pseudonym (regular Powell collaborator Emeric Pressburger writing as Richard Imrie, who worked on a script first penned by Powell and then elaborated upon by O'Grady), which is itself about the act of translating or understanding another culture. It is essentially about Nino's acculturation, his initiation into a conception of mainstream Australian culture. In particular, the Australian idiom he encounters, and whose difference is marked by behaviour (such as the peculiar rituals of drinking), language – terms such as 'schooner', 'shout', 'scone', and 'Kings *bloody* Cross', abound in the film – and specific social values. But the acculturation Nino undergoes should not be considered as directly illustrative of a process of assimilation, as it often has been. For example, the film frowns upon the exclusion of migrants because they fail to take on the ways of the dominant 'local' culture; in one scene set on a Sydney ferry the literal embodiment of this xenophobia – a drunk, ex-digger abusing a non-English speaking Italian family – is thrown overboard. Nino, in terms of his wish to understand and adapt, to swim between the flags – to follow the metaphor presented in the film's Bondi Beach-set beach scenes – can be seen as a preferred model. But other possibilities for identity-formation and adaptation abound in the film, and Powell's vision of contemporary Australia is bracingly broad-minded, encompassing and, it can be argued, forward-looking.

The book and the film are most significant for being amongst the first mainstream cultural texts to deal with the Italian or ethnic migrant experience following the large-scale post-war migration that totally transformed Australian society and cultural identity. *They're a Weird Mob*'s largely benign representation of this experience offers a very different set of impressions from the films of the independent film-maker Giorgio Mangiamele, whose work – *The Contract* (1953) and *The Spag* (1962), for example – presents a far more troubled and less populist vision of migrant life in the same period. *They're a Weird Mob* has a lighter, less confrontational tone that in essence explores characteristic or stereotypical Australian traits, rather than a view of the varied and increasingly ethnic experience of the country. Although in many respects a simple film in terms of its broad, laconic, comedy, stereotypes, relaxed tone, and reliance upon a very conventional and episodic narrative structure of a visitor confronting, interpreting, and to some degree commenting upon the idiosyncrasies of local identity it nonetheless, as critic Tom O'Regan has argued in *Australian National Cinema* (1996), adopts the interesting strategy of using the figure of the migrant as a means to 'other' the local culture. The 'weird mob' of the film's title refers not to the migrant but to the very strangeness of Australian culture as perceived via the gaze of the foreigner. Ultimately, its view of the migrant experience situates its perspective somewhere between the competing governmental policies of assimilationism and multiculturalism, defining ideologies that mark the transition from the immediate post-war era in Australia to the more encompassing migration policies and outlook of the 1970s.

Adrian Danks

Age of Consent

Country of Origin:
Australia

Production Company:
Nautilus Productions

Producers:
Michael Powell
James Mason

Director:
Michael Powell

Screenwriter:
Peter Yeldham, from the novel
by Norman Lindsay

Cinematographer:
Hannes Staudlinger

Editor:
Anthony Buckley

Art Director:
Dennis Gentle

Music:
Peter Sculthorpe

Duration:
103 minutes

Genre:
Drama

Cast:
James Mason
Helen Mirren
Jack MacGowran
Neva Carr Glyn
Antonia Katsaros
Michael Boddy

Year:
1969

Synopsis

Expatriate Australian painter Bradley Morahan becomes disillusioned with the international art scene and decides to return to Australia to rejuvenate his love of painting. After arriving in Brisbane and reacquainting himself with various lovers and hangers-on, Morahan retreats to the beachcombing life of Dunk Island, holing himself up in a rustic beach shack while awaiting inspiration. This inspiration arrives in the form of the natural world that surrounds him and in the guise of a young woman, Cora, a free spirit dogged by her mother's 'loose' reputation and the insinuating barbs of her grandmother (a figure who represents a garish and unnatural presence in such beautiful surroundings). Despite the disturbing implications of the burgeoning sexual connection between painter and model – Cora is only about to reach the 'age of consent' – and the reasonably frank but tasteful nudity that appears throughout, *Age of Consent* is actually a surprisingly chaste and innocent movie. As one commentator has suggested, the most disturbing suggestion offered in the film about this May-December romance is actually to be found in the film's closing song, whose lyrics longingly spell out the pedophilic implications of the relationship. Often played for broad laughs rather than truly-felt emotional effect, the film's episodic but wistful narrative leisurely develops the 'romance' between Cora and Morahan while providing numerous asides to a range of other, often grotesque and cartoonish supporting characters.

Critique

English director Michael Powell's second Australian film and last feature is a fairly loose adaptation of Norman Lindsay's controversial and long-banned (until 1962) 1938 novel. Full of references to the work of various Australian and international artists, it departs significantly from Lindsay's novel by shifting the action to north Queensland, emphasizing the relationship between Morahan and Cora, and updating its story to the present day. In contrast to his adaptation of *They're a Weird Mob*, Powell was very dismissive of his source material here, using it as means to help create an environment rather than for any particular insights it offered, or narrative craft he found within its pages. Shot almost entirely on location in Cairns, Brisbane and Dunk Island, it is a leisurely, picaresque and intermittently-arresting contribution to the field of films and novels that dramatize the relationship between a fading artist and the muse who acts to rejuvenate his creativity. In this regard, it is a sun-kissed and somewhat benign final work in the career of a director often preoccupied with the lives of 'artists': visionary autocrats who attempt – and gamely fail – to command and control the worlds around them. Although a significant departure from the darker realms of *Peeping Tom* (1960), *The Red Shoes* (1948), *The Tales of Hoffmann* (1951) and *A Canterbury Tale* (1944), *Age of Consent* is nevertheless an intriguing and somewhat benign late entry in this encompassing 'series'.

In many ways, *Age of Consent* is a largely-forgotten film of 1960s' Australian cinema. Although it was a relative success at the Australian box office, it met with a lack of interest on its international release. Garnering some respectable reviews, it was nevertheless seen as another significant downturn in Powell's career, with its fate also hampered by the heavy-handedness of its international production partner, Columbia Pictures. Featuring an often beautiful and quite sophisticated Balinese-inflected score by Peter Sculthorpe, its international release was marred by trims to the nude scenes, significant changes to the credits and the opening New York-based gallery scenes, and the replacement of Sculthorpe's music by a more hackneyed and patently vulgar score by Stanley Myers. Like *They're a Weird Mob*, *Age of Consent* is a relatively unsophisticated, often broad and laconic entertainment, but also, like the earlier film, it trades in Powell's characteristic preoccupation with place, the world of artists, and the conflict or contrast between the ethereal domain of ideas and thought and the corporeal demands of the body. Like *Weird Mob*, it is also an unevenly-paced film that shifts significantly in tone between the often-lyrical scenes featuring Cora, and the more grotesque, guttural, and exaggeratedly physical scenes featuring a range of character actors including Jack MacGowran, Neva Carr Glyn and Antonia Katsaros. Although often over the top, MacGowran's performance is an often-adept piece of physical comedy, but Carr Glyn severely blights the film in her unsubtle and hysterical performance as Cora's grandmother. Ultimately, the key pleasures of this Powellian idyll are to be found in the performances of Mason and, more intermittently, Mirren, as well as the exquisitely captured flora, fauna, beaches and cloud formations of Dunk Island.

Adrian Danks

Peter Weir.

DIRECTORS
PETER WEIR (1944–)

Despite working in Hollywood since the mid-1980s, Peter Weir will always be strongly linked to the rebirth of Australian cinema in the 1970s, and his Australian films will feature in any discussion of the representation of Australia or Australian character on screen. Films such as *Gallipoli* (1981), *The Last Wave* (1977) and, in particular, *Picnic at Hanging Rock* (1975) established his international reputation. Whenever a European is asked about Australian cinema, Peter Weir's *Picnic at Hanging Rock* (1975) will likely be recalled first. The evocative, mysterious and incandescent images are seared into the memory.

Weir has repeatedly expressed the opinion that film-making is a craft. However, the vast majority of critical work on his films has focused on the artistic side of his movies, and Weir has often been placed within the European *auteur* tradition. Weir's style is a mixture of intuition and professionalism, and his films display recognizable characteristic features. He is not an innovator in the sense of looking for new, non-standard ways of realization. Rather, he takes advantage of commonplace tricks and motifs, frequently combining high- and pop-culture in innovative ways. This brings him close to Stanley Kubrick, whom Weir calls his *master*; it was after watching *Dr. Strangelove* that the Australian decided to become a film-maker. The story is always in the centre of 'Weir's playground', and the director himself used to say 'I think of myself as a storyteller' (McGilligan 1986: 24). In fact, it is the spectator who decides whether it is a matter of classical *genre* story or the intriguing reflections of *auteur* art narration.

Peter Lindsay Weir was born in 1944 in Sydney. As a young man Weir did not see his future as a film-maker. First, he studied law and arts at the University of Sydney, then worked in his father's real estate business. His fascination with cinema was fired during a trip to Europe in 1965. He learnt the art of direction in practice but never attended any film schools. On a ship to Europe he met his future wife and producer Wendy Stites and, together with friends, decided to entertain himself and his voyage companions by filming short, satirical sketches which were screened over the onboard television system. After his homecoming in 1967, Weir started working in television, at Channel Seven in Sydney. Two years later he joined the Australian Commonwealth Film Unit (replaced by Film Australia in 1973) as an assistant cameraman, but in fact he was hired as a director. As he admitted later, the CFU was his film school. In 1970 Weir, along with Brian Hannant and Oliver Howes, directed a part of the feature film *Three to Go* for the CFU. Weir's contribution, *Michael*, the story of a young boy from a middle-class family who changes under the influence of rebels that he met, won the Best Film and Best Cinematography in a Non-Feature or Documentary Film (for Kerry Brown) at the 1970 Australian Film Institute Awards. The film opened the door for Weir. His subsequent film, *Homesdale*, met with even greater success, winning Best Film, Best Short Fiction Film, and the inaugural award for Best Direction at the 1971 AFI Awards.

In 1974 Weir made his feature film debut with *The Cars That Ate Paris*. The story about the inhabitants of a small town, Paris, who earn money from car crashes that they cause, is a satire on Australians' love for cars. The black humour and grotesque characters of this and Weir's other films (including *The Plumber*, 1979) place them within the so-called 'Australian Gothic' *genre*. *Cars* was also Weir's first step into an international market. The film was screened independently during the 1974 Cannes Film Festival, with the director and producers driving the iconic Volkswagen Beetle festooned with vicious spikes along the Promenade de la Croisette. Two years later Weir returned to Cannes with *Picnic at Hanging Rock*, which opened the mythical, dreamlike series in his career (*The Last Wave*, *Gallipoli*). These films display elements of the W*eir style* and iconic features of the new Australian cinema: the Australian bush, spatial landscapes, mysterious, uncanny atmosphere, archetypical characters, Aborigines, the border between dream and reality, nature and civilization, and finally 'mateship'. In 1981, Weir tackled the most important war story and national event in Australian history in *Gallipoli*, a film he regards as his unofficial diploma. The popular and critical success of *Gallipoli* permitted him to co-produce his next film, *The Year Of Living Dangerously* (1982), with an American studio. Weir admitted that, after making *Picnic at Hanging Rock*, he had been offered work in the US. He waited to move to Hollywood until after *The Year of Living Dangerously*, claiming he finally knew at that time where he was as a man and as an artist. It was essential not to get lost in the Hollywood system and to make his artistic emigration a source of new inspiration.

The film *Witness* (1985), starring Harrison Ford (fresh from the success of *Indiana Jones* and *Star Wars*), started Weir's American career. His Hollywood movies have had mixed fortunes at the box office, with *The Mosquito Coast* (1986), *Fearless* (1993) and *Green Card* (1990) performing below expectations. *Dead Poets Society* (1989) quickly became one of his most popular and successful movies, while *The Truman Show* (1998), starring Jim Carrey, was prized by film critics. In 2003 he ventured to Mexico and the Galapagos Islands to make *Master and Commander*:

The Cars That Ate Paris, Saltpaan/Afdc/Royce Smeal.

The Far Side of the World, a cumulative adaptation of several of Patrick O'Brian's Aubrey-Maturin novels set on the High Seas during the Napoleonic Wars. In 2010 he is to present his new movie *The Way Back*, an adaptation of Slawomir Rawicz' novel about soldiers who escape from a Siberian gulag in 1940. Although films made before he left for Hollywood are seen as close to European artistic cinema, Weir's Hollywood films cannot be seen as mainstream cinema, especially because many motifs from the earliest pictures are maintained. 'Hollywood is just irrelevant. They just provide the room you play in', Weir said once in an interview (McGilligan 1986: 32). This continuum, that characterizes Weir's works, needs to be emphasized. It could be seen as repeating motifs (presence of *sacrum*, a hero dumped into a closed society, nature versus civilization, searching for truth, clash of cultures, a lack of female characters, open endings) and placing him between *art* and *genre film*.

Peter Weir often cooperates with the same people, including editor William Anderson, cinematographers John Seale and Russell Boyd and composer Maurice Jarre. As he admitted once, the story and narration are for him a matter of craft, while music is an inspiration and a groundwork for film atmosphere (McGilligan 1986: 30). His score choices seem to be eclectic and, especially when working with Jarre, Weir mixes classical and electronic music. Soundtracks usually introduce dissonance in his films and create atmospheres of understatement and allusion: the sound of flute in *Picnic at Hanging Rock*; Albinoni's *Adagio in G minor* in *Gallipoli*; the *mélange* of Philip Glass, Burkhard Dallwitz and Chopin in *The Truman Show*; as well as the compositions of an Australian trio (Christopher Gordon, Richard Tognetti, Iva Davies) in *Master and Commander*.

Inspiration for Weir's experimentation also comes from other extra-cinematic sources. Weir frequently cites art, as for instance the impressionism of the

Heidelberg school in *Picnic at Hanging Rock* (particularly the motif of *The Lost Child* by Frederick McCubbin). Dutch painters have also influenced Weir, especially Vermeer in *Witness*.

Considering the problem of auteurism, in the case of Weir we can point to some characteristic elements that construct his 'auteur trademark'. Besides influences from music or art, the 'Weir hero' is such a trademark. With the exceptions of *Green Card* and *The Plumber*, Weir's film worlds are male-dominated, and, most of all, this applies to *Master and Commander*, where there are only male characters. Women are often an impulse, making heroes act and face other cultures and mystery. As a wife, a mother or an object of platonic love (Weir avoids erotic scenes in his movies) a woman is always subordinated to a man. While in his early works he creates heroes close to the 'archetypical Australian' (especially in *Gallipoli*), in Hollywood films the 'Australianness' is replaced by 'Americanness' and the 'Australian hero' by the 'American hero'. While Albert in *Picnic at Hanging Rock* or Archy in *Gallipoli* are mythologized in romantic, AFC genre style, Allie, John Book, Max or Truman constitute a dialogue or polemic with the archetype of American hero. Weir's characters are always strangers who stand against the Other (e.g. *sacrum*, dreams, nature, culture, mysteries, but also civilization or a restrictive bourgeois society) that, even if impossible to understand, must be experienced by them.

The director has often used the *star system* in his films, casting popular actors like Mel Gibson, Richard Chamberlain, Harrison Ford, Robin Williams, Jim Carrey, Jeff Bridges or Russell Crowe. World-famous actors have starred in nearly all Weir's movies. Sometimes star names have been the producers' decision – either a trump card in negotiations with studios or an element of film marketing – and sometimes they have been Weir's choice, which represented for him a chance to play with the star image; for actors – to change this image.

As he does with the star system, Weir reformulates *genres* as well. In *The Year of Living Dangerously* he exposes the romantic elements of C J Koch's novel rather than its political plots, and recalls of classical melodramas such as *Casablanca*. In *The Last Wave* or even in *Picnic at Hanging Rock* he uses mystery-thriller atmosphere and plays with a war movie in *Gallipoli*. In Hollywood films, Weir takes elements of genres like the police thriller, western (*Witness*) or romantic comedy (*Green Card*) and makes use of the American myth of multiculturalism, American hero figures, urban and rural landscapes, in order to build his own, auteur 'Weir genre'. Through genre he establishes a connection with his audience in which he expresses his feelings regarding American or modern society in general and criticizes consumerism, media culture, contemporary relativism and rationalism that exclude mystery from our lives. 'What we see, and what we seem, are but a dream. A dream within a dream' – this famous sentence opening *Picnic at Hanging Rock* can be considered the leitmotif of Weir's films. Hanging Rock and the mysterious disappearance of the girls; in the ritual stones in *The Last Wave*; *Wayang* puppets in *The Year of Living Dangerously*; suddenly-shooting spotlight instead of a star in *Truman Show*; an airplane crash in *Fearless* – all interrupt the harmonious lives of heroes, making them stop and re-think. Weir's *sacrum* is the reality of dreams and fantasy, the world of tradition, myths and beliefs. He uses formal elements like bird's eye shots, godlike heroes (Kristof, Max, Allie Fox, Capt. Aubrey) or dreamlike scenes to captivate the audience and to create a space for the intersection of *sacrum* and *profanum*. The atmosphere is meant to capture the viewer, but it also constitutes a space for the meeting of *sacrum* and *profanum*. While his Australian movies take the motifs of dreams and visions, in his Hollywood works it is life that becomes a dream, 'a dream within a dream' and it is the 'Weir hero' who has to wake up.

Picnic at Hanging Rock, Picnic/Bef/Aust.Film Commission. Photograph By David Kynoch.

It is difficult to discuss Weir as a *star* like Martin Scorsese or Steven Spielberg: he is not an auteur celebrity, as Timothy Corrigan understands it (Corrigan 1998), even though his name can be taken as a trademark that guarantees a film's quality. *Master and Commander* in some measure can be analysed as an allegory of Weir's career, and also as an autothematical story. Both Aubrey and Maturin are artists in their craft. Their good, old ship *Surprise* appears to have no chance against the modern battleship *Acheron*. And yet as an instrument in the creator's hands the *Surprise* becomes a piece of art able to overcome the *Acheron*. It is not the modern technique or spectacular means that have importance in a battle, but experience, talent and intuition. It is only the production system or formal spectacle that has changed for Weir, on his way from artistic Australian cinema to Hollywood genre movies, yet themes, motifs and atmosphere are still continued. *Master and Commander* is a proof of his constant negotiation of his status as an artist and as an auteur star.

Martyna Olszowska

Three to Go: Michael

Country of Origin:
Australia

Studio/Distributor:
The Commonwealth Film Unit

Director:
Peter Weir

Producer:
Gil Brealey

Screenwriter:
Peter Weir

Cinematographer:
Kerry Brown

Editor:
Wayne LeClos

Duration:
27 minutes

Genre:
Drama

Cast:
Matthew Burton
Grahame Bond
Georgina West

Year:
1971

Synopsis

Michael s a young office worker from a wealthy middle-class family. The novella opens with scenes of street guerrilla fights. As it turns out, these are in a movie Michael is watching. In the morning he waits at the bus station, like other men, wearing a suit and reading *The Australian* newspaper. Michael's story is intercut with the parody of a television show about young rebels entitled *Youth Quake*. During one lunch break Michael meets a hippie couple, Georgina and Graham, in a bar and starts chatting with them. After a typical Sunday – mass in a church, a barbecue with parents and Judy, his girlfriend – Michael meets up with his new friends and they wander around in the city. He invites them to his girlfriend's sophisticated birthday party, which irritates his parents. The following day Michael phones his boss and takes a day off. After a day with Graham he feels strange at the evening party with other hippies who smoke marijuana and drink a lot. He phones home to tell his parents he will be home late, and leaves the party. The film ends with Michael walking the streets of Sydney.

Critique

Michael is one of three short-length movies included in the portmanteau feature *Three to Go*, produced by the Commonwealth Film Unit. The film was intended to give a voice to the younger generation, and to present the work of three promising young directors (Weir, Brian Hannant and Oliver Howes). In fact, among this trio, only Weir went on to an international career. *Michael* won several awards at the 1970 Australian Film Institute Awards, and received critical acclaim after being broadcast on Channel 7.

Michael is the first of the series of 'Weir heroes'. He fits neither in his parents' conservative middle-class world nor in the world of the rebellious hippies. He stays between these two worlds. The novella is a good example of the feature debut where a director, making his first steps, wants to show his skills. In such a way Weir experiments with editing and music. Instead of dialogues he uses rock songs by the Cleves to express the emotion of particular scenes or feelings. Paradoxically, a lack of dialogue, as Weir once admitted, was also due to the fact that Australians were not used to an Australian accent in films. Here, though, there are already clear signs of his future style and firm reliance upon striking images to tell the story.

Weir also reveals his specific sense of humour, as *Michael* is not only a parody of the restricted middle class. When Michael is making his way to the office, he passes a TV reporter preparing an interview for a television programme. The middle-aged man in a suit, who is unable to make his introduction in front of a camera, seems to be ridiculous in the same way as is a group of young rebels, interviewed for the show, when they are asked to look angry. As a result, they look more like puppets with bored faces. Maybe an older generation, terrified by hippies and trying to understand the problem of a 'youth quake' in the TV show, compromises itself, but the same thing happens to youngsters who declaim slogans about a repressive system, social changes and a revolution which seem to be incomprehensible for them. Both the hippies' freedom and middle-class correctness are imposed by culture, so, in some measure, *Michael* becomes a satire on atmosphere of the 1960s in general.

Even though the first of Weir's film is not perfect, with over-literal pictures occasionally used to symbolize the meaning of some scenes, it is still a very successful and impressive debut for a film-maker who would go on to become one of the most interesting auteurs of contemporary cinema.

Martyna Olszowska

Homesdale

Country of Origin:
Australia

Studio/Distributor:
Experimental Film Board

Director:
Peter Weir

Producer:
Grahame Bond
Richard Brennan

Screenwriters:
Peter Weir
Piers Davies

Cinematographer:
Anthony Wallis

Editor:
Wayne LeClos

Duration:
48 minutes

Genre:
Black comedy

Cast:
Geoff Malone
Grahame Bond
Peter Weir
Phillip Noyce

Year:
1971

Synopsis

A group of six people arrives at the Homesdale Hunting Lodge, a hotel on an isolated island. A sign on the front door claims that the bizarre hotel will be 'a new experience in togetherness'. While eating dinner on the veranda the group introduce themselves. The guests include an ex-soldier, a widow with a French accent, a butcher who wants to be a rock star and the very timid Mr Malfry. The next day, the group spend time reading, chatting or killing staff members. Eventually, they go in to the bush for a 'treasure hunt'. In the evening each of them has to present a short sketch, a song or a game that shows their worst 'face' and, meanwhile, makes fun of others. Suddenly, the play gets out of the control and the hotel guests lynch Mr Malfry. The strange Manager of the hotel, who resembles Dr Frankenstein, decides to dispose of Mr Malfry's body the next morning. But in the night calm Malfry shows his 'worst face' and takes his revenge on the butcher by killing him. The movie ends with the Manager welcoming new guests and presenting staff members. Malfry is among them.

Critique

It is difficult to classify Australian Gothic as a *genre*, although it is possible to list common features for movies of the 1970s described by this term. Among them, films of Peter Weir such as *The Last Wave, The Cars That Ate Paris, The Plumber* or *Homesdale* are the most interesting instances. Weir, as an expert in dreamlike, mysterious atmosphere created in cinema, felt at home in the Gothic. While *Michael* is a débutante's play with means of expression, *Homesdale* becomes a *cinéphile's* play with genres and cinema in general. It recalls artistic experiments that took place in cinema in the 1960s with its black humour, absurdity and freedom of imagination, as in Roman Polanski's works (*Repulsion*, 1965 or *The Fearless Vampire Killers*, 1967) or that of the Monty Python comedy group, which Weir cites as an influence. Weir, as in *Michael*, makes fun of some fashions of the 1960s. In *Homesdale* he makes a mockery of psychoanalysis, when guests of the Homesdale Hotel go on the treasure hunt in the bush and meet their own inner fears and 'id'.

As in *The Plumber*, Weir, in *Homesdale*, cites the famous shower scene from the Alfred Hitchcock's *Psycho*, but in a less serious way.

While one of the guests is taking a shower, somebody tries to kill him and, at first, everything suggests that he is, indeed, murdered. But, later, the victim comes out of the bathroom with a smile on his face and advises the other guests to 'have a shower'. In fact, this is the aim of staying in the Homesdale: to experience a little thrill that allows guests to forget about everyday life.

In *Homesdale* Weir explores genres like black comedy and horror through elements such as an absurd sense of humor, grotesque characters and nightmarish events. The Manager, who resembles Dr Frankenstein, is carrying out a sort of cruel, social experiment, showing that there is a devil in each of us. In some measure, he anticipates later 'Weir heroes' like Allie Fox in *The Mosquito Coast*, Max in *Fearless* or Christof in *Truman Show* – heroes who would like to control others' lives in a godlike fashion. As well, browbeaten and unfit for reality, Mr Malfry is another version of the 'Weir hero' – the stranger in a closed society.

Only an hour long, *Homesdale* contains nearly all the elements of the future Weir style. *Homesdale* was made in the old house in which the director lived with his wife at that time, and it was made with friends like Philip Noyce, now a well-known director in his own right. Despite some lapses, an aura of good student fun emanates from this film and charms, even after thirty years.

Martyna Olszowska

The Cars That Ate Paris

Country of Origin:
Australia

Studio/Distributor:
Salt Pan Production
Royce Smeal Film Production

Director:
Peter Weir

Producers:
Hal McElroy
Jim McElroy
Screenwriter
Peter Weir
Keith Gow
Piers Davies

Cinematographer:
John McLean

Synopsis

Arthur Waldo, driving with his brother George near the small town, Paris, has a car accident. George is killed, and Arthur, unconscious, is taken to a local hospital. When he wakes up he is forced to stay in the town and live in the mayor's house. The mayor starts to treat him as a son. Arthur blames himself for his brother's death and is unable to drive, having developed a phobia after the accident. But he discovers that the accident was not only the result of bad luck: inhabitants of Paris plan and execute the car crashes and live off the wrecked cars and victims' belongings they salvage. Survivors are admitted to the weird hospital where Dr Midland keeps them in a zombie-like state. The town is terrorized by a gang of youths driving bizarre vehicles constructed from the remnants of crashed cars. In the final battle, between the older inhabitants, supported by the mayor, and young rebels, Arthur stands by the mayor's people and kills one of aggressors. Shocked by his actions, Arthur forgets about his driving phobia, takes a car and runs away from the town.

Critique

After two multi-award-winning short films, *The Cars That Ate Paris* was Peter Weir's feature film debut. He decided to direct a story from his own script that was written during his second journey to Europe. He was inspired to write the story by the experience of driving through

Art Director:
David Copping

Editor:
Wayne LeClos

Duration:
91 minutes

Genre:
Comedy
Horror

Cast:
Terry Camilleri
John Meillon
Melissa Jaffer
Kevin Miles
Max Gillies
Peter Armstrong
Edward Howell
Bruce Spence

Year:
1974

some small French villages. But when he returned to Australia, changes in the film industry were in progress. The Commonwealth Film Unit, where Weir had worked before leaving for Europe, and where he had received his directorial experience, had now become Film Australia. Australian cinema was in the throes of a revival. Although raising money for a debut feature turned to be quite a difficult challenge, Weir managed to make Cars on a A$200,000 budget in 27 days.

The Cars That Ate Paris continues some motifs and themes evident in Weir's earlier films. *Cars …* was also Weir's first step into the international market. He presented his debut during the Cannes Film Festival Marketplace in 1974 and, with his producers, he drove the iconic Volkswagen Beetle dressed up with plastic spikes along the Promenade de Croisette. Although the crazy story about the small town that makes a living from car accidents did not achieve enormous success, either at the local or foreign box office, Weir returned to Cannes two years later with *Picnic at Hanging Rock* and found receptive audiences in Europe and South America.

Signs of Weir's future interests can be seen in the stylized opening scene. A beautiful young couple is driving their new car to a cottage to buy an antique painting. They are drinking Coke and smoking Alpine cigarettes. Suddenly one of wheels falls off and the car rolls down a precipice. The scene ends with a shot of a bush that surrounds the crashed car. Nature in its silence seems to be indifferent. A criticism of consumerism, which may be discerned in this scene, shot like a lavish television commercial, and a preponderance of nature over civilization return, especially in Weir's American movies like *Mosquito Coast*.

Grotesque characters and the film's black humour, as well as horror techniques, place *The Cars That Ate Paris* within Australian Gothic. Weir's debut is also, in some measure, an auto satire on Australians' love for cars and fascination with car accidents. Other elements will recur in Weir's later films: the closed society, a hero who does not fit anywhere and a clash of two generations that, in the finale, takes a very literal and brutal form. Even though Weir's debut could seem to be a little trashy nowadays, and perhaps a little overdrawn, there are some moments that give a lot of pleasure for a *cinéphile*. A parody of the western *genre*, in particular those of Sergio Leone and Sam Peckinpah, still bring a smile to a viewer's face.

Martyna Olszowska

Picnic at Hanging Rock

Studio/Distributor:
South Australian Film Corporation
Australian Film Commission

Synopsis

1900, St. Valentine's Day. The film opens with a still shot of the monolith known as Hanging Rock. Then the scene shifts to the exclusive Appleyard's College, where a group of young schoolgirls is preparing for a picnic at Hanging Rock. During their trip, four of them decide to explore, but they disappear. Michael Fitzhubert, a young aristocrat fascinated by one of girls, Miranda, holds an investigation with a stable-boy, Albert and, one week later, they find Irma, the only one to return, but she does not remember anything. The other girls, and

Director:
Peter Weir

Producers:
Hal McElroy
Jim McElroy
Patricia Lovell

Screenwriter:
Cliff Green, from the novel by
Joan Lindsay

Cinematographer:
Russell Boyd

Art Director:
David Copping

Editor:
Max Lemon

Duration:
115 minutes

Genre:
Drama
Mystery

Cast:
Rachel Roberts
Vivean Gray
Anne-Louise Lambert
Tony Llewellyn-Jones

Year:
1975

the teacher of mathematics who followed them, are never found. The mysterious disappearance of the girls casts an anxious shadow over the school. The accident also ruins the harmony of school life. Sara, a poor orphan at the school, discriminated against by the head teacher, commits suicide when she finds out about the death of her best friend, Miranda. At the end of the film, the college is closed after the mysterious death of Mrs Appleyard at Hanging Rock.

Critique

Even though at the time of its release *Picnic at Hanging Rock* was ignored by the jury of Australian Film Institute Awards and, at first, was not distributed in the US, it is nowadays considered one of the most significant films of the revived Australian cinema. The film demonstrates Weir's directorial maturity and talent in creating a subtle atmosphere of dreamlike reality through evocative images and music.

It was the producer, Patricia Lovell (a popular television presenter at the same time), who first drew Weir's attention to Joan Lindsay's novel, which had been published in 1967. It is hard to disagree with Brian McFarlane who claims that, in fact, *Picnic at Hanging Rock* is a case of the adaptation exceeding the original story. The book is, for Weir, only a pretext to build a network of obsessions that would find their continuation in further movies.

As in *The Cars That Ate Paris,* Weir begins the movie with an opening scene that constitutes an opposition between nature and civilization and introduces an atmosphere of anxiety and understatement. The still image of monolithic rocks is contrasted with a preparation for a picnic in Mrs Appleyard's school. Soft images of young girls tying their corsets and reading poetry are accompanied by the haunting sound of Bruce Smeaton's flute. While Lindsay's novel places emphasis on differences between the upper and lower class in Victorian Australia, Weir gives his attention to a contrast between nature's inner power and freedom, foreshadowing at the same time a coming catastrophe, and the closed society with its conventions and restrictions, manifested in clothes and manners. Through Russell Boyd's cinematography, Weir creates an erotic tension without a literal eroticism. Weir searched for his actors for a long time, seeking girls with a pre-Raphaelite look, especially Miranda, who was to be like Botticelli's angel. Schoolgirls are a part of the landscape in the same way as Hanging Rock and have their part in creating the mysterious atmosphere. Their image also references the famous motif of Frederick McCubbin's painting *The Lost Child,* while the movie as a whole is indebted to the impressionism of the Heidelberg school of Australian painters who were active in the late nineteenth century.

Paradoxically, Weir builds the mystery with some common elements which would not, separately, give the same impression of the this anxiety – for instance, a watch that suddenly stops at noon, which some pupils try to explain scientifically. It is another opposition in *Picnic* and a characteristic feature of Weir's stories, where rationalism must fail in the battle with irrational mystery and with questions that do not get answers. That irrationality is connected with *sacrum*, with an unknowing that Weir heroes always experience. And puzzling the mystery out is not the aim. Weir loves open endings, because the essence of his stories is facing the Other – other reality, other cultures, other men – rather than unravelling the mystery. Although the 'magic of cinema' has become a cliché nowadays, it is difficult to find a more appropriate epithet for Weir's movies and *Picnic at Hanging Rock* is the best example of that.

Martyna Olszowska

The Last Wave

Country of Origin:
Australia

Studio/Distributor:
Ayer Production
Australian Film Commission

Director:
Peter Weir

Producers:
Hal McElroy
Jim McElroy

Screenwriters:
Tony Morphett
Petru Popescu
Peter Weir

Cinematographer:
Russell Boyd

Art Director:
Neil Angwin

Editor:
Max Lemon

Duration:
106 minutes

Genre:
Drama
Thriller

Cast:
Richard Chamberlain
Olivia Hamnet
David Gulpilil
Fred Parslow
Vivean Gray

Year:
1977

Synopsis

The film opens with a series of shots: an Aboriginal man painting mysterious signs on a cave wall, a group of Aborigines looking for a shelter although there are no clouds on the sky and only a sound suggesting a coming storm, and a small outback town where unexpectedly it is hailing. These mysterious weather conditions, with a downpour of frogs in the climax, are announced only on radio in the next part of the film. The main story takes place in Sydney and focuses on a lawyer, David Burton. The successful, middle-class man is asked to defend a group of Aboriginal men accused of killing one of their clan members, because he stole sacred stones. The victim was murdered by an old Aboriginal man, Charlie, who used the 'death bones'. During the investigation David has strange dreams and premonitions, and discovers the remnants of an ancient civilization below the city. He later learns that his dreams are warnings about the imminent destruction of the city by a tsunami.

Critique

After the success of *Picnic at Hanging Rock,* Peter Weir was able to raise a larger budget for his next movie. *The Last Wave* was written by Weir, based on his personal experience. *The Last Wave* introduced Weir to America. The film was distributed in North America and gained popularity there before *Picnic at Hanging Rock* (which was not distributed in US until 1979) perhaps because of the American star, Richard Chamberlain, perhaps in the genres that the film evokes. But looking at *The Last Wave* only from the perspective of genre can lead to a blind alley. Genre is only a frame here and the investigation is only a pretext to build a story in which dreamlike visions, irrationality, a water motif recalling Jung's theory, and Aboriginal culture interweave in a very interesting way.

'Why did you not tell me about the mysteries?' David Burton asks his stepfather, the priest. Like Max or Truman, characters in Weir's later movies, the lawyer has to go towards the light after finding his way out from the labyrinth of catacombs located under Sydney. Mystical or even religious associations abound, especially when Burton recognizes himself as a messenger who links two worlds of white and black Australia and two realities, although we cannot be sure whether it is not a result of his paranoia. Like most of the 'Weir heroes' David's job and approach is highly rational, but the case requires him to open himself to the *sacrum,* to what is unknown. A pragmatic and rational way of thinking could not help at the moment of facing another culture that appears to be an irrational world of beliefs and dreams. The Weir hero has to leave it and go beyond rational thought to find his answer. Burton wants to gain knowledge, a mystery, but, as always happens in Weir's world, he fails to connect with the other culture. The meeting of cultures opens both sides to what was unrecognized until that time. As in *Picnic at Hanging Rock* and in Weir's later movies, there are some sacred objects and mythical persons, messengers linking both realities. In *The Last Wave*, it is dreams, sacred stones and the Aboriginal man, Chris, that fulfill this role. Weir's fascination with Aboriginal traditions and beliefs is evident in *The Last Wave*. Aboriginal people are, in some measure, idealized and presented romantically as a part of the mystery.

The Last Wave, even if stamped by Weir's distinguishing marks and continuing dreamlike and mystery motifs from *Picnic at Hanging Rock*, can irritate by its literality. What, in *Picnic at Hanging Rock*, was left for viewers' imagination is made obvious in *The Last Wave*. As a result, there is little space for the mystery.

Martyna Olszowska

The Plumber

Country of Origin:
Australia

Studio/Distributor:
South Australian Film
Corporation

Director:
Peter Weir

Producer:
Matt Carroll

Screenwriter:
Peter Weir

Cinematographer:
David Sanderson

Art Directors:
Ken James
Herbert Pinter

Editor:
Gerald Turney-Smith

Duration:
76 minutes

Genre:
Thriller

Synopsis

Most of the story takes place in a small apartment of a married couple, Jill and Brian, in Adelaide. She is an anthropologist working at home on her Master's thesis on the culture of New Guinean tribes. One morning Brian reads in Jill's diary about her bizarre encounter with a shaman in New Guinea. After Brian goes to work, a plumber, Max, arrives unexpectedly. He claims he is from the university administration and has to make a routine check of drain pipes in a bathroom. Jill lets him in but after a moment she becomes suspicious. Her suspicions increase when Max starts talking about his criminal past and taking a shower without permission. His work drags on and, day by day, Jill feels more and more uncomfortable in the presence of the plumber, who is making a lot of mess. She feels unable to communicate with this uneducated, 'primitive' man. She does not know if her suspicion of Max is a result of her nervousness or is well-founded, and her husband and friend, Meg, do not believe her. She resolves to get rid of Max, and accuses him of stealing her watch.

Critique

In 1978 Peter Weir decided to take a year's break from film-making. For twelve months he watched almost all of the most important American and European pictures, silent and sound, in film history. As he admitted, after watching the films, he was glad that he had not done this before he became a film-maker, otherwise he would not have made any movies. As the director of three features, he realized he 'was at the bottom of the hill'. In fact, the television feature *The Plumber* released in 1979 was not a result of this 'film course'. It would be *Gallipoli*, made in 1981, that would allow Weir to feel he had reached maturity as a director.

Cast:
Judy Morris
Ivar Kants
Robert Coleby
Candy Raymond

Year:
1979

Weir claimed that *The Plumber*, directed for Channel 9, was made for money. Even if it is not Weir's masterpiece, and for film critics it is often a sort of interlude in his career before his next successful movie, it is, at the same time, a little gem. *The Plumber* is a modest picture with few actors, mostly made in a small apartment in Adelaide. From his own script, Weir builds a simple but attractive story. As in *The Last Wave* or *Picnic at Hanging Rock*, Weir creates an anxious atmosphere. The plot recalls one of the films by Weir's favorite director, Stanley Kubrick. As in *The Shining*, we cannot be sure if characters face a real danger or whether their suspicions and fear are, rather, the result of paranoia.

Jill is an exception in the gallery of male 'Weir's heroes', although, as always in a case of a woman in Weir's movies, an erotic tension is linked to her. In *Picnic at Hanging Rock* it was nature that symbolized this erotic freedom. In *The Plumber*, Max, like a New Guinean shaman, brings into Jill's existence a side of life that she has denied.

In some measure, Weir plays with the viewer in a very fickle way. It is not a matter of the narration and the story itself; Jill's character resembles other Weir heroes who stand between two worlds, experience a clash of cultures and are faced with a mystery. She researches a New Guinean tribe and, as we learn at the very beginning of the film, she has a strange experience with a shaman. But, as it soon turns out, it is not a primitive culture but a 'primitive' man from a lower class that will symbolize this other world and culture that she cannot understand. At the end, a question is raised: who is the real victim, Jill as a woman terrorized by a psycho, or Max as an undereducated man discriminated against by a middle class woman?

Martyna Olszowska

Gallipoli

Country of Origin:
Australia

Studio/Distributor:
The Australian Film Commission, R&R Films

Director:
Peter Weir

Producers:
Patricia Lovell
Robert Stigwood

Screenwriters:
David Williamson
Peter Weir

Synopsis

Gallipoli tells the story of the participation of Australian and New Zealand troops (ANZACs) in the disastrous Dardanelles campaign in 1915. In the Western Australian bush, Archy is trained by his uncle Jack to be a champion athlete. But the boy has his own plans. After competing in a sprint, Archy befriends another competitor, a cynical city-boy, Frank. Archy suggests that he and Frank enlist in the armed forces together, but they are not accepted because Frank is unable to ride a horse, and Archy is underage. They decide to travel to Perth, where they are unknown, to try again to join the army. They travel by train and then walk across an interior desert. Archy is an idealist and wants to join the Light Horse to protect his country. Frank just wants to earn money. After enlisting they unite again in Cairo, where the troops are trained. Eventually, they are sent out to the Gallipoli peninsula, where they have to conquer the beach defended by Turkish artillery. The battle becomes a massacre and costs the lives of many Anzac soldiers. The film ends with a freeze-frame of Archy as he sprints across the battlefield and is shot by Turkish troops.

Cinematographer:
Russell Boyd

Art Director:
Herbert Pinter

Editor:
William M. Anderson

Duration:
110 minutes

Genre:
History, Drama, War

Cast:
Mel Gibson
Mark Lee
Bill Kerr
Bill Hunter

Year:
1981

Critique

Gallipoli displays Weir's directorial self-confidence and awareness. Weir has said that the film is his least personal project, but also his favourite film. *Gallipoli* presented a commercial image of Australia in historical packaging and is acknowledged as one of the most important Australian films of the revival. *Gallipoli* took one of the most fundamental and symbolic events in Australian history to the international arena. Weir collaborated on the script with playwright David Williamson. The movie was produced by Patricia Lovell, Robert Stigwood and media magnate Rupert Murdoch – his first foray into film production in Australia.

Fifty thousand Australian soldiers fought in the Gallipoli campaign in 1915. Eight thousand died, and twenty thousand were wounded. Even though it was not the bloodiest battle of the First World War for Australia, it has enormous symbolic significance. In part through the contemporary reportage of the official war historian, C E W Bean, who compared the Anzacs to Greek gods, and in part because the battle was the first major engagement of the war for Australian troops, Gallipoli was represented as Australia's 'baptism of fire': the battle in which the nation was forged. Weir was of course perfectly aware of this.

Gallipoli is a film of a foundational, national moment, so in some measure it is impossible to ignore its contribution to Australian national cinema. Stylistically, it is a continuation of the AFC genre line with other films like *Newsfront, Picnic at Hanging Rock* or *Breaker Morant*, where the definition of Australianness is found in the past. The script was constructed on a few *leitmotifs* and some simple oppositions, where a contrast between 'us' and 'them' is the most crucial. Weir contrasts the open spaces of Australia with the narrow streets of Cairo and the tight space of the trenches. At the core of the story is Archy and Frank's friendship – a symbol of the Australian quality of mateship, and also a representation of two kinds of Australians: the naïve, strong and brave bushman, and the resourceful, cynical city boy. The film is structured as a (doomed) race against time; given the outcome of the battle, the film cannot avoid a tragic ending. The film opens and closes with the race against time: the first scene depicts Archy's training run, the final scene depicts his race towards death. It is a metonym: the running of one boy represents the thousands of young Australians who were sent to their deaths by the British High Command. The last still of dying Archy is a powerful, myth-making image.

Although sentimental, and conventional in its ideology, *Gallipoli* is a part of national cinema that aims to maintain national myths and to create a romantic metaphor of significant historical facts. Weir, situating his movie between an artistic and Hollywood style, manages to make this national myth both locally resonant and internationally appealing.

Martyna Olszowska

The Year of Living Dangerously

Country of Origin:
Australia

Studio/Distributor:
MGM, McElroy&McElroy

Director:
Peter Weir

Producer:
Jim McElroy

Screenwriters:
C J Koch from his novel
David Williamson
Peter Weir

Cinematographer:
Russell Boyd

Art Director:
Herbert Pinter

Editor:
William M. Anderson

Duration:
115 minutes

Genre:
Drama
Romance
War

Cast:
Mel Gibson
Linda Hunt
Sigourney Weaver
Bill Kerr

Year:
1982

Synopsis

Guy Hamilton, a foreign correspondent of the Australian Broadcasting Service, arrives in Jakarta in 1965, in the midst of what Indonesian President Sukarno calls 'the year of living dangerously'. This is the young and ambitious reporter's first job, and a chance to make a name for himself. He meets a half-Chinese, half-Australian midget and photographer, Billy Kwan. Kwan becomes Guy's guide as he has many useful contacts and knows the country very well. He introduces Hamilton to Jill, an Englishwoman working for the British Embassy. Guy and Jill soon fall in love. Jill wants to leave Jakarta because of the tense atmosphere in Indonesia. She persuades Guy to leave with her but, before they depart, she receives a top secret message about war supplies from Shanghai for the Communists in Jakarta. Guy decides to write a story about it. They quarrel, and split up. Guy returns to Jakarta and witnesses Kwan's suicide. He injures his eye in an accident. Eventually, he decides to join Jill at the airport as street fighting intensifies.

Critique

Peter Weir took an interest in C J Koch's novel in 1978 and bought the rights to use it. After *Picnic at Hanging Rock, The Year of Living Dangerously* (which was nominated for the Golden Palm at the 1983 Cannes Film Festival) was his second movie based on a book. The screenplay modifies Koch's novel, with Weir focusing on the love affair between Jill and Guy rather then on political plots. Billy Kwan, rather than Koch's neutral correspondent Cookie, becomes the narrator of the story.

In the 1970s the journalist as hero of adventure or criminal movies appeared in such pictures as Alan Pakula's *All the President's Men* and *The Parallax View*. In the 1980s the trend continued in Oliver Stone's *Salvador* and Roland Joffe's *The Killing Fields*. But, in contrast to the main characters in Pakula's or Joffe's films, Guy Hamilton stands outside all political activity that happens in Jakarta. He is an observer; he writes articles but, in the end, he does not support any side. In fact, such an attitude follows Weir's point of view that could be seen from the early short-length novella *Michael*. 'I've never been a joiner', he admitted once and, in fact, heroes like Michael or even Arthur in *The Cars* are at the edges of the Sixties, as Weir was himself. That is a reason why *The Year of Living Dangerously* is closer to a melodrama genre like *Casablanca* than to 'engaged political cinema'.

Although the film stars Mel Gibson, American actress Linda Hunt turned out to be the real star, winning the 1983 Oscar as the Best Actress in a Supporting Role. As male dwarf Billy Kwan she gives the narrator of the movie some metrosexual features and some sort of fluttery understatement. Kwan in voice-over becomes a main character of the story as we look at Jill and Guy through his eyes. He is a master of the wayang theatre of shadow puppets. The performance starts the story and provides a kind of commentary on Jill and Guy's love affair, as the puppets depict the love between a Prince Ajurna and Princess Srikandi. At the same time, the puppetry expresses the Eastern philosophy. 'In the West, we want answers. Everything is either right or wrong, good or bad, but in the wayang no such final conclusions exist', Billy says in the movie. This fits with Weir's other film worlds where heroes never find the answers they seek. Kwan is like characters in Weir's Hollywood films – godlike Kristof in *Truman Show*, Max in *Fearless* or Allie Fox in *The Mosquito Coast* who want to influence and direct other people's lives.

The character of Kwan also raises the issue of national belonging, as he is half-Chinese, while Guy is half-American. What does it mean to be Australian? How does it manifest in a clash with different culture? So, even if moving the focus to a love affair simplified Koch's novel, in fact it becomes only a frame in Weir's movie. As in several of his Hollywood films, Weir implies problems and issues that interest him in what appears to be a simple story. In *The Year of Living Dangerously* it is Billy Kwan who is a medium for these interests.

Martyna Olszowska

Australia (2008), 20th Century Fox/Bazmark Films.

DIRECTORS
BAZ LUHRMANN (1962–)

Like Orson Welles and Vincente Minnelli before him, Baz Luhrmann brought his prodigious talent from the world of theatre to the grander canvas of cinema. A graduate of Sydney's National Institute of Dramatic Arts (NIDA), Luhrmann's reputation was established, before he directed his first film, with his productions of Puccini's opera La Bohème, Benjamin Britten's A Midsummer Night's Dream and Lake Lost for the Australian Opera. In 2002, Luhrmann revived his production of La Bohème for Broadway, winning three Tony Awards. Luhrmann's first feature film, the ballroom-dancing romantic comedy Strictly Ballroom (1992), was originally conceived as a play at NIDA, and later developed by Luhrmann's theatre company, the Six Years Old Company. Throughout his career, on stage and in film, he has collaborated with costume and production designer Catherine Martin, who is also his wife. Martin won two Academy Awards – for Best Art Direction and Best Costume Design – for her work on Moulin Rouge! (2001).

Luhrmann has his own production company, Bazmark Inq, based in Sydney in a heritage building he calls the House of Iona. Like Francis Ford Coppola's American Zoetrope studio or George Lucas' company Lucasfilm, Luhrmann has established the base and infrastructure from which to create his cinematic visions, keeping all aspects of pre- and post-production in-house, while filming on location or in Sydney's Fox Studios as required. Luhrmann has a first-look deal with 20th Century Fox that preserves his creative autonomy. After Strictly Ballroom's success at the Cannes Film Festival, Luhrmann was courted by various studios all looking to finance his next film, but Fox was the only studio that would allow him to retain artistic independence. In interviews, he has acknowledged that this has come at a price – other studio deals would have seen him become 'seriously wealthy' – but he places a higher value on his 'freedom' (Cook 2007; Malone 1997). He describes Fox as 'curators who take care of the business side of things so that [Catherine and I] are free to manage the creative process of film-making' (quoted in Cook 2007: 10).[1] The perceived 'gamble' that Fox took in subsidizing Luhrmann's reimagining of Shakespeare paid off when William Shakespeare's Romeo + Juliet (1996) opened at number one at the American box office, ahead of the multi-star vehicle Sleepers (Barry Levinson, 1996) with Robert De Niro, Brad Pitt and Dustin Hoffmann. Luhrmann's arrangement with Fox also allows him extended development time between film projects – five years between the release of Romeo + Juliet and Moulin Rouge! with Australia (2008) released seven years later (after an earlier project on Alexander the Great was abandoned). In a 1997 interview, Lurhmann defended his artistic process:

> We are noted for doing a ludicrous amount of preparation. And we are noted for ridiculous kind of research, but this is what we like to do – the act of making must make your life rich. It's got to be interesting and fulfilling and educational and take you on a journey. They're the choices we make. (Malone 1997: 44)

Luhrmann is very self-conscious about his status as an auteur, as evidenced by his 'Red Curtain Trilogy', a term created by Luhrmann himself (rather than a term applied to his work by film scholars) to describe his first three films. Following the theatrical release of Moulin Rouge! in 2002 Luhrmann released Strictly Ballroom, William Shakespeare's Romeo + Juliet and Moulin Rouge! as a DVD box set, which was marketed as The Red Curtain Trilogy. A cynic might regard this as simply a clever marketing device for a DVD release, but Luhrmann has been explicit and consistent in his definition of 'Red Curtain' cinema, which he says is 'a theatricalised cinema-style': 'A simple, even naïve story, based on a primary myth is set in a world that is distant, exotic, and yet familiar. The audience

Australia (2008), 20th Century Fox/Bazmark Films.

participates in the telling of the story through a device. In *Strictly Ballroom* that device is dance, while *Romeo + Juliet* uses the language of Shakespeare. *Moulin Rouge!* is told through song' (Luhrmann 2002). By setting down the principles by which he and his team at Bazmark created these three films, Luhrmann is also strategically intervening in the growing auteurist analysis of his works by framing the terms of reference for critics. He exemplifies Deb Verhoeven's observations (in relation to another Australian film director, Jane Campion) of the contemporary film director who fashions themself as an 'auteur' through their interactions with the media, their choice of projects, their film-making techniques and their promotion of their films (Verhoeven 2009).

Independent of his own rhetoric, there is a unity of vision in the 'Red Curtain' films that is subsequently lost with *Australia. Australia* saw the end of Luhrmann's long-standing collaborations with his co-writer Craig Pearce (whom he met at NIDA) and editor Jill Bilcock, whose astonishing, rapid-fire editing style in *Romeo + Juliet* and *Moulin Rouge!* was justly recognized with several awards and nominations, including an Oscar nomination for *Moulin Rouge!*. *Australia* is the collective product of no less than four screenwriters and two editors; unsurprisingly, the screenplay and the pacing (at over 165 minutes) are the weakest elements in the film. In addition, Luhrmann's director of photography on *Romeo + Juliet* and *Moulin Rouge!*, Don McAlpine, was replaced by Mandy Walker, and there is a distinct lack of innovation in *Australia*'s cinematography; while the images are handsome, they show us nothing we have not seen before in countless films set in the Outback, and indeed several images border on cliché (knowingly, perhaps, given Luhrmann's pastiche style?). Registering the disappointment shared by many after the 'iconoclasm, from concept to execution' of Luhrmann's Red Curtain Trilogy, Brian McFarlane observed that *Australia* 'may well be his most conventional [film] to date' (McFarlane 2008: 10).

Despite the lukewarm reception from critics, *Australia* was a box-office success on its home territory, becoming the second highest-grossing Australian film of all time after *Crocodile Dundee* (Peter Faiman, 1986) ('*Australia* Beats *Babe* Box Office' 2009). One of the stronger elements in *Australia* is its use of source music, particularly the film's reappropriation of 'Somewhere Over the Rainbow' from *The Wizard of Oz* (Victor Fleming, 1939) to convey the hopes and dreams of a racially-divided society (as in the open-air cinema scene, for instance). This 'musicality' ties *Australia* with Lurhmann's earlier films, in which the legacy of the musical genre is evident. While this is most obvious with *Moulin Rouge!*, Luhrmann also demonstrates his love of the musical form in *Strictly Ballroom*, which resembles the backstage musical in its preparations for the dance championships, while the pop music soundtrack of *Romeo + Juliet* attests to Luhrmann's awareness of the power of song to convey characters' emotions, with songs from artists as diverse as Radiohead, Des'ree and The Wannadies integrated into the storytelling. Darragh O'Donoghue (2008) refers to this recycling of popular music as 'Luhrmann's karaoke aesthetic', where he has actors (not professional singers) performing 'classic hits' from bygone eras: for example, Nicole Kidman singing 'Diamonds are a Girl's Best Friend' from *Gentlemen Prefer Blondes* (Howard Hawks, 1953) and Madonna's 'Material Girl' alongside Ewan McGregor singing Elton John's 'Your Song' and 'The Hills are Alive' from *The Sound of Music* (Robert Wise, 1965) in *Moulin Rouge!*; Harold Perrineau lip-synching the 1970s' disco hit 'Young Hearts Run Free' in *Romeo + Juliet*; or Tara Morice singing Cyndi Lauper's 'Time after Time' on the *Strictly Ballroom* soundtrack.

It is this musicality of Luhrmann's cinematic vision that sets him apart from other Australian directors. He embraces the artifice of the musical form to serve the sincerity of emotion. This is not an easy thing to achieve and many modern filmgoers remain sceptical when characters burst into song, but Luhrmann has found various ways to 'smuggle' the musical back into contemporary cinema, reinvigorating the genre for global, as well as local, audiences.[2]

Notes

1. Cook interviewed Luhrmann during the course of her research for a book-length study of Luhrmann's films, to be released in March 2010 as part of the BFI World Directors series. See this link for more information: http://filmstore.bfi.org.uk/acatalog/info_294.html, accessed 16 October 2009.
2. On Luhrmann and the musical genre, see Marsha Kinder's review of *Moulin Rouge!* in *Film Quarterly*, Spring 2002, vol. 55, no. 3, pp. 52–59.

Fincina Hopgood

Strictly Ballroom

Country of Origin:
Australia

Studio:
M & A Film Corporation
and Australian Film Finance
Corporation

Director:
Baz Luhrmann

Producers:
Tristram Miall
Antoinette Albert
Jane Scott

Screenwriters:
Baz Luhrmann & Craig Pearce
(from a screenplay by Baz
Luhrmann & Andrew Bovell)

Cinematographer:
Steve Mason

Editor:
Jill Bilcock

Duration:
91 minutes

Genre:
Romantic comedy

Cast:
Paul Mercurio
Tara Morice
Bill Hunter
Pat Thomson
Gia Carides
Peter Whitford
Antony Vargas

Year:
1992

Synopsis

Set in the world of ballroom dancing, *Strictly Ballroom* combines a tale of rebellion and artistic freedom with the story of the ugly duckling. Scott Hastings has a promising career as an amateur ballroom dancing champion, but his creativity is stifled by the strict rules of competition that govern what kinds of steps are allowed. In the film's opening sequence at the Waratah District Championships, Scott is forced to improvise to avoid a collision with another couple. The crowd responds with applause but he and his partner, Liz, are disqualified. Enraged that they missed out on winning the championship, Liz leaves Scott for another dance partner, Ken Railings.

Scott dances his own steps in the rehearsal studio, unaware that Fran – a dowdy wallflower with glasses and pimples who is a beginner ballroom dancer – is watching him. Excited by what she sees, and with a few dance ideas of her own, Fran offers to become Scott's partner and dance 'your steps, your way'. Scott is initially sceptical, but agrees to rehearse with Fran in secret, while his pushy stage mother, Pat, and dance-hall instructor, Les, arrange a series of auditions to replace Liz. A slow attraction develops between Scott and Fran over a montage of rehearsals, which include Fran removing her beer-goggle lenses to reveal a quiet beauty beneath. Scott accompanies Fran home one night and meets her Spanish family – her widowed father, Rico, and her nana, Ya Ya. Rico ridicules Scott's attempt at the Paso Doble and proceeds to instruct him in the ways of Spanish dancing. Scott and Fran decide to incorporate these steps into their routine. Ya Ya's contribution to their performance is to give Scott Rico's bejewelled matador jacket and make Fran a resplendent red dress.

As the championships draw near, Scott is pressured to partner up with leading dancer Tina Sparkle. To persuade him, President Barry Fife reveals the tragic secret of Scott's father's past – he lost the championship title when he insisted on dancing his own steps and was devastated by the defeat. Scott's father, Doug, has been a mousy recluse ever since; he is a mute, tragic figure dismissed by everyone, including Scott. But when Doug tells Scott the true story of his betrayal, Scott refuses to bow to pressure and insists on dancing with Fran. Despite the attempts of Barry and his female assistant to thwart Scott and Fran's performance through disqualification and turning off the music, the audience cheers and the younger generation of dancers enthusiastically embrace Scott's ideas. The film ends with Fran and Scott kissing on the dance floor as all the characters – young and old, dancers and spectators – dance en masse to the strains of John Paul Young's 'Love is in the Air'.

Critique

Strictly Ballroom is often regarded as the beginning of a wave of 'quirky comedies' that characterized Australian cinema in the first half of the 1990s. These films tended to satirize Anglo Australian culture with varying degrees of affection and loathing (see, for example, *The Castle*, Rob Sitch, 1997 versus *Welcome to Woop Woop*, Stephan Elliott, 1997). With the garish make-up, fake tan and coiffed hairstyles of ballroom dance culture exaggerated to the point of grotesquery, Luhrmann is merciless in his portrayal of Anglo Australian culture as superficial and spiteful, lacking any real depth of feeling and caring only about winning, not dancing. This is contrasted with the authentic culture of Spain, as embodied by the music and passionate dancing of Fran's family. The film is significant for tapping into Australia's growing sense of itself as a multicultural nation in the early 1990s. However simplistic it may be as a narrative device, the importation of Spanish dance into the sterile world of ballroom dancing serves as a powerful metaphor for the embracing of difference and the bridging of old and new generations. This message was warmly received both locally and abroad, as the film's box office, awards and film festival screenings attest.

Strictly Ballroom has been linked with two other successful films of the nineties – *The Adventures of Priscilla: Queen of the Desert* (Elliott, 1994) and *Muriel's Wedding* (P J Hogan, 1994) – as part of 'The Glitter Cycle' of contemporary Australian cinema (Rustin 2001). These films share an obvious visual style of excess and glitz in costuming, makeup and musical performance pieces. They harness the kitsch appeal ('so bad it's good') and nostalgic pleasure associated with popular songs from the 1970s and 1980s by ABBA, John Paul Young, Gloria Gaynor, and Cyndi Lauper. These three films are also linked thematically in their portrayal of protagonists asserting their individuality in defiance of their family's expectations and the social roles demanded of them. *Strictly Ballroom* is the most conventional of the three in its recreation of the musical's utopian space of dance and the primacy of the heterosexual couple (as opposed to the re maginings of family and partnership proposed by *Priscilla*'s drag queens and Muriel with her best friend, Rhonda).

Strictly Ballroom offers a textbook example of the influence of Hollywood genre films upon Australian cinema. It shares a number of generic features with the popular dance movie *Dirty Dancing* (Emile Ardolino, 1987): the accomplished male dancer instructing the shy, awkward girl in a montage of rehearsal scenes; the inevitable romance that blossoms through dance; the familial divide that threatens the lovers' union (in *Dirty Dancing*, the issue is one of class, rather than ethnicity) and finally, the triumphant performance that marks the culmination of the romance and heals the wounds of familial discord. Writers such as Stuart Cunningham have noted Australian cinema's tendency to 'Australianise' Hollywood genres, thereby creating something both new and familiar that is embraced by audiences locally and overseas (Cunningham 1985). *Strictly Ballroom* 'Australianises' the romantic comedy and the dance movie by grafting onto these generic forms the local accents and iconic symbols of Australian urban culture: the corner milk bar run by the immigrant family; the Hill's Hoist washing line; the suburban family home adorned with trophies. The famous rooftop setting where Fran and Scott dance while Lauper's romantic ballad 'Time After Time' plays on the soundtrack is emblematic of this relation between the local and the global – the couple is framed between the metal bars of the Hill's Hoist and the glittering red sequins of a Coca-Cola sign. Indeed, this shot encapsulates Luhrmann's aesthetic, prefiguring his future film projects (both *William Shakespeare's Romeo + Juliet*, 1996, and *Moulin Rouge!*, 2001, feature the word 'L'Amour' styled in the famous Coca-Cola font) and the ongoing tension between the local and the global that characterizes his work.

Fincina Hopgood

Romeo + Juliet
(alternative title: William Shakespeare's Romeo + Juliet)

Country of Origin:
Australia / USA

Studio:
20th Century Fox
Bazmark Films

Director:
Baz Luhrmann

Producers:
Gabriella Martinelli
Baz Lurhmann

Screenwriters:
Craig Pearce
Baz Luhrmann

Cinematographer:
Donald M McAlpine

Editor:
Jill Bilcock

Duration:
116 minutes

Genre:
Drama
Romance

Cast:
Leonardo DiCaprio
Claire Danes
John Leguizamo
Brian Dennehy
Miriam Margolyes
Pete Postlethwaite
Vondie Curtis-Hall
Paul Rudd

Year:
1996

Synopsis

Shakespeare's classic play about two young lovers from feuding families is relocated to modern-day Verona Beach. The Montague and Capulet patriarchs are rivals in property development; their male off-spring hang out in gangs on the beach, in the pool hall or cruising the streets. Swords are replaced with guns; news media and pop culture references dominate, but Shakespeare's prose is retained.

Following a prologue (to be discussed below), the action commences with a stand-off between the rival Montague and Capulet gangs at a gas station, which escalates into a gun fight and fire, before culminating in the arrest of the chief antagonists Tybalt and Benvolio by police chief Captain Prince. Benvolio seeks out his cousin and Montague's son, Romeo, who is pining for his love, Rosaline, and appears alienated from the violence that surrounds him. Romeo's friend Mercutio offers to cheer him up with an ecstasy tablet ('Queen Mab') and admission to a party at the Capulet mansion. Wearing a mask, Romeo slips into the party unnoticed, but he finds the noise and colour of the spectacle overwhelming. He retreats to the bathroom, removes his mask and lingers by a fish tank, when he spies Juliet on the other side of the glass. The two playfully and wordlessly flirt between the fishes, before Juliet is whisked away by her nurse. In an earlier scene, we learn that Juliet's parents have arranged for her to be married to the governor's son and 'bachelor of the year', Dave Paris. The party is the first time Juliet meets Dave, and he courts her with a ridiculous dance, while Romeo watches bemused, continuing to exchange furtive glances with Juliet. Tybalt spies Romeo without his mask, but he is restrained from confronting him by Capulet. Romeo whispers in Juliet's ear, she responds positively, and then Romeo whisks her into an elevator where they kiss. Dragged away once again by her nurse, it is only after their embrace that each learns of the other's parentage: 'my only love sprung from my only hate.'

Undeterred, Romeo slips back into the Capulet mansion after the party hoping to see Juliet again. Unaware that Romeo is hiding beside the pool, Juliet speaks aloud of her dilemma and her love for Romeo. He reveals himself, but the surprise sees them both fall into the pool. Swimming and wading in the water together, the young couple court one another with words and kisses, and Juliet requests that Romeo arrange their marriage. Romeo enlists the help of Father Laurence who, after initially chiding Romeo for forgetting so quickly about Rosaline, sees in this union the chance to end the fighting between the two families and he secretly marries the couple.

Back at the beach, Mercutio and Benvolio are confronted by Tybalt, who is looking to fight Romeo after he gate-crashed the party. Romeo refuses to fight Tybalt, as he is Juliet's cousin, but he does not reveal why. Intervening in the confrontation, Mercutio is stabbed by Tybalt wielding a shard of glass, which was intended for Romeo. Mercutio curses the two families and dies. Enraged with grief, Romeo pursues Tybalt and begs for him to kill him, but instead he ends up shooting Tybalt. Captain Prince banishes Romeo from the city. Father Laurence advises Romeo to hide out in the waste-lands of Mantua (a trailer park) until he can send word that it is safe to return. Romeo secretly visits Juliet that night and they consummate their marriage before his departure next morning. Grieving for both her lost cousin and husband and despairing because her parents want her to marry Dave Paris, Juliet visits Father Laurence and threatens to kill herself. Father Laurence hatches a plan for Juliet to take a poison that will give her the appearance of death, so that she may escape her arranged marriage and be reunited with Romeo. Laurence sends an urgent message to Romeo advising him of the plan, but the Post Haste deliveryman is unable to deliver the package. Instead, Romeo hears from Balthasar of Juliet's death and, believing this to be true, returns to see her dead body in the church. Discovering her vial of poison, Romeo drinks it – just at the moment when Juliet wakes. Unable to revive him, Juliet takes Romeo's gun and shoots herself.

Critique

There are many impressive set-pieces in Luhrmann's radical reimagining of Shakespeare's play: the gas station fight that pays homage to the Spaghetti Western and has a jaw-dropping 185 cuts in only five-and-half minutes; the party at the Capulet mansion that is fuelled by the '1990s' revival in disco, with Mercutio, in drag, lip-synching 'Young Hearts Run Free'; the restaging of Romeo and Juliet's famous balcony scene in the pool; the desperate stand-off between Romeo and Tybalt that rivals any contemporary gangster film in tension and drama. But Luhrmann's vision for his adaptation can be encapsulated in the film's opening minutes, where we have Shakespeare's opening prologue (which traditionally summarizes the entire plot) delivered by a newsreader on a television set. This immediately signals Luhrmann's film as a sophisticated updating of Shakespeare's story, a film that is knowingly informed by the mass media and popular culture, but one that remains respectful of The Bard's prose. Sensitive to the challenge that Shakespearean language poses to a contemporary audience (particularly the youth market that the film is unapologetically aiming at), Luhrmann recapitulates the prologue with a voice-over by Father Laurence, his words visually restated by a montage of newspaper headlines, captions and magazine covers. Extending the televisual aesthetic of the film's opening shot, each of Shakespeare's main characters is introduced via freeze-frame close-up and title card, in the style of the opening credits of a prime-time soap opera. These are punctuated by explosive flash-forwards giving a sneak preview of the action to come, like a theatrical trailer on speed.

Purists may protest that the relentless pace of Luhrmann's film and the relative inexperience of his young cast (with the exception of Postlethwaite and Margolyes) 'butcher' the poetry of Shakespeare's words. But this is to overlook the raw emotion that these actors bring to their roles (for example, DiCaprio's blood-curdling delivery of 'Either I, or both, shall go with him') and the added emotional resonance of the soundtrack. Luhrmann cannily chose contemporary songs whose lyrics and mood would complement the action. This was not only a crucial part in his aim to 'translate' Shakespeare for a contemporary audience, it provided the added benefit of marketing the film via music videos and CD sales.

The critical tendency to focus on Luhrmann's MTV music video aesthetic – the quick-fire edits and pumping soundtrack – overlooks the achievements of the film's quieter moments and the sincerity with which the love story is presented. The scene where Romeo and Juliet first see each other, on opposite sides of the fish tank, is beautifully staged and photographed, and the acting is without affectation or self-consciousness. The motif of water, which provides sanctuary for the couple, has already been established when we first meet Juliet: her head is underwater in the bath, blissfully unaware of the domestic chaos downstairs. This shot is repeated when Romeo submerges his face in the bathroom sink, to escape the din of the party and the effects of ecstasy. This water motif is most fully developed in the balcony scene as Romeo and Juliet 'dance' around each other in the pool. As editor Jill Bilcock explains, the pacing of the scene is slow and luxurious so that we can enjoy the language. This scene gives the audience respite from the noise and violence of the opening scenes, and the original score effectively conveys the lovers' emotions, lending further weight to their dialogue.

The film ends as it began, with the newsreader on the television set delivering Shakespeare's final lines. Luhrmann's reinterpretation of Shakespeare assumes a media-literate audience, and his vision embraces the postmodern collapse of high art with popular culture. While critical opinion on the film was divided, it triumphed at the box office, opening in the number 1 spot in the US and taking over $150 million. It cemented Luhrmann's reputation internationally as a 'visionary director' – and this was only his second film.

Fincina Hopgood

Moulin Rouge!

Country of Origin:
Australia / USA

Studio:
20th Century Fox
Bazmark Films

Director:
Baz Luhrmann

Producers:
Martin Brown
Baz Luhrmann
Fred Baron

Synopsis

A penniless writer, Christian, arrives in Montmartre, Paris and is quickly befriended by a bohemian group of artists looking to put on a show. They take Christian to the Moulin Rouge where he sees the courtesan Satine perform. He instantly falls in love but must compete for her affections with The Duke, to whom she has been promised by the club's impresario, Harold Zidler. In return for Satine, The Duke has agreed to invest in a show, 'Spectacular Spectacular', which Christian finds himself composing on the spot when he is caught sneaking into Satine's chamber. Thus, the film proceeds as a backstage musical, with the narrative convention of rehearsals leading up to the opening night's performance juxtaposed with Christian's courtship of Satine, her return of his affections, and the threat posed to their happiness by The Duke. Their future together is further threatened by the fact that Satine is dying from consumption, although only Zidler and his assistant Marie know this. When The Duke becomes suspicious of Satine and Christian's relationship, Satine is forced to give herself to him in order to save Zidler's investment. Realizing Satine is in love with Christian, The Duke attacks her, but she

Screenwriters:
Baz Luhrmann
Craig Pearce

Cinematographer:
Donald M McAlpine

Editor:
Jill Bilcock

Duration:
122 minutes

Genre:
Musical

Cast:
Nicole Kidman
Ewan McGregor
John Leguizamo
Jim Broadbent
Richard Roxburgh
Deobia Oparei

Year:
2001

is saved by Le Chocolat, one of the dancers at the Moulin Rouge. The couple make plans to escape, but when Zidler informs Satine that she is dying and that The Duke plans to kill Christian, Satine reluctantly pretends she does not love Christian in order to save him. The story climaxes with the performance of 'Spectacular Spectacular', juxtaposed with the backstage drama of Christian being chased by The Duke's henchman. The couple are reunited on stage in song but as the curtain falls, Satine collapses and finally dies, leaving a distraught Christian to write the tale.

Critique

Moulin Rouge! is the quintessential postmodern product. In its recycling of well-known pop songs to express Christian and Satine's love, a critic of postmodernism like Frederic Jameson would argue that the film shows the inability of postmodern popular culture to say anything new or original; it can only recycle and rehash tired clichés of romantic love songs and the tragedy of lost love. A more positive view would assert that in its merging of the Hollywood musical with music videos, Bollywood iconography and the narrative conventions of opera, Luhrmann and his team have indeed created something new and alive out of a cinematic form – the musical – that many had dismissed as long since dead.

In its tragic romantic ending, *Moulin Rouge!* adheres to the narrative conventions of opera, rather than the happy-ever-after ending that we expect from the classical Hollywood musical. The narrative is clearly influenced by Puccini's opera *La Bohème* (indeed, Luhrmann mounted a famous stage production of this opera earlier in his career). *Moulin Rouge!* takes from *La Bohème* the Parisian setting, the group of Bohemian artists, and the tragic figure of Mimi, who is loved by Rudolfo but is dying of consumption. The figure of Christian also recalls the sentimental, melancholic lover of archetypal Bollywood tales such as *Devdas*, which has been made into a film three times (by P.C Barua in 1935; by Bimal Roy in 1955; by Sanjay Leela Bhansali in 2002).

Moulin Rouge! pays homage to the grand scale and elaborate style of Bollywood films through a pastiche of Bollywood conventions. The show-within-the-film 'Spectacular Spectacular' is the most obvious example. The opening number 'Chamma Chamma' is a popular Hindi song, and the staging of this musical number recalls the proscenium arch tradition of Parsee theatre, which was a major influence on Bollywood films. The choreography recreates Bollywood dance styles; the bejewelled costumes are inspired by Indian saris, salwar kameez and sherwani suits; and the setting includes a painted backdrop of the Taj Mahal. As a postmodern musical number par excellence, these Bollywood features are combined with Satine singing her theme song (for the second time in the film) 'Diamonds Are a Girl's Best Friend', from *Gentlemen Prefer Blondes* (Howard Hawks, 1953), and choreography inspired by the geometric patterns and top shots of Busby Berkeley.

Moulin Rouge!'s use of well-known pop songs also echoes the role of the song in Bollywood cinema, where songs are used as marketing tools and producers will often pre-release songs to generate awareness of their films. With their accompanying dance numbers, Bollywood producers can create promotional music videos lifted wholesale from the film. The effect upon the audience when they hear these familiar songs in the cinema is one of nostalgia, the pleasure of recognition. This is similar to the effect of the classical Hollywood musical's adaptation of successful Broadway shows. Luhrmann's choice of pop songs activates this feeling of nostalgia. Many of the songs in *Moulin Rouge!* come from the 1970s and 1980s, when the film's target demographic of 16 to 34-year-olds would have been children and teenagers.

In justifying his use of contemporary songs in a narrative set in the previous century, Luhrmann explained that he wanted to recreate the feeling 'of the time' with songs that were readily identifiable to a contemporary audience and would therefore communicate what is was like to be in the Moulin Rouge. This recalls Richard Dyer's idea (Dyer 2002: 20) that the musical conveys what utopia would *feel* like, although the utopian, heady atmosphere of the Moulin Rouge is constantly being undercut by the squalor of backstage life and the tragedy of Satine's imminent death. Luhrmann also claimed that the use of contemporary songs was a common practice in Hollywood musicals anyway, citing Judy Garland's trolley song from *Meet Me in St. Louis* (Vincente Minnelli, 1944), as an example of a big band 1940s' number sung in a film set in 1900.[1]

Moulin Rouge!'s engagement with Bollywood and pop music is not limited to pastiche; the film also revels in parody. The most notorious example is the song-and-dance duet between Zidler and The Duke, 'Like a Virgin'. Following the pattern of the musical numbers in *Starstruck* (Gillian Armstrong, 1982), *The Adventures of Priscilla: Queen of the Desert* (Stephan Elliott, 1994) and *Muriel's Wedding* (P J Hogan, 1994), here we see Australians queering the musical, as Madonna's hit song of sexual re-awakening is camped up by Jim Broadbent, Richard Roxburgh and an ensemble of male dancers. While these two men enact a parody of heterosexual courtship, the costume, iconography and choreography create an intertextual reference to Madonna's music video, through Broadbent's white veil (using the tablecloth), the gothic palatial setting and the recreation of the famous shot of Madonna on a gondola sailing under a Venetian bridge.

The film's most impressive reinvention of pop music is reserved for the 'El Tango de Roxanne', which is played straight, with the heightened drama of great tragedy. As The Unconscious Argentinian bellows the famous refrain 'Roxanne' from Sting's tortured love song, Nini Legs In The Air dances with several men. The choreography is charged with sexual tension and the threat of violence; the dark, expressionist lighting is punctuated with stark spotlights. Luhrmann employs melodramatic crosscutting throughout this performance to show us Satine's subjugation at the hands of the Duke, while Christian sings in despair 'Why does my heart cry?' This produces a powerful, doubling effect at the level of both the image track (Nini and her fellow courtesans dancing with the men; Satine trying to evade the Duke) and the sound track (The Argentinian and Christian singing in counterpoint). In this union of song, dance, lighting and editing, Luhrmann gives us the film's most memorable moment, revealing the visceral impact of the musical's darker side.

Note

1. These comments attributed to Luhrmann come from the commentary on the *Moulin Rouge!* DVD, produced by Holly Radcliffe for Twentieth Century Fox Home Entertainment (2001, region 4).

Fincina Hopgood

Australia

Country of Origin:
Australia / USA

Studio:
20th Century Fox in association
with Dune Entertainment LLC
and Ingenious Film Partners
A Bazmark Production
[Bazmark Film]

Director:
Baz Luhrmann

Producers:
Baz Luhrmann
G Mac Brown
Catherine Knapman

Screenwriters:
Baz Luhrmann
Stuart Beattie
Ronald Harwood
Richard Flanagan

Cinematographer:
Mandy Walker

Editors:
Dody Dorn
Michael McCusker

Duration:
175 minutes

Genre:
Western
Melodrama
Historical epic
War

Cast:
Nicole Kidman
Hugh Jackman
David Wenham
Bryan Brown
Jack Thompson
David Gulpilil
Brandon Walters

Year:
2008

Synopsis

Set in the Northern Territory during the early years of World War II (1939–1941), *Australia* opens with the voice-over narration of Nullah, an Aboriginal boy, who tells the story of Lady Sarah Ashley, a formal, uptight caricature of the British aristocracy. Sarah travels from Mother England to the Northern Territory to confront her husband, who has long been absent from home while tending his cattle station, Faraway Downs. Sarah intends to convince her husband to accept an offer from King Carney to buy his cattle and return home. Upon her arrival in Darwin, she is greeted by The Drover, a rough, sunburnt man of action. Each takes an instant dislike to the other, although Sarah mistakenly assumes that The Drover is attracted to her. When they reach Faraway Downs, they discover that Sarah's husband has been killed by a spear; the station manager Neil Fletcher informs them he was killed by King George, an Aboriginal leader (and Nullah's grandfather) known for his hatred of the white man. (It is later revealed that it was in fact Fletcher who killed Sarah's husband.) Sarah is visited that night by Nullah, who explains that Fletcher was secretly working for their competitor, King Carney; he also tells Sarah that Fletcher sleeps with and beats Nullah's mother. The implication is that Fletcher is in fact Nullah's biological father.

The childless Sarah is immediately charmed by Nullah and seized by a desire to protect him. She dismisses Fletcher and resolves to continue with her husband's plans to drove his cattle to Darwin and sell the herd to the Army, rather than accept Carney's under-priced offer and allow him to gain a monopoly in the region. Although they are now under-staffed with the departure of Fletcher and his men, The Drover reluctantly agrees to lead the drove, with a motley crew of riders, including Sarah, in return for the station's prize stallion. Before their departure, Sergeant Callahan visits the station looking for Nullah (during this time, the police were charged with removing half-caste Aboriginal children from their families, so that they might be raised as 'white' by church missionaries). To evade capture, Nullah hides in the water tank, but his mother, Daisy, tragically drowns. Confessing that she is not very good with children, Sarah awkwardly comforts the grieving Nullah by singing a few lines of 'Somewhere over the Rainbow' from *The Wizard of Oz* (Victor Fleming, 1939), and Nullah is entranced.

During the drove, the group encounter various acts of sabotage by Fletcher, including a fire that results in a stampede, which crushes Kipling Flynn, the station's accountant and reformed alcoholic. A romantic attraction gradually develops between Sarah and The Drover. The group survives a life-threatening journey across the desert, guided by King George. Once in Darwin, Sarah and The Drover triumphantly herd the cattle straight down the pier, loading them onto the Army's boats before Carney can load his. Sarah decides to reinvest the money into Faraway Downs and settle there, inviting The Drover to be station manager. He is reluctant to be tied down to one place, but signals his acceptance of her offer when he turns up at the society ball, clean-shaven and wearing a white dinner jacket. This causes a stir, as The Drover had been considered an outcast in white society for marrying an Aboriginal girl (who died from tuberculosis). That night, Sarah and The Drover sleep together.

Life and colour return to Faraway Downs, with The Drover away mustering for half the year, and Sarah acting as surrogate mother to Nullah. Through a montage of newspaper headlines, we learn that Fletcher engineers Carney's death (a crocodile attack) and marries his daughter, so that he can inherit the cattle empire. When Sarah refuses to sell Faraway Downs to him, Fletcher threatens both Nullah and The Drover, obliquely referring to the 'accidents' that claimed the lives of her husband and Carney. Nullah wants to go on walkabout with his grandfather, but Sarah, fearing for his safety, refuses to let him go; she argues with The Drover, and The Drover leaves. World War II intervenes and Sarah finds herself working as a radio operator in Darwin. She is mourning the loss of both The Drover and Nullah, who has finally been captured by Sergeant Callahan (under instruction from Fletcher) and taken to Mission Island. Japanese planes attack Darwin, including the island. After being persuaded to return to Sarah by his brother-in-law Magarri, The Drover arrives in Darwin to be confronted by the aftermath of the bombing. Believing Sarah is dead, The Drover and Magarri sail to Mission Island to rescue the Aboriginal children. To divert attention from the children's escape, Magarri shoots at the Japanese soldiers and is killed. Meanwhile, Sarah – who has survived the attack – is about to be evacuated when she hears the children singing 'Somewhere Over the Rainbow' as their ship sails into the docks. Sarah, The Drover and Nullah are reunited, but not before they are threatened once more, this time by Fletcher who attempts to shoot Nullah, but is killed by King George's spear. The trio return to Faraway Downs, and Sarah finally lets Nullah go on walkabout.

Critique

As the lengthy synopsis suggests, there is more than one story in *Australia*, and indeed it feels like more than one film. The first half is devoted to saving Faraway Downs from King Carney's empire, and the extended droving sequences – a combination of location photography and special effects – culminate in the impressive set piece of the cattle drive down the Darwin pier. With the consummation of the romance between Sarah and The Drover following the society ball, this seems like the 'natural' place for the film to end. But Luhrmann pushes on to tell the story of 'what happened next' to Sarah and The Drover, and this is where the film overstays its welcome. There is a shift in genre and visual tone as we move from the western to the war film, and the deep, rich browns and reds of the outback are replaced by the grey monochrome of a city under siege. Our three protagonists are separated for much of this second half, and the film is weaker for it. Much of the film's appeal lies in the interplay between The Drover and Sarah; their relationship is an archetypal clash of opposites, complemented by the impish presence of Nullah, and there is a spark in Kidman and Jackman's playing that is lacking when the two are apart.

What ties this fragmented narrative together, at least thematically, is the story of the stolen generations, which marks *Australia* as a particularly important film – even if it is a flawed one – in Australian cinema 'after Mabo'. Nullah's name seems a subtle reference to the doctrine of Terra Nullius that was overthrown by the High Court in the famous land-rights case fought by Aboriginal leader Eddie Mabo; as Nullah explains in his opening monologue, 'I belong no one', which recalls the notion of Terra

Nullius that perniciously claimed that Australia 'belonged to no one' at the time of the British invasion in 1788. As Australian film scholars Felicity Collins and Therese Davis have argued, Australian cinema since 1992 has registered in various ways the impact of the High Court's decision upon our national identity and our relationship with the land. Released in the year when the Prime Minister of Australia offered a formal apology to the members of the stolen generations, *Australia* represents a conscious, heartfelt engagement on the part of white Australians with our history and a desire to envisage reconciliation on screen.

Luhrmann's grandiose, hyperbolic vision was embraced by Indigenous Studies professor Marcia Langton for daring to give Australians 'a new past – a myth of national origin' that combines fantasy with historical accuracy: 'Luhrmann depicts with satirical sharpness the racial caste system of that time' (Langton 2008a). Her favourable review of the film was attacked by Germaine Greer, who argued that the film romanticizes a period of Australian history when Aboriginal workers were exploited by the northern cattle industry (Greer 2008). The key point of tension between these two views relates to the film's use of history – Greer sees it as Luhrmann's obligation to represent past events in a stark, realist manner, faithful to the historical record, but Langton's view is more forward-looking, advocating Luhrmann's 'alternative history' as a means to effect reconciliation through storytelling. Langton is under no illusion that this is a film, not a history book; one that expresses a hopeful vision for our future as well as telling stories of our past.

Cinematically, in terms of the film's style rather than its politics, Luhrmann spoke about the influence of Hollywood epics such as *Gone with the Wind* (Victor Fleming, 1939). But the legacy of Australian cinema is equally evident in *Australia*'s sweeping helicopter shots of the Northern Territory's magisterial landscape, which recall Gary Hansen's cinematography in *We of the Never Never* (Igor Auzins, 1982). The scene on Mission Island where Magarri single-handedly takes on the Japanese soldiers is particularly striking in relation to the history of Australian film: as he runs along the beachfront, Magarri is shot and falls down in a manner that recalls the stunning final frame of Peter Weir's *Gallipoli* (1981). Like the sacrificial figure of Archy, who is killed on the Turkish battlefield, Magarri runs from left to right of frame and as the bullet hits, his arms are raised and his back arches. Weir's emblematic image of self-sacrifice in wartime is reclaimed by Luhrmann as a testimony to brotherhood between black and white Australia. This scene has further intertextual resonance in the casting of Ngoombujarra, who earlier in his career won Best Supporting Actor at the AFI Awards for his performance in *Blackfellas* (James Ricketson, 1993). In this earlier film, Ngoombujarra's character causes a diversion by pretending to shoot at police, similarly sacrificing himself so that his friends might escape. As he lies bleeding on the road, Ngoombujarra delivers his final line: 'Free – free as a fucking bird'. This moment is echoed 15 years later in Magarri's dying words as he watches the children climbing aboard the ship: 'Drove 'em home, Drover'. Greer may legitimately protest that Luhrmann is reinforcing the stereotype of the sacrificial black man dying to save the white man here, but this overlooks the film's subversion of expectations when King George survives his incarceration in a Darwin jail and emerges as a potent *deus ex machina* in the final moments.

Fincina Hopgood

DISABILITY IN THE AUSTRALIAN CINEMA

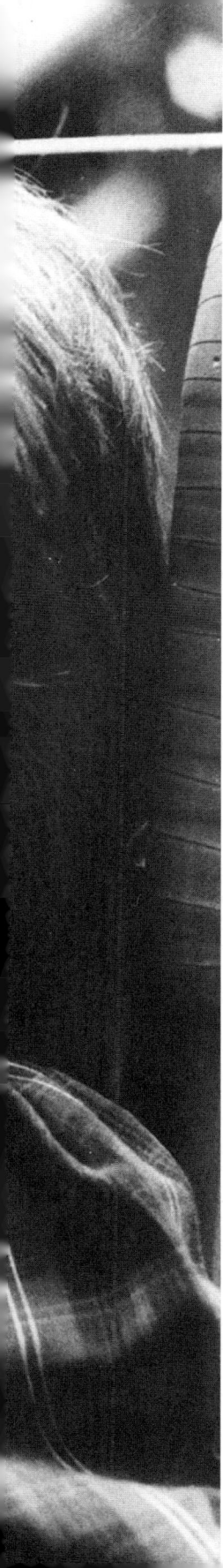

One of the theatrical posters for the 2008 Australian film *The Black Balloon* declares 'normal is relative' over an image of the autistic main character running in his underpants wearing bunny ears. The poster is bordered by smaller images of scenarios that we have come to expect in Australian national cinema: love amongst families, outdoor activities and suburban settings. The central position of disability in this film is indicative of its (changing) place throughout Australian cinema's history.

Although ever present, the ways in which disability is represented in Australian cinema have become more diverse as minority-group interests become valued and disability is increasingly recognized in terms of social restriction rather than physical ailment. Throughout this short piece I will consider the changing representation of disability in Australian cinema at key moments of the Australian film industry, focusing mainly on the post-renaissance period. Disability has always been present in the cultural imagination of Australians and has proved useful in creating a 'typical' Australian character. Perhaps due to the geographical isolation of Australia, Australian national cinema is characterized by a willingness to give scene-time to those normally considered peripheral, such as people with disability. Characteristics of disability have an affinity with the 'quirky' characterizations favoured by Australian film-makers.

Disability was used in early Australian cinema to project a unique national character.

For example, during the 1930s and 1940s Ken G Hall used disability in films such as *On Our Selection* and *The Squatter's Daughter* as a way to emphasize his creativity in a national cinema and articulate wider cultural doubts about representation itself (Verhoeven 1999b). These films, like Australian literature of the colonial period, relied on disability to create a national identity in opposition to Britain.

During the renaissance period of Australian cinema a cycle of films, including *Let the Balloon Go* (Oliver Howes, 1976), *Break of Day* (Ken Hannam, 1977), *Love Letters From Teralba Road* (Stehen Wallace, 1977), *Because He's My Friend* (Ralph Nelson, 1977) and *Tim* (Michael Pate, 1979), adopted an atmosphere of threat and/or compassion in the context of disability characterization. Representations that suggest that disability is up to the individual to overcome through hard work, determination and an exemplary personal attitude are popular in much of Western cinema and worked well with the focus on 'good taste' that dominated Australian film-making during the 1970s. By individualizing the experience of disability, these films allowed audiences to feel good about being Australian.

During the 1980s, a politicization of the way disability was represented in popular cinema was underway internationally, as critics and academics began documenting stereotypes of disability. These stereotypes, which focused on criminality, adjustment and sexuality, contributed to an individualization of disability (Longmore 1987). These three stereotypes of disability are evident throughout 1980s' Australian cinema. *Warm Nights on a Slow Moving Train* (Bob Ellis, 1988) explored an intersection of sexuality and adjustment to suggest people with disability were a drain on resources and unable to contribute to the workforce. The film is likewise characterized by an atmosphere of criminality. The feel-good film *Annie's Coming Out* (Gil Brealy, 1984) also invoked stereotypes of dependency and adjustment to perpetuate the notion that people with disability can overcome all odds through perseverance. Likewise, minor characters with disability worked in films such as the *Mad Max* cycle to create an atmosphere of threat or criminality.

Disability has appeared throughout every genre that has come to be associated with Australian national cinema. For example, disability threatened masculinity in *Hammers Over the Anvil* (Ann Turner, 1993), a film of the 'horse genre'. During the 1990s, as Australian film-makers sought a more international audience with international genres and modes of funding, the most successful film of the period *Shine* (Scott Hicks, 1996) was a typical triumph over the adversary of disability narrative with an Australian inflection.

The 1990s was an important decade in terms of the representation of disability as the growing number of culturally-diverse film-makers in the Australian film industry initiated a critical focus on minority group interests. Despite being consistently represented during this period, characters with disability were not, however, involved in the celebration of diversity, as social restrictions were rarely addressed. Disability was most often used for stylistic purposes rather than thematic reasons; it was often used to rehabilitate a previously marginalized 'other' (Ellis 2008). *Death in Brunswick* (John Ruane, 1990) recognized for its representation of a more inclusive multicultural national identity, used disability to punish bad parenting. Other marginalized groups such as gay men (*The Sum of Us*, Burton & Dowling, 1994) and unemployed youth (*Cosi*, Mark Joffe, 1995) were able to prove their worth to society via narratives involving caring for the disabled.

The tendency to use characters with disability to provide information about the main character established by Ken G Hall in early Australian cinema and carried through the *Mad Max* Cycle (in the 1970s and 1980s) continued in the 1990s with *Muriel's Wedding* (P J Hogan, 1994), *Black Robe* (Bruce Beresford, 1991), *Metal Skin* (Geoffrey Wright, 1994), *Heaven's Burning* (Craig Lahiff, 1997),

Doing Time For Fatsy Cline (Chris Kennedy, 1997), Dead To The World (1990), Muggers (Dean Murphy, 1999), Dogwatch (Laurie McInnes, 1999), Cut (Yan Toderi, 1999), The Nostradamus Kid (Bob Ellis, 1992), Welcome To Woop Woop (Stephan Elliot, 1997), and That Eye, The Sky (John Ruane, 1994). In 1996, Rolf de Heer and disabled actor and film-maker Heather Rose embarked on a project that would revolutionize the way disability was represented and reviewed in Australian cinema. Dance Me To My Song (1998) reverses the trend to use disabled characters in support of able-bodied characters as it uses the able-bodied Madeline to support the protagonist Julia (played by Rose) who has a disability.

With some few exceptions (such as Dance Me to My Song), in a cinema fascinated with social constructions, disability has been individualized. However, due to the changing nature of the Australian film industry and the international politicization of disability, a change in focus is underway. By the 2000s, Australian cinema began to include disability in terms of diversity and narratives examined both the physical difference of having a disability and the social stigma that came along with it. This redirection is evident in recent Australian films including Thunderstruck (Darren Ashton, 2003), Under The Radar (Nathan Phillips, 2003), Little Fish (Rowan Woods, 2005), Clubland (Cherie Nolan, 2006), and The Black Balloon (Elissa Down, 2007). Disability has been used in different ways throughout Australia's cinematic history and the relativity of normality can been seen in the ways this image has changed.

Katie Ellis

Annie's Coming Out

Country of Origin:
Australia

Studio/Distributor:
Film Australia Limited

Director:
Gil Brealey

Producer:
Don Murray

Screenwriters:
Chris Borthwick
John Patterson

Cinematographer:
Mick von Bornemann

Editor:
Lindsay Frazer

Duration:
93 minutes

Genre:
Biopic
Drama

Cast:
Angela Punch McGregor
Drew Forsythe
Tina Arhondis

Year:
1984

Synopsis

Based on the book of the same title written by Rosemary Crossley and Anne McDonald, *Annie's Coming Out* is a biographical account of Annie O'Farrell who was born with cerebral palsy. As a young child, Annie is misdiagnosed as intellectually disabled and placed in an institution, where she remains until Jessica Hathaway, an energetic young social worker, begins working there. Jessica, who has a tendency to 'rescue' things and take in stray animals, becomes convinced that Annie is in fact highly intelligent. She embarks on a mission to find a way to allow Annie to communicate and reveal the doctors' mistakes. Despite the personal and professional problems Jessica encounters as a result of her quest, she perseveres and ultimately takes the Victorian Health Commission to Court.

Critique

Cinematic representations of disability, particularly within the drama or biopic genres, usually present disability as a personal tragedy that requires individuals to adapt. While the narratives invoke compassion amongst the audience for the characters with disability, the important characterization of the carer invites a simultaneous message of burden and assumptions of dependency. These characterizations are designed to bestow carers with 'saintly' qualities, such as self-sacrifice, and the disabled character is used to provide information about the more important able-bodied characters. *Annie's Coming Out* exemplifies the operation of the personal-tragedy theory of disability in Australian cinema on both a literal and a metaphoric level, as Jessica is willing to give up almost anything to prove Annie's intelligence, yet we hear little from Annie herself, except for a voice-over at the beginning and end of the film.

The film is more about Jessica (Annie's carer) than Annie (the impaired character) and the impact Annie has on Jessica's life and relationship. Despite the at-times negative impact, Jessica sticks with Annie because she is a carer bestowed with saintly qualities. The characterization of Jessica as Annie's symbolic mother, who is totally devoted to the extent that she has no leisure time, reveals society's unreal expectations of mothers of children with impairments. By comparison, Annie's real mother chose not to put in the effort that Jessica did. Although Annie's parents feel guilty that they did not pick up on the misdiagnosis, they perpetuate the problem by resisting Jessica's claims because they cannot face their error.

The film rarely presents the world from Annie's perspective; with only a very limited number of point-of-view shots, the camera more often gazes at her. Although Jessica is constructed as Annie's saviour, Annie does exhibit some agency by choosing to fail the tests constantly thrown at her by doctors, Jessica and lawyers. However, we are never given an insight into Annie' inner world that is not filtered through Jessica's perspective until the end of the film, when Annie remarks via voice-over that Jessica never thought they could be normal. The film would have benefitted from a further exploration of Annie's critique of this charity perspective throughout.

Despite the stereotypical representations of disability in terms of personal tragedy and triumph, and self-sacrificing carers, *Annie's Coming Out* provides a good exposé of the institutionalization of people with disability in the Australian community as late as the 1970s. The film also highlights the importance of mental stimulation in therapy, and cautions against leaving any child behind due to preconceived notions about what they can do. However, *Annie's Coming Out* does not fully address culturally-ingrained assumptions of dependency as the negative impacts of caring for Annie on Jessica's life are continually reinforced when she loses friends and argues with her family and partner David. David is a pivotal character in this film as he articulates fear amongst the able-bodied population in dealing with the disabled, claiming he does not want to meet Annie because he knows he is only a car accident away from being like her. Notwithstanding its inadequacies, *Annie's Coming Out* is an important disability-themed film on the Australian Cinema landscape as it was made prior to the introduction of the Disability Discrimination Act (1992) and during a decade of Australian cinema that valued strength, perfect bodies and hegemonic masculinity.

Katie Ellis

Dance Me to My Song

Country of Origin:
Australia

Studio/Distributor:
Vertigo Productions Pty Ltd

Director:
Rolf de Heer

Producers:
Rolf de Heer
Giuseppe Pedersoli
Domenico Procacci

Screenwriters:
Rolf de Heer
Heather Rose
Frederick Stahl

Cinematographer:
Tony Clark

Art Director:
Beverly Freeman

Synopsis

Dance Me to My Song explores the relationships Julia, a woman with disability, has with her carer Madeline, her friend Rix and the mysterious Eddie. Julia who has severe cerebral palsy requires a carer for independence. Madeline mentally abuses Julia in an attempt to increase Julia's dependence on her. Both women fall for Eddie, a man with questionable connections, who forms a friendship with Julia. By sleeping with him first, Madeline steals him from Julia, but then Julia steals him back. By adopting a generic love-triangle storyline with a character who has a disability, this film challenges deeply-ingrained cultural beliefs regarding disability.

Critique

The film is the creation of Rolf de Heer and Heather Rose (who plays Julia). Together they worked on the script attempting to achieve a dramatic film remarkably different from just another 'disability film'. While *Dance Me to My Song* could be accused of adopting the 'super cripple' format – it has all the features of the inspirational role – the focus on disabling structures and prejudice prevents this classification.

In developing the character of Julia, de Heer sought to present her on an equal level to the able-bodied characters in the film; 'She's just Julia, no longer the disabled character any more than Madeline is the character with brown hair or Eddie is the character with the muscular body' (Urban et al. 1998). Julia, who uses a wheelchair for mobility, is only disabled when Madeline leaves her alone in the house with the lock on her wheelchair on or puts her voice synthesizer in another

Editor:

Tania Nehme

Duration:

102 minutes

Genre:

Drama

Cast:

Heather Rose
Joey Kennedy
John Brumpton
Rena Owen

Year:

1998

room. Otherwise, Julia is extremely independent: she goes outside and sits in the sun (where she met Eddie) or meets up with her friend Rix for some drinks.

Throughout the film we see the world from Julia's perspective. Point-of-view shots are restricted to what Julia sees, taking the gaze off her impaired body. Julia's self assurance can be seen in her interactions with Madeline and Rix. Despite Madeline's harsh treatment towards her, Julia understands that Madeline is experiencing a different kind of suffering. When with Rix, Julia remains constant in her identity as a drinking buddy, even trying to seduce her at one stage.

Julia's experiences of activities typical of nondisabled women, such as getting drunk with a girlfriend and telling her how much you love her, are juxtaposed with the extreme social prejudice Julia experiences on a daily basis. When Eddie and Julia go to a corner shop for an ice cream they both agree that the prices are too high but the woman working there singles Julia out, taking issue with her personal attitude. She is overly nice to Eddie and speaks to him about Julia as though Julia is not there. When Julia swears, they are asked to leave as the shop worker attempts to avoid having to gaze on a disabled person who refuses to fit in and be quiet. The film questions why disabled people are isolated from society in this way.

The cinematic tendency to present women with disability as needy and dependent is debunked as Madeline is constantly disempowered by men in her life, yet continues to pursue them. Despite Madeline's position as carer, she is more dependent on Julia than Julia is on her. After being date-raped, Madeline goes to the only safe place she knows – Julia's house – and cuddles up to her in bed. Julia comforts her by placing her hand on Madeline's. While the role reversal between popular cinematic representations of the able and the disabled is empowering in this film, the date-rape punishment goes too far. This could be seen as disempowering to all women, including women with disability, who experience a higher incidence of abuse than the general population.

Disability is politicized in this film through the heterosexual coupling of Julia (a disabled woman) and Eddie (an able-bodied man), who chose her over Madeline (an able-bodied woman). Julia, who is more confident than Madeline, is able to 'reclaim' Eddie. Whereas Madeline, who has little self-confidence despite her bravado, was only able to seduce Eddie by pretending to be Julia on the phone in order to get him to come to the house. Julia is a complex character that we come to know through her consistent personality, use of camera, and editing, rather than through exploitative gazing on her impairment. While the severity of Julia's impairments prevents her from attempting to 'pass' as nondisabled, she refuses to embrace a 'cheerful cripple' identity. She is self-assured and finds stability in her disability identity.

Super cripple stories are comforting because lack of control is terrifying, particularly if it means dependency (Morris 1997). Stories of overcoming, like *Annie's Coming Out*, *My Left Foot* and *Shine,* lessen this fear of disability and provide greater entertainment value. They also assure nondisabled people of their normality. *Dance Me to My Song* is not an 'overcoming' story; it is a story about forcing a disabling world to take respo?sibility for excluding people with disability. Although *Dance Me to My Song* highlights these important disability issues in such an effective way, it was screened at the Cannes film festival in an inaccessible location to its writer and star Heather Rose, who had to be carried up a flight of stairs to the theatre.

Katie Ellis

Shine

Country of Origin:
Australia

Studio/Distributor:
Momentum Films Pty Ltd

Director:
Scott Hicks

Producer:
Jane Scott

Screenwriter:
Jan Sardi

Cinematographer:
Geoffrey Simpson

Art Director:
Tony Cronin

Editor:
Pip Karmel

Duration:
100 minutes

Genre:
Biopic
Drama

Cast:
Geoffrey Rush
Lynn Redgrave
Sir John Gielgud
Armin Mueller-Stahl
Noah Taylor

Year:
1995

Synopsis

David Helfgott is a child-prodigy pianist who experiences a mental breakdown as a result of pressure placed on him by his father. He finally achieves the popular and personal success he seemed destined for as a child later in life. His father, a Holocaust survivor whose own dreams of musical fame were shattered, instructs David in piano and especially Rachmaninoff's 3rd piano concerto: 'the hardest piece in the world'. David's performances in local competitions rarely take the top prize but reveal a talented musician lacking the finer points of performance. Under the tutelage of Ben Rosen, David's raw talent transforms into musical genius and he is offered a scholarship to study at a prestigious American musical college. When his father forbids him to go, David seeks musical mentors outside his home and, through them, secures a place to study at the Royal College of Music in London and goes without his father's blessing. David eventually suffers a complete breakdown on stage while playing the Rachmaninoff 3, his father's favourite piece. He returns to Australia and disappears from the spotlight into a mental institution. He eventually reappears to rise in fame once again and marry Gillian, an astrologer.

Critique

While *Shine* has been compared to a number of disability-themed Hollywood films from *Rainman* to *Forrest Gump*, the atmosphere and characterizations remain distinctly Australian. Unlike these films, *Shine* incorporates naturalistic depictions of romantic and family relationships and professional failure as well as success. *Shine* Australianizes both the Hollywood melodrama and disability genres by featuring a quirky character that succeeds because of rather than in spite of their disability.

The representation of disability in *Shine*, long thought of as 'positive', is increasingly being recognized as stereotypical by disability critics. The film perpetuates several stereotypes regarding disability, including compensatory abilities, infantilization, and women as saintly carer (Shakespeare 1999). In *Shine*, disability is a personal tragedy which initially challenges but ultimately reinforces cultural ideals of the 'normal' body.

Many films present people with disability as extraordinary in other ways in order to compensate for impairment. This thematic tendency locates disability in the body rather than unadaptive social practices.

A passionate musician, David is described by his professors at the Royal College of Music as a genius. When David is successful in playing the Rachmaninoff 3 his hands and face are never framed together in the same shot until just before he collapses. As David begins to lose control in this scene, his fingers keep moving, just as they continue during his shock therapy. Later in the film as David re-enters society he is drawn to the piano and, via his extraordinary talent, becomes a contributing member of society.

David is immediately positioned as childlike at the beginning of the film when the narrative flashes back from the confused old man in the rain to the determined young boy at a piano competition. David as a 'sweet innocent' continues as the film progresses back and forward

Shine, Momentum Films.

throughout the stages of David's life. As an adult he always seems to be laughing; he hopscotches down corridors, is unable to clean up after himself, plays in bubble baths and jumps naked on a trampoline. David is pure and determined to please everyone he meets. While this leads to opportunity for young David, adolescent David is led astray and experiences a catastrophic breakdown while, finally, older David is able to re-enter society. This media infantilization of disability perpetuates the belief that people with disability are totally dependent.

The relationship between David and Gillian is often criticized for playing into the stereotype of woman as carer and ultimate deliverer of a disabled man. However, in many ways, Gillian is as socially marginal as David; she lives her life according to the stars and has previously been unable to commit to marriage. The scene in which David goes for a swim just before his first concert and gets his entire music score wet presents the relationship as a partnership rather than a carer-patient relationship. Gillian, Sylvia and Sylvia's children rally around David to support him in getting ready for his debut as his family – not as carers. Gillian is not rescuing David as a carer would, she is rescuing herself, and she is attracted to David's outlook on life.

Shine is a celebrated Australian film of the 1990s, receiving both Oscars and Australian Film Institute Awards. While many believe the film to be a positive portrayal of overcoming disability and disappointment, deeply ingrained cultural stereotypes regarding disability are utilized throughout this film. Throughout, David is presented as a childlike figure, burdened by musical genius out of his control and an overbearing father. Although refusing association amongst people with disability and rejecting the notion of a disability community, David re-enters society via community and his relationship with Gillian re-forms an unconventional family unit.

Katie Ellis

The Black Balloon

Country of Origin:
Australia

Studio/Distributor:
Black Balloon Productions
Pty Ltd

Director:
Elissa Down

Producer:
Tristram Miall

Synopsis

The Black Balloon is set within a (not so) 'typical' Australian family during the 1980s. It is a coming of age story about acceptance and fitting in. The story centres on the Mollison family, whose interactions are dominated by oldest son Charlie, who has autism and ADHD. Youngest son Thomas is a frustrated teenager who wishes for a sense of normality in his life. He resents both Charlie, who communicates through signing, plus a single word – 'duh', and his parents, because Thomas feels the brothers are held to different and unfair levels of responsibility. While this is 'just life' for parents Simon (an army dad) and Maggie (who is heavily pregnant), Thomas longs for the days when he was younger and Charlie could say 'Tom, Mum and Dad'. Their most recent move does not begin well as the neighbours immediately find Charlie weird and the other kids at Thomas' new school laugh at the 'spastic bus' that Charlie takes to school each

Screenwriters:
Elissa Down
Jimmy Jack (also credited as
Jimmy the Exploder)

Cinematographer:
Denson Baker

Art Director:
Matthew Putland

Editor:
Veronika Jenet

Duration:
97 minutes

Genre:
Drama

Cast:
Rhys Wakefield
Gemma Ward
Luke Ford
Erik Thomson
Toni Collette

Year:
2007

day. When pregnant Maggie is prescribed bed rest, Thomas is put in charge of caring for Charlie and finds that his hijinks (such as breaking into stranger's houses to use the toilet) do not always fit into Thomas' emerging relationship with Jackie.

Critique

The film is most unlike *Rainman*, the most well-known cinematic exploration of autism. Charlie has no compensatory abilities and he is presented as a boy, albeit a very difficult one to be around at times. Down's message that Charlie is just another character within the Australian family milieu is clear from the beginning, where every object from chair to Hills Hoist is labelled in the opening credits. These are just things around the people, who are not labelled with the exception of a 'boy' in the street, 'man' (their dad) on the roof setting up the television aerial and, eventually, Charlie, also tagged as 'boy'.

However, in some ways this perpetuates the cinematic infantiliza-tion of people with disability, as Charlie is actually 18 years old. Children with disability are often seen in popular culture and media via Telethons and other inspirational stories; however, adults and the social exclusion they experience are often forgotten about. Charlie is constructed as a perpetual child and is not permitted extensive experiences of his own. He is always just to the side of the screen in Thomas' key moments of adolescent life, including his first kiss with Jackie.

Thomas' own inability to swim is juxtaposed with Charlie's socially-inappropriate behaviour and resulting social exclusion. Thomas never learnt to swim because his family has moved around so much and, now, at his new school they are already up to the Bronze medallion. As Thomas struggles to swim one lap, the rest of his class snigger and laugh, yet he is forced to participate without any consideration of his lack of ability.

Despite the plethora of quirky characters or characters that exist on the fringes of the mainstream, Australian cinema has not really explored the experience of autism throughout its history. However, four years prior to *The Black Balloon*, *Somersault* (Cate Shortland, 2004) introduced a character with Asperger's Syndrome, a milder form of autism. Where *Somersault* continued to relegate autism to the sidelines by using a secondary character, *The Black Balloon* puts autism up front and as an integral part of the family. While the mes-sage of diversity is clear, as Thomas, by the end of the film, comes to accept Charlie and participate with him in his strange activities, such as banging a wooden spoon on the concrete in the backyard, this acceptance does not extend beyond the family structure in an overt way.

Ultimately, *The Black Balloon* is a significant film in the Australian cinema landscape, particularly in the context of disability, diversity and Australianness. It succeeds in making audiences feel uncomfort-able and acknowledges the diversity of Australian identity through a mosaic of characterizations: the ocker parents, the disabled brother who throws tantrums in the shop, the beautiful yet dorky girlfriend and Thomas who just wants to fit in but ultimately learns to be proud to ride on the Autistic School Bus with the brother whom he loves. This film acknowledges the changes people with disability require in order to lead fulfilling lives and, likewise, acknowledges that at times this may be difficult on the people who love them. It highlights the impact of both impairment and disabling attitudes on the lives of people with disability – but without paying undue attention to their bodies.

Katie Ellis

In Australia today, short film production is a prolific, fertile and diverse form. Shorts can be in any genre – animated, narrative fiction, experimental or documentary. They are made using a wide range of film or video gauges, stocks or technologies. A film is generally regarded as a 'short' if it is under sixty minutes, although there are films known as 'short features', which are regarded as feature films rather than shorts, (for example, Davida Allen's 1998 film *Feeling Sexy* or Ana Kokkinos' 1994 *Only the Brave*). Documentaries might also be regarded as shorts if they are less than thirty minutes, given that many are routinely made as a television half-hour (typically 26 minutes).

The significant interest in short films in Australia is demonstrated by the enormous number of short film festivals held throughout the country – more than sixty short film festivals run annually.[1] Despite the difficulties in raising funds, or recouping them from short production, many hundreds are made in Australia each year.

A number of high-profile award-winning short films have turned the global spotlight on Australian film-making. In 2003, Glendyn Ivin's live action drama *Cracker Bag* won the 'Golden Palm' for Best Short Film at the 2003 Cannes Film Festival, an award previously won by Jane Campion for her 1986 Australian Film, Television and Radio School student film, *Peel: An Exercise in Discipline*. Adam Elliot's 2003 animation *Harvey Crumpet* thrilled those at home by winning an Academy Award for 'Best Short Film' in 2004. Australian short films received Academy Award nominations in each of the following three years: Sejong Park's digital animation *Birthday Boy* in 2005, Anthony Lucas's silhouette animation *The Mysterious Geographic Explorations of Jasper Morello* in 2006, and Peter Templeman's live-action drama *The Saviour* in 2007. *Birthday Boy* and *The Saviour* were both made by teams of students at the Australian Film, Television and Radio School (AFTRS).

In Australia, the rise of the short film can be traced back to the post-war period. Among the organizations established at this time was the Realist Film Unit, which was formed in 1945 to make films on social justice issues, including a number of dramatized documentaries like *Prices and the People* (Bob Mathews, 1948), which was initially sponsored by the Communist Party of Australia, although funding was later withdrawn. The RFU went on to make a series of documentaries for the Brotherhood of St Laurence: *Beautiful Melbourne* (J G Fitzsimons & Ken Coldicutt, 1947), *These Are Our Children* (Ken Coldicutt & J G Fitzsimons, 1948), *A Place to Live* (Ken Coldicutt & J G Fitzsimons, 1950), the latter two both being dramatized documentaries. Several of the RFU's members would go on to be key figures in the development of the Olinda Film Festival, the precursor to the Melbourne International Film Festival. Organizations like the RFU, the Australian National Film Board (later to become Film Australia) founded in 1945, the State Film Centre in Victoria, which was established in

Left: *Birthday Boy* – Sejong Park/Australian Film, Television and Radio School.

Short Films   79

1948, and the Shell Film Unit, also formed in 1948 with the backing of Shell Oil, played significant roles in maintaining film production in Australia, particularly documentary film-making. The most intense flush of the short-film form came in the 1960s and after, particularly in Melbourne and Sydney, where enthusiasm for film was establishing both a lobby and a climate for the renaissance of the industry in the early 1970s. Two prominent short film-making groups at this time were Ubu, an avant-garde films group which made, exhibited and distributed experimental films, and which emerged in Sydney in 1965, and a loose group of film-makers who clustered in the inner-Melbourne suburb of Carlton in the 1960s including Nigel Buesst, Brian Davies, Gil Brealey, Giorgio Mangiamele, Dusan Marek and Paul Winkler. Representative examples of the work of these two groups includes Albie Thoms' 1967 scratch film *Bluto* (1967), which was made as part of the Ubu collective and reflected artist Paul Klee's concept of taking a line for a walk; Paul Winkler's 1973 experimental film *Dark*, which was filmed at an Aboriginal Land Rights demonstration and powerfully evokes that clash through juxtaposing images of the protest and tourist slide of an Aboriginal warrior; and Nigel Buesst's 1971 *Come Out Fighting*, another film picking up on the issue of the Aboriginal struggle, but through narrative fiction.

Short films have long been regarded as stepping-stones for budding film-makers on the path to feature film production, but many have argued that the form itself has value, that there is something intrinsic about the short film form as a unique and poetic art form. This may explain why many feature film-makers often return to the short film despite having successful feature careers. For example, after making six features, and two years after announcing that she would take a four-year break from film-making, Jane Campion made a short called *The Water Diary* (2005/2006). The film was one of eight shorts made by leading film-makers from around the world to promote the United Nations Millennium Development Goals.

Film-makers themselves have argued that 'short films are not "mini-features," they have unique creative parameters',[2] and are 'little works of poetry'.[3] John Polson, an actor, director, and founder of the highly successful 'Tropfest' short film festival has written that short films are not just stepping-stones, they 'can be satisfying in a way that the best features never can'.[4] The esteem with which shorts have been regarded has been evident for some decades; for example, in a 1990 report to the AFC, Stuart Cunningham interviewed a number of industry professionals regarding short film production in Australia and found that shorts were 'held in high regard by distributors and exhibitors. Their cultural significance, aesthetic value, and innovations in style rank them highly by international standards' (Cunningham 1990: 8).

Anna Dzenis has outlined the diversity of stylistic incarnations of the Australian narrative and experimental short film: (1) postmodern pastiche; (2) personal, subjective, diaristic and autobiographical; (3) representations and analysis of experiences of ethnic and Indigenous film-makers; (4) stylized narratives which experimentally tackle pressing contemporary issues; and (5) the 'gag' film. Jackie Farkas' *Amelia Rose Towers* (1993) is an example of a postmodern pastiche, as is Emma-Kate Groghan's *Sexy Girls, Sexy Appliances* (1992). Personal, subjective, diaristic and autobiographical films have been particularly favoured by women film-makers, across a range of genres – for example, Corrine Cantrill's self portrait, *In this Life's Body* (1984), Merelee Bennett's experimental *A Song of Air* (1987), Anna Kannava's short documentary *The Butler* (1997), and Sarah Watt's animated short *Small Treasures* (1995). Examples of films by Indigenous Australians which explore Aboriginal experience include Ivan Sen's shorts *Tears*

(1998), *Wind* (1999) and *Dust* (2000) and Richard Franklin's historical narrative, *Harry's War* (1999). Monica Pellizzari's films explore ethnic experience, for example her study of second generation Italians in *Rabbit On The Moon* (1987), while Teck Tan's 1991 *My Tiger's Eyes* reveals the strangeness of a new country for Chinese immigrants. Dzenis' fourth category: stylized narratives that experimentally tackle pressing contemporary issues, include films such as Kay Pavlou's *The Killing of Angelo Tsakos* (1990) about a police killing of a youth, or Tracey Moffatt's symbolic representation of the 'stolen generation'[5] in her 1989 film, *Night Cries: A Rural Tragecy*, or her earlier film *Nice Coloured Girls* (1987) which counters dominant representations of Aboriginals at the time it was made, and explores (and counters) the history of black/white relations in Australia. Examples of the 'gag' film include Gregor Jordan's *Swinger* (1995), Lynn-Maree Danzey's *Fetch* (1998), and Tony Rogers' *Wilfred* (2002). The latter film, about a talking, overprotective, dope-smoking dog, subsequently formed the basis of a television comedy series.

The Australian film industry is policy-led, and the policies of State and Federal Government film-funding bodies have played a significant role in shaping the form of Australian short films – as they do (arguably more so) in the feature sector, which is heavily dependent on government support. Some funding bodies identify funds for the express purpose of funding shorts, but short film is generally conceived as a training ground for feature film-making and is highly competitive.

The visibility of a number of directors whose short films launched them into successful feature careers has also been responsible for the view of shorts as a pathway to feature production. Examples most notably come from film schools, which provide an important contribution to short film production; these include Robert Luketic, a graduate of the Victorian College of the Arts (VCA), whose short musical, *Titsiana Booberini* (1997) caught the attention of Hollywood and he went on to make *Legally Blonde* (2001), and other films such as *Monster-in-Law* (2005). Another example is Gregor Jordan, also a graduate of the VCA. He picked up the Jury prize for 'Best Short Film' at the 1995 Cannes Film Festival with his 1995 gag film *Swinger*, and he then went on to direct features in Hollywood – *Buffalo Soldiers* (2001) and, at home, *Ned Kelly* (2003).

The largest and most significant producer of short films in Australia in recent decades has been the national film school, the Australian Film, Television and Radio School. The AFTRS was founded in 1973, and among its more than 2000 alumni are many of the best-known names in Australian cinema. Short student films produced at the AFRS helped launch the careers of directors Philip Noyce, Jane Campion, Gillian Armstrong, Alex Proyas, P J Hogan, Rolf De Heer and David Caesar, among many others. In addition, a host of film-makers who are less well known but equally important to the success and vitality of Australian screen culture have honed their craft on short films produced at AFTRS.

Short films have provided an important vehicle for Indigenous people to tell their stories, explore their own concerns, and to enter into what Langton has described as 'intercultural dialogues' (Langton 2003: 46). Prior to the 1990s, the bulk of production by Aboriginal people had been documentaries. While there were some excellent contemporary initiatives that produced interesting documentary work,[6] in more recent times, Indigenous organizations such as the Central Australian Aboriginal Media Association (CAAMA) have turned to drama production, as well as new media.[7] Indigenous production has received particular assistance from public broadcasters, often in collaboration with Aboriginal media organizations and government-funding agencies. In the late 1990s the most significant advance in regard to Australian Indigenous short film drama production occurred when it received a boost with a series of shorts funded via the Indigenous Drama Initiative (IDI) of the Australian Film Commission.[8] It gave Indigenous film-makers creative opportunities to make drama, it developed the skills of Indigenous film-makers and actors, and it got Aboriginal faces on the screen in representations they had constructed themselves. Their films reflect on identity, relationships, culture, tradition and representation from historical and political perspectives. Titles funded by the IDI initiative include Sally Riley's *Confessions of a Headhunter* (2000) – a film that won 'Best Short Fiction' at the 2000 Australian Film Institute 'AFI Awards' – and films by numerous other Aboriginal film-makers who have become important figures in the industry, including Richard Frankland, Darlene Johnson, Ivan Sen and Warwick Thornton.

Like the feature film sector, which, despite close geographic proximity, has seen few productions set in South-east Asia, the shorts sector has not exploited the region for locations (most likely due to smaller budgets and the fact that the film-makers are more often at entry level). However, there are a small number of film-makers producing features – Clara Law's *Floating Life* (1996) and Solrun Hoaas's *Aya* (1990); and shorts – Teck Tan's *My Tiger's Eyes* (1991) and Cate Shortland's *Flower Girl* (1999); and short documentaries – Tony Ayers's *China Dolls* (1997) and Safina Uberoi's *My Mother India* (2002) exploring the experiences of Asians, Asian-Australians, or in the case of *My Mother India*, Australians in Asia – although they are not always films by Asian-Australians themselves (Hoaas is from Holland, and Shortland was born in Australia).

Short film is a significant and valued art form that has been vitally important for the development of several generations of Australian film-makers. Short films have also helped build audiences for Australian cinema. They have enjoyed popular success and awards at film festivals in Australia and internationally, and this success translates into acclaim and kudos for the industry as a whole. Australian short films present a microcosm of the wider industry in terms of the themes and tropes, and are influenced by the same policy directions. As an accessible medium, the form has provided a noteworthy voice for multicultural, or bi-cultural, Australia and is a site of intense creative production.

Lisa French

Notes

1. For online links to short film festivals, see http://www.australianshortfilms.com.
2. Hugh Short quoted in Australian Film Commission 'Introduction' *Australian Short Films 1995-1996*. Woolloomooloo, NSW: AFC, 1996.
3. Jackie McKimmie quoted in Julie James Bailey *Reel Women: Working in Film and Television*. Sydney: AFTRS, 1999, p.223.
4. John Polson quoted in Australian Film Commission 'Foreword' *Australian Short Films 1995-1996*. Woolloomooloo, NSW: AFC, 1996.
5. Government policy was that Aboriginal children were forcibly removed from their families if they were of mixed race.
6. See for example the National Indigenous Documentary Fund (NIDF) project at http://www.abc.net.au/ipu/nidf.htm.
7. See Australia Council. 'Australia's Indigenous Arts.' Report. http://www.ozco.gov.au/resources/publications/artform/aia_newmedia.pdf.
8. See in particular the first four packages titled: *Sand to Celluloid*, *Shifting Sands*, *Crossing Tracks* and *On Wheels*.

Birthday Boy

Country of Origin:
Australia

Director:
Sejong Park

Producer:
Andrew Gregory

Screenwriter:
Sejong Park

Editor:
Adrian Rostirolla

Genre:
Animation
War
Short

Duration:
9 minutes

Cast:
Joshua Ahn
Jin Sook Lee

Year:
2004

Synopsis

An on-screen title sets the action in Korea, 1951. The film tells the story of a young boy, Manuk, who roams a seemingly-deserted town to glean and recycle the debris of war. We first meet him in the wreck of an aeroplane, looking for a particular piece of war refuse – a bolt – to turn into a toy soldier for his collection. He sings a song about a bear. Upon hearing the unmistakable low whistle of a train in the distance he runs to the track and places the bolt on the rail. The train thunders past on its urgent mission to carry tanks to the front. Manuk stands mesmerized, and grins widely. Once the train has passed he retrieves the bolt which has become magnetized. He makes his way through the town, pretending to be a soldier engaged in house-to-house fighting, until his attention is captured by the drone of aeroplane engines. Silently he watches them slowly cross the sky. His war game begins again as he crouches behind rocks on a ridge overlooking an area with houses jumbled together. A postman cycles down the road below Manuk's hiding place. Manuk imagines he is with his dad, pinned down by enemy fire. 'Dad, there are too many of them,' he cries as the sound of machine guns and artillery fire fill his head. 'But we are braver than them,' his father replies in the game. Manuk picks up a rock as if it is a hand grenade, expertly pulls the pin with his teeth and hurls it at the enemy crying 'Dad, get down!' He waits, crouched, fingers in ears for the explosion which never comes. Instead we hear the postman cry in surprise and pain, before crashing his bicycle and shouting at his unseen tormentor. Manuk slinks away, and climbs the hill towards his home. He takes a key from a special hiding spot, and approaches the veranda in front of his house. He notices a parcel, and hurries to open it. He pulls out an old leather wallet containing a faded black and white photograph of a man crouching with a child dressed as Manuk is now, but much younger. Manuk gently caresses the photograph with his thumb. He then pulls out a set of dog tags, and an old boot. He marches up and down in front of his house, wearing the boots, as if he is a soldier on guard. Later, inside the house, he plays with the toy soldiers and tanks he has made from bits and pieces of metal he has found, and falls asleep on the floor. His mother appears at the door, saying 'Manuk, Mum is home'.

Critique

Birthday Boy has won over 40 awards at film festivals around the world including Best Animated Short at the prestigious SIGGRAPH Computer Animation Festival in 2004 which qualified the film for the 2005 Academy Awards even before Park and fellow students had graduated from the Australian Film, Television and Radio School (AFTRS). It was subsequently nominated for the Oscar for Best Animated Short Film, losing to another extraordinary short, Chris Landreth's tribute to pioneering Canadian animator Ryan Larkin, *Ryan*. Other awards include the Prix Jean-Luc Xiberras at the Annecy International Animated Film Festival in 2005 (which had a special focus on Korea) and Best Short Animation at the 2005 BAFTA awards.

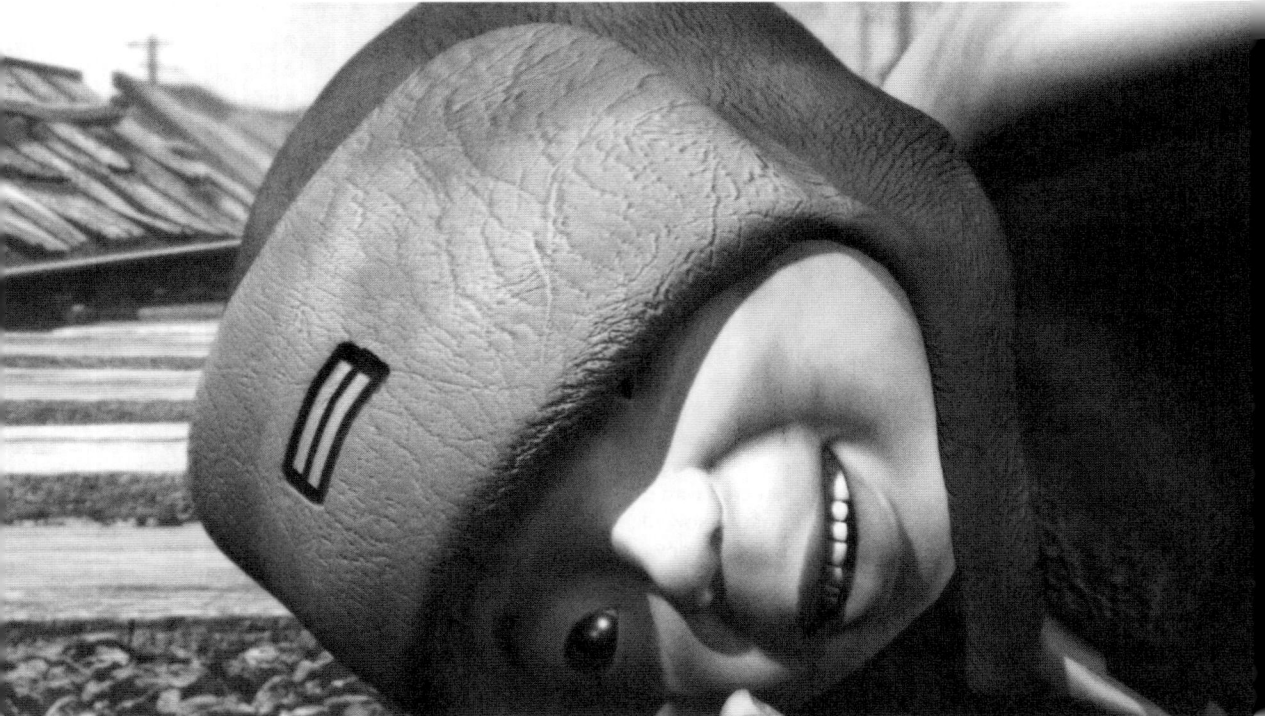

Birthday Boy – Sejong Park/Australian Film, Television and Radio School.

It has screened at over 100 film festivals around the world, and is the most awarded film in the almost forty-year history of the AFTRS.

Dynamic and subtle camera moves are a feature of the film. These are not, of course, real camera moves at all, but rather computer-generated approximations and recreations. The movement of the camera within a shot acts to identify the work as digital rather than hand-drawn 2D animation, but the principal purposes of the camera moves are to reinforce the storytelling and enhance mood cues. The first two shots of the film majestically swoop from a close-up of a butterfly on the crown of a roof down over the roof and tracking in to the fuselage of a crashed aeroplane to end facing Manuk, who is sorting through the ruins of war. The transition between shots is masked by the film's title, first written onscreen in Hanja (Korean adaptations of Chinese characters), dissolving to 'Birthday Boy' in capital letters, in English, in a slightly stylized typeface. The next shot is a brief overhead which, rising slowly, frames Manuk through a hole in the fuselage as he walks out into the sunlight. (This shot will be repeated in the next sequence as the train passes, and again, heart-wrenchingly in the epilogue where, along with the dissolves between shots, the gradual upward lift of the overhead shot completes our separation from Manuk that had begun when he saw the parcel.) In a long, locked-off wide shot we then watch Manuk exit the wreck of the plane and walk towards the camera, the shot ending with a close-up of his face, reinforcing his importance in the story and allowing contemplation of the accomplishment of the animation.

The film uses a naturalistic, earthy colour palette, full of greens, browns and rusty reds; like the camerawork the colours are not garish or showy as in many animated films. Even the sky is yellowish rather than blue or grey. Apart from the wide shot of the train track running off into the mountains, the only natural flora or fauna seen in the film (insect noises are heard throughout) is the butterfly in the opening shot, an unidentified white and orange pieridae, which is disturbed by a metallic clang. Its flight launches the camera backwards over the wooden roof of a traditional Korean building. In Korean culture the butterfly can symbolize happiness, perhaps an allusion to Manuk's impending happiness at finding the bolt and making the toy, although this may be one of many moments in the film which invite a cross-cultural reading. The Greek word for 'butterfly' is 'psyche', which also means the soul or the form that a person takes in the afterlife. The flight of the butterfly here in Birthday Boy might then be the flight of the soul, perhaps the soul of Manuk's soldier father who, we will learn, has recently been killed. Manuk is oblivious.

We are first introduced to Manuk through sound as the butterfly is disturbed by Manuk's clatter through the debris in the aeroplane in search of a particular piece of metal, before we hear him singing. This is fitting, as the sound design and sound editing, along with the score, are critical to the telling and comprehension of the story. In the absence of English dialogue (Manuk's song, his game, the postman's cries and his mother's greeting are all sung or spoken in Korean, with English subtitles), the work that must be done through sound effects, atmosphere and foley is amplified. And it is through sound that we identify and are aligned with Manuk at two critical moments: first, as the train passes Manuk its noise diminishes, leaving only the wind and his heartbeat between the boy and the train; and, second, in his war game leading up to the assault on the postman when he talks with his father and we hear the sounds of explosions and gunfire in his head. When he throws the rock/hand grenade, we hear it spiralling to earth, but then it abruptly stops and instead of the anticipated explosion we hear a dull thud followed by the anguished cries of the postman crashing his bicycle. The use of atmospheres is also notable here, particularly the sound of insects, birds and frogs which runs through the film, dropping out only when overpowered by other sounds, and in the epilogue when the soundscape is cleared to leave only the sound of Manuk sleeping, and the wind whistling through the house. The use of the sound of the wind in this final scene gestures back both to the incident with the train and to the opening scene where the wind whistles through the aeroplane. In the epilogue the wind is made more eerie, ominous and other-worldly by the removal of other environmental noises.

Music is used sparingly but effectively in the film. After metallic clangs and rhythm set by the sounds of insects and frogs, the first music in the film is Manuk's song, which is heard twice in the setup. The song appears before Manuk, so initially it functions to provide information about character and setting and to alert us that the film's first language is not English. The first instrumental note is not heard until the transition from the setup to the complicating action when a combination of gongs, chimes, bells that are bowed or struck, and plucked string instruments are used to play an apparently arrhythmic motif. This motif appears again in variations at the start of the development and again at the beginning of the climax. The eerie strangeness of the music is discomfiting, and raises concern for Manuk's well-being at each spot it appears. Music is used most consistently in the climax. As Manuk discovers the parcel the pattern of short bursts of a single or few notes is broken. A low, drawn out, deep resonating note ominously signals the power of the box's contents, and the music ceases completely in the transition to the epilogue as Manuk marches up and down wearing his father's presents, the boots and dog tags. They are reunited at last, but forever destined to be apart.

Ben Goldsmith

The Mysterious Geographical Adventures of Jasper Morello

Country of Origin:
Australia

Director:
Anthony Lucas

Producers:
Anthony Lucas
Julia Lucas

Screenwriter:
Mark Shirrefs

Production Designer:
Anthony Lucas

Editor:
David Tait

Genre:
Science Fiction
Short

Duration:
26 minutes

Synopsis

Jasper Morello is an aerial navigator in a world of steam-powered airships and mechanical computers, but he lives in disgrace after a terrible accident caused by an error in judgement. A terrible plague is ravaging his city, Gothia, and Morello's wife becomes infected.

On a mission to distribute weather beacons, Morello's airship, the *Resolution*, is wrecked in a collision with an abandoned airship, the *Hieronymous*. The crew is able to take over the *Hieronymous* but, when one of the crew is discovered to have the plague, the captain decides to head home. It is now that they discover a levitating island. On this island the crew of the airship discovers a species of creature that lures people in to traps in order to drain their blood. Morello is very nearly killed by one of the creatures, but another of the crew arrives just in time and shoots it dead. The crew feast on the body, then discover that the cooked flesh has the power to cure the plague. Pupal young of the creatures are taken aboard the airship. Only one of the pupae survives, but it hatches and thrives. On a nightmare voyage back to civilization, Morello discovers that the ship's scientist, Dr Belgon, is feeding the crew to the growing creature. With everyone else dead, Belgon dies in a struggle with Morello. The navigator is now left with the prospect of feeding his own blood to the creature in order to get it back to his country so that he can stop the plague and save his wife.

Critique

While there have been plenty of Australian Academy Award nominees (and even a few winners) for their contributions to science fiction and fantasy films, The *Mysterious Geographical Adventures of Jasper Morello* was the first – and so far only – such film to receive a nomination in its own right. In terms of plot, this is effectively a feature-length film presented in less than half an hour. In addition, an astonishing depth of characterization is achieved, and an entire world is also displayed.

Cast:
Joel Edgerton
Helmut Bakaitis
Tommy Dysart
Jude Beaumont

Year:
2005

There is a definite feeling of the Victorian Gothic revival about this film. The dark and shadowy silhouette animation suggests the same brooding gloom of such nineteenth-century works as *Dr Jekyll and Mr Hyde*, *Dracula* and *Frankenstein*. This impression is reinforced by the mechanistic technology, floating architecture, and pervasive iron lace and gears. The iron-airship technology parallels that of the oceangoing nineteenth-century steamships. This is a world where islands defy gravity as easily as the unlikely airships, yet it is not hard to suspend disbelief and accept this.

The central theme concerns the value of human life. The vampire-creatures need to be nourished with blood, and on the voyage home there is only human blood available. Thus, some must be sacrificed if many are to live. For Dr Belgon there is no moral conflict, and the crewmen are no more than feedstock as far as he is concerned. Morello, by contrast, has the role of everyman: he has a stronger sense of morality, but this makes his dilemma more intense. Saving people is clearly good. Sacrificing people is clearly bad. Sacrificing some people to save others is a very difficult call. Oddly enough, by the end of the film Jasper is in a much more clear-cut position. He is the only survivor in the ship, so he only has to decide whether or not to sacrifice himself. His blood can keep the vampire-creature alive long enough to save his wife and many others.

In our own society we are witnessing the beginnings of a parallel situation. Factory workers are exposed to toxins in order to produce consumer goods more cheaply. Not good, but we generally buy the goods and try not to think why they are so cheap. Pharmaceuticals are priced out of the reach of some so that others may have a higher return on investment. The temptation to buy shares in the pharmaceutical company is strong. You donate a kidney so that your child may live. That is a personal decision. You need a liver transplant and a black market liver is available. Did someone die so that you may live?

Like *Dark City* (Alex Proyas, 1998), *The Mysterious Geographical Adventures of Jasper Morello* is a stunning but isolated achievement in Australian cinema. The talent to make many more such films exists. As yet, the backing does not.

Sean McMullen

BUSHRANGER

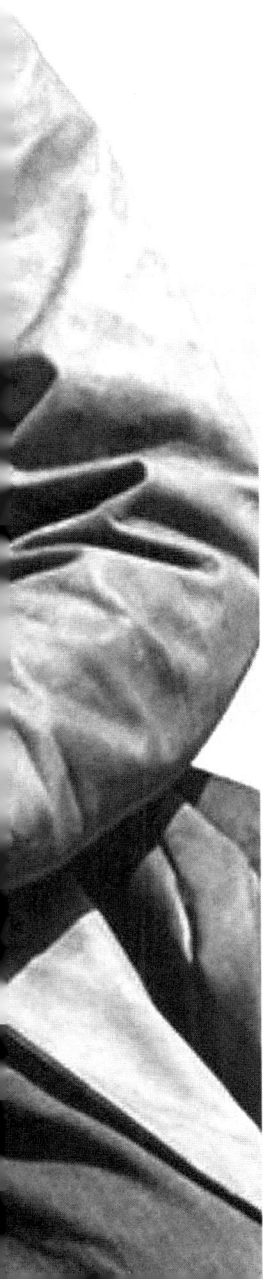

Bushranging films have appeared at regular intervals throughout the history of Australia's national cinema. Yet, this genre
has suffered from enormous critical neglect. For many historians, bushranging films are located in that hazy field known
as the 'historical film'. Bushranger films are certainly historical
for they generally narrate the exploits of famous people and
tend to be set in the past (usually the nineteenth century), but
they sit awkwardly in a category that in Australia includes a
large number of costume dramas or 'period films'. Bushranger
movies are a distant cousin of the American western, sharing
a tradition of celebrating bad men and outlaws, but there
are also significant differences between the two genres.
Bushranging stories are often set in a debauched political and
social climate. In a landscape where the state apparatus of
judges, politicians and police are the real villains, bushrangers who plunder, murder and terrorize are represented as folk
heroes.

Bushranging in North Queensland was probably Australia's first bushranging film. Shot in 1904, it was produced by
Joseph Long for the Limelight Division of the Salvation Army.
The Limelight Division was the largest Australian film production organization in the first years of the twentieth century,
and was known both for its religious epics such as Soldiers of
the Cross (1900), and for its documentaries of major secular
public events including The Inauguration of the Commonwealth of Australia (1901) and the official record of the Royal
Tour of Australia in the same year. It may seem surprising
that such an organization would make a film about notorious
outlaws, but perhaps this reveals something about the fascination with bushranging and with Australian subjects in this
period. Film historian Chris Long (1995b) has suggested that

Joseph Long may have been inspired by American film-maker Edwin S. Porter's 1903 film *The Great Train Robbery*, although Bill Routt (2001) notes that this may be assuming too much since the first documented screening of Porter's film in Australia was not until February 1905.

On 26 December 1906, the Tait Brothers premiered *The Story of the Kelly Gang* at the Athenaeum Theatre in Collins Street, Melbourne. Widely regarded as the world's first feature-length narrative film, the film tells the story of the life of the legendary Australian bushranger, Ned Kelly. Over time, much of the film has been lost, but in 2007, the National Film and Sound Archive released a DVD of the surviving minutes, together with a book detailing the range of historical material around the film, interrogating previous studies, and analysing the film's content and style (Bertrand & Routt 2007). In 2007, 101 years after it was made, the film was placed on UNESCO's Memory of the World register of internationally significant documents.

Also touring in 1906 was another film on Ned Kelly which Ina Bertrand has dubbed the 'Perth Fragments'. As the name suggests, very little of this film remains. William D Routt claims that it was adapted from the 1898 melodrama, *The Kelly Gang or the Career of Ned Kelly, the Ironclad Bushranger of Australia*. It seems that 'The Perth Fragments' toured under the title 'The Kelly Gang'. So, distinguishing it from *The Story of the Kelly Gang* is difficult and, given that the Taits switched between promoting their feature as either 'The Story of the Kelly Gang' or 'The Kelly Gang', differentiating the films is almost impossible. However, the fact that that Dan Barry and Robert Hollyford presented a movie entitled *The Kelly Gang* at the Hobart Town Hall on the same evening as the Tait's Melbourne premiere at least affirms that more than one Kelly production was in existence. The Olympia theatre announced a screening of *Ned Kelly the Iron-clad Bushranger*, and a journalist reviewed the splendid Kelly film *Bail Up*. These suggest a variety of Kelly gang films, although they could just be the result of inventive wording to arouse interest in the other Kelly films.

Due to the overwhelming success of *The Story of the Kelly Gang*, film producers were eager to make their own bushranging films. In 1907, Charles MacMahon produced *Robbery Under Arms*, the first of several adaptations of Rolf Boldrewood's 1888 novel. In 1910, the Taits reshot their 1906 feature and released it under the same title. While some claim that this was the 1906 movie repackaged, images on the theatrical poster suggest that this edition included a different cast and was shot at different locations. Sadly, verifying whether it was an entirely different production is difficult as only fragmented scenes remain from this version. Still, this 1910 release sparked one of Australia's great booms of feature film-making. For about ten months, bushranging films flooded Australian movie theatres.

In 1910, S A Fitzgerald produced *The Life and Adventures of John Vane, the Notorious Australian Bushranger*. Vane was a member of the Ben Hall Gang, who turned his back on his bushranging mates for a lawful life. The film received positive reviews and played to large audiences. Yet, the most significant aspect about this movie was that it marked the first recorded involvement in narrative film production of pioneer exhibitor and producer Charles Cozens Spencer. Also in 1910, John Gavin directed two popular bushranging films: *Thunderbolt* and *Moonlite*. Unlike Fitzgerald's movie in which Vane renounced his evil ways, Gavin's bushrangers were violent and fierce, and treated the police force with contempt and malice. Gavin described *Moonlite* as 'a bushranging saga in the grand manner, with enough dead troopers to warrant a severe censorship'. These were prescient words, as bushranging films were banned in 1912 in New

South Wales and Victoria, in large part because of their depictions of successful criminal activity and negative portrayals of police and authorities.

Gavin was a particularly prolific producer of bushranging films before the ban was introduced. In early 1911 he directed and starred in *Ben Hall and His Gang*, and later the same year he played the lead in *Frank Gardiner, the King of the Road*. When censorship was enforced, Gavin left Australia for Hollywood where he appeared in a number of B-Westerns. He returned to Australia in 1922 with the intention of producing a serial based on Ned Kelly. But when he ran in censorship problems he again found refuge in Hollywood.

Routt claims 'about 11 films in which bushrangers were the featured attraction' were made in the first and greatest boom in production between November 1910 and July 1912 (Routt 2001). In 1911, Alfred Rolfe directed two bushranging films for Cozens Spencer's company (Spencer's Pictures). The first was *Captain Midnight, the Bush King* and, alongside Rolfe, it starred up-and-coming director Raymond Longford, who would also star in Rolfe's next bushranging feature *Captain Starlight, or Gentleman of the Road*. Directed by Rolfe and produced by Cozens Spencer, it was another film loosely based on Boldrewood's popular novel *Robbery Under Arms*. Rolfe was known for his sympathetic representation of bushrangers as chivalrous and gentlemanly, and his films in particular spurred the campaign by police and others against bushranging films on the grounds that they romanticized crime.

In an attempt to challenge claims that bushranger films celebrated the country's most depraved criminals, Gaston Mervale changed the name of his forthcoming film from 'Ben Hall, the Notorious Bushranger' to the more anodyne *Tale of the Australian Bush* (1911). Mervale even promoted his Ben Hall saga as a 'clean tale ... that will please the masses and not offend anybody' in an attempt to stave off mounting criticism of the genre. But while directors like Mervale were trying to sanitize the genre, others were celebrating all its blood and gore. Spencer's Pictures *Dan Morgan* (1911) was brutally and remorselessly violent. Not only does Morgan kill his gang members in cold blood, he destroys anyone or anything in his path. Its massive success was the final straw for authorities in New South Wales and Victoria. Bans were introduced in the two states in 1912, remaining in place until the 1940s.

In the age of censorship, producers who had nothing to lose and no reputation to destroy were generally the ones game enough to make bushranging films, and some were passed by the censors if they portrayed bushrangers as criminals and the police and judicial system in a positive light. In 1920, unknown Welsh director Harry Southwell made *The Kelly Gang*, which to the dismay of the South Australian government received censorship approval in Victoria and New South Wales. In 1922, Southwell made another Kelly film, *When the Kellys Were Out*, however this film did not fare so well with the censors, Southwell was not deterred and in 1934 he returned with yet another Kelly film, *When the Kellys Rode*, but this too was banned. In 1920, a young Kenneth Brampton produced another adaptation of *Robbery Under Arms*. Originally Raymond Longford was given the option to direct the movie, but he passed, fearing the taboo of bushranging could severely tarnish his credibility. In 1946, Ken G Hall flirted with the idea of making a Ned Kelly film, but chose instead to make the much more politically-acceptable bio-pic *Smithy* about pioneering Australian aviator Sir Charles Kingsford Smith.

By the late 1940s, censorship on bushranging films eased but the boom was long gone. Bushranging films appeared here and there, but nothing that would suggest a renaissance. Rupert Kathner did not help the popularity of the genre with his terrible 1951 Kelly film, *The Glenrowan Affair*. A financial and critical debacle, it was Kathner's last movie. Cecil Homes brought some credibility to the genre in 1953 with *Captain Thunderbolt*. Filmed in the New England area of New South Wales, and starring a young and handsome Charles 'Bud' Tingwell, it had a loyal following both in Australia and overseas. In 1957, Jack Lee directed the first sound version of *Robbery Under Arms*. Featuring the internationally-famed Peter Finch as the charismatic Captain Starlight, it also enjoyed some box-office success overseas.

The arrival of television provided a new medium for bushranging films. In 1960, William Sterling directed the ABC television adaptation of Douglas Stewart's popular play *Ned Kelly*. Also in 1960, Ned Kelly became a popular subject for short films. Gary Shead directed *Stringybark Massacre* and Tim Burstall made his AFI Award winning *Ned Kelly*. Shead and Burstall each had ideas to direct their own Kelly feature but, in a climate where bushrangers were considered outdated, neither could raise the necessary funding.

At the end of the 1960s, British director Tony Richardson and Mick Jagger came to Australia to make *Ned Kelly*. Jagger's puny body and laughable attempt at a bog-Irish accent did not fare well with the critics but, still, the feature did reasonably well at the box-office. In 1974, Hollywood star Dennis Hopper came to Australia to make *Mad Dog Morgan* for director Philippe Mora. Based on the book *Morgan the Bold Bushranger* by Margaret Carnegie, the film was highly inventive and referred to Morgan's supposed homosexual affair with his Aboriginal traveller, played by David Gulpilil.

In 1977, the ABC produced the telemovie *The Trial of Ned Kelly*. A ratings bonanza in Australia, it was also successful in Britain. The following year Fred Schepisi adapted Thomas Keneally's book *The Chant of Jimmy Blacksmith*. The film told the story of famous Aboriginal bushranger Jimmy Governor, acknowledging that bushrangers were not only white settlers or the sons of immigrants. In 1980, the television mini-series *The Last Outlaw* was aired to coincide with the centenary of Ned Kelly's death. Written and produced by historian Ian Jones, it depicted Kelly as a gentleman bushranger. Following a similar pattern was the 1985 feature *Robbery Under Arms*, which cast Sam Neill as the courteous and well-mannered Captain Starlight.

Since the early 1990s, a number of comedies have had great fun with the genre. Films such as *The Nun and the Bandit* (1992), *Reckless Kelly* (1995) and *Ned* (2003) all transport the principles and codes of nineteenth-century bushrangers into a modern-day social and political climate. While none of these films were hugely successful, they did provide a refreshing look at the genre. After a huge promotional campaign, in 2003 came the latest Ned Kelly feature. Starring Heath Ledger, and featuring Geoffrey Rush, Naomi Watts and Orlando Bloom, it was a box-office hit, even though there were some complaints that the sanitized representation of bushrangers in recent times had dulled the once highly immoral and wicked genre. Still, not all was lost. In 2006, John Hillcoat's *The Proposition*, written by Nick Cave, featured all the blood, gore and depravity that saw bushranging films banned in the first place. Winning the Best Film at the 2006 AFI Awards, it painted a vivid image of the debauched social climate that spawned bushrangers during the nineteenth century.

Stephen Gaunson

The Story of the Kelly Gang

Country of Origin:
Australia

Director:
Charles Tait

Producers:
W A Gibson
Millard Johnson
John Tait
Nevin Tait

Screenwriter:
Charles Tait

Duration:
60 minutes (original)

Genre:
Bushranger

Cast:
Frank Mills
Sam Crew
John Forde
Jack Ennis
Will Coyne
Lizzie Tait
Charles Tait (early
documentation does not name
the cast and it is quite possible
that more than one person
played Ned Kelly, or any role)

Year:
1906

The film premiered on 26 December 1906 at the Athenaeum Hall, Melbourne and was said to be six reels long, or close to 60 minutes. If this is true, then it makes it the longest narrative film for its time. Sadly, film deterioration has destroyed all but 16 minutes of original footage. So a complete synopsis of the film is difficult. The programme booklet that was sold for 6d at the original screenings fills in some of the missing content. A copy of the booklet is now preserved by the National Film & Sound Archive. As this film predated intertitles and sound, the programme booklet would have helped audience members follow the narrative. The programme booklet breaks the film into 6 scenes/sequences, which follow the main exploits of the historic Kelly Outbreak.

Synopsis

Scene 1: Fitzpatrick Mystery. Constable Fitzpatrick arrives with a warrant to arrest Dan Kelly for cattle stealing. Fitzpatrick manhandles Mrs Kelly and attempts to molest Kate Kelly. 'Just one kiss Kate, dear, and I'll let Dan go', Fitzpatrick begs. As protection for the women, Ned shoots the trooper in the wrist. Held at bay by Kate with a loaded revolver, the Kelly brothers and two friends (Joe Byrne and Steve Hart) flee into Victoria's Wombat Ranges.

The last part of this scene remains. The footage begins with a distraught Mrs Kelly led into the house by Kate. When Kate returns, Fitzpatrick gropes and roughly shoves her. From the house, the Kelly Gang emerge. As Fitzpatrick goes for his gun, Ned shoots him in the wrist. Kate holds her molester at gun point as the gang casually ride into the distance.

Scene 2: Stringybark Creek. The Kelly Gang bail up the police officers Lonigan (misspelt in the booklet as Lonergan) and McIntyre (misspelt as MacIntyre). McIntyre surrenders but Lonigan is shot dead as he runs for cover. Waiting for the other officers to return, the gang help themselves to afternoon tea. Later Kennedy and Scanlon return to the camp. Given the option to bail up, they also are shot by the gang. During the gun fight, Lonigan escapes on Kennedy's horse. The gang fire shots at him, but to no avail.

Fragments of this scene remain. The gunfight reveals no sign of the gang giving the police any chance of bailing up, as the programme booklet asserts. The manner in which the gang devour the officers' provisions represents them as uncouth, uncivilized and wild.

Scene 3: The Gang hold up Younghusband's station. Everybody on site is rounded up and held hostage. Ned instructs Steve to go through the male hostages' pockets. Ned boldly announces 'we do not rob women or children'. However, they do rob the poor Scottish hawker Sandy Gloster (whose actual name was James). Despite Gloster's pleas not to loot his hawker van, the gang help themselves to his clothes, alcohol and cigars. Joe Byrne is left to guard the hostages as the others ride into town and rob the Euroa bank. The gang do not share their loot with any of the hostages.

DEATH OF DAN KELLY & STEVE HART

The Story of the Kelly Gang, J & N Tait/Johnson And Gibson.

Recently, fragments of this long sequence were uncovered. The footage mainly deals with the early part of the hold up and arrival of Sandy Gloster. As Gloster is held at gun point, the outlaws take his goods. This scene does little to support Kelly's image as a noble robber. Here the gang cruelly humiliate Gloster in front of the hostages. To the delight of the cheering hostages, Kelly comically kicks Gloster in the rear.

Scene 4: This seems to be a long sequence of many small scenes edited together. Kate Kelly shows her horse prowess as she escapes from a group of police. Black trackers look for the gang in the Strathbogie Ranges. Friend of the Kellys, Aarron Sherritt is seen assisting the police. Joe arrives at Aaron's shanty and cries 'death to all traitors' as he shoots Sherritt dead. The police who hide underneath Sherritt's bed quake in fear. Excusing their cowardice, the programme booklet includes the line 'this is the only Blot on the police'.

Nothing of this sequence remains, however an image of the black trackers appears in the programme booklet. The National Film and Sound Archive also hold some stills from this sequence, such as Kate Kelly riding through a pond.

Scene 5: The Glenrowan siege. Kelly forces the platelayers to tear up the Glenrowan train tracks. Schoolmaster Thomas Curnow who is held hostage along with many others inside the Glenrowan Inn reveals to Ned that the station master has a loaded gun. For his deceit, the station master is beaten 'rather Roughly'. Curnow flees from the Inn and warns the driver of Special Police Train about the derailed tracks. Officers descend from the train and surround the Inn. The reckless shooting by the police kills a young male hostage. To ensure that no outlaw survives the battles, the police set fire to the inn.

Fragments of this sequence remains. Most of the remaining footage though is terribly damaged. The death of Joe Byrne for example is barely visible. The clearest shot is the police firing towards the Inn. Refusing to be taken prisoner, Steve and Dan shoot one another in a suicide pact. Heroically Father Gibney runs into the burning inn and saves a wounded platelayer from death.

Scene 6: The final scene is Ned Kelly's gallant gun battle with the police. Bullets ricochet off Ned's armour, as he takes on the entire army of officers. A shot into Ned's leg brings the armoured outlaw to his knees. At the mercy of the officers, Ned weakly begs that his life be spared.

Thankfully, this seminal scene has been preserved. The figure of Kelly staggering towards the police in his makeshift armour is an instantly recognizable, even iconic, image.

Critique

For years it was believed that all the footage from the film was destroyed. In the mid 1970s ten frames were discovered. In 1979 a variety of negatives from the film were found, and a further 400 feet in 1931. During research for the film's Centennial Restoration, the National Film and Sound Archive uncovered 11 more minutes of the film. The footage mostly concerns the Kellys at Younghusband's Station. This footage however is more significant as it includes an entire unbroken sequence. For the first time, the footage could be watched without any gaps.

The Story of the Kelly Gang was produced by the Tait family. The Taits were certainly involved in the international exhibition of bush-ranging plays prior to their film. In addition to holding the rights for the Kelly 'Flesh and Blood Show', they toured Hiener's *The Bushrangers* around Britain. In 1904 the Taits made their first substantial move into film exhibition. At Melbourne Town Hall, they divided one of their programmes between imported newsreels and gramophone recordings by Nellie Melba. From 29 March 1906 they had a highly successful run with a documentary, *Living London*. By the year's end, they premiered *The Story of the Kelly Gang*. John and Nevin Tait acted as producers and their brother Charles directed. The Taits joined forces with two chemists, William Gibson and Millard Johnson, who knew how to develop film. Johnson acted as the cameraman and Gibson handled the processing work. Several members of the Tait family played key roles in the film. Elizabeth Tait, Charles's wife, played Kate Kelly. The chief location for their shoot was the estate of the Taits at Heidelberg, Melbourne. The nearby train station at Rosanna Station became the Glenrowan Station, and the Victorian Railway Commissioner provided a train and gangers to rip up the tracks.

Despite the Tait's theatre background, and lack of experience in film production, the film is sophisticated and innovative in its mix of deep and lateral staging of action, and in the (albeit tentative) use of the pan. Such camera movement was highly unusual for the time. Most of the film consists of long shots, which allow coverage of several planes of action. There are some notable cuts to closer views, although there are no close-up shots. The lack of close-ups in the movie places greater importance on the role of costumes and settings for identifying characters and following the narrative. It also allowed the Taits to interchange the actors. It is widely believed that an anonymous Canadian stunt actor played Ned Kelly in a few scenes. The screenings of the film also allowed the Taits to embellish their flair for theatrics. As the film played, a narrator would have explained onscreen action as others performed live sound effects such as shooting guns and galloping horses. Still, this was not to everyone's liking. In a review in 1907, *The Bulletin* growled, 'there is a deal too much racket in connection with the show'.

On its release, the film was billed at 'The Sensation of the year – the greatest most thrilling, and sensational moving picture even taken'. It was a phenomenal success and in a matter of weeks it had recouped its production budget of around £1000 (A$2500). Despite its romanticization and evasion of certain facts, reviews generally appreciated the film's historical retelling.

Today, *The Story of the Kelly Gang* is discussed more as an historical artefact than actual film. This is mainly because of its missing footage and significance as the world's first feature-length moving picture. In 2007, Ina Bertrand and William D Routt wrote a monograph celebrating the film's importance in the history of world cinema. Entitled 'The Picture That Will Live Forever', it was released together with a DVD of the remaining footage, restored by The National Film and Sound Archive and the Haghefilm laboratory in Amsterdam.

Stephen Gaunson

The Glenrowan Affair

Director:
Rupert Kathner

Producer:
Rupert Kathner

Screenwriter:
Rupert Kathner

Cinematographers:
Harry Malcolm
Rupert Kathner

Editor:
Alex Ezard

Duration:
70 minutes

Genre:
Bushranger

Cast:
Bob Chitty
Albie Henderson
Ben Crowe
Bill Wright
Charles Tingwell

Year:
1951

Synopsis

Over the top of unilluminating black-and-white footage of Victoria's northeast the narrator – Charles 'Bud' Tingwell – introduces the milieu of 'Kelly Country'. Next, he introduces the character of Dan Kelly. Yet, this is not Dan Kelly the young robust bushranger, but Dan Kelly the old withered man. Dan did not die at Glenrowan in 1880 with the other members of the Kelly Gang, but escaped to tell his tale. Apart from this deviation, *The Glenrowan Affair* follows an almost identical story as narrated in the earlier Kelly features. After the Kelly Gang shoot dead three police officers at Stringybark Creek, they become the subject of a nationwide police hunt. The criminal outbreak, which includes bank raids and the murder of Kelly ally Aaron Sherritt, culminates at Glenrowan where Ned in his armoured suit confronts the Victoria police. Things end disastrously for Ned, but his brother Dan escapes to tell his tale.

Critique

The multi-talented Rupert Kathner cast Victorian footballer Bob Chitty as Ned Kelly. Regarded as a fearsome competitor, Chitty in many regards was an appropriate choice. Footballer Jack Dyer even joked, 'it was the first time Chitty ever needed armour'. For the role of Aaron Sherritt, Kathner cast himself under the pseudonym 'Hunt Angels'. *The Glenrowan Affair* is riddled with historical errors, yet perhaps the most peculiar is an intertitle early in the film that announces the year as 1887. Surely those with even a hazy memory of the Outbreak remembered that Ned had died on 11 November 1880. Kathner must have been having a laugh when he marketed his film as 'The True Story of the Kelly Gang'. As a review from the *Sunday Herald* in August 1951 declared, this film demonstrates 'less than the minimal requirements of film craft'.

The *Glenrowan Affair* began in 1947 as a Harry Southwell project entitled, *A Message to Kelly*. Southwell was certainly an old hand at producing Kelly films having previously directed *The Kelly Gang* (1920), *When the Kellys Were Out* (1922) and *When the Kellys Rode* (1934). Like Kathner, Southwell is remembered as a fairly incompetent director. When Southwell heard that Kathner had plans to shoot his own Kelly production, he hired him as co-director. Earlier, in 1935, Kathner worked as the artistic director on Southwell's film *The Burgomeister* (Harry Southwell, 1935). For their Kelly project, they scrounged together a budget of £6000 and formed the production company, Benalla Film Productions. Within weeks they had shot over 1000 feet of film. However, when Southwell discovered that once the production wrapped Kathner still had plans to shoot his own Kelly feature, he immediately dumped him from the project. Ironically, though, a few weeks later, Southwell ran out of money and abandoned the picture. Footage from this feature is now held at the National Film & Sound Archive. In 1950, Kathner was back in Benalla shooting *The Glenrowan Affair*. Since parting ways with Southwell, Kathner had begun his own production company – Australian Action Pictures – and written his own script. Marred by shonky direction and factual errors, the film did nothing to enhance Kathner's already poor reputation.

The biographical docudrama based on Kathner's career, *Hunt Angels* (Alec Morgan, 2005) champions *The Glenrowan Affair* as his crowning achievement. Beyond capturing his style and attitude, *Hunt Angels* employs Kathner's filmmaking ingredients such as re-enactments, voice-over narration and interviews. Fittingly, this docudrama is also crammed full of baffling untruths. In one instance, it declares *The Glenrowan Affair* as the only Australian feature released in 1951, despite films such as *Wherever She Goes* (Michael S Gordon, 1951) also premiering that year.

Importantly, *Hunt Angels* celebrates Kathner's ineptness as his most enjoyable feature. Throughout this docudrama, clips from Kathner's movies are interspersed with experts discussing his shonky methods, bad luck and financial restrictions. The audience is certainly encouraged to laugh at Kathner's productions, but *Hunt Angels* proposes *The Glenrowan Affair* as a neglected gem. While acknowledging that Kathner's film received a 'dreadful' reception in Sydney, *Hunt Angels* draws attention to its 'fabulous' premiere in Benalla, claiming that Kelly descendants appreciated the film in ways that city slickers could not. Not surprisingly, this is an absolute and categorical lie. Not only did Kelly descendants not appreciate this film, they lobbied to see it banned in 'Kelly Country'. They argued that the Dan Kelly escape myth was unfounded and deliberately offensive. Reports indicated that every time the withered Dan character appeared on screen, the audience booed and hollered.

Stephen Gaunson

Ned Kelly

Studio/Distributor:
Woodfall film productions

Director:
Tony Richardson

Screenwriters:
Tony Richardson
Ian Jones

Producer:
Neil Hartley

Cinematographer:
Gerry Fisher

Art Direction:
Andrew Sanders

Synopsis

After being released from jail following a 3-year sentence for an unspecified crime, Ned Kelly returns home to his family in the rural outback of late nineteenth-century Australia. During his incarceration the matriarch of the family has taken up with a new man, George King, an American whom Ned is initially wary of. Before long, Ned is back to causing trouble, antagonizing the local English landowner Mr.Whitty and fighting with the police. After Ned and his gang steal Whitty's horses, a reward is offered for their capture. While hiding in the surrounding outback, the gang learn that Mrs. Kelly has been sentenced to 3 years in prison in a clear miscarriage of justice. After his request to exchange himself for his mother's freedom is flatly refused, Ned and the gang turn to more serious crime, at first in order to raise money to support themselves, but they soon begin to believe the popular mythology growing up around them that casts the gang as defenders of the poor against the colonial establishment. As the Kelly gang's crimes escalate, so does the reward on their heads. The police employ Aboriginal trackers in their quest to bring them to justice. The gang is surrounded at the Glenrowan Hotel, where they make their final stand.

Composer:
Shel Silverstein

Editor:
Charles Rees

Duration:
99 minutes

Genre:
Action
Bushranger
Historical drama

Cast:
Mick Jagger
Clarissa Kaye-Mason
Mark McManus
Ken Goodlet

Year:
1970

Critique

Oscar winning director (for *Tom Jones*, 1963) Tony Richardson's take on the legend of *Ned Kelly* is a curiously flat and unengaging affair despite its subject being one of Australia's most notorious historical figures. Mick Jagger in his first screen role gives an instantly recognizable face to the iconic Kelly, Jagger being globally renowned as the frontman of the band The Rolling Stones. Jagger's well-publicized brushes with the law aligned him with the outlaw Kelly, and he just about pulls off the role, even if his accent is suspect and varies wildly from scene to scene. *Ned Kelly* appears almost quaint in its depiction of life in Australia during the nineteenth century; its portrayal of the landscape is picturesque and the inhabitants appear to be little more than caricatures: the rogue Irishmen, the aristocratic English, and the mostly drunken, bawdy locals. Aboriginal people appear as coach drivers and police trackers. The film's portrayal of violence is also somewhat out of keeping with its contemporary movies, Arthur Penn's *Bonnie & Clyde* (1967) and Sam Peckinpah's *The Wild Bunch* (1969) being much grittier period pieces.

Ned Kelly suffers from a lack of fully-fleshed-out characters. The story moves along briskly, encompassing a variety of events in the lives of Ned and his gang, but no real insight into their transformation from petty criminals to outlaws. Ned's sporadic speeches on the tyranny of English rule and the loyalty he feels to the Irish flag could have been expanded upon, as they are the key to getting under the skin of the man. These issues are not fully investigated as the film is determined to keep up its essentially jaunty tone and, as a result, it fails to ignite and engross the audience. There is an over-reliance on the folk and country songs sung by Waylon Jennings and composed by Shel Silverstein, which sometimes dominate the scenes they accompany. Richardson's direction and Gerry Fisher's cinematography are solid and unspectacular. Notable, though, is the film's opening, which depicts the hanging of Ned Kelly in black and white, with the swift wipes between scenes typical of contemporary editing techniques in British and American cinema. These stylistic choices were, however, highly innovative in Australian cinema at a time when the revival in feature film production was still in its very early stages.

Ned Kelly is not without its saving graces, it scoots along at an entertaining pace, and it is hard not to feel little affection for Jagger's amiable take on Kelly. The film mythologizes this self-styled rebel, as Kelly is portrayed as the sympathetic everyman standing up to the colonial ruling classes. The one truly memorable image comes at the climax of the movie as we see Kelly in his home-fashioned armour and helmet facing off against what seems to be the entire Australian police force: a bizarre post-medieval knight making one last stand against his enemies.

Neil Mitchell

The Proposition

Studio/Distributor:
First Look Pictures

Director:
John Hillcoat

Screenwriter:
Nick Cave

Producers:
Chiara Minage
Cat Villers

Cinematographer:
Benoit Delhomme

Art Direction:
Bill Booth
Marita Mussett

Composers:
Nick Cave
Warren Ellis

Editor:
Jon Gregory

Duration:
104 minutes

Genre:
Bushranger

Cast:
Guy Pearce
Ray Winstone
Danny Huston
John Hurt
Emily Watson

Year:
2005

Synopsis

In late nineteenth-century rural Australia, Captain Stanley and his men apprehend two members of the Burns gang, brothers Charlie and Mikey. The gang, led by oldest brother Arthur, are responsible for the savage murders of a local family, the Hopkins. To save his younger brother from being executed on Christmas Day and to gain a pardon for them both, Charlie Burns is asked by Captain Stanley to find and kill Arthur in the nine days before the holiday. Charlie is freed to carry out his ultimatum whilst Mikey is incarcerated in the town's police station.

The townsfolk and Stanley's wife Martha are desperate for the outlaws to be brought to justice, as is Stanley's superior Mr. Fletcher, who, on visiting the town, confronts him over his offer of clemency for the brothers and orders Mikey to be flogged. Stanley fails to convince anyone around him that the flogging will spark a wave of retribution from the Burns gang. Arthur, having saved Charlie from attack, becomes aware of the situation after probing him for answers as to his younger brother's whereabouts. As Stanley and his wife prepare for Christmas Day the Burns gang make their move, with Charlie having an impossible decision to make.

Critique

John Hillcoat's third feature after *Ghosts ... of the Civil Dead* (1988) and *To Have and to Hold* (1996) relocates the Western to rural Australia, the period detail of late nineteenth-century life providing a suitably primitive setting for this harsh and bloody tale. With a screenplay by Nick Cave, who also provides the film's score with long-time collaborator Warren Ellis, *The Proposition* is a taut, strung out, almost Biblical tale of the lives led by the inhabitants of a small town in an untamed land under colonial rule. As Captain Stanley proclaims at the beginning of the movie, 'Australia, what fresh hell is this'. The rule of law is under constant threat, epitomized by the murderous Burns gang and their massacre of the Hopkins family. Stanley's proposition to Charlie is the film's driving force. Everything revolves around Charlie's dilemma: which brother will he save, and will he stop Arthur Burns' murderous spree in time to save Mikey from the gallows.

Featuring strong performances from all involved, including a great turn by John Hurt as a crazed bounty hunter, the pared-back script is brought to life by the cast and bolstered by stunning photography of the landscape: all dusty plains, rocky mountains and unforgiving heat. Cave and Ellis' score of melancholy violins, throbbing bass and portentous vocals perfectly captures the sense of tension that runs throughout the movie. Hillcoat's stately, unfussy direction lets the events play out gradually, with the sporadic outbursts of violence underlining the viciousness of the times.

Cave's screenplay is unflinching in its portrayal of life in Australia during this period. Aboriginal people are routinely racially abused and treated as 'rebel blacks' by the police and the colonial establishment. Stanley's men are portrayed as barely more refined than the outlaws, and the whole notion of civilizing a land is put into question by the brutal and inhumane treatment dished out to detainees. Ray Winstone gives a compelling performance of a man under extreme duress from all angles, his shaking hands in some scenes a sign of his inner turmoil. Trying to keep his wife shielded from the brutalities of the environment around her, keeping his men on the right side of the law and dealing with an obnoxious and cold superior who masquerades as a man of civility, becomes harder throughout the film. His pleading that Mikey's flogging will be 'a death sentence' on the town falls on deaf ears. Photographic omens of impending violence appear throughout: Stanley in his bed, with the whole room flooded with the light of a blood-red setting sun, and the heat finally giving way to a rainstorm following Mikey's flogging. The climax of The Proposition is as brutal as the outbursts of violence that have come before. The outlaws attack Stanley and Martha in their own home as they sit down to Christmas dinner, thus striking at the very essence of what represents Western civility.

Cave and Hillcoat's movie is a lean depiction of the struggles to maintain justice and humanity in an inhospitable land during an ugly and barbaric time. The greatest strength of The Proposition is its unflinching portrayal of a society struggling to establish itself, with its people riven by conflicts of ideology while at the same time trying to maintain law and order in the face of the outlaw gangs that threaten its very foundations.

Neil Mitchell

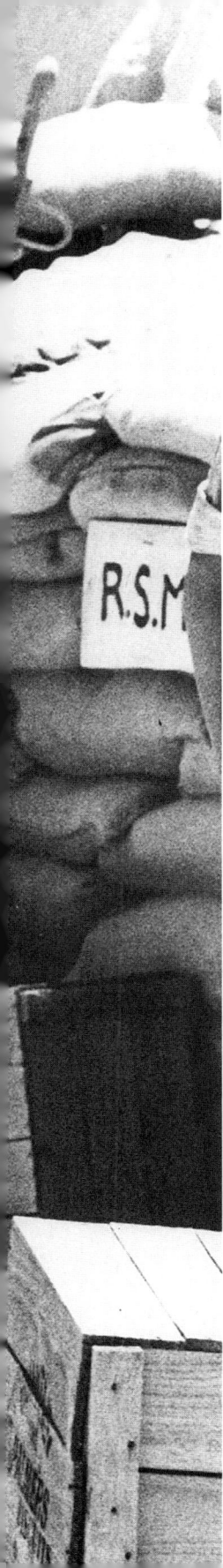

Australia's war cinema forms part of a broader discourse on the Anzac legend, alongside a prolific literature of books and pamphlets, as well as oral memory, war memorials, returned soldiers' clubs and public celebrations such as Anzac Day. It also forms a significant thread in its cinema, with about 40 movies devoted to the subject, not to mention many documentaries and television dramas.

The role of the cinema in the development and dissemination of the Anzac legend should not be underestimated. At many key points in its history, the story of Anzac has been propelled forward, or given significant shaping, by cinema representations. Many of Australia's finest writers, directors and actors have played their part in bringing Anzac to the public, often in new and forceful ways.

Australia's first war movies were closely modelled on British war films, with an emphasis on spies, rapacious Huns and upper-class Britons. The success of the short recruiting film *Will They Never Come?* (April 1915), though set in Europe, was credited with contributing to the surge of enlistments that followed the electrifying reports of the Anzac landings. In mid-July, two Gallipoli movies were huge box-office hits, attracting attention from audiences and critics who read them almost as if they were documentaries. *The Hero of the Dardanelles*, by one of the leading silent directors, Alfred Rolfe, and *Within Our Gates* were from the two leading rivals in Australian film production: Australasian Films and J C Williamson. Both films were melodramas, portraying the ideal Australian soldier in typically British terms, while *The Hero*'s restaged landings at Sydney's Tamarama Bay have survived to be shown virtually every Anzac Day as if they were footage of the real thing. In December 1915 two more films from the

Left: *Gallipoli*, Assoc R&R Films/Paramount.

rival houses emerged, this time on the topic of the sea battle between the Royal Australian Navy cruiser HMAS *Sydney* and the German warship SMS *Emden* off the Cocos Islands in November 1914. Rolfe's restrained film was far more convincing than the Monte Luke-directed Williamson production.

The pinnacle of wartime features came with John Gavin's wildly successful *The Martyrdom of Nurse Cavell* (January 1916). Literally written overnight by Gavin's wife Agnes, and released within weeks, it capitalized on the outrage of the German execution of the British nurse who helped Allied prisoners escape. Other war films followed from producers keen to cash in, but they only struck a popular backlash, as by mid-1916, audiences were tired of jingoistic melodramas, preferring documentaries such as *Australia Prepared* (July 1916) or the official British war documentaries. While strict censorship from the increasingly-paranoid government of Billy Hughes ensured that any domestic war movies took a suitably hysteric tone on the potential of the Hun ravaging Australian women, audiences increasingly stayed away, and production slumped dramatically. Two cunningly-marketed films were successful in 1918: *The Enemy Within* marketed its spy thriller as 'not a war film' and starred the popular all-round athlete Reg 'Snowy' Baker performing spectacular stunts, while Beaumont Smith compensated for his sloppy direction with superb marketing by getting his film banned for its portrayal of soldiers in dens of vice, then subsequently released 'uncut', which generated enormous free publicity.

Unlike the developing Anzac literature, Australian wartime films were slow to depict a distinctively Australian soldier character, instead portraying him in conservative, imperial British and triumphalist terms. Between the wars, this began to change as films focused on what made the Australian soldier different from his British counterpart. Several other qualities mark these films: a tendency to comedy as the most acceptable way to portray the horrors of the war to a post-war generation tired of war talk; a continuation of the portrayal of the war in positive terms, in contrast to the cynical and despairing representations popular in Europe; and the portrayal of the Australian and British as different-but-equal partners in the war, both of them the objects of affectionate humour. These films also saw the association of iconic Australian actors with Anzac roles, and the emergence of two key Australian directors. *Ginger Mick* (1920) and the less successful *Fellers* (1930) starred Arthur Tauchert, who had made his reputation as The Sentimental Bloke, the stocky, larrikin, urban, archetypical Australian. In 1928, Ken G Hall made his directorial debut, adapting a German film to Australian tastes with *The Exploits of the Emden*. *Diggers* (1931) and *Diggers in Blighty* (1933) were fairly successful comedies based on New Zealander Pat Hanna's stage plays, whose lean comic bushman Anzac moved the archetype in a new and permanent direction. Charles Chauvel's *Forty Thousand Horsemen* (1940), Australia's biggest box-office success at home and internationally to that point, introduced Chips Rafferty, whose laconic image was built on Hanna's. Chauvel and Rafferty followed up with another hit, *The Rats of Tobruk* (1944), which was the first Australian film to be set during the Second World War. More sombre and realistic, the story covered Australia's two legendary battles of the war, Tobruk and Kokoda. Rafferty went on to embody the typical Australian in international films for three more decades.

After World War II, Australian war movies languished in the wake of Australia's relatively low-key participation in the war, the virtual death of Australian film making and the glut of heroic war movies from Hollywood and Britain. With the revival of Australian media production in the late 1960s came the first attempts through television to re-engage the Anzac legacy. Productions veered from the simply heroic to the anti-war sentiments popular at the time. However, the movies and television productions of the 1970s and 1980s depicted a new development in the Anzac legend. The British had slipped to the status of hated and incompetent enemy, while the Australian image was consolidated as the ultimate casual, anti-authoritarian bushman soldier. *The Odd Angry Shot* (1979) set the theme of Aussie mateship in Vietnam, while Bruce Beresford's far more successful *Breaker Morant* (1980) gave real impetus to anti-British sentiment with its Boer War story. The most successful and influential of all Australian war films, however, was Peter Weir's elegant and elegiac *Gallipoli* (1981), although David Williamson's script offered a largely uncritical and reverential presentation of the Anzac story. Perhaps because of this, it has probably reached a larger contemporary audience than any other single text about Anzac, and the power of its tragic story continues to define the meaning of Anzac for new generations of Australians. A plethora of television productions, the most influential being *Anzacs* (1985), have tended to reinforce a simplistic tale of Australian bush virtue undone by snobbish British incompetence, so much so that few films have emerged in the years to follow. *The Lighthorsemen* (1987) was an earnest failure, *Paradise Road* (1997) was a rare excursion into women in war, and *Kokoda* (2006) and *Australia* (2008) finally brought the New Guinea and Darwin campaigns to contemporary Australian screens.

Daniel Reynaud

Will They Never Come?

Country of Origin:
Australia

Director:
Alfred Rolfe

Genre:
War

Year:
1915

Synopsis

The first Australian war film to represent Australians, albeit in a hypothetical battle, was the short recruiting film *Will They Never Come?* It was based on a popular and much republished recruiting poster of the period showing desperate, wounded soldiers looking across the seas to their sports-playing compatriots, longing for their assistance. The story was of two brothers, one an athlete whose devotion to sport kept him at home, while his 'namby-pamby' bookish brother volunteered, went off to fight, was wounded and returned home a hero and the centre of female attention, especially that of his brother's girlfriend, persuading the sportsman to sign up before he lost his girl.

Critique

Alfred Rolfe directed the film for Australasian, Australia's largest film company, which was accused of monopolistic practices, having recently absorbed several small rivals. Australasian made a grovelling patriotic offer to the Government to make a recruiting film at its own cost, which helped deflect criticism, and incidentally made patriotism very profitable, since the film was a hit. Set in Europe, the story was of a desperate last stand by a small group of soldiers needing reinforcement to fight off the Germans. Typically of the period, it made the enemy out to be war criminals, and it connected manhood with war. Even a lad 'devoid of real fibre', as the script described him, could become a real man in battle, and leave athletes behind him in the battle to marry and propagate the British race. It won the approval of the Prime Minister and the Minister of Defence, as well as popular and critical acclaim. It was also credited with stimulating recruiting, although the jump in the following months probably had more to do with the heroic press reports of the Gallipoli landings. A tiny sequence, several seconds long, survives as a flashback in *The Hero of the Dardanelles*, showing soldiers retreating under fire, against a skyline that looks suspiciously like gum trees.

Daniel Reynaud

The Hero of the Dardanelles

Country of Origin:
Australia

Director:
Alfred Rolfe

Screenwriters:
Phillip Gell
Loris Brown

Synopsis

This film, a sequel to *Will They Never Come?*, featured the sportsman leaving his bat and racket for a rifle, bidding farewell to family and friends, being trained, then taken to Egypt and finally Gallipoli, where on the first day he confronts a Red-Cross-sniping Turk, wrestling him over a cliff and drowning him in the sea. Hospitalized because of his injuries, he is repatriated and marries his sweetheart, taking up a farm.

Critique

Prompted by a suggestion by Prime Minister Hughes, Australasian Films made the sequel, which was released in July while the Gallipoli

Genre:

War

Cast:

Guy Hastings

Loma Rossmore

C Throoby

Ruth Wainwright

Fred Francis

Year:

1915

campaign was still under way. The screenplay was loosely based on reports of the Gallipoli landings. Many of the extras were soldiers in training from the Liverpool Camp, later themselves to end up on Gallipoli and there was extended actuality footage of the Liverpool Camp and of Egypt woven into the narrative, as was common at the time. The landings were restaged at Tamarama Bay in Sydney.

The film was a huge commercial and critical success, the press lauding the film as both extremely realistic and comparable to the best British and American films, a common touchstone for Australian critics of the time. Audiences lapped up the opportunity to see a representation of their soldiers in action. It was also released with some success in Britain, and press accounts of the film, by now passed off as a true story, amused soldiers on Gallipoli who recognized its improbability.

This film idealizes the Australian soldier as an upper-class, rather English-type man, who has the makings of a good officer. The contrast with the current image of the Anzac could not be greater.

A 20-minute partial reconstruction of this film exists in the Australian National Film and Sound Archive, marrying footage preserved in various sources with stills and other images, based on the original screenplay. Footage of the boats landing soldiers is regularly screened each year on Anzac Day as if it is documentary: it is in fact taken from a documentary that lifted the scenes from *The Hero of the Dardanelles*. Surviving footage suggests that Rolfe was a good director, making effective use of the close-up and backlighting when these techniques were still very new.

Daniel Reynaud

Within Our Gates (also known as Deeds that Won Gallipoli)

Country of Origin:

Australia

Director:

Frank Harvey

Screenwriter:

W J Lincoln

Cinematography:

Monte Luke

Genre:

War

Synopsis

A villainous German spy who is blackmailing Max, a German-Australian, is himself in turn exposed by his step-daughter who is in love with Edgar, the War Minister's son. Both Max and Edgar enlist in the Australian army. At Gallipoli Max redeems himself by losing his own life to save Edgar's.

Critique

J C Williamson Ltd, Australasian's rival, released this film two days after *The Hero of the Dardanelles*. Like their counterparts at Australasian, Harvey and his crew had the cooperation of government and military officials in the making of *Within Our Gates*. The film is a typical melodrama, with all the predictable heroes and villains, but topical and sufficiently well-made to succeed at the box office. Critical reviews were also positive, rating it among the best Australian productions, and considering it a realistic story, although the review of the left-leaning *Bulletin* magazine gave its realism a tongue-in-cheek endorsement. Within a year, films like this were ignored by critics and audiences alike as they tired of obvious propaganda. But in July 1915, Australian audiences were still innocent enough to enjoy it. The

Cast:
Cyril Mackay
Leslie Victor
Frank Harvey
Dorothy Cumming
John Ralston
Norman Easty

Year:
1915

How We Beat the Emden

Country of Origin:
Australia

Director:
Alfred Rolfe

Genre:
War

Year:
1915

landings were restaged in Obelisk Bay, inside Sydney Harbour, and the surviving six-second clip of the film is of soldiers charging ashore. The film's subtitle was 'Deeds that Won Gallipoli', evoking a popular pre-war book *Deeds that Won the Empire*. This and the overtly British imperial advertising for the film reflect how this now-archetypically Australian battle was at the time seen firmly in the British imperial tradition.

Daniel Reynaud

Synopsis

A young cadet from the training ship HMAS *Tingira* recounts to his former classmates the story of how HMAS *Sydney* sank the German cruiser *Emden* off Cocos Island in late 1914. Much of the story is told in flashback.

Critique

The third war picture from prolific silent director Alfred Rolfe was again based on historical events and also made extensive use of actuality footage. Several cadets were aboard the *Sydney* in November 1914 when the ship battered the *Emden* until it ran aground and surrendered. Rolfe made use of footage of the *Tingira* with recruits coming aboard and undergoing basic training. He also used footage of the wreck of the real *Emden*, taken from a documentary released in June called *The Fate of the Emden or How We Fought the Emden*. The battle scenes featured model ships, which were not entirely convincing even to contemporary audiences.

Critical response considered the film realistic (except for some caveats about the models), and the film enjoyed some success overseas. Its significance is in two things: first, surviving sequences add to the reputation of Rolfe as a competent, and even innovative, director, and second, it marked a direction in which the Anzac legend would strangely not go. Despite Britain being the model for Australian military heroics at the time, the Australian public proved not to be susceptible to developing a myth of naval supremacy like that around the Royal Navy, rather waiting for land-based Gallipoli battles to begin the process of national military myth-making.

Continuing the rivalry, J C Williamson released a *Sydney-Emden* film on the same day, titled *For Australia*. It was a crudely-filmed flimsy melodrama, and wooed neither audiences nor critics. However, both films were edited into a single movie and released in Britain to modest success. This compilation survives in the national Film and Sound Archive. With remarkable foresight, Australasian attempted no further war films, thus avoiding the failures that marked almost all other excursions into the genre to 1918.

Daniel Reynaud

The Martyrdom of Nurse Cavell

Country of Origin:
Australia

Directors:
John Gavin
C Post Mason

Screenwriter:
Agnes Gavin

Cinematography:
Lacey Percival

Genre:
War

Cast:
Vera Pearce
Harrington Reynolds
C Post Mason
Percy Walshe
John Gavin

Year:
1916

Synopsis

A beautiful young, heroic nurse caught behind German lines in Belgium helps British soldiers escape captivity and make their back to British lines. She is caught by the Germans, tried and executed by firing squad.

Critique

John Gavin's timely movie cashed in on the international outrage at the German execution of Nurse Cavell, an event which British propaganda exploited to cement the image of the brutal Hun. Agnes Gavin, John's wife, wrote the screenplay overnight, and the film was released just weeks later. An outlay of £450 reaped over £25,000 worldwide as the film moved audiences around the globe. The stout, middle-aged nurse of history was transformed into an angelic figure in the film, bravely and calmly facing the firing squad. The Germans were stereotypical bullies, the 18-stone Gavin himself playing a menacing officer. Advertising took the tone of hysterical propaganda, with exaggerated descriptions of the German menace. Most critics warmed to its theme, praising the technical and artistic features of the film and calling it realistic, though one bold critic noted how much Belgian homes resembled a Sydney suburb, and suggested that the story was 'history as you may wish it taught', rather than the literal truth.

This film was the high water mark of Australian war films in World War One. Having exploited to the full the outrage generated by Cavell's execution, the film appears to have satiated audience appetites for simplistic, extreme, patriotic propaganda. Two Cavell films by a rival company failed at the box office just weeks later, and other war films also sank without a trace, including an Anzac Day release of a film about Simpson and his donkey. Gavin attempted to reprise his success with another atrocity movie in 1917 (*The Murder of Captain Fryatt*), but without any success at all.

Daniel Reynaud

The Enemy Within

Country of Origin:
Australia

Director:
Roland Stavely

Producers:
Franklyn Barrett
Roland Stavely

Synopsis

German spies, supported by warships cruising off the coast of Australia, work with trade unionists and sinister industrialists plotting to over throw the government. A special agent, Jack Airlie, thwarts their actions. Airlie uncovers the plot, rescues his girl from their clutches and captures the key conspirators in a series of daring and spectacular stunts.

Critique

The action of the movie takes place in the Australia of Prime Minister Hughes' fevered imagination. For several years Hughes had attacked workers groups as 'nests of spies' in increasingly rabid and hysterical tones,

Screenwriter:
Roland Stavely

Cinematographer:
Franklyn Barrett

Art Director:
Rock Phillips

Genre:
War
Thriller

Cast:
Reg 'Snowy' Baker
John Faulkner
Lily Molloy
Nellie Calvin
Sandy McVea

Year:
1918

denouncing anyone who contradicted him. Hence the film pleased government censors. However, by starring Reg 'Snowy' Baker, the renowned multi-discipline athlete, Olympian and, for a short time, matinee idol, the film also offered a popular hero that audiences could identify with. The general context was clearly the war, but there were virtually no references to it in the film, allowing audiences to read it simply as an action-packed thriller. Baker performed all his own stunts, which were daring by the standards of the time, and critics welcomed a local production that appeared sophisticated – a backlash against the low-brow bush comedies that had become popular with both audiences and film companies in recent years. The film actually marketed itself as 'not a war film' in order to reassure jaded audiences, and it was a successful approach, despite the clear parallels to contemporary contexts. Baker epitomized the resourcefulness and courage of the Anzac, but in civilian clothes. The film survives in its entirety, one of the earliest complete Australian movies. Snowy Baker made several more films in Australia, later moving to Hollywood to play in action films and westerns, but his success was cut short by his clearly inadequate acting skills.

Daniel Reynaud

Ginger Mick

Country of Origin:
Australia

Director:
Raymond Longford

Screenwriters:
Lottie Lyell
Raymond Longford, adapted from the verse narrative The Moods of Ginger Mick by CJ Dennis

Cinematographer:
Arthur Higgins

Genre:
War
Comedy

Cast:
Gilbert Emery
Arthur Tauchert
Lottie Lyell
Jack Tauchert
Queenie Cross
George Hartspur

Year:
1920

Synopsis

The Sentimental Bloke recounts the story of his larrikin friend Ginger Mick, the rabbiter from the outskirts of Sydney. He has problems with alcohol, various run-ins with the law, but eventually finds work, and love with Rose. Despite his opposition to war profiteers, he enlists and, on Gallipoli, he conducts himself with honour, dying heroically at Sari Bair. A clergyman breaks the sad news to Rose, and The Sentimental Bloke mourns his lost mate.

Critique

Directed by Raymond Longford, one of Australia's most important silent film-makers, *Ginger Mick* was a sequel to his hugely successful *The Sentimental Bloke* (1919), also based on C J Dennis' popular verse narratives. Longford and his partner Lottie Lyell were responsible for some of Australia's most innovative and best films of the period, but they were shunned by Australasian, the monopolistic film combine, which eventually forced them out of the film business. The film contained much of the charm of its predecessor: the sentimental warmth of its characters, its distinctive Australian dialect and humour, and a relatively naturalistic acting style, as well as excessive subtitling that made it something of a chore to watch. The core cast from *The Sentimental Bloke* carried through to this film, with Arthur Tauchert again playing the Bloke, a part he played with total conviction as his own life reflected aspects of the stocky Australian urban larrikin role. Lyell played Doreen, now the Bloke's wife, while Gilbert Emery reprised Ginger Mick. It achieved both critical and commercial success. The film managed to reconcile the conflicting ideologies of the war: the working class versus big business, and the nationalistic Australian versus British imperial interests. In doing so, the film advanced the representation of Anzac, permitting for the first time a truly Australian character within a larger British context. Its humour also became a key feature of future Anzac productions. Tauchert by now had established himself as the archetypical Australian screen character, and in *The Digger Earl* (1924) and *Fellers* (1930) he put this character in Anzac uniform, though neither film was a great success.

Daniel Reynaud

The Exploits of the Emden

Country of Origin:
Australia, Germany

Directors:
Ken G Hall (Australian sequences)
Louis Ralph (German original)

Producer:
Ken G Hall

Screenwriters:
R Werner
Ken G Hall

Editor:
Ken G Hall

Cinematographers:
Ewald Daub
Werner Bohne
Arthur von Schwertfuehrer
Josef Wirsching
Claud C Carter
Ray Vaughn

Art Directors:
Ludwig Reiber
Botho Hoefer

Genre:
War

Cast:
Louis Ralph, Fritz Greiner, Jack Mylong-Muenz, Charles Willy Kayser, officers and men of the Royal Australian Navy

Year:
1928

Synopsis

The German cruiser *Emden* is based in China before the start of the First World War. An officer sends for his wife to join him, but the war forces him to sea. Fortuitously, he meets his wife when his ship rescues passengers from a sinking ship. The *Emden* meets HMAS *Sydney* in battle and is sunk, but the officer escapes and eventually rejoins his wife.

Critique

Bought sight unseen by First National Pictures (the new name for Australasian), the documentary-style film was acceptable enough except for its sequences on HMAS *Sydney*. German actors made unconvincing Aussie sailors, so publicity director Ken G Hall was commissioned to write and direct new sequences to replace the 'German propaganda'. With the help of a former *Sydney* crew man, Hall stitched together some sequences and filmed them on board the *Sydney*, with members of the actual crew playing various roles. The film was a modest success, and introduced several new elements to the telling of Anzac stories. Given its German origins, it is unsurprising that the Germans were portrayed sympathetically; nevertheless, this was a first for an Anzac movie, and advertising trumpeted its 'perfect fairness'. But it was also overtly patriotic about the great British Empire and its navy, and reviewers felt that this would make it attractive. Interestingly, it also tried to appeal to the anti-war lobby by proclaiming the film to be a 'powerful argument against war'. The other factor that makes the film important is that it introduced Hall to directing. Having never previously done anything more than plan publicity releases, Hall's excursion into scripting and directing eventually led to a distinguished career as one of the two great Australian directors of the 1930s, alongside Charles Chauvel. However, his efforts in this film are undistinguished, with stiff performances from the amateur cast, and laboured humour. A reconstruction of the film exists in the National Film and Sound Archive, consisting of about two-thirds of the Australian adaptation. Many of the German sequences are missing.

Daniel Reynaud

Diggers

Country of Origin:
Australia

Director:
F W Thring

Screenwriters:
Pat Hanna
Eric Donaldson

Cinematographer:
Arthur Higgins

Art Director:
W R Coleman

Duration:
61 minutes

Genre:
War

Cast:
Pat Hanna
George Moon
Edmund Warrington
Cecil Scott
Norman French
Guy Hastings

Year:
1931

Synopsis

A battalion reunion dinner leads to three flashbacks of wartime episodes. In a hospital, two chums pretend to be sick but are exposed by a perceptive doctor. In the next scene they conspire to steal rum from a British quartermaster, and in the final scene, set to a melancholy rendering of 'Mademoiselle from Armentieres', a soldier tries to romance a French waitress in an estaminet.

Critique

Made by F W Thring's new film company Efftee, *Diggers* was a showpiece for Pat Hanna and his successful touring 'Diggers' theatre troupe. The three episodes of the film were established stage routines. Thring changed the sequence of episodes to finish with the melancholy estaminet scene, despite Hanna's desire to finish on the brighter hospital scene. Hanna was so upset that he formed his own company to make a sequel, *Diggers in Blighty* (1933). Discounting a couple of hasty and incompetent productions, *Diggers* can be considered Australia's first full-length talkie feature. While sound was an innovation, it resulted in stodgy direction, making for a rather laboured comedy. It fared poorly on its initial release in Melbourne but did better in the country, developing enough momentum to make a successful return to metropolitan screens. The film ultimately realized a useful profit. Hanna represents a real advance in the development of the Anzac image, building on Tauchert's embodiment of the lean, comic bushman. The film also highlights differences between the typical Australian and the typical Englishman, continuing a process of separating the Anzac from his British counterpart, although, unlike written versions of the legend, the screen Anzac was not anti-British at this point. Both national characteristics were played for laughs, with a sense of mutual respect. In *Diggers in Blighty*, the two lead Australian characters marry the two lead English characters, and there is still a strong sense of imperial unity. By dealing with the war in largely comic terms, the film allows a war which is still a painful memory to be acceptable to Australian audiences.

Daniel Reynaud

Forty Thousand Horsemen

Country of Origin:
Australia

Director:
Charles Chauvel

Synopsis

Three light horsemen get up to mischief in Cairo before becoming involved in the Sinai battles and Gaza, where two of the mates, Larry and Jim, perish. In the meantime, Red Gallagher has met Juliette, a French girl disguised for her safety as an Arab boy, and been captured by the Turks. A daring escape before the Battle of Beersheba allows him to pass on vital information and participate in the successful Light Horse charge. He is reunited with Juliette in Jerusalem as the Light Horse march past, singing.

Forty Thousand (40,000) Horsemen, Goodwill Productions.

Producer:
Charles Chauvel

Screenwriters:
Charles Chauvel
Elsa Chauvel

Cinematographers:
George Heath
Frank Hurley
Tasman Higgins
Bert Nicholas
John Heyer

Editor:
William Shepherd

Art Director:
Eric Thompson

Genre:
War

Cast:
Grant Taylor
Betty Bryant
Chips Rafferty
Pat Twohill
Harvey Adams
Eric Reiman

Year:
1940

Critique

Director Charles Chauvel had learnt his craft in minor roles in Hollywood, having worked there for Snowy Baker. He returned to Australia determined to make distinctively Australian films. In partnership with his wife, he produced several movies with modest success, despite the resistance of some of the major players in the Australian film industry, who were lukewarm in their support for local productions. *Forty Thousand Horsemen* was Chauvel's first box office hit. He understood the culture of the light horse as his uncle was the notable General Harry Chauvel, and others in his family also served. Red Gallagher, played by Grant Taylor, was the conventional romantic heroic lead, but the most memorable character was Chips Rafferty's Jim. Rafferty's lean, comic bushman, played with instinctive and occasionally improvised skill, established him as the heir to Pat Hanna and the new iconic Australian in feature films for several decades. The film was still reasonably respectful of the British but gave more play to distinctive Australian behaviour and, hence, represents a further advance in the development of the screen Anzac. It was given a more patriotic turn to suit the start of the Second World War, and played to very receptive audiences in Australia and Britain, achieving some success even in America. It was for some time Australia's most successful film on the international market. This was partly because of its topicality, and partly because the charge and battle scenes were well executed and moving, despite the somewhat silly love tale wedged into the story.

Daniel Reynaud

CRIME

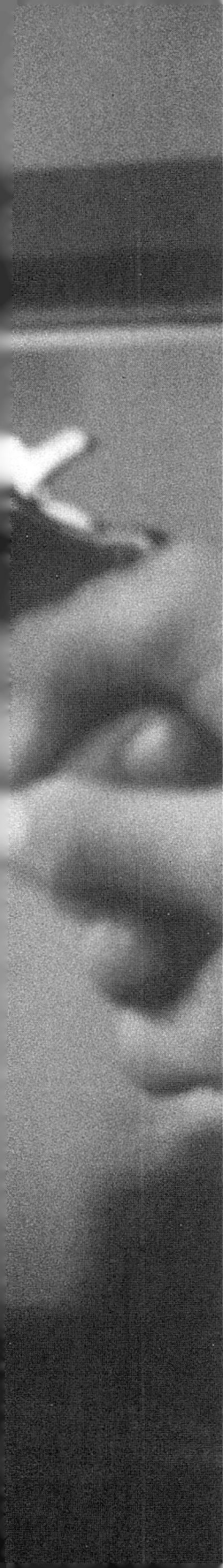

Although they occupy a marginal position in the national cinema canon, crime films have been a consistent feature of Australian screen production for more than a century. The Australian crime cinema tradition extends back to the 1900s, when locally-made bushranger and adventure films were massively popular with settler audiences. Charles Tait's 1906 film *The Story of the Kelly Gang*, arguably the world's first narrative feature, was the *Scarface* of its day – an ultra-violent glorification of a criminal outlaw. Tait's film and others like it were so popular that, in 1912, Victoria and New South Wales placed a ban on bushranger films, fearing an upsurge in anti-social behaviour. This crime cinema boom fizzled out in the mid-1910s when Australian production entered a slump that would last fifty years. Early bushranger mythology has, however, been revisited in films such as Philippe Mora's *Mad Dog Morgan* (1976), Gregor Jordan's *Ned Kelly* (2003), and John Hillcoat's postcolonial Western *The Proposition* (2005).

The guardians of the Australian cinema revival of the 1970s, assessors and officers of state and federal film funding agencies tended not to look favourably on genre cinema. Crime movies and the Australian New Wave overlapped only on rare occasions, as in Bruce Beresford's heist film *The Money Movers* (1979) and Phillip Noyce's conspiracy film *Heatwave* (1982). Commercial crime-film production did reappear in the 1980s when new government tax breaks fuelled an influx of private capital into the industry. As a staple of genre production, the crime film was seen as a suitable vehicle for investment. Minor 1980s' thrillers and action films like Mark Joffe's *Grievous Bodily Harm* (1988) and Brian Trenchard-Smith's *Day of the Panther* (1987) are characteristic of this fast-and-cheap approach.

The late 1990s saw the beginning of a cycle of mid-budget Australian crime films with broad appeal and commercial ambition. Gregor Jordan's romantic gangster film *Two Hands* (1999) offered a fast-paced tour through the Sydney underworld, featuring a typically menacing performance from Bryan Brown as a Kings Cross strip-club owner. Andrew Dominik's *Chopper* followed in 2000, establishing Eric Bana as a serious dramatic actor. Other films from this period include *Risk* (Alan White, 2000), *The Bank* (Robert Connolly, 2001), *The Hard Word* (Scott Roberts, 2002), *Bad Eggs* (Tony Martin, 2003) and *Gettin' Square* (Jonathan Teplitzky, 2003).

Released towards the end of this cycle, David Caesar's *Dirty Deeds* (2002) is a rare attempt at a big-budget Australian gangster movie. Aimed squarely at multiplex audiences, the film is set in Sydney during the Vietnam War and follows the misadventures of two foot soldiers from the Chicago mafia (played by American actor John Goodman and Australian actor Felix Williamson) as they try to expand their racket into territory controlled by homegrown mobster Barry Ryan (Bryan Brown). The film's central narrative device (a transnational criminal turf war) and generic identity (US gangster movie in vernacular mode) speak to its industrial context – namely, the local film community's anxiety about the 'invasion' of American runaway productions in the lead-up to the Australia-US Free Trade Agreement (which came into force in 2005).

The many sub-genres that make up crime cinema have been unequally represented in Australian productions. Idiosyncratic crime-comedies have been a strong suit. Films like *Two Hands*, John Ruane's *Death in Brunswick* (1991), and the two Shane Maloney telemovies *Stiff* and *The Brush-Off* (Seven Network, 2004) explore the dodgy side of Melbourne and Sydney with a deft comic touch. There are a number of gangster films that depict the workings of organized crime and chart the rise and fall of the gang boss, while many more films feature gangster characters, often in comic mode. Among the former group of films is Kevin Dobson's *Squizzy Taylor* (1982), which tells the (partly) true story of the rise and fall of the eponymous 1920s' Melbourne hoodlum. Honourable mention must also go to Geoffrey Wright's adaptation of William Shakespeare's *Macbeth* (2006), which transposes the action to present-day Melbourne, where crime boss Duncan is overthrown by his lieutenant Macbeth in a clear allusion to the gang war which gripped Melbourne in the mid-2000s and which is dramatized in the television series *Underbelly*. Wright might be seen to have taken a lead from Baz Luhrmann's Shakespeare adaptation *Romeo + Juliet* (1996) which is also set in the midst of a present-day gang war. Other films dealing with gangs who occasionally engage in criminal behaviour (as distinct from gangs whose sole purpose is crime) include Geoffrey Wright's *Romper Stomper* (1992), which focuses on a neo-Nazi skinhead gang, and Sandy Harbutt's *Stone* (1974), which follows an undercover policeman investigating the murders of several outlaw motorcycle gang members. Gangsters also feature as key supporting characters in a number of crime-comedies, including David Bilcock and Rob Copping's ocker comedy *Alvin Rides Again* (1974), and two films written by lawyer Chris Nyst and set on the Gold Coast: *Gettin' Square* (2003), and *Crooked Business* (2008), which Nyst also directed.

Heist movies and robberies are the subjects, or parts of the plot, of a wide range of Australian films, including *The Hard Word* (2002), in which three brothers are 'freed' from prison to undertake a series of daring robberies culminating in a cheeky heist on Melbourne Cup day. David Caesar's *Idiot Box* (1996) follows a couple of disaffected, unemployed suburban youths who decide to rob a bank to relieve the boredom of their lives, with tragic consequences. In Craig Lahiff's *Heaven's Burning* (1997), a bungled heist provides an opportunity for a discontented Japanese honeymooner to escape the confines of a marriage she regrets when she is taken hostage by the getaway driver. The cross-country chase that ensues is mirrored in several road movies in which fugitives try to stay one step ahead of the police, including Bill Bennett's *Kiss or Kill* (1997), Stavros Kazantzidis's *True Love and Chaos*, and most recently Glendyn Ivin's *Last Ride* (2009).

Films in which detectives or police officers are the lead characters are fewer in number. In addition to Matthew Saville's 2007 story *Noise*, about a police officer struggling with tinnitus while manning a temporary investigation office at the site of a mass murder on a suburban train, notable recent examples of the detective and police procedural film include Craig Monahan's *The Interview* (1998), which begins with a police raid on an apartment but is predominantly set in a police interview room, and Jon Hewitt's low-budget feature *Redball* (1998), which follows a group of police whose investigation into a series of child murders threatens to expose corruption within the force when a police officer is implicated in the killings. Another remarkable example of a detective-police procedural is the lesbian private-eye film *The Monkey's Mask* (2000) by Samantha Lang, one of the few female directors to try their hand at this blokiest of genres. *The Monkey's Mask* was adapted from a novel of the same name, written in verse, by Australian poet Dorothy Porter. After critics excoriated her young adult novel *The Witch Number* for its depictions of menstruation and witchcraft, Porter turned back to poetry. She later wrote:

> I wanted ingredients that stank to high heaven of badness. I wanted graphic sex. I wanted explicit perversion. I wanted putrid language. I wanted stenching murder. I wanted to pour out my heart. I wanted to take the piss. I wanted lesbians who weren't nice to other women. I wanted glamorous nasty men who even lesbians want to fuck. I wanted to say that far too much Australian poetry is a dramatic cure for insomnia. But I still wanted to write the book in poetry. (Porter 2000)

The crime genre provided the perfect outlet, and the film is faithful to the book's form, intentions and confronting subject matter.

A number of Australian films of the last twenty years have used crime narratives as launching pads for social commentary and formal experimentation. At one end of this spectrum lies a series of what could be called Australian 'art-crime' films. Bill Bennett's innovative road movie *Kiss or Kill* (1997), Rowan Woods' minimalist psychodrama *The Boys* (1998), Matthew Saville's experimental police-procedural *Noise* (2007), and possibly Geoffrey Wright's acclaimed *Romper Stomper* (1992), are reference points here. Woods' extraordinary *Little Fish* (2005), starring Cate Blanchett, manages to be a crime film, a drug epic, a love story, a tragedy, and a family melodrama all at once. The most commercially-successful director in this pack is Ray Lawrence, whose humanist dramas *Lantana* (2001) and *Jindabyne* (2006) both feature multi-character network narratives structured around a mysterious death.

At the other end of the market is a trio of recent low-budget digital films which rework aspects of the crime genre. Khoa Do's *The Finished People* (2003), Dee McLachlan's *The Jammed* (2007), and David Field's *The Combination* (2009) received minimal theatrical exhibition but found an audience on DVD and online. In different ways, and with varying results, all three films use black-market trade in people and drugs as an entry point to explore marginalized ethnic communities in contemporary Australia, drawing on the iconography of crime but using it in the service of social analysis. Films such as these are indicative of new directions in crime cinema as the Australian film industry makes the transition to digital production and distribution models.

Ramon Lobato

Jindabyne

Country of Origin:
Australia

Director:
Ray Lawrence

Producer:
Catherine Jarman

Screenwriter:
Beatrix Christian

Cinematographer:
David Williamson

Editor:
Karl Sodersten

Production Designer:
Margot Wilson

Duration:
123 minutes

Genre:
Crime

Cast:
Gabriel Byrne
Laura Linney
Chris Haywood
Deborra-Lee Furness
John Howard
Simon Stone

Year:
2006

Synopsis

A young Indigenous woman driving through a deserted brown land-scape, singing as she goes, is, unknown to her, being pursued by an enigmatic and oddly-alarming man in a truck. This cryptic encounter – Who is the girl? Why is this grizzled truck-driver pursuing her? – gives way to an early morning sequence in Claire and Stuart's house, which appears to establish a close, loving family, with hugs for young son Tom, and talk of the upcoming fishermen's weekend away. Then the film moves to another household in which an older couple, Jude and Carl, are concerned that their granddaughter is not in her bedroom. Quite quickly it is clear that neither of these households is quite what it seems, that there is lurking unhappiness and less-than-perfect trust at work among the occupants. There are two other couples involved in the network of intersecting lives that will be traumatically disrupted by the events of the fishing weekend.

Stuart, Carl, and two other friends set off on a fishing trip deep in the wilderness of a national park. Soon after they start to fish they find a body, that of the young Indigenous woman seen at the start of the film. What the four fishing friends in *Jindabyne* are required to do is to consider their priorities and they signally fail to recognize these, or, if they do, they put them to one side. Billy, the youngest, reports that he is 'not getting any reception' on his mobile phone, and this seems reason enough for the friends to go ahead and enjoy the weekend and report the body in the water upon their return a few days later. The men are unprepared for the rage that is unleashed in the town. 'It's about all of us,' Claire tells Carmel, girlfriend of Rocco, the fourth of the fishermen. Claire determines to come to a kind of reconciliation with the Indigenous community, even at the risk to her own marriage.

Critique

New Australian cinema from the 1970s depended quite heavily on pre-existing stories. At first, national 'classics', and, more recently, less-reverentially-regarded modern fictions such as *Candy* and *Loaded* (filmed as *Head On*, Anna Kokkinos, 1998) have been adapted for the screen, but almost never have Australian film-makers of the modern era taken on literary works whose roots are other than Australian. *Jindabyne* is derived from US-author Raymond Carver's minimalist short story, 'So Much Water So Close to Home', which has also been the inspiration for songwriter Paul Kelly's song of the same name. The source of the story alone would make the film a matter of interest, exhibiting a pleasing anti-parochial turn of mind among its makers. Director Ray Lawrence relocates the story to the Snowy Mountains. The moral dilemma at the story's core is retained, while at the same time Lawrence and screenwriter Beatrix Christian give it a powerful local inflection. There is surely no reason why Australian film-makers should feel limited to adapting Australian literature; and there is no point in adapting *any* literary work to the screen unless the film-maker has something new to say about it. This is where *Jindabyne*'s real distinction lies.

Jindabyne, April Films.

Jindabyne, in Christian's elegant and eloquent screenplay, is essentially a study of individual lives and relationships, how these resonate in the community at large and, here, beyond the community to touch on a vein of sensitive national feeling. The lives of the four men are shaken up by the suppressions of their weekend, and Claire gradually emerges as the film's moral voice. Unstable as she has been regarded, it is she who cannot let the men's feebly self-interested prevarications rest. And, in her attempts to reach the Indigenous girl's people, in her unwanted collection of money for the funeral, asking the priest to pass it on for her, she runs herself into danger from the murderous Gregory (in a sequence that parallels the opening) as she goes to attend the outdoor burial ceremony. What, by unobtrusive metaphoric extension, she is doing here, by comparison with her community at large, is to critique the national negligence of its Indigenous population and the official unwillingness to effect real reconciliation. The film is not in the least preachy about this or anything else, but it is so richly textured that such wider meanings ripple out from the specificities of the plot. The film does not end on a note of unrelieved bleakness, any more than Carver's story does. 'I want you to come home, Claire,' says Stuart who has come to the ceremony, as a mourner sings one of Susan's last songs.

Director Ray Lawrence is a strange, maverick figure in Australian cinema; his sparing output makes Terence Malick look prolific. In 1985 he directed and co-wrote (with the novel's author Peter Carey) the maddeningly-pretentious *Bliss*; maybe it was ahead of its time but certainly *in* its time it was hard to bear, though it did win AFI awards for film, screenplay and director. One can only surmise that this was a dud year for Australian films; unruly Cannes audiences left noisily, and the failure of this stylistically-incoherent black comedy-cum-fantasy probably accounts for Lawrence's not filming again for sixteen years. In 2001, he made *Lantana*, arguably one of the finest films ever made here, an absorbing account of interlocking suburban lives. In *Jindabyne*, he has again adopted the omnibus approach, exhibiting a real capacity to understand and represent what is going on in a relationship, and to suggest how communities, because they are never anything but relationships, are always fragile.

In relocating Carver's story to the Snowy Mountains, Lawrence has resisted the temptation to mere pictorialism. Whereas Carver can do without filling in the physical setting of America's mid-West, the mimetic demands of film mean that Lawrence does not have this choice. He creates a powerful sense of community – both that of the town's white inhabitants and that of the Indigenous settlement at its edges – and of how they interact with the physical ambience. Though the film makes valuable use of its diversity of natural setting, Lawrence and Christian have focused very firmly on the strands of the community, with the affiliations and undercurrents, and, very importantly, the Indigenous community just outside Jindabyne. In this latter respect, the film, as I have suggested, has a significance that ripples beyond the specificities of place so sharply drawn.

The film was nominated for nine AFI awards and inexplicably won none. Given that the two top-billed actors, Laura Linney and Gabriel Byrne, both nominated, were imported from overseas, one would hope that xenophobia was not involved. However, the ensemble cast behaves as an ensemble should – that is, without any sense of straining towards star delivery at the expense of the sense of interaction and of community under threat which are at the heart of the film's meaning. *Jindabyne* sets its characters some tough moral challenges, some dodged, some met and others in the process of being worked through. From start to finish, it is a film made with grown-ups in mind; if it asks a lot of its characters, it is also a demanding and rewarding experience for its viewers.

Brian McFarlane

Macbeth

Country of Origin:
Australia

Director:
Geoffrey Wright

Producer:
Martin Fabinyi

Screenwriters:
Victoria Hill
Geoffrey Wright

Cinematographer:
Will Gibson

Editor:
Jane Usher

Production Designer:
David McKay

Duration:
109 minutes

Genre:
Crime
Gangster

Cast:
Sam Worthington
Victoria Hill
Steve Bastoni
Matt Doran
Lachy Hulme
Gary Sweet

Year:
2006

Synopsis

In contemporary Melbourne, gangland rivalries are running dangerously hot. Macbeth, acting on the orders of mob boss Duncan, destroys Macdonwald's drug-trafficking gang. With his ally, Banquo, Macbeth kills Cawdor, whose club he takes over. When three young witches foretell the drug-fuddled Macbeth's ascendancy in the gangland hierarchy, his ambition is fired. Encouraged by Lady Macbeth, he kills Duncan and sends two thugs to murder Banquo and his son Fleance because the witches had prophesied that Banquo's children would succeed the sonless Macbeth. Banquo is murdered but Fleance escapes. Macbeth, now irrevocably embarked on a murderous career to secure what his ambition has led him to grab, orders the unmotivated slaughter of Macduff's wife and children. Finally, Macduff and Duncan's son, Malcolm, lead a mob which surrounds Macbeth's house and, in the gunfire that ensues, Macduff tracks Macbeth to the cellar of the house and stabs him. He dies by the corpse of Lady Macbeth, from whom he has become remote and whose sanity has collapsed under the strain of her complicity in Macbeth's rise to power. As the witches had foretold, Fleance now assumes leadership of the mob and in the film's last moments he walks off with Macduff.

Critique

Australian cinema has shown little interest in adapting Shakespeare to the screen – or, indeed, non-Australian works of any kind. It is interesting to speculate why this should be so. Surely it cannot be because they think Shakespeare irrelevant to antipodean life? It surely cannot be anything as narrow-visioned as that, when you consider all those other non-British countries that have filmed the very greatest plays: think of Russian Grigori Kosintzev's stunning black-and-white *Hamlet* (1964), or the Japanese *Throne of Blood* (1957), Akira Kurosawa's savage samurai version of *Macbeth*, or even the MGM sci-fi reworking of *The Tempest* as *Forbidden Planet* (Fred M Wilcox, 1956). I draw attention to these merely to suggest that there is no reason why an Australian film-maker should feel daunted by the prospect of Shakespeare, any more than Russian, Japanese, American, and many others have, and also no reason why a film adapted from Shakespeare cannot be relocated not just to another country but also to another genre.

In addition to Baz Luhrmann's *Romeo + Juliet* (1996), which was shot in Mexico with a largely non-Australian cast, Neil Armfield's *Twelfth Night* (1986) is the only other modern Australian film derived from Shakespeare, and that was more or less a filming of his own stage production and received only very limited screening. Geoffrey Wright has relocated Shakespeare's *Macbeth* from the warring clans of long-ago Scotland to the underworld of present-day Melbourne, with rival gangs seeking ascendancy in the local drug trade. Whereas Edward Dmytryk's *Broken Lance* (1954) transferred *King Lear* to an American-western setting, drawing on the iconography and narrative motifs of the western genre, Wright has accommodated the drama of Shakespeare's swift and complex tragedy to the generic mode of urban action thriller.

In one key sense he has been more daring than Dmytryk: he has retained Shakespeare's blank verse in this new time and place. This is a major problem confronting the film-maker who aspires to 'capture' Shakespeare on screen: the plays belong to a non-realist category of drama, and film has so accustomed us to a level of realistic depiction of the actual world that it demands quite a lot of its audience to accept characters speaking in iambic pentameters. Wright has had the cheek to do this. And not only to retain the verse but, further, to have actors speak it with a range of Australian accents which are convincing in the context of the relocated drama. Perhaps some of the poetry is lost in the transfer but, by compensation, its essentially low-key delivery works well enough in realist vein. The actors give the verse a conversational quality that helps to effect the transition from the conventions of the drama to those of the screen's greater and easier naturalism. In view of this one can forgive the odd improbability of, say, thuggish types addressing each other as 'My lord' or Macbeth's wife somehow answering to the title of 'Lady Macbeth'.

What essentially matters in the film, as in the play, is the personal drama of the corrupting potential of powerful ambition and this seems as much at home in the night streets and by-ways of Melbourne as in twelfth-century Scotland, the predominant darkness and bloody deeds articulating in realist terms the play's insistent images of night and blood. Wright's and actor Sam Worthington's Macbeth is – like Shakespeare's – a nature divided against itself. From the graveyard opening where Macbeth's sonless state is announced, there is a thread of allusion to fathers and sons which goes some distance to explaining the rift in Macbeth's nature. The feeling between him and Lady Macbeth (Victoria Hill) is intensified by this opening image of shared grief, and there is pathos, if not perhaps tragedy, in the way they draw apart. Unusually for any performance of Macbeth, one of the scenes that stay in the mind is that between the doctor (Kim Gyngell) and Lady Macbeth's housekeeper/maid (Katherine Tonkin), who give us necessary glimpses of lives not caught up in the pervasive bloodshed and darker impulses, as they attend her decline towards death. Their professional solicitude strikes an aptly realist note in a film that also aims to make the supernatural figures of the witches believable as figments of Macbeth's increasingly-disturbed mind.

The graveyard opening prefigures the theme of parents and children, which Wright's film stresses: through the resurgence of Duncan's son Malcolm, through Macduff's child brutally killed, and implied again in the final moment in which Macduff and Banquo's son Fleance walk off into the dawn, suggestive of fragile hope for a future in which familial bonds may be more secure. Of course, not everything in this venturesome film works – some of the main action sequences, for instance, lack clarity – but Wright has shown again the feral talent at work which made his feature debut, Romper Stomper (1992), so properly unnerving an experience.

Brian McFarlane

The Square

Country of Origin:
Australia

Director:
Nash Edgerton

Producer:
Louise Smith

Scriptwriters:
Joel Edgerton
Matthew Dabner

Cinematographer:
Brad Shield

Production Designer:
Elizabeth Mary Moore

Editors:
Nash Edgerton
Luke Doolan

Duration:
105 minutes

Genre:
Crime
Melodrama

Cast:
David Roberts
Claire van der Boom
Joel Edgerton
Anthony Hayes
Bill Hunter

Year:
2009

Synopsis

Ray, the site manager of a new housing development (The Square of the title) fixes a large contract in order to receive a kickback from concreter Barney, to pay for a new life with his mistress Carla. Carla, meanwhile, has discovered a bag full of money – the proceeds of an unspecified crime – that her partner Greg has hidden in the roof of their house. The windfall emboldens Carla to press Ray to leave his wife. Ray hires arsonist Billy to set fire to Greg and Carla's house so that Greg will think the money has been destroyed, but unbeknown to the plotters, Greg's mother is asleep in the house and is killed in the blaze. After the fire, Ray receives a card from a blackmailer. He suspects Leonard, a mechanic who has been working on The Square, after Leonard witnesses one of Ray and Carla's assignations. Ray accidentally kills Leonard, and hides his body under an area of The Square which is about to be concreted, but torrential rain and a freak workplace accident delay the cover-up. Ray continues to receive cards from the blackmailer. He breaks in to Billy and Lily's flat, now believing Lily is the culprit, and confronts her. Ray's foreman Jake suspects that Ray has caused some unexplained damage to the site and secretly inspects the area where Leonard is buried. But Ray has followed Jake to the site, and realizes that the scale of his deception is about to be uncovered. After a scuffle, Jake drives off at high speed. Ray chases him, calling out for a chance to explain what has happened. Ray swerves to avoid a tree and accidentally knocks Jake's car off the road. Ray saves Jake's baby from the wreck, but Jake dies in hospital. Ray goes to meet the blackmailer, but is intercepted by his boss, Gil, who has been tipped off about the arrangements. Together with the local police sergeant, they apprehend the blackmailer, who turns out to be the concreting contractor Barney who had earlier paid Ray the kickback. Ray hurries to meet Carla, only to find that Billy is holding her at gunpoint. Billy confronts Ray with one of the blackmailer's cards that Ray had cropped when he accosted Lily; Billy believes that the arson has been discovered. Ray and Carla try to explain about the kickback, and tell Billy about Greg's bag of money. Greg unexpectedly arrives, and a brief shootout ensues. Billy shoots Greg, but is wounded himself. Ray tries to wrestle the gun from Billy but, in the struggle, the gun goes off, fatally wounding Carla. Billy escapes with the money. Ray stumbles out to the street in a daze as police sirens approach.

Critique

The Square is the feature film debut of director Nash Edgerton, well-known in Australian film circles not only for his award-winning music videos and short films *Deadline* (first prize winner at Tropfest in 1997) and *Spider* but also for his work as an actor, editor, producer, writer and stuntman on countless Australian films and television programmes. The film was co-written by Edgerton's regular partner and brother Joel, who also plays the arsonist Billy. Joel is familiar to Australian and international audiences for his television work in *The Secret Life of Us* as well as numerous film roles.

The Square is reminiscent of Sam Raimi's film blanc *A Simple Plan*, not only in the terrible consequences that flow from the chance discovery of a bag full of cash, and the tragedies that befall characters who make questionable moral choices, but also in the blank-visaged, vapid intensity of the lead characters Ray (*The Square*) and Hank (*A Simple Plan*). For both of these characters, survival is ultimately a greater punishment than the terminal fate so many of those around them suffer as a consequence of their actions. David Roberts' Ray is uncharismatic and difficult for viewers to connect with: for someone engaged in an affair with a much younger woman he is oddly passionless, but given the various deceptions he is practising it is perhaps fitting that his facial expressions and manner give little away. Like the shark-infested river that separates Ray and Carla's houses, on the surface Ray is equable and unremarkable, but below the surface deadly forces lurk. The theme of hidden dangers is literalized in the unfortunate demise of Carla's dog that we first encounter in the opening scene locked in Carla's car, watching her tryst with Ray in his car. The dog regularly swims across the river to be with Ray's dog until one day he disappears half-way across, a victim of the unseen shark.

This contemporary immorality play deploys familiar cinematic energies – greed, infidelity, serendipity – to great effect in its cautionary tale of respectable people brought to ruin by ethical transgressions and the deadly, seductive power of large sums of money. Both the deliberate and the fortuitous interventions in the circulation of capital in the film have disastrous consequences for the main protagonists and all those around them: Ray's request for a kickback kicks off the blackmail plot, while Carla's chance discovery of Greg's bag of loot indirectly causes the chain of accidental deaths culminating in her own farcical demise. As in *A Simple Plan*, the ill-gotten gains magnify Ray and Carla's duplicity; the money and all it promises takes control of them and ultimately destroys their lives.

Claire van der Boom in her first feature film role makes Carla immensely likeable, despite her complicity in the series of criminal acts that punctuate the film. On one level, her attraction to Ray is hard to comprehend, and we are given little insight into the origins of their affair, but her desire to escape her relationship with violent bully Greg is ultimately the only explanation we need for her actions. Anthony Hayes as Greg demonstrates once again a remarkable screen presence; his air of quiet menace and imminent potential for savage violence is reminiscent of Oliver Reed at his most threatening.

Ben Goldsmith

The Jammed

Country of Origin:
Australia

Director:
Dee McLachlan

Producers:
Sally Ayre-Smith
Andrea Buck
Dee McLachlan

Screenwriter:
Dee McLachlan

Cinematographer:
Peter Falk

Editor:
Anne Carter

Art Director:
Emma Wicks

Duration:
89 minutes

Genre:
Crime
Thriller

Synopsis

An illegal immigrant, Crystal, is interviewed by federal agents investigating the trafficking of women to Australia to work as prostitutes. A series of flashbacks reveal that she arrived from Indonesia expecting to find work as a dancer to pay off family debts, only to be forced into working in the sex trade. Crystal's story is intercut with that of Ashley, who, while picking up a friend from the airport, meets an old woman, Sunee, who has travelled from China in search of her missing daughter. Unwillingly at first, Ashley is drawn in to Sunee's search. After being raped and beaten by a man who collects her at Sydney airport, Crystal is taken to Melbourne with two other women, Rubi and Vanya, to work in a brothel run by Vic Glassman. One night, Rubi passes out in the brothel. Vic orders his henchmen to dump her 'anywhere', but Vanya manages to take Rubi to hospital. Vanya finds one of Sunee's posters, and realizes that Rubi is the woman she is looking for. She telephones Ashley with the location of the brothel. Ashley discovers that the building is owned by Glassman's wife; Ashley contacts Glassman, and arranges to buy Rubi back. Ashley and her former boyfriend Tom secretly follow one of Glassman's henchmen, Lai, as he transports the women from the brothel to their accommodation. Ashley distracts Lai, enabling Crystal and Rubi to escape, but Vanya is caught by Lai. The escapees are taken to a hotel, where Sunee is reunited with Rubi. Rubi is apoplectic, shouting that her mother sold her to a trafficker in Bangkok. The next morning, Crystal awakes in the room to discover Rubi has jumped to her death from the window. Crystal is taken to immigration detention, where the interview that begins the film takes place. Ashley forces her way in to the brothel to rescue Vanya. Together they go to the opening of Mrs Glassman's art gallery. Ashley confronts Mrs Glassman, saying 'Tell your husband Vanya wants her passport back'. Outside the gallery, Vanya gives Ashley Vic's notebook that she has stolen from the brothel, and runs away. In the detention centre, Crystal waits to be deported.

Cast:
Emma Lung
Veronica Sywak
Saskia Burmeister
Sun Park
Amanda Ma
Andrew S. Gilbert

Year:
2007

Critique

One of the strengths of Dee McLachlan's shocking and moving film is the extensive research undertaken in pre-production, which grounds the film in a reality of which many Australians are unaware. The film opens with a caption stating that it was inspired by court transcripts and closes with an intertitle stating that, in 2001 and 2002, two sex-trafficked victims died in Villawood Detention Centre. The film makes it clear that human trafficking and the coercion of women into prostitution are as much problems in Australia as anywhere: Project Respect, an organization that acts on behalf of trafficked sex workers, has estimated that about 1000 women are illegally brought to Australia to work as prostitutes each year. The film's title is taken from the term used by support workers to describe how the women are 'jammed' between their captors and the authorities: their illegal status and often heavy indebtedness, coupled with their innate fear of authority figures and the captors' threats to their families back home, deter them from escaping or going to the police. The latter course of action may only lead to incarceration and deportation, as it does for Crystal in *The Jammed*. They are also deterred from speaking out by the implied (and often real) collusion between the traffickers and the authorities. While she is held in an apartment shortly after she arrives in Australia, Crystal threatens to call the police, only to be told by her captor 'my best friend is the police'.

The Jammed joins a growing roster of feature films and documentaries from around the world that take this sordid trade as their subject. Like Amos Gitai's *Promised Land* (2004) about the trafficking of Estonian women to Israel, and Marco Kreuzpainter's *Trade* (2007) about the kidnapping and sale into sex slavery in America of a young Mexican girl, but unlike higher-budgeted thrillers on the same subject like Pierre Morel's *Taken* (2008) and David Cronenberg's *Eastern Promises* (2007) or the American television miniseries *Human Trafficking*, there is no happy ending in *The Jammed*. While some of the perpetrators may face justice, the trafficked women in *The Jammed* die (Rubi), are incarcerated and deported (Crystal), or face an uncertain future on the street (Vanya), while the trade simply moves on. This lack of closure and avoidance of the temptation to end the film positively was a deliberate strategy by the film-makers to reflect the fact that prosecutions are rare in Australia – and successful prosecutions even more so – and laws to counter sex trafficking remain manifestly inadequate. The inaction and ambivalence of the authorities also explains the choice of an ordinary person – office worker Ashley – to lead the investigation, rather than making the film a police procedural with a detective as a main character.

Although *The Jammed* marks a departure from her previous work, which includes *The Second Jungle Book: Mowgli and Baloo* (1997) and *Born Wild* (aka *Running Wild* 1992), both of which were directed under her birth name, Duncan McLachlan, Dee McLachlan's film is a stylishly and skilfully-executed ultra-low-budget thriller. Peter Falk's cinematography – the film was shot on HDV – deserves special note, with many scenes taking place outside at night or in cramped spaces, each of which present challenges in lighting and framing the action. The score by acclaimed South African composer Grant McLachlan, is hauntingly beautiful. The cast consists of largely unknown actors, who collectively are pitch-perfect. Serendipity and strong word-of-mouth helped overcome the film's struggles with distribution, which are well-documented in interviews with director McLachlan. From a short run on a single screen in Melbourne, positive audience reaction propelled the film to a national release and widespread acclaim as one of the finest Australian films of 2007.

Ben Goldsmith

PRISON

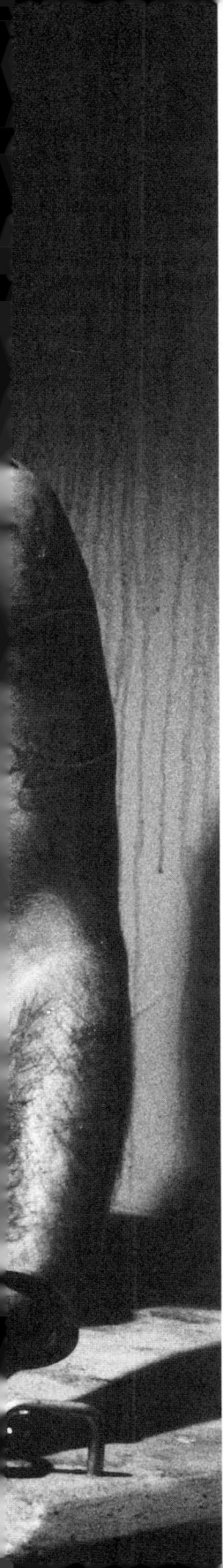

The prison casts a long shadow over Australian cinema. Literal
or metaphorical imprisonment features in a wide variety of
genres. A large number of films, particularly in the crime
genre, contain scenes or sequences set in prisons, and many
other films tell stories about characters who have either
recently been imprisoned or are heading back there, or, in
some other way, are trapped or limited by social expectations, family ties or institutional rules. In the early years of
Australian cinema, adaptations of novels and plays about
convict life were relatively numerous and generally popular,
albeit not as popular as films about the exploits of outlaws
beyond prison walls. Since the revival, there have been a
number of films and television series set in the convict era,
alongside several which interrogate contemporary prison life,
and others – including a number of international productions
made in Queensland – which imagine carceral regimes and
correctional institutions of the near future.

In one of the most important studies of the production of
Australian stories in literature and on film, Graeme Turner
argues that the 'construction of the condition of enclosure,
restriction and entrapment' is a characteristic and constitutive
feature of Australian narrative (Turner 1986: 51). Turner sees this
condition as the result of the individual's subordination to the
environment (which may be 'naturalised' as much as 'natural'),
to the point where the individual is rendered powerless to
'affect or change his condition' (ibid). This condition of entrapment or imprisonment is rendered literally in the convict dramas
that were popular in the early Australian cinema, culminating in
the big budget, special-effects-laden blockbuster adaptation
of a nineteenth century novel, For the Term of His Natural Life,
made in 1927 by American director Norman Dawn.

Left: *Ghosts...Of The Civil Dead,* Correctional Services.

The earliest images of Australia in late eighteenth-century British popular culture depicted the penal colony at Botany Bay as a hell on earth. Stories of the misery of convict life and the brutal punishments that awaited transgressors at Moreton Bay, in Van Diemen's Land or on Norfolk Island, were told in street ballads, pamphlets and illustrated penny broadsides as warnings to working-class Britons. Such stories were popular and lucrative throughout the nineteenth century, and it should be no surprise that despite considerable ambivalence about the legacy of 'the convict stain' Australian film-makers seeking local stories and large local audiences turned to convict narratives in the first decades of the twentieth century. Of the more than 50 films produced in Australian cinema's annus mirabilis of 1911, eight had convict themes. Many of the films set in the convict era, and particularly those from the early period (1908–1927), cast the central convict character as an innocent victim whose initial 'crime' that led to their transportation was either committed by someone else (Devine/Dawes in *For the Term of His Natural Life*), was disproportionate to their punishment (in *The Assigned Servant* (John Gavin, 1911), for example, a character is transported for poaching rabbits) or not committed at all, with several films featuring characters who have been 'set-up' by jealous or unscrupulous authority figures (*Conn, the Shaughraun*, Gaston Mervale, 1912; *His Convict Bride*, John Gavin, 1918; *The Tenth Straw*, Robert G. McAnderson, 1928).

Few of the prison films made since the revival in Australian production beginning in the 1970s suggest that their principal characters have not committed the crimes for which they are inside, or that they are unjustly imprisoned. Instead, the focus in films like *Stir* (Stephen Wallace, 1980), *Ghosts … of the Civil Dead* (John Hillcoat, 1989), and *Everynight… Everynight* (Alkinos Tsilimidos, 1994) is on their maltreatment within the prison. Their original crimes are irrelevant. While the lead characters in these contemporary prison dramas survive their ordeals, all are left with uncertain futures, having failed to effect substantive change in the system. At the end of *Stir* the prisoners are transported away in a convoy of prison vans at dawn from the gaol they have destroyed. As they share a cigarette, one prisoner reassures his fellows: 'One good thing about being in the slot [prison], you're always prepared'. The prisoners know what awaits them in the next institution: more of the same. In *Ghosts … of the Civil Dead* Wenzil ends the film out of prison, but it is clear he will soon be back inside. As Wenzil prepares to leave prison in the penultimate sequence, another prisoner in solitary confinement explains how he became a pawn of the system, 'trained' by the institution and those that ran it to commit crimes in order to maintain an atmosphere of fear in the general population that, in turn, made the extension of police powers and reinforcement of the penal system politically acceptable. The cutting between this prisoner's testimony and Wenzil preparing to leave the prison clearly implies that he has also been 'trained' to instil fear in the community. The final shot of Wenzil ascending an escalator behind an unsuspecting woman leaves little doubt that he will soon offend again. At the end of *Everynight, Everynight*, Dale, Brennan and Bryant are taken from their cells after appearing to have won their psychological battle with the guards and the governor, but an onscreen title and off-screen dialogue reveal that, although a Board of Inquiry found that officers used brutal methods of discipline against them, the charges against the prison officers were dismissed by a magistrate. Once again, the implication is clear: the system prevails, and it looks after its own.

Similar themes and outcomes are played out in the futuristic prison dramas *Turkey Shoot* (Brian Trenchard-Smith, 1982, released as *Escape 2000* in the

US and *Blood Camp Thatcher* in the UK), *Dead End Drive-In* (Brian Trenchard-Smith, 1986), *Fortress* (Stuart Gordon, 1993), *Escape from Absolom* (Martin Campbell, 1994, titled *No Escape* for US release) and *The Island of Dr Moreau* (John Frankenheimer, 1996). The last three films are international productions made in Queensland. *Turkey Shoot* and *Dead End Drive-In* were both directed by Brian Trenchard-Smith, a leading figure in the 'Ozploitation' genre whose films are notable for their energetic action sequences and spectacular stunts. In *Turkey Shoot* Australia has been taken over by a totalitarian regime, and 'social deviants' (or anyone the regime dislikes) are sent to prison camps for 're-education'. The camp authorities hunt and kill prisoners for sport, and an uprising is ultimately quelled by a napalm strike. In *Dead End Drive-In*, it is teenagers who are targeted by an unseen authoritarian government and detained in camps converted from their former use as drive-in cinemas. While the lead character Crabs survives the drive-in, like his fellow survivors the Brennicks in *Fortress*, Robbins in *Escape from Absolom*, and Edward Douglas in *The Island of Dr Moreau*, his future is far from certain.

One characteristic feature of contemporary prison films is that they draw on actual events, or make use of the experience of former inmates and others with intimate knowledge of the prison institution. *Stir* was written by Bob Jewson and based in part on his experience in prison in the early 1970s, including his time as an inmate during a notorious uprising at Bathurst Gaol in 1974. The director and producer of *Ghosts ... of the Civil Dead* spent a number of years researching 'corrective services' in Australia and in the United States, and some of the film was based on correspondence with long-term American prisoner Jack Henry Abbott, whose book about his time in jail, *In the Belly of the Beast*, provided the title for the Australian film. *Everynight, Everynight* lightly fictionalizes the story of Australian hit-man Christopher Dale Flannery, focusing on the period he spent on remand and, after sentencing, in the 'most secure place in Australia', H Division of Pentridge Gaol. Much of *Chopper* (Andrew Dominik, 2000), the stylish bio-pic of infamous criminal Mark 'Chopper' Read, is set in prison (and partly shot in the now-decommissioned Pentridge prison), including scenes faithfully recreating Read's deadly attacks on other prisoners, and an episode in which he persuades another prisoner to cut off one of his (Chopper's) ears in order to avoid an attack planned by fellow inmates.

As these examples illustrate, Australian prison films focus almost exclusively on the experience of male prisoners, with only Tom Cowan's film about a group of escaped women convicts *Journey Among Women* (1977) breaking the mould. This is not the case in Australian television, however; the most prominent television prison drama series, *Prisoner* (or *Prisoner Cell Block H* as it was titled in the UK) which ran for almost 700 one-hour episodes from 1979, was set in a women's prison. An attempt by the production company Grundy's to capitalize on the popularity of *Prisoner* with a series about a men's prison called *Punishment*, was unsuccessful.

As Graeme Turner notes, characters in Australian films are not only entrapped or imprisoned in convict or prison dramas. The outback environment and the hell of small, isolated towns function as a kind of prison for the English schoolteacher John Grant in *Wake in Fright* (Ted Kotcheff, 1971), the American criminal on-the-run Teddy in the homage to ocker comedies of the 1970s *Welcome to Woop Woop* (Stephan Elliot, 1997), and the stranded car-crash survivor Arthur in the gothic horror film *The Cars That Ate Paris* (Peter Weir, 1974). And the real outback (in this instance the other-worldly landscape around Coober Pedy in South Australia) is transformed into an alien planet on which the crew and passengers of a space transporter are marooned and terrorized in *Pitch Black* (David Twohy, 2000). The tropes of capture and deprivation of liberty by crazed individuals are standard features of Australian horror films like *Wolf Creek* (Greg Mclean, 2005), while several historical and science fiction films revolve around the capture and trials (both literal and metaphorical) of their lead characters by unsympathetic regimes. The Boer war drama *'Breaker' Morant* (Bruce Beresford, 1980) centres on the British military justice meted out to three Australian soldiers accused of killing Boer prisoners, while *Paradise Road* (Bruce Beresford, 1997) tells the story of a number of women taken prisoner by the Japanese after the fall of Singapore in 1942. An earlier film, *Blood Oath* (Stephen Wallace, 1990), which focuses on the trials of Japanese soldiers for war crimes after the Second World War, also contains a number of scenes set in a prisoner of war camp. In the science fiction features *Dark City* (Alex Proyas, 1995) and *The Matrix* (Larry and Andy Wachowski, 1999), the latter an American film made at Fox Studios in Sydney, the lead characters discover that they are being held prisoner and their worlds are not quite what they seem.

Scenes or experiences in prisons and police cells are pivotal to the plots and to characters' experiences in many other Australian films. The discovery of an Aboriginal prisoner hanging in a cell in a remote outback police station is the catalyst for a powerful exploration of Indigenous/non-Indigenous relations in the thriller *Dead Heart* (Nick Parsons, 1996). In the road movie *Doing Time for Patsy Cline* (Chris Kennedy, 1997), aspiring country musician Ralph finds himself in jail after hitching a ride with a glamorous couple. He decides to take the rap for something he did not do – in part as a moral stance but mostly because he feels the experience will give him wonderful material for the songs he plans to write. In the outback western *The Proposition* (John Hillcoat, 2005), Mikey Burns waits in police custody, terrified and abused by his guards, as his brother Charlie hunts their older sibling Arthur in order to win Mikey's freedom. In the heist movie *The Hard Word* (Scott Roberts, 2002) brothers Dale, Mal and Shane are periodically 'released' from prison to commit robberies at the behest of their crooked lawyer. Escaped prisoners play key roles in a diverse group of films, including Ivan Sen's debut feature *Beneath Clouds* (2002), the comedy vehicle for Irish comic Jimeoin *The Craic* (Ted Emery, 1999), and the rarely-seen *DeVil's Tas Mania* (Di Nettlefold, 1993). In the low-budget social-realist feature *27A* (Esben Storm, 1974), the lead character escapes several times from a psychiatric institution where he is treated, violently and ultimately unsuccessfully, for alcoholism. The comedy *Gettin' Square* (Jonathan Teplitzky, 2003, written by Gold Coast criminal lawyer Chris Nyst) and the pre-crime drama *The Boys* (Rowan Woods, 1998, which tells the story of the period leading up to a brutal crime) feature characters that have recently been released from prison. In the latter film, lead character Brett Sprague, like Wenzil in *Ghosts ... of the Civil Dead*, will not remain a free man for long.

Many of the films set in the convict era, and the majority of contemporary prison films, highlight systemic injustices through depictions of undeserved or disproportionate punishments and violence against convicts or prisoners. Prison officers are almost universally unsympathetic and often despicable characters, even in those films that acknowledge that they too may be victims of the system. Even rare exceptions like Norton in *Stir* whose remorsefulness drives him to seek the forgiveness of a prisoner he has previously abused, cannot be completely redeemed. Violence is endemic in Australian prison films, though it tends to be 'blue on green' (prison officer on prisoner) rather than 'green on green' (prisoner on prisoner). In *Ghosts ... of the Civil Dead*, violence between prisoners is tolerated and even encouraged by the prison authorities, although it is the violence committed by the officers that leaves the greater impression. As in *Stir* and *Everynight, Everynight,* the violence of individual officers represents the violence of the system as a whole; it is used to bring into question the morality and practice of the penal system. In films like this, the principal intention is to provoke the audience into reflection on the ethics and rectitude of the regime of punishment. For film-makers whose intention is to make political arguments or to explore philosophical questions, the prison is a potent setting. It is an equally powerful location for film-makers whose priority is dramatic storytelling, since it permits the exploration of characters' reactions to the stress and fear that inevitably accompanies incarceration.

Ben Goldsmith

For the Term of His Natural Life

Country of Origin:
Australia

Studio/Distributor:
Australasian Films/National Film
and Sound Archive

Director:
Norman Dawn

Producer:
Norman Dawn

Screenwriter:
Norman Dawn, adapted from
the novel *For the Term of His
Natural Life* by Marcus Clarke

Cinematographers:
Len H Roos
William Trerise
Bert Cross

Editors:
Katherine Dawn
Norman Dawn
Mona Donaldson

Art Director:
Norman Dawn
Dorothy Gordon

Duration:
Originally 10,000 feet (c.160
minutes), Restored and
incomplete 102 mins

Genre:
Convict
Prison

Cast:
George Fisher
Eva Novak
Dunstan Webb
Marian Marcus Clark
Jessica Harcourt
Arthur McLaglan
Mayne Lynton

Year:
1927

Synopsis

British aristocrat Richard Devine is transported to Australia after being wrongfully convicted of murdering his biological father, Lord Bellasis. Devine accepts the punishment in order to protect his mother's name, telling the authorities that he is Rufus Dawes. En route to Australia, Dawes inadvertently foils an attempt by convicts, led by Gabbett, to take over the ship. In retribution, Gabbett claims Dawes was their ringleader. Among the convicts is Bellasis' real murderer, his son John Rex, who bears a striking resemblance to Dawes. In Tasmania, Dawes lives in isolation on an island. After an attempt to commit suicide by diving into the ocean, Dawes avoids being transported with the other convicts to the notorious penal settlement at Port Arthur. Rex succeeds in taking over one of the ships. A British officer, Frere, along with the wife and daughter of the commanding officer Major Vickers, are abandoned by the convicts. Dawes stumbles across the abandoned group, and helps them to make their way to Port Arthur. Dawes falls in love with Vickers daughter, Sylvia, but her sudden amnesia means that his heroism goes unrecognized and he is returned to prison. Years pass. Frere marries Sylvia who, despite several encounters with Dawes, does not remember his role in her salvation. Rex is captured and put on trial. Frere's mistress (and Rex's lover) Sarah Purfoy blackmails him to give evidence that will save Rex from execution. Sarah helps Rex and Gabbett escape. Dawes gives Rex a letter to deliver to his mother, Lady Devine. Rex reads the letter and decides to return to England to impersonate Richard Devine, and claim the family fortune. Dawes has been transported to Norfolk Island, a harsh penal settlement now under Frere's command. In England, Lady Devine realizes that Rex is an impostor, and forces him to confess to the murder of Lord Bellasis. On Norfolk Island, Dawes is helped to escape by Reverend North who had witnessed Lord Bellasis' murder and is wracked with guilt for his failure to tell the truth about what he had seen. Impersonating the Reverend, Dawes boards a ship taking Sylvia back to the mainland. On the Island, Frere is killed during a convict uprising. The ship is wrecked in a storm, but Dawes and Sylvia are reunited. Her memory returns as they drift on a makeshift raft towards land.

Critique

For the Term of His Natural Life was one of the last Australian silent films, and also one of the most significant in the history of Australian cinema. At the time of its production, controversy raged over its depiction of convict life, its scale and cost, which was reported to be around £50,000 at a time when most Australian films had budgets of less than £2,000, (Pike &Cooper 1998: 139) and the fact that the director, several of the crew and the leading cast members were American. Australasian Films launched a publicity campaign of unprecedented scale to counter opposition to the film's subject matter and the charge that they were 'seeking to make capital out of the drab and sordid days of Australia' (Tulloch 1981: 307). The film's expense was turned into a virtue: hundreds of unemployed men were used as extras, while the film also provided work for many within the Australian film industry and, according to Australasian, enabled the establishment of new production companies. The American imports, who earlier had been accused of being 'party to the slaughtering' of the Australian film industry, were fêted for their artistic contributions, and the concerns raised in federal parliament about an American 'invasion' were deflected by claims about what the local industry could learn from those with Hollywood experience (*Sydney Truth* 1926, cited in Shirley & Adams 1989: 90). The publicity campaign was successful as the film proved enormously popular at the Australian box office in its initial run. But the coming of sound film in 1928 had a considerable impact on audiences for silent films like *For the Term*, and its early local success was not repeated in subsequent seasons or in overseas markets.

The film has since gained notoriety for a scene featuring a burning ship; the fire was fuelled by 'over two tonnes' of old film, much of which was likely to have come from Australian productions of the time (Routt in Sabine 1995: 62). Watching this scene now, we can imagine the history of Australian cinema going up in smoke in front of our eyes. The film's director, Norman Dawn, also produced, adapted the screenplay, provided art direction and oversaw the many special effects in this bloated, tedious and often unintentionally comic epic. Dawn, who had taken over responsibility for the film from Raymond Longford at the request of the studio Australasian Films, had worked in Hollywood for much of the previous two decades. In Hollywood, Dawn had gained something of a reputation for innovation in special effects, and is credited with inventing the glass shot, a much used technique in which details missing from a location (such as the roofs of ruined buildings at Port Arthur) are painted on a glass slide which is positioned in front of the camera to provide a composite picture (Fielding 1965: 30). In Australia, he was given extraordinary freedom to make this film. Lengthy location shoots, large-scale set-piece scenes featuring hundreds of extras, and expensive attention to historical detail in costumes and props, mark the film out from other films made in Australia at this time.

The film's narrative, criticized in contemporary reviews for its complexity and eventfulness, deploys many of the themes popular in fiction at the time of its source novel's publication in 1874, including transportation or migration to avoid family shame, mistaken identity, imposture and double cross. Like the novel, the film relies on coincidences and contrivances of plot and, while the film retains the novels 'underlying recognition that the prison is not a world apart but a revealing expression of social power' (Hergenhan 1993: 48), the film is more intent on exploiting the melodramatic and spectacular elements of the novel than it is in reinforcing the original social message.

Ben Goldsmith

Stir

Country of Origin:
Australia

Director:
Stephen Wallace

Producer:
Richard Brennan

Screenwriter:
Bob Jewson

Production Designer:
Lee Whitmore

Editor:
Henry Dangar

Director of Photography:
Geoff Burton

Duration:
100 minutes

Genre:
Prison

Cast:
Bryan Brown
Max Phipps
Dennis Miller
Gary Waddell
Phil Motherwell
Edward Robshaw
Robert Tex Morton
Ray Marshall
Paul Sonkkila

Year:
1980

Synopsis

Two prisoners are beaten up in their cell by warders. One of the prisoners later appears on television talking about the beatings, which came in the aftermath of a sit-in protest by inmates. Norton, one of the warders who administered the beating, watches the television interview at home, drinking heavily. Three years later, the same prisoner, China Jackson, is on his way back to the same prison after a conviction for shoplifting. He discusses the beatings and the ineffectiveness of his whistle-blowing with his fellow prisoners. At Gatunga Gaol, Jackson and the other prisoners are intimidated and treated violently by warders, with beatings and punishments meted out for trivial or manufactured offences. On several occasions Norton tries to befriend Jackson, and attempts to apologize for the earlier incident. Jackson repeatedly refuses to accept the apology. A delegation of prisoners fruitlessly complains to the Governor when rations are inexplicably reduced. Prisoners stage a protest; Jackson talks them into backing down after receiving a promise from Norton that there will be no reprisals. The promise is broken and several prisoners are shanghaid – transferred to other prisons in the middle of the night. The instigator of the protest, Alby, is badly beaten by guards. Jackson and others resolve to burn the prison to the ground. At a film screening, one prisoner throws a makeshift petrol bomb but others lose their nerve. The prisoner is singled out and taken away to be beaten; hearing his screams the other prisoners begin to riot. The warders take up arms and shoot several prisoners as the gaol is systematically destroyed. The prisoners surrender, but the promise that there will be no reprisals is broken once again. Prisoners are herded into special yards. In the middle of the night, warders throw tear gas into the cages, open the doors, and bash the prisoners as they are herded into prison vans. Norton is taunted by a fellow warder as a crim-lover. Jackson is the last prisoner to leave the special yard. He tries to fight the warders but is overcome by numbers before Norton brutally bashes him. In a long convoy of prison vans and police cars with sirens wailing, the prisoners are taken away.

Critique

Stir was written by a former prisoner, Bob Jewson, who had witnessed first-hand a notorious riot at Bathurst Gaol in New South Wales in February 1974, the second serious disturbance at the prison in four years. In 1979, prisoners at Parramatta Gaol staged a peaceful sit-in to protest against the New South Wales government's decision not to pursue criminal charges against prison officers for their actions during the 1974 Bathurst riot. The bashing of China Jackson and his cellmate in the first scene of *Stir* follows a sit-in, with the rest of the film drawing heavily on events around the 1974 Bathurst riot. The director later claimed that he wanted to call the film *The Riot at Bathurst Prison*, but was persuaded by nervous bureaucrats to apply the veneer of fiction. The film was retitled *Stir*, and set in the fictional Gatunga Gaol. Like other films in this genre, *Stir* draws heavily on the experiences of former prisoners and warders. The Prisoners Action Group played a leading role in the planning and preparation of the film, and many former inmates and guards were employed as extras. And in common with many films in this genre, *Stir* is concerned to humanize the plight of prisoners. Through the depiction of the routines of punishment, violence and retribution by which order in the institution is maintained, and through careful evocation of the atmosphere of fear and intimidation that prisoners (and warders) live with every day, *Stir*, again like other films in this genre, blames the authorities and the system itself for events like those portrayed here. As producer Richard Brennan says in an interview on the 2005 DVD release of the film, 'prisons create monsters'.

For the most part the film is shot in a naturalistic style, although several artistic flourishes stand out – for instance, the initial bashing in the opening pre-title sequence is shot with a blue wash to indicate events at night. The colour scheme is maintained in the subsequent scene, in which one of the warders, Norton, watches Jackson being interviewed on television. The only contrasting colour is the yellow of the alcohol that Norton gulps down as he tries to swallow his feelings of cowardice and guilt. Later, scenes of warders striding ominously past rows of cells to administer another punishment are accompanied by repeated one- or two-note phrases played on a cello, xylophone or piano, accompanied by sustained metallic noises which combine eerily with the sharp reports of bolts being pulled back, the clanging of the iron cell doors, and the jangling of the enormous bunches of keys carried by the guards.

Stir was nominated for 11 AFI awards in 1980, but was unsuccessful in every category. It is notable for its sympathetic treatment of homosexual relations between prisoners. In one scene, as Jackson and his mate Redford discuss the latter's conquests in the prison, Redford says 'Of course I'm into women on the outside, but it's different in here'. Later Redford arranges for first-time prisoner Andrew to be transferred to his cell and, after some persuasion, succeeds in seducing the young inmate. Unlike many other prison movies, the threat and fear of homosexual assault is entirely absent in *Stir*.

Ben Goldsmith

Ghosts ... Of the Civil Dead

Country of Origin:
Australia

Studio/Distributor:
Umbrella Entertainment

Director:
John Hillcoat

Synopsis

The film depicts events leading up to a lengthy period of lockdown (in which prisoners are confined to cells for 23 hours per day) at a new-generation, maximum-security institution, Central Industrial Prison, located in the middle of a desert. The story is told in part through a series of intertitles detailing the findings of a subsequent report by the Committee on the Judiciary. A group of new prisoners arrive, including Wenzil, who enters the General Population Unit, and guard-killer Grezner, who enters the maximum security Administrative Segregation Unit. Various guards vow to avenge their slain colleague; a police officer posted outside his cell ensures Grezner's safety, for now. Another

Producer:
Evan English

Screenwriters:
Gene Conkie
John Hillcoat
Evan English
Nick Cave
Hugo Race

Cinematographers:
Paul Goldman
Graham Wood

Production Designer:
Chris Kennedy

Editor:
Stewart Young

Duration:
89 minutes

Genre:
Prison

Cast:
David Field
Mike Bishop
Vince Gil
Dave Mason
Nick Cave
Chris De Rose
Kevin Mackey
Bogdan Koca

Year:
1988

prisoner, Glover, is in Solitary Confinement. Drugs and pornography are freely available, despite the constant, omnipresent surveillance. Wenzil attacks another prisoner and steals a radio. In retribution, two prisoners assault him as he is being tattooed. He regains consciousness to find the word 'Cunt' has been tattooed on his forehead. Special Operations officers search all cells and confiscate all property belonging to Administrative Segregation Unit prisoners. Televisions are banned from the General Population Units. More violent prisoners are brought into the prison, including the psychopath Maynard. A prison guard kills himself. Wenzil kills a transvestite prisoner. Grezner is found hanging in his cell after the police officer mysteriously leaves his post one night. A guard is killed by a maximum security prisoner. Outside the prison, a news reporter gives details of the lockdown, the killings and the increasing tension in the prison. Intertitles announce that in response to the violence 30 inmates were transferred, and five released, Wenzil among them. Glover, in voice over, says 'They [the authorities] bred me to create fear. And I just did what I was supposed to do. People are scared. They're scared of each other because of people like me.' Now out of prison, Wenzil follows an unsuspecting woman out of a train station.

Critique

Drawing heavily from the book *In the Belly of the Beast* by American author and long-term prisoner Jack Henry Abbott, as well as from the historical and philosophical work of Michel Foucault (the credits include Foucault Authority, Simon During), *Ghosts … Of the Civil Dead* is a searing critique of the so-called new generation prison system developed in the United States and recently introduced in Australia. Director John Hillcoat and producer Evan English conducted extensive research for the film, including spending time at the National Institute of Corrections, a think-tank in Colorado, and visiting numerous institutions like the new Alcatraz at Marion Illinois and other maximum security prisons across the United States. Using a mix of professionals and non-actors, including former prisoners and prison guards, the story was workshopped during a lengthy rehearsal period with many actual events and experiences of participants incorporated into the film. The end result deliberately blurs the line between American and Australian prison experience to make the political point that what had happened in the US – from where many events and characters, and much of the architecture and design of the prison are drawn – was beginning to happen in Australia. The film emphasizes the vicious cycle of institutionalization, and highlights the role state authorities play in manufacturing, provoking and manipulating violence and fear both in prisons and in wider society as a means to augment policing and surveillance of the population, to oppress the working classes, and to maintain the political status quo.

In its exploration of the influence of the American penal system in Australia, the film is a significant departure from earlier convict and prison films that drew on British precedents and influences. English and Hillcoat initially sought the rights to adapt Abbott's book, which consists of a series of letters written by the prisoner to Norman Mailer as Mailer researched his book *The Executioners Song*. Eventually this proved impossible, and the film, instead, uses a mixture of documentary and dramatic techniques to develop what producer English, in an interview included in the 2003 Australian DVD release, described as a cumulative narrative. Rather than focusing on the experiences of a goal-oriented protagonist, the film concentrates on evoking mood and atmosphere through a series of scenes intended gradually to build awareness and understanding in the audience. Prison exteriors were shot in Nevada, with interiors shot in a Melbourne warehouse on sets made largely of cardboard. The voice that introduces the prisoners and the audience to the institution, and the news reporter who gives details of the lockdown at the end, are both female Americans. All other characters are male Australians, and the clear implication is that the prison is somewhere in outback Australia.

The film is notable for the multiple involvements of Australian musician Nick Cave, who contributed to the screenplay and the score (along with Mick Harvey and Blixa Bargeld from Cave's band the Bad Seeds). Cave also played the role of a psychopathic prisoner who is brought in to the prison to stir up his fellow inmates and the increasingly tense and powerless guards. Cave subsequently wrote the score for Hillcoat's next film *To Have and To Hold*, and later wrote both screenplay and score for Hillcoat's third feature film, *The Proposition*.

Ghosts … Of the Civil Dead screened at several major international film festivals, including Cannes and Venice. At the latter festival the film gained significant publicity following the arrest of the director, as he illegally put up posters for the film around the city. Apprehended on terrorism-related charges, Hillcoat was later fined and released.

Ben Goldsmith

Everynight … Everynight

Country of Origin:
Australia

Director:
Alkinos Tsilimidos

Producer:
Alkinos Tsilimidos

Screenwriters:
Ray Mooney
Alkinos Tsilimidos, adapted from a play by Ray Mooney

Editors:
Cindy Clarkson
Alkinos Tsilimidos

Synopsis

Dale, a prisoner on remand, is sentenced to an indefinite term in H Division, the gaol-within-the-gaol of Pentridge Prison in Melbourne. He is physically and sexually assaulted by several prison warders and ordered to break rocks. At night, another inmate, Bryant, calls out to Dale, warning him not to dob, or inform on anyone including the prison officers. Berriman, one of the warders, bashes a third inmate, Barrett. A prison doctor offers to help if Dale makes a complaint, but he steadfastly refuses to blame the prison warders for his injuries. At his trial, Dale is sentenced to four years' imprisonment and returned to H Division. Dale receives a letter from his sweetheart, Lorraine. He asks warder Kert for permission to write a special letter. Kert forces him to beg on his knees. Dale is told that Lorraine has come to visit him, but the visitor turns out to be Dale's former teacher, a priest. The priest has come to seek Dale's forgiveness for abusing him when Dale was a child, but Dale ignores him. Later, Dale is again told that Lorraine has come to visit. At first he does not believe the warder. Eventually he is convinced and makes his way to the visiting area, but another warder prevents him going in and tells him there is no

Director of Photography:
Toby Oliver

Production Designer:
Steven Meier

Duration:
92 minutes

Genre:
Prison

Cast:
David Field
Bill Hunter
Robert Morgan
Phil Motherwell
Jim Daly
Jim Shaw
Simon Woodward
Theodore Zakos

Year:
1995

visitor. Dale demands to see Lorraine, and is forcibly restrained. In his cell, Dale catches a small lizard, which pretends to be dead. Dale lets it go and it springs back to life. Dale is taken to the Governor, charged with insolence and making unnecessary noise. Dale strips off, and announces 'I'm no longer part of this world. I've resigned'. The Governor orders him on to a diet of bread and water until he conforms to regulations; Dale refuses to eat 'until you conform to humanity'. Dale encourages the other inmates of H Division to follow his example. They repeatedly taunt Berriman, who realizes that the physical and psychological hold that the authorities had over the prisoners has been broken. Dale, Bryant and Barrett are removed from H Division. Another prisoner, Driscoll, is found hanging in his cell. Over the final credits, voice-over and intertitles reveal that a subsequent Board of Inquiry found that the officers used unlawful and brutal methods of discipline, but charges against them were dismissed in a magistrate's court. Final intertitles announce that Dale went on to become Australia's most notorious hitman, but is currently missing; Bryant tried to bomb state police headquarters, and is back inside never to be released; and Barrett was certified.

Critique

An opening title states that *Everynight ... Everynight* is a true story, but due to 'legal implications', the characters have been fictionalized. Another title dedicates the film to the memory of Christopher Dale Flannery, an infamous underworld figure known as Mr Rent-a-Kill who spent time in H Division in the 1970s and 1980s. Originally from Melbourne, Flannery was a major figure in the Sydney gang wars of 1984–85, dramatized in the television series *Underbelly: A Tale of Two Cities* (2009). He disappeared in mid-1985; there are several conflicting stories about his fate. The character of Bryant appears to have been based on Stan Taylor, who had spent time in H Division with Flannery. Taylor was sentenced to life imprisonment without parole in 1988 for the 1986 bombing of police headquarters in Melbourne.

Like many other films in this genre, *Everynight ... Everynight* draws heavily on real-life experiences and events, and shares a common intention to raise public awareness of the brutal treatment of inmates in Australian prisons and, by implication, to condemn a system of institutionalized violence. Unlike some other prison films, *Everynight ... Everynight* makes no attempt to suggest that prison officers are also victims of the system. None of the authority figures in the film, with the exception perhaps of the prison doctor who features briefly in an early scene, question the treatment of the prisoners or the justice or morality of their own actions. They are mere ciphers, simple agents of the system, as inhuman as the sledgehammer that Dale uses to break rocks. The prisoners are gradually broken down and reduced to rubble by the endless, routine humiliations and constant, petty cruelties that they are forced to endure. The ludicrous charges and disproportionate punishments that the prisoners receive for breaching often arbitrary rules similarly wear down the viewer. And in the end we, too, are broken, exhausted, brutalized by what we have witnessed and, ultimately, left with no choice, no way to redeem the system other than to resign from it, and refuse to succumb to its violence or to participate in its power games.

Stylistically, *Everynight ... Everynight* is unlike any other prison film I have seen. A variety of artistic techniques are used to powerful effect, most notably the chiaroscuro cinematography. The blackness that literally and metaphorically inhabits the prison repeatedly spills out of the frame obscuring the boundary that separates the film world from ours, and denying the comfort of objective, distanced viewing. It is fitting that the film is shot in black and white, as there is no room for equivocation or misdirected sympathies here. The prisoners, for all their sins, are undeserving of the violence they suffer, and the authorities are unremittingly evil.

The choice of black and white gives the film a timeless quality. The prisoners' uniforms, the cold, stone walls of the Victorian prison, the ancient punishment of rock breaking, the hierarchy of power and pattern of oppression and abuse, situate the action in an uncertain (or endless) historical moment; only small details – a rifle, a radio – suggest a specific timeframe. Religious symbols and indices abound: the tattoo of a crucifix that covers Dale's back, the repeated orders to prisoners to stand 'on the cross' in their cells, the priest begging forgiveness. This could be purgatory, not Pentridge.

Ben Goldsmith

Chopper

Country of Origin:
Australia

Director:
Andrew Dominik

Screenwriter:
Andrew Dominik

Producer:
Michele Bennett

Editor:
Ken Sallows

Director of Photography:
Geoffrey Hall
Kevin Hayward

Production Designer:
Paddy Reardon

Genre:
Crime
Prison

Synopsis

1991. Notorious standover man Mark Brandon Chopper Read watches himself being interviewed on television from his prison cell. Flashback to 1978. In Pentridge Gaol, Chopper launches an unprovoked attack on a fellow prisoner, a senior trades' union figure, stabbing him repeatedly in the face and neck. Chopper denies any involvement but, after the prisoner dies, a contract is put on Chopper's head. He is attacked by his cellmates Jimmy and Bluey but survives. In hospital, Chopper initially refuses to make a statement until he learns that Jimmy has made a statement against him and filed a claim for compensation through the victims of crime fund. Chopper requests a transfer to another prison, fearing further attacks, but prison authorities refuse. He convinces another prisoner to cut off his ears in order to secure the transfer. 1986: Chopper, recently released from prison, takes his girlfriend Tanya, a prostitute, to Bojangles nightclub. Neville, a former associate who Chopper kneecapped some years earlier, approaches him. Neville is friendly and forgiving, but Chopper is suspicious and leaves the club after drawing a handgun and firing several shots into the ceiling. Chopper argues with Tanya, accusing her of sleeping with Neville. Tanya storms off, but Chopper kicks down her front door and beats her up. In a bar, Chopper gives information to two police officers, believing that they will turn a blind eye to his activities. Chopper goes to Neville's mansion to apologize. Reluctantly, Neville lets him in, but becomes angry when Chopper asks for money. Chopper shoots Neville in the stomach and, then, helps Neville's

Duration:
94 minutes

Cast:
Eric Bana
Simon Lyndon
Dan Wyllie
Vince Colosimo
Kate Beahan

Year:
2000

henchmen take him to hospital. Chopper goes to see his former cell-mate Jimmy who is now a junkie living with his heavily-pregnant girl-friend Mandy in a squalid apartment. Chopper pulls a gun on Jimmy, and demands to know if Jimmy is planning to kill him on Neville's behalf. Jimmy manages to talk him down. Back at Bojangles night-club, Chopper meets Sammy the Turk. Believing he is being set up, Chopper follows Sammy outside to the car park and shoots him in the head, unaware that Mandy has been watching. In the bar, Chopper tells the police a different version of events, but feels insulted when they disbelieve him. Mandy turns crown witness and testifies against Chopper. He is acquitted of murder, but sentenced to five years for malicious wounding. 1991: In the prison yard, Chopper is interviewed by a television journalist following the publication of his memoirs. In his cell, he watches the interview on television with two prison officers. They leave, and Chopper is left alone, staring at the wall.

Critique

Andrew Dominik's stylish and disturbingly-amusing film about real-life violent criminal Mark Chopper Read begins with a title that announces: 'This film is a dramatization in which narrative liberties have been taken. It is not a biography.' This loosely fictionalized film forms part of a minor but important strain of Australian screen culture: dramatizations of the lives or exploits of real-life outlaws. This almost true-crime subgenre includes the various films about Ned Kelly, and Kevin Dobson's 1982 feature about eponymous 1920s' Melbourne gangster *Squizzy Taylor*. The subgenre has become a staple part of Australian television drama in the last decade – due, in some part no doubt to the success of *Chopper* – with, first, the 2003 telemovie *The Postcard Bandit* about bank robber and serial escapee Brendan Abbot, and most recently the three *Underbelly* television series (2008–10).

Adapted from Read's best-selling memoirs, which now run to twelve books, *Chopper* makes clear at an early stage that, while the central character is a gifted storyteller and raconteur, he is far from a reliable narrator. Throughout the film the same events are presented several times, *Rashomon*-like in slightly different versions. The murder of Sammy the Turk is replayed three times, once with the main characters (including the unfortunate Sammy) recounting their parts direct to camera in lilting, rhyming prose. What is depicted onscreen is often at odds with the stories Read tells the police and others during the film. This is consistent with the shifting mythology that has grown around Read, much of it created by the man himself. By his own admission, he has killed 19 people and injured many more, although, as he proudly and repeatedly observes, no 'innocent characters' were ever hurt. Read's books have sold thousands of copies, and he regularly tours his live show around Australia.

Chopper is notable for its visual style and its play with time. The opening titles play across low-angle time-lapse shots of clouds scud-ding across the sky above a prison, and several scenes are speeded up for comic effect: first as a visual representation of characters who have just snorted speed, and later in the poetic retelling of Sammy

Chopper, Australian Film Finance Corp.

the Turk's murder to emphasize the way in which this event rapidly entered popular folklore. The lighting of different scenes is expressive and arresting. The sequences in the prison cells and exercise areas contrast the grey-blue of the actors' faces and clothes, the colour of cigarette smoke, with the bright, white walls. The brothel bedroom in which Chopper hooks up with Tanya, following his release from prison, is a luscious red that is almost painful to look at, and this palette is carried through to the interior of the night-club. The lounge room in Chopper's father's house is the colour of nicotine-stained fingers, while the kitchen is bathed in a mouldy blue-green light. A similar contrast is used in the scene in which Chopper visits Jimmy and Mandy's wretched apartment: the stairwell and front door are dirty brown, while the interior of the apartment is a sickly, unnatural green.

The film is full of images and moments that have already achieved iconic status, although perhaps the most memorable does not feature in the film itself. The image that adorned the film's publicity materials and the DVD cover features Bana shirtless, with his tattoo-covered arms crossed over his similarly-illustrated chest, holding two revolvers, his face expressionless but menacingly powerful with trademark handlebar moustache and aviator sunglasses clinging to his earless-head. Along with the thrice-told murder of Sammy the Turk, perhaps the most extraordinary scene in the film is that in which an unsuspecting Chopper is repeatedly stabbed by his cellmate and long-time accomplice Jimmy Loughnan. At first, Chopper thinks Jimmy is playfully sparring with him. 'A bit early for kung fu, isn't it?', he asks. Jimmy plunges the knife again and again into the stunned Chopper, who calmly admonishes him 'Now Jimmy, if you keep stabbing me, you're going to kill me'. Rather than fighting back, Chopper hugs his assailant as if he cannot quite believe what is happening. Jimmy stabs him again and they end up face to face in a close embrace, as if they are about to kiss each other. Chopper removes his clothes to inspect his gaping wounds, then collapses into Jimmy's arms. This extraordinary scene is made more remarkable when it is later revealed that Chopper is only in prison because he held a judge hostage in an attempt to have Jimmy released from gaol.

To date, director Andrew Dominik has only made two feature films since graduating from Swinburne Film School in 1988. *Chopper*, his first film, reportedly took seven years to make, much of which was spent convincing nervous investors that the morally-repugnant but compelling stories by and about Read were worth committing to celluloid. It would be another seven years before Dominik's next film, *The Assassination of Jesse James by the Coward Robert Ford* (2007), was completed. Dominik's second film about a notorious outlaw is as visually striking as his first, but while he won a number of awards including Best Achievement in Direction at the 2001 Australian Film Institute Awards for *Chopper*, and despite the plaudits deservedly heaped on cinematographer Roger Deakins for *Jesse James* (including the 2008 Academy Award for Best Achievement in Cinematography), Dominik's achievements in *Jesse James* were largely, and unjustly, overlooked.

As well as directing both films, Dominik wrote the screenplays for *Chopper*, and *Jesse James*. His first film magnificently captures Chopper Read's characteristic, mannered delivery and verbal dexterity, and the film is full of beautifully-crafted exchanges between Chopper and his associates. 'You're fucking sick, Read. You're insane,' yells Keithy George shortly before his grisly demise. 'Beethoven had his critics,' Chopper replies. 'See if you can name three of them.' After he fails to convince the police of his involvement in the murder of Sammy the Turk, he disconsolately tells his father 'I used to be Chopper Read. Now I can't get arrested in this town.'

In contrast with Dominik's stop-start film career, lead actor Eric Bana has gone from strength to strength following his unforgettable performance as *Chopper*. He was cast, first, in a supporting role in Ridley Scott's *Black Hawk Down* (2001), before his first Hollywood lead as Bruce Banner/the Hulk in Ang Lee's much maligned 2003 version of the comic-book classic. Bana, a former (and much loved) stand-up and television comedian, has consistently proven his talent and versatility with major parts in such diverse films as Wolfgang Peterson's *Troy* (2004, as Hector), Steven Spielberg's *Munich* (2005, as Avner), Justin Chadwick's *The Other Boleyn Girl* (2008, as Henry Tudor), J J Abram's *Star Trek* (2009, as Nero) and Robert Schwentke's *The Time Travellers Wife* (2009, as Henry DeTamble). In between his Hollywood roles, Bana has regularly returned to Australia to lend his talent and profile to local feature films and to make a documentary about his obsession with cars, *Love the Beast* (2009).

Ben Goldsmith

PERIOD

The 1970s was a decade of renewal in the Australian film industry that is often characterized as a 'renaissance', or 'new wave'. A huge increase in film production was spurred on by political and cultural shifts, including the creation of national funding bodies such as the Australian Film Development Corporation (AFDC 1970–75) and later its successor the Australian Film Commission (AFC 1975–2007); the establishment of the first state film agencies (the South Australian Film Corporation in 1972, the Victorian Film Corporation in 1976, the Queensland Film Corporation, the Tasmanian Film Corporation and the New South Wales Film Corporation in 1977, and the West Australian Film Council in 1978); and the foundation of a national film school in 1973. One of the most prominent genres in the Australian 'New Wave' from the mid-1970s was the historical costume drama or 'period film', sometimes called the 'nostalgia film'. Cultural critics of the 1980s somewhat disparagingly termed these films 'the AFC genre' because of the active role the Australian Film Commission had taken in promoting European-style art cinema rather than the ocker comedies that were so popular in the early 1970s. These films have been characterized as 'Foregrounding their Australianness through the recreation of history and representations of the landscape; lyrically and beautifully shot; and employing aesthetic mannerisms such as a fondness for long, atmospheric shots, an avoidance of action or sustained conflict, and the use of slow motion to infer significance' (Turner 1989).

Beginning with the defining film of the genre, Peter Weir's *Picnic at Hanging Rock* (1975), and *Sunday Too Far Away* (Ken Hannam, 1975), *The Chant of Jimmie Blacksmith* (Fred Schepisi, 1978), *The Getting of Wisdom* (Bruce Beresford,

1978), *My Brilliant Career* (Gillian Armstrong, 1979) and *Gallipoli* (Peter Weir, 1981) through to the more saccharine *We of the Never Never* (Igor Auzins, 1982) and *The Man from Snow River* (George Miller, 1982), this collection of films is united by a very determined use of the Australian landscape not just as a backdrop but as a fundamental theme within the film. As Ross Gibson argues:

> ... by featuring the land so emphatically in the stories, all these films stake out something more significant than decorative pictorialism. Knowingly or unnkowingly, they are all engaging with the dominant mythology of white Australia. They are all partaking of the landscape-tradition which, for two hundred years, has been used by white Australians to promote a sense of the significance of European society in 'the antipodes'. (Gibson 1992: 64)

The Australian landscape tradition begins with painting and follows through to the period films. These films were heavily influenced by the iconic depictions of golden light, lost children and weary drovers painted by the so-called Heidelberg School of painters towards the end of the nineteenth century. Many of the members of the Heidelberg School, including Tom Roberts, Arthur Streeton and Frederick McCubbin, had been born in Australia and delighted in breaking with previous traditions of representation that owed much to classical European approaches to landscape. These painters enthusiastically embraced Impressionism, choosing to paint 'on location', and observing and recording the effects of light upon the landscape. Their paintings are typified by the relationship of figures to the landscape, and they were particularly interested in sunshine and glare, or as Streeton described it in a letter to McCubbin in 1891, 'the palpitating summer sunlight'. Their preferred subject matter was the bush, the figures were often lost women and children, and working men: bushmen, shearers and drovers. The reality of drought and hardship were idealized into a sense of the mythic aspects of survival in this 'harsh but beautiful' land. The mythologizing of the Australian bush had commenced in a way that resonated strongly with certain parts of the population as the Australian colonies moved towards Federation.

This mythic iconography of Australia translates directly to the period films, and indeed many of the films were set in the late nineteenth century, around the time that the Heidelberg painters were active. Several of the period films begin by dramatizing this mythic dialectic of nature and culture in their first frames: *Picnic at Hanging Rock* opens with the rock appearing out of the mists of dawn, and perhaps time, monolithic and primitive. As the music begins, the scene shifts to the green lawns and European propriety of the College – an anomaly in the rugged Australian landscape. *My Brilliant Career* begins with Sybylla trying to write, her cultural aspirations interrupted by an enormous dust storm, the forces of nature drawing her away from her intellectual pursuits. *Sunday Too Far Away* opens with Jack Thompson driving through the monotony of inland Australia. Lulled into sleep, he crashes his F J Holden and the car rolls over and over through the red dust. But the shearer is unruffled, he grabs his kit from the ruined vehicle and begins to walk, the vast expanse of countryside all around him.

The cinematography of the period films draws heavily upon the visual motifs of the Heidelberg school. *Sunday Too Far Away*'s cinematographer Geoff Burton expressed a sense of responsibility to pay homage to the paintings of Tom Roberts, to the extent that compositions such as 'Shearing the Rams', are carefully recreated within the film. Russell Boyd, often described as the 'Heidelberg cinematographer', was motivated by a concern with capturing the particular quality of Australian light in the manner of the painters of the late nineteenth century:

> It's something one becomes conscious of as a kid, to the extent where I guess the light's something you can't easily escape in Australia. And I guess when you transfer that to using that quality on film, one has to be prepared to suffer the rigours of the hard Australian light, and also try and not only communicate those on film but also to control the contrast of it, by either lighting or placement of subject against the sun or using early morning light or late afternoon light … it's certainly far different from the European, which is obviously softer and more diffused, and much more in fact controllable. (Boyd in Baxter 1986: 113–4)

Boyd's cinematographic approach to *Picnic at Hanging Rock* is suffused with this sense of light – the picnic scenes at the base of the rock are particularly painterly, recalling two paintings of the same theme and title, *Lost,* by McCubbin and Roberts. Indeed this scene had to be filmed over a number of days as direct sunlight only fell upon the picnic location for a few hours each day. Such was the concern for capturing this particular light, the schedule was arranged to accommodate the cinematographer. Boyd amplified the effects of the light by using a fine net (like that used for bridal veils) behind the lens to diffuse the light, making the image softer, and the backlight more glowing – a common technique at the time. But in a show of Australian ingenuity, Boyd dyed the white net with tea, to add an overall golden tint to the image, which was then further enhanced in the colour grading.

The Chant of Jimmie Blacksmith (Fred Schepisi, 1978) is an excoriating view of the treatment of a half-caste Aboriginal man by the white colonial society around Federation. Jimmie has been brought up by a white pastor to aspire to white society, and the film uses landscape to amplify the sense that Jimmy has lost his connection to the land through the forces of colonization. Nature is framed as potent force; there are many macro shots of cicadas and other fauna, which contrast with the immense scale of Jimmy dwarfed by the land, as he searches for work and respect from the white colonists. Even when he retreats into the bush after he murders a white family (possibly the most visceral scene from any of the films of this time – white lace splattered with blood), the land that he is alienated from seems merciless: huge rock faces, boulders filled with undefinable terror. In his flight Jimmie comes across an Aboriginal sacred ground that has been desecrated – the way he has – by white culture.

By the early 1980s, films such as *We of the Never Never* (Igor Auzins, 1982) seem to romanticize the landscape. The use of crane shots, backlight, and silhouettes against the sky gives an impression of clichéd pictorialism, the freshness of the earlier films subsiding to photographic tropes. No more apparent is this desire for the romantic than in *The Man from Snowy River* (George Miller, 1982). A frontier melodrama based on a Banjo Paterson poem, the film was extremely successful in Australia and in America, but its simplification of the Australian landscape into a 'hard land that makes hard men' is grandly trite. Ross Gibson neatly sums up the films of this time and the underlying nationalist imperative:

> The idea of the intractability of Australian nature has been an essential part of the national ethos … a notion perpetuated to this day by myriad legends of the Bush, that mythic region of isolation, moral simplicity, homelessness and the

> terrible beauty of 'nature learning how to write' … Because it has been pre-
> sented as so tantalizing and so essentially unknowable-yet-lovable, the land has
> become the cultural centre of the nation's myths of belonging. (Gibson 1992: 62)

According to Claude Lévi-Strauss, the function of myth is to play out resolutions of conflicts that in reality cannot be resolved. Unpicking the categorization of these films in particular as 'nostalgia films' allows a deeper understanding of the myth-making imperatives at work. The critique of nostalgia has been that it is a conservative force, idealizing the difficulties of the past with the rosy glow of hindsight. But the word nostalgia has origins that can lead us to a different understanding of the term. Coined in the late seventeenth century by a Swiss physician, Johannes Hofer, from the Greek 'nostos' – return home, and 'algia' – longing, nostalgia was a medical term used to describe the symptoms of intense melancholia and sadness suffered by Swiss soldiers fighting abroad, who, desir-ing to return home, drifted away from reality, became indifferent to their sur-roundings, confused past and present and even hallucinated ghosts and voices.

A more metaphorical notion of homesickness informs a new understanding of the period films. Perhaps these films are nostalgic, but in the sense that they are longing for a sense of home, that the fixation with the landscape and the recycling of the mythic Heidelberg images and a time in the past are symptoms of an unease with their place within it. Can you be homesick when at home? If you do not feel that you belong, perhaps so. The 1970s was a time when the issues of Land Rights and Indigenous culture were moving toward the centre of national debate. The desire for a sense of belonging that these films dramatize, speaks of the problems of a colonial culture still unreconciled with its Indigenous population. As Svetlana Boym writes: 'Nostalgia is a sentiment of loss and dis-placement but it is also a romance of one's own fantasy' (Boym 2001: xiii). Both these impulses seem to operate within the films and lead us to see that perhaps it is not the Australian landscape that is filled with 'weird melancholy', as Marcus Clarke wrote at the end of the nineteenth century, but rather that its film-makers were, as they framed up the landscape of Australia in the 1970s in the hope of finding something of themselves within it.

Bonnie Elliott

Caddie

Country of Origin:
Australia

Director:
Donald Crombie

Producer:
Anthony Buckley

Screenwriter:
Joan Long, adapted from
the autobiography *Caddie: A
Sydney Barmaid*

Cinematographer:
Peter James

Art Director:
Owen Williams

Editor:
Tim Wellburn

Genre:
Period Drama

Duration:
103 minutes

Cast:
Helen Morse
Takis Emmanuel
Jack Thompson
Jacki Weaver
Melissa Jaffer
Ron Blanchard

Year:
1976

Synopsis

Sydney, 1925. A young, middle-class woman learns that her husband is having an affair with her best friend. After a fight, she leaves
him, taking their two young children with her. They live in a series
of squalid boarding houses and dilapidated rented rooms while she
works as a barmaid to support them. A friendly fellow barmaid, Josie,
helps her learn the ropes. Ted, the local SP bookmaker, nicknames her
'Caddie' after his brand new Cadillac, because she, like his car, has
'beauty and class'. Caddie's daughter contracts diphtheria and almost
dies. Josie goes to an illegal abortionist to terminate her pregnancy.
Ted takes Caddie to a dance where a woman who claims to have
been 'knocking around' with Ted for two years threatens her. She
ends her relationship with Ted, and decides to find a new job. Josie
convinces Caddie to put her children in a children's home. A few years
later, Caddie is working in an upmarket pub. Her colleague Leslie
invites her to a party, and on the way she meets Peter, a handsome,
married Greek businessman. Peter and Caddie become lovers, but
he is called back to Greece when his father falls ill. Two years later, in
the midst of the Great Depression, Caddie brings her children to live
with her again, but she is forced to claim unemployment assistance
when she loses her job. After falling ill with malnutrition and nervous
exhaustion, she is helped by Bill, who ekes out a living selling rabbit
meat. After staying with Bill and his brother Sonny for some time to
recuperate, Caddie's fortunes improve when she again finds bar work
and is employed by an illegal bookmaker. She receives a letter from
Peter telling her he has divorced his wife and asking her to come to
Greece to live with him but because her own divorce is not finalized
she cannot take her children with her. She stays in Sydney. Through a
final intertitle we learn that Peter later returned to Australia to live with
Caddie, but was killed in a car crash before they could be married.

Critique

Caddie was one of the first of the swag of period dramas that have
become synonymous with the second half of the 1970s and which collectively make up the so-called 'AFC genre'. These films deliberately
departed from the contemporary, blokey world of the ocker comedies, not only to the extent that they were set in the past, but also
in their tendency to draw on Australian novels in order to gain both
from their cultural cachet and from the audience's familiarity with their
stories. In a further mark of distinction and difference from the ocker
comedies *Caddie*, like four other key period films – *Picnic at Hanging
Rock* (Peter Weir, 1975), *The Getting of Wisdom* (Bruce Beresford,
1978), *My Brilliant Career* (Gillian Armstrong, 1979), and *We of the
Never Never* (Ivor Auzins, 1982) – was based on a book by a woman,
about the experience of women. As Dianne Kirkby has argued in an
article on *Caddie*, these films provide insights into women's history,
and illuminate issues around gender politics both in the periods
they depict and at the time they were made, when women's experiences and points of view were often secondary to men's. *Caddie* has

been criticized for its sprawling shape, and for its lack of dramatic action. Indeed, perhaps the most dramatic and emotionally-affecting moment in the film is told rather than shown: a closing onscreen title announces that Peter returned to Caddie, but died in a car accident before they could marry. Rather than ending on this powerful, if down-beat, event, Crombie chooses to finish the film some years before, as Caddie realizes she cannot leave her children and travel to Greece to be with Peter. She throws herself disconsolately onto her bed, only to be interrupted by her two children who are playing dress-ups. Her mood is transformed by their playfulness and sense of fun, and the credits roll over images of Caddie and her children laughing. The implication is clear: at the heart of Caddie's story is her commitment to her children, and although it is dramatically unsatisfying, this is a positive and appropriate final scene. It is consistent with the concentration throughout the film on the choices Caddie must make and the challenges she faces. This kind of low-key ending, with further explanatory detail provided in an end title, is typical of the AFC genre and featuring in a number of films, including *Picnic at Hanging Rock*, *My Brilliant Career*, and *Sunday Too Far Away* (Ken Hannam, 1975).

Unlike many of the AFC genre films, which were either written or set in the period around the turn of the twentieth century, and which consciously drew on the imagery and sensibilities of Australian art and literature of that period and depicted aspects of life in the outback or in regional Australia, *Caddie* is set in the working-class suburbs of inner-city Sydney in the late 1920s and early 1930s. More than any of their contemporaries, Crombie, his producer Anthony Buckley and screenwriter Joan Long drew on early Australian films like Raymond Longford's *The Sentimental Bloke* (1919) and *Sunshine Sally* (Lawson Harris, 1922) to inform the look and ambience of *Caddie*'s period setting. Like these earlier films, *Caddie* is an affectionate portrait of the urban working class, and includes depictions of familiar routines of the period, like the 'six o'clock swill'. At this time, hotels or pubs in Australia were forced to close at 6pm to encourage working men to return to their families. As a result, the public bar became rowdier and more unruly than usual in the minutes leading up to closing time. In one scene, Caddie, not long a barmaid, is bewildered and almost overcome by the crush of men desperately trying to buy a last drink. Later in the film, Caddie's lover Peter voices his disgust over the 'uncivilized' drinking habits of Australians. Caddie takes this observation of cultural difference as a slight on her countrymen and on her profession, and mounts an impassioned defence of both. As this episode shows, like the main characters in Beresford's, Armstrong's and Auzins's films, Caddie is a determined, strong-willed, independent woman who struggles with social and environmental constraints, and whose ultimate triumph is to endure the circumstances in which she finds herself. In many ways, Caddie is the quintessential little Aussie battler: self-sufficient, stoic, yet able to draw when necessary on the kindness and community spirit of those around her.

Two scenes in the film are particularly memorable. The opening, pre-title sequence, in which Caddie prepares to leave her middle-class home, comprises a series of long, lateral tracking shots along the front of the house which parallel Caddie's movements inside as she walks from room to room collecting her belongings. As the camera tracks languidly from side to side looking towards the house from outside, Caddie and the children are glimpsed through windows and through the open front door. A considerable amount of screen time is taken up with views of the external brick walls of the house as the camera moves between the windows and the door. Many directors would have chosen not to shoot the walls, or to edit out what might be considered 'dead space'. But these views of the bricks not only break up our contemplation of the as-yet unexplained goings-on in the house, their tidy uniformity sets up a neat contrast with the run-down, mostly wooden dwellings that Caddie and her children will occupy for the rest of the film. The other memorable shot contains no camera movement. When Caddie hands over her son to the matron at the children's home, we see the boy in a head and shoulders shot at his eye level as he looks up at the women who are standing either side of him discussing his fate. They are only visible from the waist down, emphasizing how small and powerless he is, and his quiet despair is heartbreaking to see.

Caddie is based on the autobiography, *Caddie: A Sydney Barmaid*, which was published in 1953. Edited and with an introduction by Dymphna Cusack, herself a novelist, colleague and collaborator with several of the leading Australian literary figures of the first half of the twentieth century, the book quickly became a best-seller. The film was equally successful both in Australia (where it was one of the highest-grossing films of 1977) and overseas, particularly in Argentina, where it enjoyed a 14-week run in cinemas. The film also won a number of Australian Film Institute awards for the actors Helen Morse (Best Actress), Drew Forsythe (Best Supporting Actor), and Jacki Weaver and Melissa Jaffer, who shared the Best Supporting Actress prize. First-time director Donald Crombie, who won the Jury Prize at the San Sebastian Film Festival for *Caddie*, went on to make another important period drama, *The Irishman*, in 1978 with many of the same crew.

Ben Goldsmith

My Brilliant Career

Country of Origin:
Australia

Director:
Gillian Armstrong

Producer:
Margaret Fink

Screenwriter:
Eleanor Witcombe (from the novel by Miles Franklin)

Synopsis

Sybylla Melvin is a young woman with bigger dreams than life as a wife and mother in the bush – she wants to write. However there is little time for this in her day-to-day life on the drought-stricken farm she lives on with her family. There is only time (as she says in voice over as she milks a cow) to work and sleep. The financial woes of the family lead her mother to send her away to her rich grandmother's home. So begins Sybylla's complicated journey toward selfhood. At the lush green homestead of Caddagat she grapples with how behave in a ladylike fashion, and how to reconcile herself to the social order. When Sybylla falls in love with the well-to-do landowner, Harry Beacham, she is faced with her toughest decision when he asks for her hand in marriage. But ultimately Sybylla cannot agree to marry, as she fears she will never fulfil her dream to write if she does. Unable to

Composer:
Nathan Waks

Cinematographer:
Donald McAlpine

Editor:
Nicholas Beauman

Production Designer:
Luciana Arrighi

Duration:
100 minutes

Genre:
Period Film

Cast:
Judy Davis
Sam Neill
Wendy Hughes
Robert Grubb
Max Cullen
Aileen Britton
Peter Whitford

Year:
1979

settle for a life in the bush, 'having a baby every year', she chooses her 'brilliant' career over love, and writes her novel.

Critique

My Brilliant Career is based on the novel of the same name published in 1901 by Miles Franklin. Miles Franklin was a female writer who wrote of themes close to her heart – the difficult choice faced by women between personal creative fulfilment and the traditional domestic role of wife and mother. This was a theme that resonated strongly in the 1970s, as more women entered the workforce in the aftermath of the Women's Liberation movement of the 1960s, and discovered that equal opportunities often translated into a choice between work and marriage. The transposition of these contemporary themes into the Period film was a canny manoeuvre by female producer Margot Fink and female director Gillian Armstrong. *My Brilliant Career* has a freshness of theme that resonates to this day, helped enormously by the charismatic performance of Judy Davis in her first major role.

My Brilliant Career very actively engages with the powerful mythology of the Australian outback – nature and culture are seen as two distinct oppositional forces. Sybylla longs to be away from the bush, to be immersed in culture, in the world of music, ideas and language. As she says to her sister in an early scene of the film: 'Don't you dream of more than this? Living out in the bush, I might as well be dead!' The first scene of the film opens with Sybylla beginning to write her story, only to be interrupted by the primal force of nature outside as a huge dust storm engulfs the farm, forcing her away from her desk. The theme of drought is established early – the opening shot of the film is a wide shot of the family farm in bright sunlight, the landscape bleached and pale, a frame very reminiscent of Arthur Streeton's painting *The Selectors Hut* (1890) with its huge expanse of sky. Don McAlpine's cinematography powerfully contrasts the harsh dry landscape of Sybylla's family farm with the seductive lushness of her grandmother's verdant English-style home and gardens. In this section the compositions are very painterly, recalling the palette and design of French Impressionism, which is carried through by the art direction of the interiors at Caddagat. Luciana Arrighi uses fresh floral tones in the wallpaper, and arrangements of fresh green leaves in vases. Cultivated nature is ever present in the frame, contrasting with the sombre earthiness of the farm.

Breaking up the simple dialectic of nature versus culture is Sybylla herself, who seems to operate as a force of some other kind, disrupting the accepted order of things. Her Aunt Helen tells her that she has 'a wildness of spirit that is going to get you into trouble all your life. So you must try and learn to control it, and try and cultivate a little feminine vanity.' This wildness in Sybylla is symbolized by water throughout the film. In a scene following her *My Fair Lady*-style makeover, she is presented with a bunch of flowers by a possible suitor as she reads delicately by a picture-perfect lake – only to give in to her own sense of life and throw the flowers in the lake. Drops of rain begin to fall, and she jumps up, allowing herself to revel in the downpour soaked to the skin. Sybylla longs for water after so many years of her drought on the family farm, but it is also a metaphor for her *self*. And it is this irrepressible nature of hers that literally rocks the boat, when she is being punted around a lake in an elegant courtship by Harry, she purposefully capsizes the punt, and they are submerged – Sybylla rejecting this mirage of happiness in favour of unknown depths. This is perhaps what is so powerful about *My Brilliant Career* – it is a story that could be Australia's version of *Pride & Prejudice*, though it upends Jane Austen's novel, inserting a thoroughly-modern character into the outback mythology. Gillian Armstrong and Margaret Fink stood up for Miles Franklin's original ending to the novel when film investors were unsure, and the bold image of Sybylla alone at the gate, after posting her novel, looking off into the setting sun, is an image that subtly recalls the iconic moment of Vivien Leigh standing alone in a technicolour sunset in *Gone with the Wind*, saying 'I will go on'. *My Brilliant Career* is a film that does not simplify the complexity of Sybylla's decision, and its themes continue to resonate strongly today.

Bonnie Elliott

We of the Never Never

Director:
Igor Auzins

Producer:
Greg Tepper

Screenwriter:
Peter Schreck, adapted from the novel by Mrs Aeneas Gunn

Cinematographer:
Garry Hansen

Music:
Peter Best

Editor:
Clifford Hayes

Production Designer:
Josephine Ford

Duration:
134 minutes

Genre:
Period Film

Synopsis

We of the Never Never tells the story of the newly-married Jeannie Gunn who follows her husband Aeneas out into the vast Northern Territory outback as he takes over the running of a cattle and horse property, Elsey Station. Jeannie is greeted by coldness and suspicion from the white stockmen who believe that the outback is no place for a woman. But Jeannie refuses to give in, and tries hard to win their respect. Isolated, she turns to the Aboriginal women of the station for friendship, and slowly she finds her sense of belonging, although it is tested by death and tragedy.

Critique

Based on the popular autobiography of Mrs Aeneas Gunn published in 1908, *We of the Never Never* is a classic fish-out-of-water story. The underlying theme of the film is place – first of Jeannie finding 'her place' as a marginalized woman in a sexist male word and, more generally, for all the people of Elsey Station. Jeannie is confronted by the racism of the white stockmen towards the Aboriginal people of the station, and tries in her own way to change the situation, asking 'Why does it have to be them and us? Why can't we live together?' However she rarely respects the actual cultural systems of the Aboriginal characters, often meddling in matters like a missionary. When she attempts to adopt the young half-caste girl Bett Bett, it is mostly because she needs her to assuage her own loneliness. The film clearly wants to tackle the issue of race relations, yet it never really gets under the skin of the matter. The film-makers give us a fairly one-dimensional portrait of the Aboriginal characters in the film, never

Cast:
Angela Punch McGregor
Arthur Dignam
Martin Vaughan
Lewis Fitz-Gerald
John Jarratt
Tommy Lewis

Year:
1982

allowing us to really know them – there are many onscreen dialogues in Aboriginal languages which are never sub-titled. The closest we get is to the character of Goggle Eye, who delivers the pithiest line in the film around the issue of land ownership. Sitting around two nearby campfires, one for the whites, one for the blackfellas, they discuss how the stars were made, and he tells a traditional Aboriginal creation story. Mrs Gunn tries to convince him that it is God who made everything, including the stars. Goggle Eye replies if 'Whitefella god made everything, then why didn't he make whitefellas some bush of their own?'

We of the Never Never is a romantic film. It romanticizes the pioneering life and aims for an epic feel. Huge cattle musters, horses thundering through the backlit dust, countless crane shots that rise up to reveal the vast scale of the landscape, conspire to create this romanticized vision. Shot in cinemascope anamorphic for the wide screen, cinematographer Garry Hansen really milks the idea that a big country needs a big frame. Wide-angle lenses are often used, most notably in the helicopter shot that runs underneath the credits as the

Caddie, Roadshow/Buckley.

camera flies over tracts of empty land to finally find a lone horse-man traversing the landscape, the horizon line curving in space. The grandiose visuals are often matched with a somewhat overwrought score. Strings swell, harmonicas strain for emotion, the didgeridoo gets added for drama, and the melody of Waltzing Matilda even makes a brief appearance, making the overall tone of the film quite cloying at times. The desire to tell an epic tale of our settlement is an impulse that has not gone away – Baz Lurhmann's recent attempt with *Australia* (2008) shares a surprising amount of story points, themes and visual style with this earlier effort from Igor Auzins.

The uncertainty of one's place was indeed an appropriate theme for a white film-maker to tackle in the early 1980s, as the Aboriginal land rights movement grew in strength, leading to the 1992 Mabo decision which overturned the legal fiction that Australia was 'terra nullius' or an empty land and therefore able to be colonized without recompense to the traditional owners and occupiers. *We of the Never Never* explores the issue of colonization to some degree, but this is mostly subsumed into the overall 'plucky woman' story it tells, the film settling for a celebration of Jeannie's sympathy towards the Aboriginal people, despite her behaviour being misguided and patronizing. More frustratingly, the film never really attempts to give any depth or complexity to the Aboriginal characters, or perspective within the story; they are as silent as the many termite mounds that surround the homestead at Elsey station, bearing mute witness to the histrionics of the whitefellas.

Bonnie Elliott

COMEDY

Comedy has been a significant genre of Australian cinema since the silent film period. A perennially popular staple genre of international cinema, in Australia, film comedy has sometimes served as an index of the local industry's resurgence in the face of the overshadowing influence of other film industries, particularly Hollywood. Australian comedy film can be understood in relation to Australian humour as a more general national propensity, identified by Dorothy Jones (1985) in earlier literature and other print works, and also in relation to the textual forms and modes of the comedy genre, through which Australian film has long engaged with a range of media that includes vaudeville theatre, radio and television.

In histories of Australian silent film, most of the attention given to humour has centred on films that seek to represent uniquely Australian subject matter. Such examples as Raymond Longford's *The Sentimental Bloke* (1919) and *On Our Selection* (1920) are undoubtedly important comedic and romantic film narratives about urban and rural Australian life. Yet these films have tended to receive more attention for their Australian subject matter and literary origins (in works by C J Dennis and Steele Rudd, respectively) than for their possible contributions to the comedy genre. Moreover, silent Australian cinema includes a wider range of short and feature-length comedies that includes less acclaimed rural narratives, and films with origins in theatrical farce or vaudeville that place less emphasis on uniquely Australian subject matter. Such films as *Our Friends, The Hayseeds* (Beaumont Smith, 1917), *The Laugh on Dad* (A C Tinsdale, 1918), *The Waybacks* (Arthur W Sterry, 1918), *Algie's Romance* (Leonard Doogood, 1918) and *Hullo Marmaduke* (Beaumont Smith, 1924) reflect the diversity of early Australian film comedy and the local industry's capacity to produce inexpensive, lightweight entertainment that does not seem to take nationalist or elitist concerns seriously: traits that form a general precedent for the proliferation of locally-made exploitation comedies in the 1970s.

Hollywood's economic domination of the local film industry from the 1920s onwards threatened local production but did not put an immediate end to local comedy films. Indeed, films produced in the 1930s by local studios, Efftee Film Productions and Cinesound Productions, reflect an active investment in humour and constitute this as one of the most prolific periods for Australian comedy film. Examples of the wide range of comedies produced in this period are F W Thring's and Ken G Hall's broad versions of, respectively, The Sentimental Bloke (1932) and On Our Selection (1932); the films starring local vaudeville comedians George Wallace and Roy Rene; service comedies such as Diggers (F W Thring, 1931); and the comedy of manners in It Isn't Done (Ken G Hall, 1937). A significant lapse in local production of comedy films occurred only after Cinesound ceased feature production in 1940 because of the war, a decision that affected all genres of Australian feature film-making.

Although continuity between Australian comedies produced before and after World War II is not immediately apparent, closer examination qualifies this perception. For instance, radio is a point of continuity between the post-war success of Roy Rene and George Wallace in this medium and the subsequent career of Graham Kennedy, whose work in radio, television and film typifies how the film industry's revival in the 1970s drew personnel from other local media industries. Such prominent contributors to post-war comedy as Graham Kennedy, Tim Burstall and Max Gillies have acknowledged the legacies of Wallace and Rene as vital influences. Among very few comedies produced in Australia between 1940 and 1970, the prominent example of They're a Weird Mob (Michael Powell, 1966) forms a link between the prewar period and the industry's revival in the 1970s. While Tom O'Regan has noted that this film 'forges a path for later comedy films and humourists' (O'Regan 1996: 251), the othering of the Australian and the ethnic humour in They're a Weird Mob have precedents in Strike Me Lucky (Ken G Hall, 1934), the only film starring Jewish-Australian comedian Roy Rene.

As though reflecting inversely the proliferation of Australian film comedies during the film industry's struggle in the 1930s, the industry's revival in the 1970s was initially driven by comedy. The 'ocker' film cycle of this period was fuelled by the box office success of The Adventures of Barry McKenzie (Bruce Beresford, 1972) and Alvin Purple (Tim Burstall, 1973). Characterized by 'unabashed celebration of the "Australian", particularly the vernacular, whether in speech, content, or action' (O'Regan 1989: 76), and tending to emphasize traits associated with working-class Australians, the ocker films reflect the resurgent nationalism of a period when Australia was becoming more cosmopolitan and gradually discarding the 'cultural cringe' associated with its historical relationship to Britain. The influence on the ocker cycle of personnel and textual strategies derived from variety television, comedy revue, experimental and avant-garde theatre and bestselling books position this cycle at the nexus of various emergent cultural developments (O'Regan 1989: 79).

Notwithstanding the difficulty of defining the ocker cycle in terms of any particular textual strategy, this predominantly comedic cycle is important for being so profitable as to revive the local film industry, and for its subsequently pivotal role in a major shift in government film funding policy. Curtailed by the Australian government's decision in the mid-1970s to redirect funding away from comedy films[1] and towards period and art films that were more acceptable to middle-class audiences, the ocker cycle has recently been a focus of renewed interest. Viewed in historical perspective, the ocker films are receiving greater recognition for their exceptionally vivid portrayals of Australian identity, their close relationship to a resurgence of Australian nationalism around the period of Gough Whitlam's government, and for the injustice of the cycle's demise, a shift in Australian film history that seems, today, to highlight the salience of the ocker cycle and the daring with which it confronted Australians' perceptions of class identity and class difference within their own society.

Although the term 'ocker' is associated specifically with films made in the 1970s and, more particularly, with middle-class stereotyping of working-class Australians, the assertion of distinctively Australian behaviour through comedy forms a link between the ocker cycle and Australian comedies of earlier and later periods. In films made before World War II, for instance, the urban settings and vernacular language of films made in the 1970s are prefigured in *The Sentimental Bloke* and the 1930s' comedies of George Wallace. In *They're a Weird Mob*, made by British director Michael Powell in 1966, the Italian protagonist's adoption of the language and other customs of working-class Australians provides further precedents for the 1970s comedies. The legacy of the ocker cycle is suggested in a scattered range of subsequent Australian comedies that include behaviour redolent of characters in the 1970s' comedies. Examples are the exaggeratedly- aconic, masculine demeanour of the protagonist in *Crocodile Dundee* (Peter Faiman, 1986); the portrayal of the Kerrigan family in *The Castle* (Rob Sitch, 1997) as naively proud working-class Australians; and the vulgar assertion of recent immigrant identities as performative variations on brash Australian masculinity in *The Nog Boy* (Aleksi Vellis, 2000) and *Fat Pizza* (Paul Fenech, 2003).

Aside from these predominantly masculine trajectories of Australian screen culture, comedy has also been central to other late twentieth-century developments in Australian film. For instance, Felicity Collins (2002) has shown that romantic and grotesque comedy are used to explore female social and familial roles in a number of Australian films written and directed by women in the 1980s and 1990s. Prominent examples are *Sweetie* (Jane Campion, 1989) and *Love and Other Catastrophes* (Emma-Kate Croghan, 1996). Loosely contemporaneous with these explorations of female relationships are two high-profile film adaptations of Australian novels about girlhood by women, *Puberty Blues* (Bruce Beresford, 1981) and *Looking for Alibrandi* (Kate Woods, 2000). Depicting experiences that range from disjunctive sexual relationships to unfulfilling sexual encounters and the emotional challenges of familial relationships and social exclusion, uses of humour in Australian films about female perspectives resonate with the idea, expressed by Dorothy Jones, that Australian humour is frequently a response to failed aspiration and hope (Jones 1985: 79). As though answering the ocker cycle's crude assertion of Australian masculinity, later Australian films that are shaped by women display no less affinity for comedy but posit romance and relationships with family and with other women as themes of greater importance than beer consumption, urination and male sexual fantasy.

Such developments have been paralleled by an encompassing debate about the significance of suburbia and its associated lifestyles as subject matter for Australian entertainment. Sue Turnbull has drawn attention to the recurrent significance of comedy in this debate, which, even in the early twentieth century, saw suburban women being satirized as proponents of a 'politics of niceness' (Turnbull 2008: 19). The division between cultural elites' preference for the bush and the fact that a majority of Australians inhabit suburbs may be seen to underpin the high cultural value attributed to such works as *On Our Selection*. The directing of satire at Australian suburban lifestyles and aspirations become more pronounced after World War II in the work of Barry Humphries, however, whose alter ego of Dame Edna Everage Turnbull views as a predecessor to the television series *Kath and Kim* (2002–). At the same time, the abundance of Australian comedic depictions of suburbia, satirical or otherwise, encompasses a much wider range of works that includes *Puberty Blues*, *The Castle* and *Muriel's Wedding* (P J Hogan, 1994), to name but a few. The ambivalence that Turnbull identifies by asking if Australian comedy about suburbia is 'perceived to be a critique or a celebration' (Turnbull 2008: 28) highlights an issue of longstanding significance in Australian society and remains open to further exploration.

Note
1. The first national film agency, the Australian Film Development Corporation, provided financial backing for several ocker films, including the entire $250,000 budget of *The Adventures of Barry McKenzie*. The replacement of the AFDC by the Australian Film Commission in 1975 marked the turning point. See Ben Goldsmith 'Government, Film and the National Image: Reappraising the Australian Film Development Corporation,' in *Australian Studies* vol 12 no 1 (1997).

Lesley Speed

His Royal Highness

Country of Origin:
Australia

Studio:
Efftee Film Productions

Director:
F W Thring

Screenwriters:
C J Dennis
George Wallace

Cinematographer:
Arthur Higgins

Art Director:
W R Coleman

Duration:
90 minutes

Genre:
Musical Comedy

Cast:
John Dobbie
George Wallace
Byrl Walkley
Marshall Crosby

Year:
1932

Synopsis

Tommy Dodds, an aspiring vaudevillian who is infatuated with a stage actress, Molly, obtains employment as a stagehand. Backstage, a disgruntled employee hits Tommy on the head and the protagonist finds himself back in the streets of Fitzroy, where two men recognize him as the lost heir to the throne of Betonia. The voyage from Australia to Betonia reveals how ill-prepared Tommy is for this new role, however. After coronation, Tommy causes chaos by seeking to have his friend appointed to an official position, teaching the Prime Minister to roller skate and arousing the envy of a pretender to the throne, Torano, who arranges for him to be poisoned. Yet the King survives and takes control of the palace by playing cards with his footmen and taking Betonia to war. With the subsequent arrival of the true heir to the throne, Tommy is unceremoniously ejected by court officials. Recovering consciousness backstage in Australia, Tommy resumes nursing his longing for Molly as she leaves the stage door with another man.

Critique

His Royal Highness is the first of five feature films starring comedian George Wallace and the first of three Wallace films that F W Thring directed for his Efftee Film Productions. A successful stage comedian from the 1920s onwards, Wallace's vaudeville popularity was exceeded only by that of Roy 'Mo' Rene. In film, however, the financial success and duration of Wallace's career eclipsed Rene and positions Wallace as the most significant star of Australian comedian comedy films before World War II.

Thring's goal to produce a film record of Australian vaudeville performers is both historically valuable and a source of textual incoherence, exemplified by the relative lack of narrative motivation for a vaudeville routine by Wallace. Indeed, Thring's limited artistic aspirations occasionally undermine the historic value of his work. While the film's obtrusive background noise and abrupt shifts in volume may be attributed to the relative newness of sound-film technology, poor directorial judgement must be blamed, at least partly, for the omission of Wallace's feet from view during his tap dance. Notwithstanding these shortcomings, and the tendency for the impoverished *mise-en-scène* to suggest inferior imitation of Hollywood, the narrative and themes of *His Royal Highness* are of considerable interest.

The film both echoes international styles and suggests Australia's strained relationship to Britain in the Great Depression. *His Royal Highness* is an early example of a proliferation of English-language comedy films set in fictional countries that appeared in the period from 1930 to 1940. This independently-conceived satire anticipates developments in 1930s' Hollywood comedy. Differing from contemporaneous American films set in fictional countries that are not monarchies, the fictional setting of *His Royal Highness* also contrasts with British royal formality through incorporating musical numbers, pratfalls and roller-skating. The film thus envisages an empire that is

His Royal Highness, Efftee Film Productions.

an alternative to Britain, suggesting Australia's remoteness and lack of commitment to Europe. The film defies a perception of 1930s' Australian film-making as conservative by depicting an ordinary Australian's introduction of chaos into monarchy. If the narrative's ultimate reinstatement of Tommy's original circumstances reinforces a class status quo, his longing for the unattainable Molly suggests persistent unfulfilment rather than acceptance of circumstances. In *His Royal Highness*, anarchy wrought by the protagonist is linked to empowerment and failed accession to maturity.

Lesley Speed

Harmony Row

Country of Origin:
Australia

Studio:
Efftee Film Productions

Director:
F W Thring

Screenwriter:
George Wallace

Cinematographer:
Arthur Higgins

Art Director:
W R Coleman

Duration:
80 minutes

Genre:
Comedy (the title card includes the subtitle 'a farce-comedy')

Cast:
Bill Kerr (credited as Willie Kerr)
John Dobbie
George Wallace
Thelma Scott
Marshall Crosby

Year:
1933

Synopsis

Nicknamed 'Dreadnought' because of his reputation as a boxer, Tommy Wallace joins the Victoria Police force. His first posting is to the inner-city slum neighbourhood of Harmony Row, which is under threat from a bully named Slogger Lee. Spending much of his time conversing and becoming drawn to a local woman named Molly, Dreadnought's ineptitude at police work is revealed when he is threatened by locals, robbed by a young boy, and encounters a wanted criminal. Posted then to an affluent neighbourhood with a lower crime rate, the protagonist enters a house that is thought to be haunted and becomes drawn into intrigue involving missing jewels, culminating in an encounter with Slogger Lee. Posted back to Harmony Row, Dreadnought's troubles return when he is involved in a brawl with an abusive husband and then with the man's wife. Losing patience at the man's persistent failure as a police officer, Dreadnought's superior officer asks him to fight Slogger Lee in a boxing match. Although his opponent is much larger, Dreadnought ultimately triumphs after reconciling with Molly.

Critique

Harmony Row is the second of three films starring comedian George Wallace and directed by F W Thring. Like Wallace's previous collaboration with Thring, the film has a loosely-structured narrative that is subordinated at times to episodes that are little more than filmed vaudeville routines, clearly intended to showcase the star's comedic skills. The sequences, in which the protagonist enlists in the police force and starts with his first day at work, showcase Wallace's characteristically naive 'fish out of water' persona and his playfully-comedic use of language. Although the direction is often undynamic, including long takes that unfortunately emphasize the artificial sets of urban Harmony Row, the haunted-house segment makes more elaborate use of *mise-en-scène,* and the boxing sequence is both convincingly staged and ably shot and edited. While the narrative premises of the inexperienced policeman and the undersized boxer are redolent of films of Charles Chaplin, the film is nonetheless noteworthy as an example of market-driven Australian film-making in the 1930s.

Harmony Row exemplifies how Wallace's films engage with international cinematic developments, deriving their Australianness from local performers and passing allusions to local entities rather than clumsy or conspicuous use of such overtly Australian iconographic elements as outback settings and indigenous fauna. Independent by virtue of being produced outside the major Hollywood studios, Wallace's films display production and marketing strategies that are redolent of production of 'B' films by small American film companies. The latter opted for modest budgets and emulation of genres familiar from major studio productions. Equally, the scene of the 'haunted' house in Harmony Row, including secret panels and a hidden skeleton, can be read as an attempt to capitalize on the recent success of such foreign horror films as *The Cat and the Canary* (Paul Leni, 1927) and *Dracula* (Tod Browning, 1931). The film is thus a relatively early example of a comedic variation on the horror genre.

Although comedic representations of ghost stories had appeared previously in cinema, slapstick treatments of horror subject matter did not proliferate until after World War II in Hollywood. In this context, Dreadnought's comedic encounters with a hidden skeleton, secret doors and a zombie-like character who resembles Frankenstein's monster seems rather imaginative for its period. Harmony Row thus highlights the resourcefulness of Australian film-makers by exemplifying how Wallace's films utilized low-budget film-making strategies similar to those being used abroad. Produced in a period in which Australian films included little reference to the Depression, this film suggests that local film-makers were nonetheless attentive to contemporary film developments and the potential box office appeal of comedic treatments of other genres.

Lesley Speed

A Ticket in Tatts

Country of Origin:
Australia

Studio:
Efftee Film Productions

Director:
F W Thring

Screenwriters:
George Wallace
John P McLeod

Cinematographer:
Arthur Higgins

Art Director:
W R Coleman

Editor:
W Albrecht

Genre:
Comedy

Duration:
88 minutes

Synopsis

George is employed as a delivery man at a general store. He appropriates sugar from a customer's order to feed his favourite racehorse Hotspur, a Melbourne Cup contender that is stabled at a nearby stud farm. When George visits the farm to see Hotspur and his sweetheart, a servant named Marjorie, he is scolded after his whistle prompts Hotspur to win a tryout race. The next morning, George is left in charge of the store and causes havoc by mishandling food, offending a customer, knocking a man unconscious and causing shelves to collapse. Consequently losing his job, George obtains employment as a stable hand at the farm. Meanwhile, a subplot develops about an aristocratic romance that involves two men competing to marry the stud farmer's daughter Dorothy. The stable hands discover a plot to sabotage Hotspur's performance in the Melbourne Cup, prompting George to seek information by posing as a singing waiter at a nightclub where the criminals meet. Although Hotspur's jockey in the Melbourne Cup is in league with the criminals, the horse wins at the last minute after George whistles. The film ends with the unions of George and Marjorie and Dorothy and her beau.

Critique

A Ticket in Tatts is the last of three feature films starring comedian George Wallace that were directed by F W Thring. Whereas their previous films were filmed largely in studios and only intermittently integrate Wallace's routines into overarching narratives, *A Ticket in Tatts* is a significant departure from filmed vaudeville sequences. The film's more developed *mise-en-scène* includes outdoor scenes at the store, the stables, the Summers' mansion and Flemington Racecourse. The film also includes an elaborately-staged nightclub scene, although the latter is now particularly outdated. Indeed, little entertainment

Cast:
Thelma Scott
George Wallace
John Dobbie
Frank Harvey
Campbell Copelin
Marshall Crosby

Year:
1934

can be derived today from the scene's inclusion of a song that refers to 'darkies picking cotton' and a comedic skit about female soldiers. Notwithstanding the largely-historical significance of some sequences, the film is noteworthy for including another engaging performance by George Wallace and for a narrative that centres on a characteristically Australian interest in sport, in the form of horseracing.

Of Wallace's films, *A Ticket in Tatts* is one of those that contribute most clearly to his status as a distinctively Australian star of comedian comedy films, a tradition associated most strongly with US cinema. The comedian comedies' usual accommodation of contradiction between the fictional story and the star's persona accounts for the lengthy grocery store scene in *A Ticket in Tatts*. While this episode fulfils narrative functions, the amusement it generates in spectators has less to do with its narrative role than with Wallace's skills as a vaudeville performer. Throughout the film he gathers even insignificant plot elements into a characterization that juxtaposes spontaneous foolishness with deliberately failed seriousness. A brief sequence, in which George clutches opportunistically at Marjorie while they watch a horse race, is imbued as clearly with Wallace's naive comedic persona as a pivotal narrative episode in which the protagonist reveals to a pair of criminals the security measures taken to protect Hotspur. Indeed, the latter episode is a masterfully-comic evocation of a calculating manoeuvre in ingenuous form.

Within a framework of comedian comedy, *A Ticket in Tatts* alludes to a model of Australian masculine identity that is characterized by informality, egalitarianism, an attachment to the outdoors and an interest in sport. The film's positioning of George's enthusiasm for horseracing as ultimately more effective than the work of professional horse trainers exemplifies a longstanding Australian tendency to privilege activities of ordinary, working-class people over those of professionals and intellectuals. In the nightclub scene, the comedic ineptitude of Wallace's juxtaposing of tap dancing with pratfalls equally suggests an Australian aversion to flawless displays of professionalism even though this trademark of Wallace's work was unusual among performers both within and outside Australia. Episodes in which George and his fellow stable hands (including the star's frequent collaborator, John Dobbie) engage in practical jokes are imbued with Australian traits of easygoing humour and disregard for hard work. Although overtly-Australian entities are not emphasized in *A Ticket in Tatts*, only casually evident in the narrative role of the Melbourne Cup and references to such entities as Flemington Racecourse and Phar Lap, the film nonetheless constitutes an Australian variant of comedian comedy.

Lesley Speed

Strike Me Lucky

Country of Origin:
Australia

Studio:
Cinesound Productions Ltd

Director:
Ken G Hall

Screenwriters:
Victor Roberts
George D Parker

Cinematographers:
Frank Hurley
George Heath

Art Director:
Fred Finlay

Editor:
William Shepherd

Genre:
Musical Comedy

Duration:
87 minutes

Cast:
Bert Le Blanc
Molly Raynor
Dan Agar
Alex McKinnon
Eric Masters
John D'Arcy
Lorraine Smith
Roy Rene
Yvonne Banvard
Pamela Bevan

Year:
1934

Synopsis

The plot centres on the character of Mo McIsaacs, whose pursuit of profit prompts an episodic series of encounters with urban capitalists, aristocrats and gangsters. Mo picks up a dropped purse, searches for a rural gold mine and takes up short-lived employment as a tailor's assistant, a surf lifesaver at Bondi beach and a door-to-door vacuum-cleaner salesman. The film loosely intertwines Mo's quest for wealth with other plotlines involving secondary characters. These include aviator Larry McCormack's courtship of aristocratic Margot Burnett; young Miriam Burnett's pretence at being a street urchin in an effort resolve her father's financial problems; an impersonation of Hollywood star Mae West by a gangster's woman named Kate; the kidnapping of Miriam by Al Baloney and his gangster circle; and Kate's collusion with Larry to arrive at the gold mine before Baloney does. The plot ends with Mo marrying Kate and both presiding over a Jewish Home for Bankrupt Bookmakers' Children.

Critique

Ken G. Hall's *Strike Me Lucky* is of interest principally because it stars Roy 'Mo' Rene, Australia's pre-eminent vaudeville theatre performer in the period from 1920 to 1950. While the presence of Rene in the film prompted high expectations, *Strike Me Lucky* was a disappointment at the box office and only much later recovered its production costs. The film has long been largely dismissed by critics and historians because of this perceived financial failure and the film's lack of success in replicating Rene's vaudeville persona or popularity on the screen. *Strike Me Lucky* is unavailable commercially and rarely screened but is due for critical re-evaluation on the basis of features that render this film unusual among Australian screen productions before World War II.

Although the intermittent comedic effectiveness of Rene's performance on screen is consistent with contemporary commentators' view that he had difficulty performing to a camera, *Strike Me Lucky* is also of interest for its succession of outlandish comedic episodes and vivid portrayals of secondary characters. The latter include memorable performances by Yvonne Banvard, who convincingly impersonates Hollywood star Mae West, and Bob Le Blanc's portrayal of a stereotyped Jewish tailor.

Strike Me Lucky is a rare example of an Australian film that centres on a prominent Jewish-Australian comedian, forming an early instance of Australian ethnic screen humour. The film's inclusion of a stereotyped Jewish tailor and intermingling of Jewish references with comedic allusions to Scottish, Greek and Irish identities prefigures by decades the ethnic comedy of Australian films produced in and around the multicultural period, including *They're a Weird Mob* (1966), *The Wog Boy* (2000) and *Fat Pizza* (2003). In *Strike Me Lucky*, as in these later films, the protagonist embodies a working-class Australian type of masculinity that is sometimes referred to as the 'ocker'. At the same time, *Strike Me Lucky* defies a perception of 1930s' Australia as culturally homogeneous and Anglocentric by presenting a range of Australian identities that is strikingly diverse in speech and action. An example is a scene in which Mo and his Scottish friend, Donald, attempt to become surf lifesavers. Although the protagonists are presented here as clearly unsuited to the job – gauche and unathletic – a sequence in which they attempt to revive a man rescued from drowning presents athletic Australian masculinity as other – mechanical and perverse – rather than an unquestioned norm.

The film is also significant for presenting Australians as engaging in more irreverent and complex ways with Hollywood cinema and modern capitalism than the nationalist orientations of many historical readings of Australian film have suggested. *Strike Me Lucky* presents a playful view of contemporary urban Australia in which females embrace modern consumer culture with abandon. On one hand, the film alludes to a local tension between international modernity and nationalist parochialism by suggesting a degree of tension between female consumption and Mo's estrangement from the modern consumer society. On the other hand, a sequence in which Mo becomes a door-to-door vacuum cleaner salesman suggests the difficulty of reconciling this tension with economic survival , positioning the protagonist as both defiantly working-class and a scapegoat in a backlash against modern capitalism during the Depression.

Lesley Speed

Crocodile Dundee

Country of Origin:
Australia

Director:
Peter Faiman

Producer:
John Cornell

Screenwriters:
John Cornell
Paul Hogan
Ken Shadie

Director of Photography:
Russell Boyd

Editor:
David Stiven

Production Designer:
Graham 'Grace' Walker

Synopsis

American journalist Sue Charlton travels to the Northern Territory to interview Mick 'Crocodile' Dundee, a local man who survived a crocodile attack. They journey from Walkabout Creek Hotel back to the site of Dundee's legendary escape from the crocodile, which has long since become a Tall Story. On the way, they encounter a wild buffalo, a kangaroo hunting party, a hungry croc, and an urban Aborigine. Sue convinces Mick to go back with her to New York where he encounters and defuses a series of urban threats – including not only pickpockets and pimps but also the hazard of a sophisticated, wealthy, urban 'elite'. Transformed by his encounter with Dundee, Gus, the bemused chauffeur (of 'Harlem Warload' tribe), emulates Aussie ingenuity by using a makeshift boomerang to rescue Dundee from a hiding. And in the final scene, NY commuters turn themselves into a 'bush telegraph' to get Sue's message – I love ya' – through to Dundee, bringing the film's inter-continental walkabout to a happy conclusion.

Critique

If *Crocodile Dundee*'s central character, Mick Dundee (Paul Hogan) can be described as 'a residual Australian' – a character leftover from an outdated version of the national type – then the plot of this blockbuster comedy might well be described as the residue of three cultural forms. The film's loosely-composed sequence of adventures is derived from prose literature's picaresque genre; its hokey visual and

Genre:

Comedy

Duration:

102 minutes

Cast:

Paul Hogan
Linda Kozwolski
David Gulpilil
John Meillon

Year:

1986

verbal gags owe much to live television's off-the-cuff sketch comedy; and its central romance (between a high-class New York newspaper reporter and a low-class crocodile poacher from Walkabout Creek) draws on the bare bones of classical Hollywood's romantic or screwball comedies. These familiar structures create a secure narrative space for the viewer to accompany New Yorker Sue into the wilds of the Australian outback (in the first half of the narrative), and to go along for the ride when Dundee boards a jumbo jet to become a fish out of water in the 'lunatic asylum' of New York. What is remarkable about the plot structure of this canny Australian film is the complete lack of suspense, compared for instance with New Hollywood's seminal high-concept blockbuster, *Jaws*.

In contrast, the ambling pace of *Crocodile Dundee* invites the viewer to go 'walkabout' – a whitefella term derived from Aboriginal culture to encompass the nomadic wanderings of Sue and Dundee. Rather than advance the narrative, their picaresque encounters with an Indigenous Australian and a variety of local wildlife set the stage for a series of comic punch lines, such as the cut-out cardboard kangaroo firing a rifle to scare away the brutal roo hunters. In the second half of the film, the genial 'walkabout' motif is extended to Dundee's ventures into the streets, bars, alleyways, galleries and mansions of New York. The outcome of these encounters is never in doubt: Dundee's naïve, down-under view of the world stands him in good stead and he gets the girl – while teaching New Yorkers a thing or two along the way.

The phenomenal, blockbuster success of *Crocodile Dundee* (1986) in both the Australian and US markets has turned the film into something of a behemoth, looming over a relatively-puny national industry. The purported feat of beating Americans at their own game – by adopting New Hollywood's blockbuster marketing strategies – has made critical evaluation of the film more or less redundant. Only Baz Luhrmann's 2008 film *Australia* (with a much higher production budget) has approached the benchmark set by the team behind *Crocodile Dundee*. Almost 25 years after the film's release, the aura of box office success has not faded. Indeed, this aura has supplanted the original experience of viewing the film. But there is no need to rediscover *Crocodile Dundee* by re-viewing it. Unlike most films, it has not slipped quietly into the vaults of history. To see it again is not to see it afresh. It confirms, rather, the original experience, the lingering memory of an inexplicable gap between the disarming ordinariness of the film and the extraordinary amount of money it made at the box office.

Indeed, it is not possible to re-view the film without puzzling over its much-touted blockbuster status. As a picaresque romance indebted to sketch comedy, *Crocodile Dundee* lacks the key aesthetic elements of the blockbuster film, i.e., special effects embedded in an action-packed, star-studded, suspenseful narrative that takes the audience on a spectacular three-act ride, culminating in an aurally- and visually-engulfing finale. Instead, it offers the viewer a strong dose of home-grown dagginess. Like a B-grade Roger Corman film, it revels in the cheapness of its major special effect: the long-dead, stuffed crocodile. As an ocker comedy it tones down the verbose larrikinism of the Bazza McKenzie films, just as the Paul Hogan show on commercial television toned down the more transgressive antics of the Aunty Jack and Norman Gunston shows on the national public broadcaster. And, as a romantic comedy, it dispenses with the struggle for true erotic recognition between the central screwball couple – New York newspaper heiress, Sue, and wildlife poacher from Walkabout Creek, Mick Dundee. If the film's humour could be translated into an ethos it would be this: disarming is the best form of attack. The point of every sequence, every encounter (whether in the Australian outback or a New York alleyway) is to culminate in a lame joke: 'You call that a knife? This is a knife!' says Dundee, revealing his over-sized hunting knife to a mugger wielding an under-sized pocket knife. It is not the passage of time that has made these jokes lame: the central concept of the film is a redundant national type who outwits his critics at home by making a huge splash in the US. But the fact that this fantasy paid off at the box office does not automatically grant the film entry into the canon of the blockbuster: an innovative aesthetic category as well as an industrial one.

As a looming behemoth, *Crocodile Dundee* has been more or less protected from criticism because of its blockbuster status. Like the lame humour of Mick Dundee, the success of the film has disarmed even those whom it attacks. The target of the film is the urban elite and its sacred cows, represented in the film by Sue, the New York reporter whose Daddy owns the newspaper and whose boyfriend is the chief editor. In the final scene, Dundee literally walks on the heads and shoulders of his natural confrères, ordinary New York subway commuters, to answer Sue's 'cooee' – a call for help from the liberal enclave deep inside the urban jungle. In this regard, *Crocodile Dundee* has more in common with the high concept film (refined by producers such as Jerry Bruckheimer and Don Simpson) than with the blockbuster films of Hollywood movie brats such as Francis Ford Coppola and, later, James Cameron. Aesthetically and ideologically, *Crocodile Dundee* is aligned with lame-but-disarming high-concept films, such as *Flashdance* and *Top Gun*, rather than *The Godfather* and *Jaws*, definitive blockbusters which transformed Hollywood cinema in the 1970s. As a landmark, one-off film event, *Crocodile Dundee* can claim no such transformative role in Australian cinema. We remember it with some affection, but we do not need to see it again.

Felicity Collins

Muriel's Wedding

Country of Origin:
Australia

Director:
P J Hogan

Screenwriter:
P J Hogan

Producers:
Lynda House
Jocelyn Moorhouse

Cinematographer:
Martin McGrath

Production Designer:
Patrick Reardon

Editor:
Jill Bilcock

Genre:
Comedy

Duration:
101 minutes

Cast:
Toni Collette
Rachel Griffiths
Sophie Lee
Bill Hunter
Jeanie Drynan
Matt Day
Daniel Lapaine

Year:
1994

Synopsis

At a wedding reception in the beachside town of Porpoise Spit, Muriel catches the bouquet thrown by bride Tania, much to Tania and her catty bridesmaids' dismay. Later, Muriel stumbles on the groom and one of the bridesmaids *in flagrante delicto*. Another guest realizes that Muriel is wearing a stolen dress, and calls the police. Muriel's father Bill, a local politician, convinces the policemen to drop the investigation. At a local nightclub, Tania is consoled by her girlfriends after her husband admits various indiscretions. The girls convince Tania to go on holiday with them to Hibiscus Island instead of going on her honeymoon. Muriel is dumped from the gang because they feel she is not 'on their level'. Muriel's mother Betty gives her a blank cheque, made out to cash, to buy cosmetics from her new employer Deirdre, with whom Bill is having an affair. Muriel uses the money to pay for a holiday to Hibiscus Island, where she meets an old school friend, Rhonda, who has also been treated miserably by Tania and her gang. The gang humiliate Muriel and try to prise Rhonda away from her; Rhonda tells Tania about the bridesmaid's affair with her husband. Rhonda and Muriel win a talent quest with their rendition of the ABBA song 'Waterloo'. Muriel returns to Porpoise Spit to learn that her deception has been discovered, and immediately runs away to Sydney.

She moves in with Rhonda, changes her name to 'Mariel' and finds a job in a video store. Mariel's first date with the clumsy Brice ends in disaster when Rhonda inexplicably falls to the ground and is unable to move her legs. A tumour is discovered on Rhonda's spine, and she is confined to a wheelchair. Mariel phones home to discover that her father is under investigation for official graft. Rhonda makes Mariel promise that they will never go back to Porpoise Spit. Mariel visits all the bridal wear shops in Sydney to try on wedding dresses and indulge her marriage fantasies. She gains the sympathy of shop assistants by making up terrible stories about her family so that they will take a photograph of her in the dress. Rhonda finds Mariel's album full of photographs, and confronts her in a bridal shop. Mariel cries that she wants to get married in order to leave the old Muriel behind. Rhonda is told that her cancer has returned, and that she will never walk again.

Responding to an advertisement in a singles column, Mariel meets South African swimmer David who must marry an Australian to gain citizenship in order to fulfil his dream of swimming in the Olympics. Mariel and David are married in a sumptuous ceremony. Rhonda refuses to be a bridesmaid, and tells Mariel she has betrayed her, as Rhonda now must go back to Porpoise Spit to live with her mother. Mariel's mother Betty only just arrives in time to see the wedding vows; she also sees Deirdre on Bill's arm. In a supermarket back in Porpoise Spit, Betty is arrested for absent-mindedly shoplifting a pair of shoes. Bill again convinces the police to drop the charges, telling the sergeant in his wife's hearing 'You can see she's not right in the head'. Bill tells Betty he is leaving her for Deirdre, and blames Betty and his family for his failings as a politician. Betty commits suicide.

At her funeral, a telegram of condolence from former Prime Minister Bob Hawke is read out; Bill has arranged this for the benefit of the press who are covering his ongoing trial. Mariel rushes out of the church, overcome by her father's insensitivity and self-centredness. She is reunited with David, and they spend the night together. In the morning, Mariel tells David she does not love him. She goes back to her family home, where Bill pressures her to stay and help him raise her siblings. She refuses, and pays back some of the money she stole from him. Mariel goes to Rhonda's house to take her back to Sydney. Together, Mariel and Rhonda leave Porpoise Spit forever.

Critique

Muriel's Wedding is one of the most important Australian films of the 1990s. Along with films like *Strictly Ballroom* (Baz Luhrmann, 1992) and *The Adventures of Priscilla, Queen of the Desert* (Stephan Elliott, 1994), *Muriel's Wedding* helped define the 'quirky comedy', a subgenre of Australian cinema that met with great success domestically and internationally in the 1990s. The film also launched the careers of many of its leading players. After her first feature film role in *Muriel's Wedding*, Toni Collette built her reputation with a string of strong performances in Australian features including *Lilian's Story* (Jerzy Domaradki, 1996) and *The Boys* (Rowan Woods, 1998) before she was chosen by director Todd Haynes to star alongside Ewan McGregor in the 1970s' glam rock film *Velvet Goldmine* (1998). The following year marked her Hollywood breakthrough, with her Academy Award-nominated role in M Night Shyamalan's blockbuster hit *The Sixth Sense* (1999). In 2010, Collette won a Golden Globe award for her role in the American television series *The United States of Tara*.

Muriel's Wedding also marked the feature debut of Rachel Griffiths, who plays Muriel's best friend Rhonda. After a supporting role in director P J Hogan's next film, the Hollywood comedy *My Best Friend's Wedding* (1997), Griffiths worked around the world on a variety of Australian and international films and television programmes, before settling in Los Angeles and landing a starring role as Brenda in the acclaimed HBO series *Six Feet Under*. Matt Day, who plays Muriel's first boyfriend Brice, also made his first feature film debut here.

Muriel's Wedding is an ugly duckling story about a fantasist and habitual liar who seeks an escape from the dullness of her family life and from the pain of being ostracized by the cool girls in the music of ABBA and in dreams of marriage. Regularly humiliated by her father, a crooked local politician, who publicly abuses Muriel and her slothful siblings as 'useless' and 'dead weights', Muriel suffers further indignity when she is cruelly shunned by the awful Tania and her gang for her unfashionable hairstyle and clothes, for her size, and worst of all, for listening to 1970s' music. It is only after she meets Rhonda, a free spirit who accepts Muriel for who she (says she) is (because Muriel cannot help herself, and deceives Rhonda just as she deceives everyone else), that Muriel gains self-confidence and the will to escape the small-minded, selfish, small-town attitudes of Porpoise Spit. Dancing with Rhonda and miming to ABBA's 'Waterloo', dressed in a blonde wig and stunning white outfit, Muriel is given the first glimpse of the swan that she can become.

For a time, her friendship with Rhonda and her new life in the big city keeps her obsessive-compulsive disorder at bay but, when Rhonda is diagnosed with cancer and Muriel becomes her carer, Muriel quickly lapses back into a world of ABBA, lies, and wedding fantasies. Ultimately it takes the death of her mother and her father's attempts to turn this, like everything, to his personal advantage, to make her realize that her own selfishness and deceptions have almost destroyed the one thing that can save her – her friendship with Rhonda.

Muriel's Wedding turns on Muriel's transformation and, ultimately, on her realization that her fantasy of a traditional white wedding and marriage will not bring her the happiness she craves. Her decision, to reject her perfect husband and choose, instead, life with her friend Rhonda, subverts the romantic comedy convention of resolving the narrative through the (re)union of a heterosexual couple. And her choice of mateship over matrimony also invests this celebrated Australian trait with a new value, as Muriel clearly rejects the older, male-centred mateship practised by her father in his dealings with the police, with developers, and with his political mentors. In these things the film is respectably radical, but the film is not beyond resorting to well-worn caricatures of small town Australians, who are variously presented as ugly, slothful, bitchy, venal, unfaithful, and shallow. The city, and specifically Sydney ('City of Brides' as an on-screen title announces), is, by contrast, a place of excitement, love, passion, and the future. Australian audiences have shown time and again, from the ocker comedies onwards, that they are prepared to laugh at, and sometimes with, ugly Australian characters. Overseas marketing also played on this stereotype: the tagline for the French poster was 'Elle est grosse, elle est bête, elle est Australienne' ('She is fat, she is stupid, she is Australian'). Of course, by the end of the film, her size is no longer an issue, and she is clearly not stupid, but she remains, inevitably, an Australian. Muriel's transformation is physical as much as mental, evident in the contrasting shots of her face as she travels by taxi at various points in the film. Returning from Hibiscus Island she is sunburnt, pimple-nosed and dowdy; leaving for Sydney with Rhonda at the end of the film she is delicately made-up, and glowing, with a beatific smile playing on her lips.

Mention must also be made of the tragic character Betty, Muriel's mother, who suffers with stoic dignity her husband's verbal abuse and infidelity, who arrives late at her daughter's wedding only to be passed unseen when Muriel walks up the aisle out of the church after the service, and whose absent-mindedness leads to arrest and humiliation in the police station. In the car on the way home, after being released from custody, her desperate, heartfelt request to her husband for help in coping with the pressures of their family life is brutally cut off in mid-sentence when he dismissively turns on the radio. And in a final indignity, after Bill announces that he wants a divorce, she is assaulted by her own son Perry. When she commits suicide, Bill manages to turn it to his advantage, believing that claiming she died of a heart attack will aid his case in court and with the press, just as he uses her funeral as a platform for his own interests. Ultimately, though, she has the last word: she sets fire to the back garden – the sacred quarter acre block – because Perry would not mow it, leaving the iconic Hills Hoist with the singed remnants of a load of washing forlornly hanging amid the smoky waste. This is a powerful image, suggesting the devastating bush fires that regularly ravage country areas, but, alongside the destruction and the almost sacrilegious attack on the washing line, there is also the promise of new growth through the fire's regenerative potential.

Ben Goldsmith

COMING OF AGE

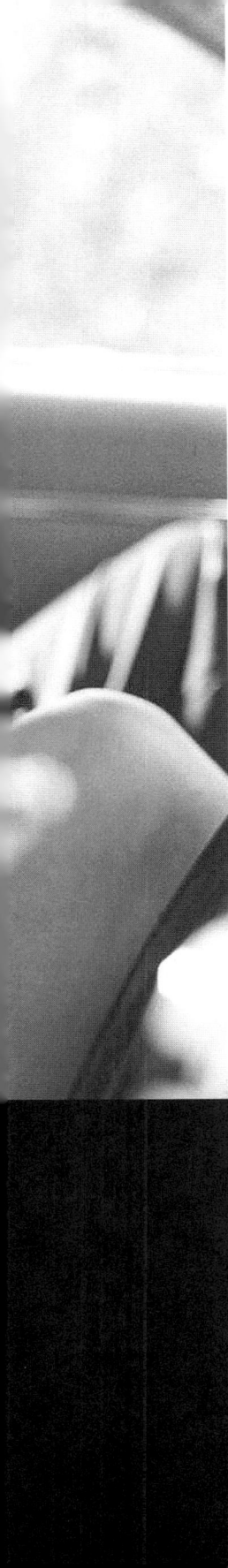

It is often said that the Australian film industry is obsessed with coming-of-age films because stories about tentative youth, unstable and struggling over their identity, are metaphors for our national film industry and, indeed, the nation itself. The story of youth becoming adults, as it is told in Australian film, is about young people having to go through sometimes funny, but often painful, rites of passage, negotiating a dramatic series of events that sometimes end happily, sometimes in sober catharsis, and sometimes in defeat and death.

Coming-of-age films from the mid-1970s were often adapted from novels. *Picnic at Hanging Rock* (1975) and *The Getting of Wisdom* (1977), for example, both followed privileged young women at 'upper-crust' ladies' colleges in the Victorian period. Whereas the biggest threat to the exquisite Miranda and her girlfriends in Peter Weir's *Picnic* lies outside the walls of their school in the 'wild' and 'uncultivated' Australian bush, Bruce Beresford's *Wisdom* demonstrated that school was no place for free-spirited, working-class, poor, unbeautiful, lesbian girls with 'innocent' and kind hearts like Laura Tweedle Rambotham.

Suffering under the oppression of the school, heartless teachers and other authority figures is a common theme in coming-of-age films. In Fred Schepisi's *The Devil's Playground* (1976), Tom's sense of self and desires are often in direct conflict with the old-fashioned mores of his strict, Catholic school in 1950s' Victoria. Danny in John Duigan's *Flirting* (1991) also discovers that it is unacceptable for someone of his age to be sexually active, and, as he painfully learns, having sex with a black girl in 1960s' Australia, is even more 'licentious'. Here the loss of virginity ends in public humiliation and further social exclusion. Not all films portray school-life as uniformly bleak; in several films, sympathetic teachers play pivotal roles in the lives of students on the cusp of adulthood. Disturbed 13-year-old Tom in Michael Caulfield's *Fighting Back* (1983), and volatile Nick in *The Heartbreak Kid* (Michael Jenkins, 1993), are both saved from self-destruction by fiercely-determined teachers. In *The Heartbreak Kid*, Nick and his teacher Christina's clandestine affair is not only the sign of his coming of age, but also the vehicle for her to escape a stultifying suburban marriage. Although their affair is discovered and they are subjected to public shame and humiliation, the film treats the couple extremely sympathetically, ending with the suggestion that they will reunite at some point in the future.

Sex is not only central to the young person's coming of age but also key to breaking convention and traditional roles in a large number of films. Three teenage friends hit the road in search of their first sexual experience in Western Australia in 1957, in the comedy *Love in Limbo* (David Elfick, 1993). 13-year-old Norman comes of age at his *bah mitzvah*, which magically turns him into 'a man' with the sexual prowess and charms of someone twice his age in *Norman Loves Rose* (Henri Safran, 1982). Confident and virile, he succeeds in impregnating his sister-in-law, Rose. In the nostalgic and quirky semi-autobiographical comedy *The Nostradamus Kid* (Bob Ellis, 1992), intellectual Ken struggles to reconcile his Seventh Day Adventist upbringing with his boundless sexual desire, as the Cuban Missile Crisis unfolds. In *The Night, The Prowler* (Jim Sharman, 1978), based on a novel by Patrick White, Felicity takes to the streets at night dressed in black leather to take out her (sexual) aggression on the men she comes across after she is raped by an intruder. Felicity's rape is the catalyst for her rejection of the conservative values epitomized by her over-wrought middle-class mother and, ultimately, the assertion of her own personal sexual revolution. For 19-year-old Ari in *Head On* (Ana Kokkinos, 1998), it is the clash between his sexuality and the expectations of his over-bearing radical activist Greek family that trigger a crisis. Ari acts out aggressively, recklessly taking drugs and having rough sex with strange men in dirty back alleys as he struggles to be true to himself and his family.

Since the 1970s, many coming-of-age films have been hard-hitting social-realist dramas. In John Duigan's film, *Mouth to Mouth* (1978), Sam struggles to make a life for herself after being released from a girls' remand centre, but the harsh reality of going it alone and the unwelcome attentions of abusive bent cop Brady makes this a mighty challenge. More recently, *Mallboy* (Vincent Giarrusso, 2001), documents the travails of 14-year-old Shaun, growing up in a broken home where the only entertainment is hanging around the local mall with a gang of young mates.

Some of the most powerful social-realist coming-of-age films have been films about Indigenous youth. Determined and ambitious Trilby wants a better life for herself and her family in Bruce Beresford's *The Fringe Dwellers* (1986). She persuades her family to move from their community to a white, middle-class suburb. But never able to feel at home in the new neighbourhood or at school, her dream comes unstuck. When she falls pregnant, her determination (and sanity) is tested, with devastating results. In *Yolngu Boy* (Stephen Michael Johnson, 2000) three young boys, Botj, Lorrpu, and Milika, struggle to come to terms with the demands of the modern (white) and ancient (black) worlds. The tribal home in the bush is presented as the place where young boys can reach their full potential as powerful Indigenous men. The city, by contrast, is a place of corruption, crime, alcohol and temptation. When Botj discovers that his father is a drunk, living on a riverside squat, he goes on a destructive bender with heartbreaking results. By contrast, the film suggests that there is hope for Milika who comes of age through traditional rites of passage, and lives a righteous (anti-city, anti-drugs) life. In *Beneath Clouds* (Ivan Sen, 2002); *Australian Rules* (Paul Goldman, 2002); *September* (Peter Carstairs, 2007) and *Samson & Delilah* (Warwick Thornton, 2009) hope for the future for Australia's Indigenous youth is clouded in ambiguity. But, importantly, hope is not lost altogether.

Young female protagonists are often placed in situations in which they must take on adult responsibilities at an early age because of parental conflict, family breakdown, environmental plunder or general adult corruption and madness. The eponymous lead character of Don McLennan's *Mull* (1988) is forced to take on the role of parent to her demanding siblings when her mother falls ill and her father is rendered incapable by his own selfish obsessions. In Stuart McDonald's *Stranded* (2005), Claudia's experience is similar to Mull's, not because her eccentric father is overbearing but, rather, because he is too easy-going and spiritless. A string of films including Donald Crombie's *Playing Beatie Bow* (1986), *Beneath Clouds*; Craig Monahan's *Peaches* (2004); Cate Shortland's *Somersault* (2004); and Sandra Sciberras's *Caterpillar Wish* (2006), depict girls who, on the brink of womanhood and often in conflict with their mothers, leave home in search of absent fathers. The girls often travel great distances, both metaphorically and literally, as the search for Daddy becomes the search for self. Some of these films end with the daughter and father's reconciliation. Others, however, show the girl 'growing up', and realizing that her father is worthless and that she (and her mother) are better off without him. For the most part, however, the single mother, positioned variously as selfish, insecure, reckless, unstable, sick, infantilized, is the root of the daughter's coming-of-age crises and the father's abandonment. This theme is played out in *Playing Beatie Bow*, *Beneath Clouds*, *Peaches*, *Somersault*, and *Caterpillar Wish*.

At the other end of the spectrum are funny and tender comedies of coming of age. In *The Big Steal* (Nadia Tass, 1990), *Crackers* (David Swann, 1998), *The Rage in Placid Lake* (Tony McNamara, 2003) and *Hating Alison Ashley* (Geoff Bennett, 2005), the protagonists learn that you certainly cannot choose your family or the lot you have been given. The lead characters' coming of age occurs when they realize that in spite of their families' eccentricities and embarrassments, and even in their less than satisfactory suburban worlds, everything will turn out well in the end. In other comedies including *The Mango Tree* (Kevin James Dobson, 1977), *The Year My Voice Broke* (John Duigan, 1987), *Fistful of Flies* (Monica Pellizzari, 1996), *Australian Rules*, and *Muriel's Wedding*, (P J Hogan, 1994), young characters realize that they must escape toxic family relationships and claustrophobic small towns in order to 'dance their own steps'.

Coming-of-age films about boys often require them to go on an heroic quest before they can legitimately enter manhood. *The Man from Snowy River* (George Miller, 1982) tells the story of Jim, who, after the tragic death of his father has to prove himself to the spirited Jessica and her rich, snooty father. After an exciting chase through the beautifully-wild Snowy Mountains, Jim captures the prized colt that got away, wins the girl and becomes not only a man but *the* man from Snowy River. *The Coolangatta Gold* (Igor Auzins, 1984) uses the sports contest – in this case the Iron Man surf life-saving competition – as a catalyst for a male youth's coming of age. Proving his worth to his bullying father, and with burning resentment for always being put in his brother's shadow, 19-year-old Steve defies the odds and beats his father at his own game, asserting his true passion and becoming his own man.

Several recent Australian films depict the lives of 'Gen X' youths who struggle to grow up. *Love and other Catastrophes* (Emma-Kate Croghan, 1996) is a comic tale of 20-something university students in Melbourne. Alice is in crisis because she cannot finish her thesis, find a good man or figure out who she is or what the rest of her life holds. Mia's obsession with her male professor takes priority over her relationship with her girlfriend Danni. Both are ultimately redeemed through a healthy relationship and healthy state of self, and are able to transition into 'normal' adults. Larrikin Eddie 'Mullet' Maloney in David Caesar's *Mullet* (2001), returns home to the seaside town of Coolawarra from the city where he has been hiding from life for three years. Trying to smooth things over with his ex-girlfriend, Tully, who is now pregnant and married to his brother Peter, and looking to reconcile with his estranged parents, Mullet is trying his best to 'be a man'. In the end he may be saved from his apathy and masculine 'childishness' from the love of a good woman, a local barmaid.

The love of a good woman saves another hapless man in one of the quirkiest coming-of-age films, Rolf de Heer's *Bad Boy Bubby* (1993). 30-something Bubby has lived his whole life in a dirty hovel with his abusive mother until, one day, he escapes into the world. Thrust into a noisy, colourful, strange, and largely hostile environment, the impressionable Bubby goes through a series of explosive and often painful sexual, emotional and existential experiences. In his own manic manner, Bubby tries to find his way, to work out who he is, and what is his place in the world. Eventually he finds a sympathetic nurse, Angel, and settles down to live a 'normal' life in the suburbs.

Australian coming-of-age stories are as numerous as they are varied. Our obsession with them may have something to do with our fledging film industry, or with an idealized sense of national identity. Many of these films display a certain anxiety. Young protagonists often have heavy burdens to bear, and it is no wonder then that they are so often seen to fall short of everyone's expectations, including their own. But then, this is only half the story. As many Australian coming-of-age films show us, in all their serious, funny and iconic ways, young people may be dangers to society, or in danger from it, if they are allowed to run wild. However, they are also engaging, exciting and intriguing, and their youthful spirit symbolizes all our society's hopes and dreams. Is it no wonder, then, that we revisit these stories again and again – we do not want to ever see them 'grow up'.

Kristina Gottschall

The Year My Voice Broke

Country of Origin:
Australia

Director:
John Duigan

Producers:
Terry Hayes
George Miller
Doug Mitchell

Cinematographer:
Geoff Burton

Screenwriter:
John Duigan

Editors:
Neil Thumpston

Production Designer:
Roger Ford

Genre:
Coming of Age
Comedy

Duration:
103 minutes

Cast:
Noah Taylor
Leone Carmen
Bruce Spence
Ben Mendelsohn
Malcolm Robertson
Judi Farr

Year:
1987

Synopsis

Growing up in a sleepy NSW country town circa 1962, 15-year-old Danny Embling is forever uncool no matter how hard he tries. Nerdy, funny-looking and more than just a little bit different, Danny is an outsider. Preferring romantic poems to sport, Danny is constantly bullied by the boys at school and laughed at by the girls. Largely alienated due to his difference, he has few friends bar a pretty and free-spirited local girl with a bad reputation, Freya, and wannabe erotic novelist, the alcoholic Jonah. Spending many hours together alone in their special place on Willy Hill overlooking the golden countryside, Danny and Freya share their thoughts and day-dreams. It is their retreat, a utopian sanctuary from the deceitful and destructive adult world. In love with Freya since he can remember, Danny silently suffers under the burden of unrequited love. No matter how hard he tries, including attempting to hypnotize her, or channel sexual desire through telepathy with a pair of her knickers pressed against his head, the mysterious Freya is always out of his reach. When Freya starts to fall for the brutish yet popular football star and local bad boy, Trevor, Danny becomes incensed and his emotional turmoil escalates. But he, too, eventually comes to tolerate the recklessly-childish Trevor, and can only stand back as Freya and Trevor's relationship kicks up a gear. Danny's parents run the local pub where the hypocritical men of the town stand on the veranda passing judgement. Overhearing bits of conversations and arguments between the deceitful adults, Danny uncovers the town's dark secret, the ramifications of which embroil him and his friends in set of events with devastating results.

Critique

Written and directed by John Duigan, *The Year My Voice Broke* is a nostalgic, bitter-sweet coming-of-age story that is almost without exception lauded by critics as an Australian classic. Winner of five AFIs, the film has been described as 'timeless', 'honest', 'warm', a delicate balance of light and dark, and a uniquely Australian story.

An emotional character in itself, the golden browns of the countryside and sense of place are vivid, as are the evocative ideas of place as a 'museum', magically capturing the events and the emotions of its inhabitants: desire, shame, fear, love, pain. Far from frivolous or silly, Danny's coming of age is profound and life-changing. There are moments of humour but, like Danny himself, a melancholic mood dominates and, in the end, it is an incredibly sad story about loss, grief and disappointment. At the same time that the countryside is represented as beautiful, it is also alienating and harsh, and the film savagely critiques the rural town, positioned as small-minded, hypocritical, oppressive, hateful. The town and the bigots in it are the things that destroy Danny and Freya's youthful utopia, and Trevor's rebellious spirit. Ultimately we learn that this is no place for those who are different, and in the end Freya leaves, never to return, and Danny attempts escape to a Sydney boarding school in the sequel *Flirting* (1991). A story primarily about youth, the adults in the film are as interesting as they are irredeemable: Freya's abusive alcoholic stepfather Nils, hateful pub-big-noter and local football coach Tom, and even Danny's guilty but deceitful father. What the women in the film demonstrate is that there are only two options available for their gender in this place at this time: suppress one's true desire for the oppressive and unhappy role of wife (like Danny's mother and Freya's adoptive mother), or risk being labelled the 'town bike' (Freya's dead biological mother), and, then, either live in permanent isolation from the town (like old Mrs O'Neil) or leave permanently (like Freya). If only Freya's grandmother could speak, what would she tell her granddaughter with whom she seems to have an inexplicable bond? So often only recognized as Danny's coming of age, *The Year My Voice Broke* is Freya's coming of age too, and, I argue, one that is twice as painful.

Kristina Gottschall

The Rage in Placid Lake

Country of Origin:
Australia

Director:
Tony McNamara

Producer:
Marion Macgowan

Screenwriter:
Tony McNamara

Cinematographer:
Ellery Ryan

Editor:
Lee Smith

Production Designer:
Roger Ford

Genre:
Coming of Age
Comedy

Synopsis

A classic outsider, 17-year-old Placid has a tough life. Since the day he was encouraged by his mother to go to school in a dress to challenge people's preconceived notions, he has been the source of ritual beatings at school by the thuggish Bull and his dumb mates. Placid's self-centred, neurotic, suburban, hippy parents – Sylvia, a bi-sexual international documentary maker, and Doug, a men's counsellor who cannot get angry – feebly dismiss Placid, ineffectually promoting 'calmness' and 'love' even when Placid comes home covered in purple bruises. After graduation Placid has a particularly lofty revelation, and decides to reinvent himself in order to 'fit in' in an attempt to become a functioning member of mainstream society. After reading a few self-help books, Placid cuts his hair, buys a suit and, to his parent's horror, embraces life as a drone working for a soulless insurance agency. Taken under the wing of the boss of the agency, the wryly acidic Joel, Placid is fast-tracked into the world of petty office jealousies and ambitiously-unemotional stationery-room sex. Meanwhile, Placid's only friend, the intellectually brilliant Gemma, tries to understand Placid's latest hare-brained plan. But Gemma is having her own existential problems. Prepped as the 'future Marie Curie' by her overzealous single Dad, Bill, the tightly-wound Gemma starts to question if she really wants to be a squeaky-clean Doris Day-esque scientist. While Placid and Gemma wrestle with their respective

Duration:

89 minutes

Cast:

Ben Lee
Toby Schmitz
Miranda Richardson
Garry McDonald
Christopher Stollery
Rose Byrne
Nicholas Hammond

Year:

2003

crises, juggle their wacky parents and try to find a place for themselves in a hostile world, they learn many important things as they come into their own. Most importantly, perhaps, they learn to embrace the rage.

Critique

Sounding like a teen slasher-thriller, *The Rage in Placid Lake* is an unseen little gem of a movie: quirky, smart and warm-hearted. The feature debut of Sydney Theatre director Tony McNamara based on his 1998 play *The Café Latte Kid*, is also the acting debut of musician Ben Lee. The choice of Ben Lee is an interesting one, and either love him or hate him, he makes an apt Placid, in spite of his self-conscious acting style. Rose Byrne is effortlessly appealing as Gemma, playing her with equal amounts of sass and vulnerability. But it is the fabulous ensemble cast that makes the film: Doug (Garry McDonald), Sylvia (Miranda Richardson), Joel (Christopher Stolley), even the psychotically-blank Anton (Francis McMahon) at the insurance agency. Some critics have been disappointed by the second half of the film, slower and more serious in pace, but this balance is needed, showing that *The Rage in Placid Lake* is more than just a collection of one-liners. There are so many absurd scenarios and laugh-out-loud dialogue that it might be easy to forget that the film highlights some serious, even dark issues. Whether it be his teachers, the school bully, his parents, or the 9 to 5 grind, Placid exposes the inauthenticities of the contemporary world. Similar in quirkiness to the Australian coming-of-age films *Hating Alison Ashley* (2005) and *Hey Hey It's Esther Blueburger* (2008), (notwithstanding the late John Hughes' US teenpics), *The Rage in Placid Lake* shows that, even in spite of their own difference, and their families' eccentricities and embarrassments, the young person *will be ok*. The final scene where Placid, and his parents, finally embrace the rage, leaving the bullies nursing their wounds and bruised egos, is a classic moment in Australian cinema. And in Placid's coming of age.

Kristina Gottschall

Somersault

Country of Origin:

Australia

Director:

Cate Shortland

Producer:

Anthony Anderson

Screenwriter:

Cate Shortland

Synopsis

16-year-old Heidi is a deep-thinking, complex emotional girl. Intensely lonely, Heidi reaches out to her mother's boyfriend, with tragic results, and, after an ugly confrontation with her mother, Heidi runs away to the frozen wilderness of ski-resort town, Jindabyne, in the Snowy Mountains. With little money and apparently without a friend in the world, Heidi recklessly and desperately tries to find a safe and loving place for herself with an unhappy succession of unknown young men. With disastrous effect, every man that comes across Heidi is all too ready to exploit or abuse her, and this seemingly comes as a

Cinematographer:
Robert Humphreys

Editor:
Scott Gray

Production Designer:
Melinda Doring

Genre:
Coming of Age
Drama

Duration:
106 minutes

Cast:
Abbie Cornish
Sam Worthington
Erik Thomson
Lynette Curran
Nathaniel Dean
Leah Purcell

Year:
2004

shock to Heidi, who is dangerously naïve and vulnerable. Heidi meets local boy, Joe, a son of well-off farmers, who quickly sleeps with Heidi but is cold and distant. The motel proprietor Irene takes pity on Heidi, allowing her to stay in a back-room. Heidi proudly gets a job at the BP servo and befriends local girl Bianca. As much as Joe tries to avoid Heidi, he cannot stay away from her, and their affection for one another grows. While they do experience some light-hearted moments together, their relationship is generally full of angst, embarrassment and mismatched emotion, Joe particularly unable to articulate his feelings. Ignored by his father and ridiculed by his jealous, small-minded mate Stuart, who calls Heidi 'a bit of rough trade' and a 'cheap fucking slag', Joe cannot confide in anyone. He starts to open up a bit, though, to a caring, gay neighbour Richard, but remains largely confused and self-destructive. Eventually, and quite painfully, Heidi learns that Joe cannot meet her on a deep emotional level and, after a tearful confession to Irene, reconciles with her mother and returns home, having learnt a valuable life-lesson.

Critique

Reportedly taking a decade to make it to the big screen, *Somersault* is Australian director Cate Shortland's feature debut. Premiering at Cannes and then going on to collect a record thirteen AFI awards, *Somersault* was the most lauded Australian film of 2004. Beautifully filmed and delicately told, this coming-of-age story is as sad as it is intricate. The fragile icy setting, the colour palettes of blues and whites with splashes of red in key scenes, and an ethereal sound-track by Sydney band Decoder Ring, provide a moody and otherworldly feel to this contemporary story of young love and angst. Slowly paced and sparse in dialogue, the audience must piece together what they can from shots of a glistening crystal charm around a rear-view mirror; the world through red-coloured ski goggles; warm breath in the cold air; leaves being blown in the wind. Interestingly, but perhaps predictably, critics have largely been preoccupied with Heidi's promiscuity, understanding her burgeoning sexuality as 'at risk', dangerous and even, amazingly, predatory. In these critics' hands Heidi is the subject of moralizing and moral panicking, pathologized as having 'a big fucking problem' (as Joe tells Heidi in the film). Arguably, many critics are locked into this reading at the cost of recognizing the profound comments made by Shortland regarding the complex and often fraught nature of relationships between men and women. Sam Worthington's Joe, is also such an interesting and tortured character. He feels deeply but is perhaps incapable of expressing it due to the obstacles of everyday life in a masculinist rural Australian setting. This, in itself, makes *Somersault* an important film, yielding significant comment on contemporary Australian manhood. Some critics have also been left unsatisfied by the ending of the film, suggesting that Heidi

has learnt nothing during her time in a harsh landscape. This
is an unfortunate oversight; the scenes with Bianca and her
autistic brother, the scenes with Irene, the threesome scene
with the two drunken tourists, and the scenes with Joe in
the latter stages of the film, demonstrate the lessons Heidi
learns as she comes of age. In many respects, Heidi's personal redemptive story, the self-healing and self-forgiveness
that occurs is also cathartic for the other 'lost souls' she
encounters.

Kristina Gottschall

Caterpillar Wish

Country of Origin:
Australia

Director:
Sandra Sciberras

Producer:
Kate Whitbread

Screenwriter:
Sandra Sciberras

Cinematographer:
Greig Fraser

Editors:
Jason Ballantine

Production Designer:
Robert Webb

Genre:
Coming of Age
Drama

Duration:
100 minutes

Cast:
Wendy Hughes
Susie Porter
Victoria Thaine
Robert Mammone
Philip Quast
Khan Chittenden

Year:
2006

Synopsis

Seventeen-year-old Emily is growing up in a seaside village
full of secrets and lies. Living with her single, topless-barmaid
mother Susan, Emily has never known her father, her mother
telling her he was a 'tom cat' who blew into town and blew
out. Secretly taking photos of male visitors to the town, Emily
tries to find her father by studying their faces for signs of
recognition. But Emily also doubts her mother's story, coming
to suspect that her father might actually be a local man. Emily
also secretly tries to track down her estranged grandparents,
her stubbornly independent mother refusing contact with
them since she gave birth to Emily at fifteen. As she comes
of age, the beautiful, intelligent and curious Emily tries to
piece together the truth about 'where she came from' and
the secrets of the past. She has a sweet and loving relationship with a sensitive local boy, Joel, and they meet in secret to
share intimate moments with each other. Joel's father, Carl is an
arrogant policeman who bullies his eldest son, leers at young
girls, and cheats on his wife Elizabeth. He also has a secret
past. Elizabeth lives in denial about her cheating husband,
pretending everything is ok, just like she pretends everything
is ok with her tragically-widowed brother, Stephen. Stephen
wants to keep his growing affection for Susan a secret because
he knows his sister disapproves of her. Susan secretly longs not
to have to do it all on her own. In the course of Emily's quest
for her father and the quest to find herself, the secrets and
lies of this little community are exposed, with shattering and
ultimately, transformative effect.

Critique

Writer-director Sandra Sciberras' debut feature, *Caterpillar Wish*
is, for the most part, a beautifully- and carefully-crafted film. Each
character has their own story to tell and demons to exorcise,
and the unfolding narrative is perfectly paced in this slow-burn
of a film. The stunning shots of the sleepy coastal setting around
Robe, South Australia, and the sad, lilting soundtrack make
for a moody and atmospheric backdrop to the story of people

trapped in the pain of past relationships, and the lies they tell themselves to get by. The adolescent girl protagonist, 'the caterpillar soon-to-be butterfly', brings about the transformation and 'growing up' of the adults in her life in painful, but necessary ways. Contemporary society so often understands young, beautiful girls like Emily as intelligent, caring, and ultimately altruistic. Girls like Emily are positioned primarily as mechanisms for social cohesion in popular narratives, restoring order, truth and even happiness to people's miserable and shambolic lives. Emily is also a wide-eyed ingénue, sharp-witted, articulate, deeply emotional and wise beyond her years. Indeed, she is more honest and 'good' than the adults in her world, ultimately teaching *them* how to be decent human beings. Emily is also her mother's moral guardian, telling her with regards to her latest boyfriend: 'If you keep giving him treats [Mum], he'll just come back for more'. But it is not the sex that Emily has the problem with, it is the disconnected, uncommitted sex that Emily chastises her mother about. Refreshingly, teenage sex is not demonized here, either: Emily and Joel's relationship is loving and intimate, rather than a source of clichéd 'discovery' or 'turmoil', including mismatched desire, parental outrage or unwanted pregnancy. It is also noteworthy that the rural town in which the film is set is not positioned as claustrophobic or deficient, and our protagonist does not need to escape it in the end to live the life they want to live, as in so many other Australian coming-of-age films (see for instance: *The Fringe Dwellers*, 1986; *Year My Voice Broke*, 1987; *Australian Rules*, 2002; *Beneath Clouds*, 2002). Sciberras was perhaps heavy-handed in the Brontesque metaphors of unwelcoming winter, raging storms and clear bright summer which echo the protagonist's state of mind. The glossy ending is also, perhaps, too polished, where not only does everyone look airbrushed and bathed in a glowing fuzzy light but so, too, is Susan and Stephen's relationship, as they are suddenly content in each other's arms. While the film makes some interesting and perhaps progressive choices with regards to the way teen sex or rural life is represented – for instance, the figure of the single mother still remains a tragic one. In the end, it seems as though Emily finally finds the nuclear family she always wanted – and a handsome 'prince' for her 'terribly sad' mother. And so they lived happily ever after. Something tells me, though, that that does not include working at the topless bar.

Kristina Gottschall

Suburban Mayhem

Country of Origin:
Australia

Director:
Paul Goldman

Synopsis

Nineteen-year-old Katrina Skinner is an unemployed, single mother living in the suburbs. Spinning between boredom, anger, recklessness, craziness and vulnerability, Katrina is a 'hurricane' who moves at a heady pace, wreaking havoc as she goes. After she dumps her baby Bailee on someone, she loves nothing more than doing drugs in the toilet at the mall; shop-lifting and bag-snatching at the shops; bragging and preening at the local beauty salon; 'picking up' at the traffic-lights; having sex with a stranger in his ute at the lookout; and driving really, really fast. The whole suburb knows about Katrina's cold-hearted, selfish and manipulative ways. Aunty Diane criticises her, teen-beautician, Lilya

Producers:

Jan Chapman
Leah Churchill-Brown

Cinematographer:

Robert Humphreys

Editor:

Stephen Evans

Screenwriter:

Alice Bell

Genre:

Coming of Age
Black Comedy

Duration:

95 minutes

Cast:

Emily Barclay
Mia Wasikowska
Genevieve Lemon
Steve Bastoni
Robert Morgan
Laurence Breuls
Michael Dorman
Anthony Hayes

Year:

2006

secretly wants to be her and local cop Sergeant Andretti wants to get (with) her. Her long-suffering and devoted dad, John, has been raising Katrina and her brother Danny on his own since their drug-addicted mother abandoned them long ago. After Danny is locked up in jail for life for a bungled robbery in which he decapitated a petrol-station attendant for calling Katrina a slut, Katrina becomes incensed. She *really* loves her brother and needs money for an appeal to get him out of jail, so she figures that the family home might be worth something and sets about orchestrating her father's death to get the inheritance. Her boyfriend Rusty seems reluctant to do the deed, so she employs Danny's dim-witted mate Kenny, who is rendered powerless by Kat's sizzling sexuality. When John is found beaten to death in his bed, Katrina side-steps accusations of her involvement in the murder and becomes a local celebrity, relishing the attention. As director Paul Goldman states, 'She's the perfect poster-girl for these raunchy, reactionary, mean times of ours – for our psychopathic society' (Goldman, production notes).

Critique

Stylistically a mix of mockumentary, flashbacks, gritty realism, black comedy, parody, music video and comic book, *Suburban Mayhem* is a unique powerhouse of a film. Scenes which bring together slick editing, blasting rock-chick music (Suzi Quatro, Adalita, Fur, The Spazzys, Little Birdy), rich writing and iconic scenes, like Katrina stealing Rusty's Charger, make for a wild and entertaining ride. Written by self-confessed true-crime addict, 20-something Alice Bell, *Suburban Mayhem* is a *tour de force* of sex, murder and mayhem. We hear about Katrina through key characters in the film, grotesquely mocking and judging her with (faux) moralistic tones, accompanied by episodic flashbacks about the events that surround Katrina's father's death. Without one redeeming feature, Katrina is presented as truly evil and wholly immoral, a contemporary take on the femme fatale, young and sexy but deadly. Through the characters in the film, the film-makers criticize and mock Katrina, while simultaneously celebrating her as a transgressive female character. It is the ambiguity that underpins the film that is most interesting. Is Katrina a one-dimensional stereotype or a transgressive figure? Are we meant to condemn her or celebrate in her wild misadventures? Are we shocked and saddened or do we laugh at the black humour and/or join in the ridicule? On one level the film is cynical and hard-hitting, making rather conservative comments about, for instance, vain, pretty girls, fame-seeking teens, evil femmes fatales. It also demonizes teenage mothers, 'banal', 'ugly' suburbia and working-class 'bogans'. But at the same time, so much of it is about rejoicing in the kitsch (anti)glamour they provide, and we see that suburbia is far from boring or cultureless. And in the end, Katrina does get away with it all. The main criticism of the film is that there was potential to give Katrina more depth (like in the scenes where her brother rejects her or when she is strung out after a three-day bender), to show Katrina's vulnerabilities, and to let the audience in on her motivations. Instead the film chooses to present us with a hyperreal, over-the-top, grotesque girl who is wild and stunning, but ultimately superficial: unfortunately, a bit like the film itself.

Kristina Gottschall

HORROR

The Australian horror film is a fascinating specimen. While the genre has antecedents in the silent era of cinema and has, at times, produced popular and commercially-successful titles, horror films have existed in the shadows of Australian cinema. For much of the last four decades, genre films have not been considered worthy parts of a national cinema funded largely by public subsidy with the objective of fostering a sense of national identity and Australian distinctiveness. Despite their popularity among film-makers and audiences, horror movies in particular have existed at the margins of Australian screen culture, largely ignored by public funding agencies, and either overlooked or despised by mainstream critics.

Razorback (Russell Mulcahy, 1984), *Patrick* (Richard Franklin, 1978), *Turkey Shoot* (Brian Trenchard-Smith, 1982) *Roadgames* (Richard Franklin, 1981), *Long Weekend* (Colin Eggleston, 1978), and *Howling III* (Philippe Mora, 1987) among others, have achieved far greater levels of commercial and critical success overseas, particularly in video and cable-TV markets. While numerous titles have won prestigious international awards in competition with much higher profile titles – *Patrick* won the Avoriaz Fantastic Film Festival's Grand Prize over the US classic *Halloween* (John Carpenter, 1978), for example – and have gone on to become popular cult titles worldwide, horror along with other 'Ozploitation' films were ignored by those assessing or determining the boundaries of Australian cinema. In recent years, however, the status of the horror genre within Australian cinema has undergone a major transformation from a marginal and despised trash genre to an increasingly naturalized commercial genre for low-budget film-makers.

The origins of an Australian horror tradition are often traced back to horror-infused thrillers *The Bells* (WJ Lincoln, 1911), *The Strangler's Grip* (Cyril Mackay, Leonard Willey and Sydney Stirling, 1912), *The Face at the Window* (Charles Villiers, 1919), and ghost stories *The Guyra Ghost Mystery* (John Cosgrove, 1921) and *Fisher's Ghost* (Raymond Longford, 1924). Nevertheless, only a handful of horror-related titles emerged during the first seven decades of Australian cinema.

Left: *Wolf Creek*, True Crime/Best Fx.

The Australian film industry experienced a major renaissance in the 1970s and horror movies, like Ozploitation films more generally, emerged as an undercurrent to mainstream Australian cinema. The first Australian horror movie of the renaissance was Terry Bourke's *Night of Fear* (1972) about a woman terrorized by a mute hermit sex-predator. Largely a silent movie, 54 minutes in length, the film is a curio. While playing off international market cycles and influenced by American and British horror movies, most early Aussie horror movies were quirky genre movies and, in many cases, far from conventional horror fare.

Bourke's second film *Inn of the Damned* (1975), revolving around a bounty-hunter's investigation into disappearances near a remote inn in the 1890s, is predominantly a western spliced with generic elements of the gothic film (a remote inn and haunting ghosts) and the horror movie (victims are crushed to death in their sleep by a medieval-esque death trap). *Thirst* (Rod Hardy, 1979), a movie about a woman held captive by an aristocratic vampire cult attempting to convince her she is of vampire ancestry, is among the quirkier vampire films in horror cinema history with pulsating walls, blood showers, and blood-filled milk cartons.

The 1980s saw a surge in Australian horror production. Shifting the financial burden from government funding agencies to private investors, the government introduced the infamous 10BA tax incentive in 1981. For many commercially-oriented producers, the horror genre offered the potential of commercial returns and international audiences. A key title was Russell Mulcahy's *Razorback* (1984) set in a degenerate community terrorized by a giant boar in the isolated Australian outback. Another 1980s' cult-favourite is Richard Franklin's Hitchcockian *Roadgames* (1981) about a truck driver and a young female hitchhiker playing 'cat and mouse' games with a serial killer. Other titles included *Nightmares* (John Lamond, 1980), revolving around a female actress in a play whose cast are being murdered, *The Survivor* (directed by British actor David Hemmings, 1981) about a plane crash and a passenger's mysterious survival, and *Houseboat Horror* (Kendal Flanagan and Ollie Martin, 1987), a slasher film set on a houseboat during a rock band's video shoot. Most 1980s' horror films were B-movies produced for drive-ins, limited theatrical release, cable and video markets.

The 1990s marked the lowest point in the history of Australian horror films. With few exceptions, commercial production dried up. The 10BA tax break was wound back in 1987, cutting off the predominant source of finance fuelling Australian horror films. The saturation of global markets with trite horror fare and the exhaustion of the slasher sub-genre by the mid-1980s also contributed to shrinking markets for local product. Only two mainstream horror titles emerged in the 1990s: the slasher *Bloodmoon* (Alex Mills, 1990) and the splatter film *Body Melt* (Philip Brophy, 1993), both savaged by critics and dismal failures at the box office. An Australian horror film tradition was sustained by low-budget underground film-makers, with *Bloodlust* (Jon Hewitt, Richard Wolstencroft, 1990), about urban vampires who double-cross mobsters, produced on a budget of A$300,000 and shot on video: typical of the period. Other low-budget titles included *Deep Sleep* (Alec Mills, 1990), about carnage in a deep-sleep clinic; and *The Min-Min* (Carl T Woods, 1990), about the violation of a sacred Aboriginal burial ground and Dreamtime spirits. Only a handful of underground titles reached niche trash audiences; many failed to receive release.

By contrast, the 2000s has been a golden period for Australian horror movies. The Australian film industry's integration into global audiovisual networks, an inflow of international finance, the rise of low-cost digital video and the growth in DVD and online niche markets have fuelled unprecedented growth in Australian horror movies. There has been a major boom in production with the number of horror flicks rising to over 70 films in the 2000s. A constant stream of B-grade titles have flowed onto national and international markets. The worldwide cult success of *Undead* (2003), and the mainstream success of *Saw* (James Wan, 2004) – which was created by Australian film-makers and which has gone on to become one of the most successful horror franchises of all-time – and *Wolf Creek* (Greg Mclean, 2005), forged a global reputation for Australian horror flicks in terms of audiences, critical reception and interest from transnational distributors. Fan culture is developing around local horror movies that simply did not exist in previous decades – from fanzines such as Digitalretribution.com, online fan groups, to Sydney's *A Night of Horror* Film Festival – fuelling grassroots development and audiences.

Wolf Creek (2005), *Black Water* (David Nerlich & Andrew Traucki, 2008), *Undead* (2003), *Storm Warning* (Jamie Blanks, 2006), *Lake Mungo* (Joel Anderson, 2009) *Dying Breed* (Jody Dwyer, 2008), and *Feed* (Brett Leonard, 2005), have all achieved varying degrees of cult success and/or commercial returns in global markets. However, since the worldwide success of *Wolf Creek* – which earned over A$50 million in worldwide revenue from a budget of A$1.4 million – no Australian horror title has achieved commensurate returns in cinema markets and, as critics point out, *Rogue* (2007) and *Dying Breed* (2008) were commercial failures at the domestic box-office. Nevertheless, the majority of Australian horror films are released straight-to-video, they often make gross returns in video markets, and many titles (courtesy of low budgets) go into profit through presales.

Since the 1970s, a key thematic concern for distinctively-Australian horror flicks has been the struggle for survival against a 'monstrous landscape' – the portrayal of landscape as a dangerous entity functioning as a character in its own right rather than purely a setting for action. An ethereal supernatural force emanating from an ancient landscape abducts a group of schoolgirls on a picnic in 1900 in the Australian gothic film *Picnic at Hanging Rock* (Peter Weir, 1975), while an entire ecosystem annihilates human trespassers in *Long Weekend* (Colin Egglestone, 1978; Jamie Blanks, 2008). In other movies, the monstrous landscape is literalized in the form of dangerous animals from giant boars (*Razorback*) and killer crocodiles (*Dark Age*, Arch Nicholson, 1987; *Black Water*; *Rogue*), to marsupial werewolves (*Howling III*).

Indigenous themed horrors – usually made by non-Indigenous film-makers – have been a common feature of terror Australis. Such movies explore tensions between white-Australians and Indigenous Australians, Indigenous spirituality and the mythology of the Dreaming, supernatural forces and black magic. Such films include *The Last Wave* (Peter Weir, 1977), *Zombie Brigade* (Carmelo Musca & Barrie Pattison, 1987), *Kadaicha* (James Bogle, 1987), *The Dreaming* (Mario Andreacchio, 1988), *The Min-Min* (1990), and *Prey* (Oscar D'Roccster, 2009).

A theme incredibly popular in recent years is the idea that 'Australia is a dangerous place for a holiday' for foreigners and outsiders. The theme has been explored in a long list of Australian horror films such as *Wolf Creek, Rogue, Storm Warning, Lake Mungo, Long Weekend, Gone* (Ringan Ledwidge, 2006), and *Dying Breed*. 'Foreigners' are often the central victims in such films, although 'Australians' are sometimes collateral damage. For example, those suffering the most at the hands of serial killer Mick Taylor in *Wolf Creek* are English backpackers Liz and Kristy, while their companion, Australian Ben Mitchell, is left to rot in an abandoned mine shaft. Conversely, Australian characters, generally from the city, who venture into the remote and isolated outback are often victims of nature's revenge (*Black Water*), or malevolent Indigenous Australian forces (*Prey*).

Mark David Ryan

Black Water

Country of Origin:
Australia

Production Company:
Prodigy Movies

Directors:
David Nerlich
Andrew Traucki

Producer:
Michael Robertson

Screenwriters:
David Nerlich
Andrew Traucki

Cinematographer:
John Biggins

Production Designer:
Aaron Crothers

Editor:
Rodrigo Balart

Duration:
85 minutes

Genre:
Horror (survival thriller/horror)

Cast:
Diana Glenn
Maeve Dermody
Andy Rodoreda
Ben Oxenbould

Year:
2007

Synopsis

Grace, her boyfriend Adam, and younger sister Lee are on a fishing trip when a crocodile capsizes their boat. Scrambling to the safety of a tree, they confront the dire reality of their situation. They are trapped in a mangrove swamp on a remote waterway; no one knows they are gone. Their tour guide Jim has been taken by the croc and their boat is firmly stuck upside down tantalizingly close to their sanctuary. But to reach the boat, they have to wade through open water, and the crocodile is waiting. Stranded, with little chance of rescue, the three tourists find themselves in a horrific struggle for survival against Australia's most deadly predator.

Critique

Black Water and *Rogue* (Greg Mclean, 2007) are killer-crocodile movies based on real events. But while the latter's budget of A$28 million – phenomenally high for an Australian film, and especially for a horror film – allowed the use of sophisticated CGI and high-profile actor, for many, *Black Water* with a A$1 million budget and using physical effects and real crocodiles, is a far better film. *Black Water* is a psychological survival thriller rather than a typical creature feature, and it is disturbingly realistic. In a similar vein to Mclean's first feature, *Wolf Creek*, audiences are forced to confront the question *What if I were in the same situation*? The answer sends a cold shiver down a viewer's spine. The killer crocodile movie generally revolves around a gargantuan crocodile devouring unsuspecting victims. But the killer croc, the star of the movie, typically has limited personality – it kills for food, defends its territory or, in some cases, it is a primeval protector of a sacred place. But in *Black Water,* the killer croc is extremely clever, and the most apt analogy is that it 'toys' with victims like a sadistic killer. The crocodile's attacks are unpredictable: sometimes it attacks, other times it waits, but it is always watching. Victims wake on mudflats beside mutilated companions surrounded by swamp water – their only escape is back through murky water where the predator waits for them as though playing a game. In a shocking scene, Lee and Grace attempt to muffle the sound of snapping bones and tearing flesh as the crocodile feasts on Adam nearby in darkness. The film explores age-old themes: the survival instinct, primal fears of the unknown, and man versus nature. A moral of the story is that humanity's relentless encroachment on nature has dangerous repercussions. In an intertitle, the movie is introduced by the text: 'the Salt Water Crocodile population in Northern Australia is expanding, so is the human population'. Crocodiles in this movie are tourist attractions; their natural habitat is a playground for tourists. Crocodiles are hunted or farmed for their skins with 'four feet being the optimum size for the handbag market'. When Lee asks their tour-guide why he brought a handgun on a fishing trip, Jim replies 'it's just Barry's insurance policy. He can remember the old days before all the crocs had moved out of here. But now they've all either been shot or taken to farms.' In *Black Water*, with the crocodile population growing, a rogue crocodile has returned to this placid waterway to reap revenge on humans. After a spate of recent deaths from crocodile attacks in 2009, this movie is a chilling reminder of the dangers crocodiles pose to humans … and vice versa.

Mark David Ryan

Cut

Country of Origin:
Australia

Production Company:
Mushroom Pictures
Beyond Films
MBP (Germany)

Director:
Kimble Rendall

Producers:
Martin Fabinyi
Bill Bennett

Screenwriter:
Dave Warner

Cinematographer:
David Foreman

Production Designer:
Steven Jones-Evans

Art Director:
Richard Hobbs

Editor:
Henry Dangar

Duration:
80 minutes

Genre:
Horror (slasher)

Cast:
Molly Ringwald
Frank Roberts
Kylie Minogue
Jessica Napier
Stephen Curry

Year:
2000

Synopsis

Charlie is left alone by his parents with his older sister Chloe when the family home catches fire – she escapes, he is horribly burned. Disfigured, mute and demented, the killer Scarman is born. A sword melded with a pair of garden shears his weapon of choice, Scarman has one simple agenda – kill his family! Have revenge! The movie is *Hot Blooded*, a schlock B-grade 1980s horror flick in production. When a psychologically-unhinged actor playing Scarman brutally murders director Hilary Jacobs, production is stopped and never completed. Many years later, a group of ambitious film students set out to remake the slasher. For producer Hester Ryan this is an opportunity to hit the 'big time', while for director Raffy Carruthers this is the chance to finish her mother's movie. Returning to the original location and persuading *Hot Blooded's* lead, American actress Vanessa Turnbill, to complete her original role, the film shoot begins. But the film is cursed. Whoever has previously attempted to finish the movie has died horribly. The characters soon discover that when *Hot Blooded's* production begins, the fictional character Scarman becomes a terrifying reality, brought into existence by negative energies caused by the horrific events of the original film shoot. Scarman has a new agenda – kill everyone! Ensure the movie is never completed! As the film's tagline puts it 'they just have to finish the film … before it finishes them'.

Critique

The slasher *Cut* (2000) was a commercial Aussie horror flick ahead of its time. Promoted as an 'Australian *Scream*', though it was ironically *Scream 3* (2000) that blew it out of the water at the box-office, *Cut* was the first mainstream Australian horror movie in almost a decade. The movie is heavily influenced by the late 1990s' US teen slasher cycle (a trend that was dominating mainstream horror cinema at the time), particularly *Scream* (Wes Craven, 1996), *Urban Legend* (directed by Australian Jamie Blanks, 1998), and *I Know What You Did Last Summer* (Jim Gillespie, 1997). Like most of these films, a young 'hip' cast, a 'clever' twist as to the slasher's identity, and the referencing of the horror genre were key ingredients. Few classic horror titles escape reference – 'who wants to make a mainstream slasher movie bigger than *Halloween* (John Carpenter, 1978), creepier than *Friday the 13th* (Sean S Cunningham, 1980), more blood and guts than *The Texas Chain Saw Massacre* (Tobe Hooper, 1974)?' For hard-core horror aficionados, Scarman's back story is a laughable combination of plot elements from *Halloween* and *A Nightmare on Elm Street* (Wes Craven,

1984). *Halloween's* Michael Myers kills his sister with a butcher's knife after a parent's night out, and *Nightmare's* Freddy Krueger is a supernatural burns victim back for revenge. Yet despite strong international influences, many of the central thematic concerns are Australian. A key theme of the film is the tension between government film agencies and film-makers producing popular movie genres such as action, adventure, science-fiction and horror movies, among others. Throughout the 1990s, the majority of Australian films were financed by government bodies that explicitly favoured 'quality' art-house films at the expense of 'debased' popular genre movies because the former were considered more culturally worthy. As such, *Cut* is a movie conscious of the difficult position it occupied in Australian cinema during the early 2000s. The character Lossman is a university lecturer whose perspective on cinema arguably reflects attitudes prevalent within Australian film culture and screen education since the 1970s. Lecturing on the murder of Hilary Jacobs, inferring that horror films inspire violent behaviour, Lossman reminds his students, 'that's why I don't include the slasher genre in my course'. When Raffy and Hester express an interest in remaking the film, Lossman snaps 'you two have more important things to say, don't waste your time doing trash!' A key message is that horror movies *do* have a place within Australian cinema. As Raffy puts it, 'a horror film can be as political as *Priscilla* (*The Adventures of Priscilla, Queen of the Desert,* Stephan Elliott, 1994) or *The Piano* (Jane Campion, 1993). But even if it's not, what's wrong with making a scary film and giving people a bit of a fright'. For Hester, 'it's time we graduated into pop culture boys and girls'. In terms of the movie's commercial performance, *Cut* sold into territories around the world, and commentators tipped it to be a box-office smash. The film opened number two at box-offices in France and Hong Kong, performed solidly on video in the United States, but failed dismally at the Australian box-office. Overall reviews were mixed, most domestic reviews were shocking. The film can be understood as a schlock B-grade horror spoof of 1980s' B-grade horror, or a terrible movie that tried hard to be cool but failed miserably. For many Aussie commentators it is the latter. A major domestic criticism is that it is a 'contrived' horror movie, packaged by producers in an attempt to crack the horror market, rather than crafted by creative talent with expertise in the genre horror genre. Despite a high body-count and plenty of dismembered limbs, the film never rises above silliness, and rarely creates tension or genuine terror. The film is not bad enough to be – as the adage goes – 'so bad it's good', but then again it is not bad enough to be so terrible that nobody remembers its existence, leaving it somewhere in between ... which is still pretty bad.

Mark David Ryan

Dying Breed, Ambience.

Dying Breed

Country of Origin:
Australia

Production Company:
Ambience Entertainment

Director:
Jody Dwyer

Producers:
Michael Boughen
Rod Morris

Screenwriters:
Michael Boughen
Jody Dwyer
Rod Morris

Cinematographer:
Geoffrey Hall

Synopsis

Dying Breed interweaves two intriguing facets of Australian folklore: the extinct Tasmanian Tiger and the story of the cannibal convict Alexander Pearce. The Tasmanian Tiger was officially hunted into extinction by the 1930s, but rumours and unconfirmed sightings continue speculation that deep in the unexplored wilds of Tasmania the species has survived. An Irish convict and bushranger, Alexander Pearce escaped the brutal Tasmanian penal colony of Sarah Island with several inmates in 1822 and later confessed to killing and eating them to survive in the wilderness. After a second escape he was recaptured with human flesh in his possession despite having adequate (non-human) food provisions. Pearce was hung in 1824 for cannibalism. *Dying Breed* is a fictional story loosely based on these two legends. Zoologist Nina, her boyfriend Matt, his friend Jack and his girlfriend Rebecca, travel to Tasmania in search of the Tiger after Nina discovers a photograph proving the species' existence taken by her sister. Reaching the isolated township of Sarah, surrounded by rugged hills notorious for tourist disappearances and Nina's sister's final destination before her mysterious death, the protagonists prepare for their expedition. But having entered the domain of Alexander Pearce's descendents, who uphold his cannibal heritage, the protagonists find

Production Designer:
David Mackay

Art Director:
Janie Parker

Editor:
Mark Perry

Duration:
88 minutes

Genre:
Horror (backwoods horror)

Cast:
Nathan Phillips
Leigh Whannell
Bille Brown
Mirrah Foulkes
Melanie Vallejo

Year:
2008

themselves in a desperate struggle for survival against modern day cannibals. Lured into the hills in search of the Tiger, tourists are game on which the township feed, and women are needed by the clan to breed. No outsider leaves Sarah alive, and tourists always arrive in search of the Tiger.

Critique

Dying Breed is one of the best Australian horror films of the decade, though receiving mixed critical reception overseas, and mostly negative critical reception in Australia. Unfortunately, Australians are the harshest critics of their own films – particularly local genre movies – and tend to focus on what is wrong rather than what is right with a local film. *Dying Breed* is a solid B-grade film; nothing more, nothing less. A major criticism is that *Dying Breed* is derivative, borrowing from *Deliverance* (John Boorman, 1972), *Wrong Turn* (Rob Schmidt, 2003), and *The Hills Have Eyes* (Wes Craven, 1977; Alexandre Aja, 2006), bringing little new to the well-worn 'backwoods horror' sub-genre. The legends of the Tasmanian Tiger and Alexander Pearce had potential to renew backwoods horror themes rather as *Wolf Creek* (Greg Mclean, 2005) renewed slasher conventions, but the film rarely strays from established conventions. The creepy little girl, like the deformed boy, the folk music scene, boating scenes surrounded by wild forests, and even the crossbow, are highly derivative of *Deliverance*. But are the derivativeness and borrowings really a problem? Most contemporary horrors flicks are derivative in one way or another and few B-grade horror flicks are perfect. But what is right with the film? Plenty! Once the carnage begins, there is nasty gore and cannibalism that made audiences scream and peer at the screen through trembling hands. Such elements are not exactly a measure of quality for an arthouse film, but for a B-grade horror with the sole objective of frightening audience, the more horrific and terrifying the better. At times *Dying Breed* is a tense, brooding film. The Tasmanian wilderness is breathtakingly, hauntingly beautiful, rugged and wild. The visual feel of the film is brilliant – dark, gloomy and ominous. A key talking point for fans is the rabbit scene. Nina zooms in on a cute bunny rabbit sitting on a rock with a high-powered photographic lens. Suddenly it disappears, and looking up from her camera, she stares aghast at a rabbit twitching in its death throes impaled on a tree by an arrow.

The film does suffer somewhat from the shortcomings of its various subplots. Nina's investigation into her sister's death, and her secretly unauthorized trip to discover the Tasmanian Tiger, often tangle and slow the narrative's drive. The Tasmanian Tiger is superfluous to the plot, and other than luring tourists into the wilds, contributes little to the story. Not a film for everyone, but for horror fans, *Dying Breed* is a slick B-grade backwoods horror, and a standout contemporary Australian horror movie.

Mark David Ryan

Lost Things

Country of Origin:
Australia

Production Company:
Agenda Film Productions
ISM Films

Director:
Martin Murphy

Producer:
Ian Iveson

Screenwriter:
Stephen Sewell

Cinematographer:
Justine Kerrigan

Production Designer:
Karla Urizar

Editor:
Benita Carey
Karen Johnson

Duration:
80 minutes

Genre:
Horror (psychological horror/
supernatural)

Cast:
Leon Ford
Charlie Garber
Lenka Kripac
Steve Le Marquand
Alexandra Vaughan

Year:
2003

Synopsis

Two teenage couples, Emily and Brad, Tracy and Garry, travel to a secluded beach for a surfing weekend. Not long into their getaway, no matter what the distraction – from love games to drinking – they cannot shake the feeling that something is wrong with this stretch of beach. When the couples meet Zippo, a strange beachcomber who warns them to leave, this feeling only intensifies. They begin experiencing déjà vu, and clues to the murder of three teenagers begin to appear. Before long their weekend descends into madness: at night their campsite is haunted by spirits from an ancient burial ground; they experience disturbing flashbacks; and any sense of the rational is shattered when they learn that Zippo is a demon preying on victims lured to the beach. In a final twist, Gary, Brad, Emily and Tracey discover that they are dead, and trapped in a reoccurring nightmare.

Critique

Lost Things is a supernatural horror film based on Friedrich Nietzsche's principle of the 'eternal return': the philosophical idea that an individual is continuously reborn to relive existence over and over again. As director Martin Murphy explains in the special features: 'Imagine a demon creeps into your bedroom and whispers into your ear "all moments past have already happened and will happen again and again for all time … what are you going to do?"' While the movie begins like countless slasher films – a group of teenagers arrive at a remote location where all is not well – Lost Things is not your regular horror movie. The story is non-linear, revolving around teenagers reliving a sequence of their lives that ultimately leads to their murders. A useful analogy is that the teenagers are trapped in a reoccurring time-loop, where the past and present overlap with the current succession of events. For example, in their current trip to the beach, which has already happened, the teenagers witness fragments of their previous murders, as well as glimpses of the actual present as mourning parents ay flowers on their sandy graves. In this 'twilight-zone', the killer is not a masked madman or a typical demon from hell but, rather, a demon in the guise of a stereotypical mullet-sporting, thong-wearing, Aussie yobbo. Rather than formula-driven, the storyline is character- and dialogue-driven, resulting in a movie consisting almost entirely of five characters, a van, and a desolate beachfront. Lost Things is one of the few horror films set predominantly in daytime, opting for sunlight and sun-bleached exteriors over the foreboding shadows and darkness iconic of classic horror cinema. Thematically, like numerous Australian horror movies, the landscape is portrayed as a dangerous entity from which the characters are alienated. The beach is desolate and dangerous; crows squawk eerily among twisted trees, deadly snakes lie hidden among the dunes waiting for victims. This idea of the 'monstrous landscape' is a common trope in Australian horror cinema, popularized by Picnic at Hanging Rock (Peter Weir, 1975) and most recently exemplified by Wolf Creek (Greg Mclean, 2005). One of the more 'frightening' elements of the movie is the eeriness Murphy evokes from little more than a shot of a desolate beachfront and a sinister score. While the 'already dead' twist can be seen coming from a long way off, the film's underlying creepiness compensates for any disappointment arising from the twist's predictability, and is a standout feature of the movie. *Lost Things* is an exemplary case of indie film-making for aspiring film-makers looking to independently produce their own feature films. The movie was shot in just 12 days. It was financed predominantly by private investors, and cast and crew payments were deferred until the film's sale to distributors. Despite its low budget, the film received an Australian cinema release, sold into over 20 countries around the world, and at one point producers were negotiating with a Hollywood major for a US remake.

Mark David Ryan

Prey

Alternative Title:
Dreamtime's Over (USA)

Country of Origin:
Australia

Production Company:
Top Cat Films

Director:
Oscar D'Roccster (George Miller)

Producer:
Robert Lewis Galinsky
Elizabeth Howatt-Jackman

Screenwriter:
John V. Soto
Robert Lewis Galinsky
Elizabeth Howatt-Jackman

Cinematographer:
Andrew Topp

Art Director:
Harvey Mawson
Lance Whitehouse

Editor:
Geoff Hitchins

Duration:
84 minutes

Synopsis

Three couples set out for a holiday driving across the desert. Refuelling at a remote petrol station, an enigmatic bushman gives Kate a magical charm and lures the group off the highway. Lost and losing all sense of direction, the couples find themselves trapped in an eerie stretch of desert. The couples have been led by a human servant onto the sacred grounds of an ancient Indigenous Australian spirit, and it is feeding time.

Critique

Houseboat Horror (Kendal Flanagan & Ollie Martin, 1989) and *Bloodlust* (Jon Hewitt & Richard Wolstencroft 1992) have long been regarded as the worst Australian horror movies ever made, but the supernatural horror *Prey* directed by George Miller (director of the Australian cinema classic *The Man from Snowy River* (1982) and not to be confused with *Mad Max*'s (1979) George Miller) and starring pop-star and *So You Think You Can Dance Australia* host Natalie Bassingthwaighte, is a very serious contender for the title. The film's production was a horror story in its own right, far more frightening than the actual movie. The film somehow received the same title as a terrible South African horror film released in 2007 about a pride of lions on a killing spree. Miller, after demanding last-minute script changes, allegedly self-destructed during the shoot. As producer Robert Lewis Galinsky wrote on Twitter in September 2009, the 'making of *Prey Exclusive* [Melbourne Underground Film Festival 2009 premiere] shows the disintegration of the original psychopathic director'. There were investor problems, line producers threatened to quit, and Bassingthwaighte injured her ankle, causing shooting delays. After disagreements with producers, George Miller relinquished his director's credit and withdrew from production, and post-production commenced without direction. Original footage was lost and a post-production team worked with offline, low-resolution material. While some of the greatest movies of all time have made it through

Genre:

Horror (supernatural)

Cast:

Natalie Bassingthwaighte
Jesse Johnson
Natalie Walker
Ben Kermode
Christian Clark
Kristin Sargent

Year:

2009

disastrous film shoots to become critically-acclaimed masterpieces, *Prey* was not so lucky. Yet for the lovers of trash cinema, this film may be 'so bad it's good'. This potential has been recognized by distributors, with the movie's promotional strategy changing dramatically between pre-release and release, from 'spooky supernatural horror starring Natalie Bassingthwaighte' to 'camp trash horror comedy', or as the movie poster tag-line puts it – 'the most horrifying movie since *Spice World* (1997) the movie'. At times the acting and visual feel resemble bad television; dialogue is poor, and attempts made by Miller to scare audiences are amateur at best – more proof that frightening an audience is far more difficult than many people believe. The storyline is incoherent and confusing. An audience is fairly sure the storyline has something to do with a 'Kaditcha' considering the human servant spends a good part of his screen time shouting, 'Kaditcha!', 'Kaditcha!' For Indigenous Australians, a 'Kaditcha man' (or similar variations depending on regional dialects) is a tribal lawmaker associated with 'black magic', similar to a witch doctor. But in *Prey*, the term appears to mean some kind of Dreamtime spirit, presumably a snake, who, through his human servant, lures victims into the desert to feed .. and to impregnate Bassingthwaighte's character. But a viewer cannot be entirely certain. The story contains no discernable generic rules. It is never explained how characters become possessed; they just become possessed. It is never explained why some corpses breathe and blink and why others do not. Are they continuity errors? Why can snakes operate a 4WD handbrake? Many of the greatest films ever are remembered for a single scene, such as the giant white pointer bursting from the ocean in *Jaws* (1975); bad and mediocre films are typically just forgotten; but absolutely terrible films that develop cult status are remembered for moments of extremely inept and bizarre film-making. *Plan 9 from Outer Space* (Edward D Wood Jr, 1959), for example, is often remembered for shaking cardboard gravestones, weird dialogue, and flying saucers on string. *Prey* has a classic 'so bad it's good' scene. Kate is a doctor. Matt (Kermode) has been attacked by a swarm of snakes and is covered in snake bites. Reaching his side, Kate makes a snap-diagnosis – Matt is suffering from an allergic reaction, though one would assume a medical practitioner should be able to distinguish between sets of holes oozing blood and an allergy. His head swelling to the size of a watermelon, Kate stabs him in the neck to clear his airway, when suddenly his head explodes. Sitting with a headless corpse in her arms, covered in brain matter, she changes her prognosis – 'snake bites'.

Mark David Ryan

Rogue

Country of Origin:
Australia

Production Company:
Dimension Films
Village Roadshow Pictures
Emu Creek Pictures

Director:
Greg Mclean

Producers:
David Lightfoot
Matt Hearn
Greg Mclean

Screenwriter:
Greg Mclean

Cinematographer:
Will Gibson

Production Designer:
Robert Webb

Editor:
Jason Ballantine

Duration:
95 minutes

Genre:
Horror (creature feature)

Cast:
Radha Mitchell
Michael Vartan
Sam Worthington
Caroline Brazier
Stephen Curry
John Jarratt

Year:
2007

Synopsis

Arriving in Australia's wild Northern Territory, American travel writer Pete McKell joins a river cruise to take a closer look at the dangerous salt-water crocodile. After a scenic tour through picturesque gorges and idyllic landscape, the boat's skipper Kate Ryan responds to a distress signal in a remote waterway. Passing primordial Indigenous Australian rock-paintings warning of an ancient creature guarding the gorge, the boat is violently rammed by a gargantuan crocodile. The boat is beached and the tourists are stranded on a small island. But in a tidal river system, the water levels are rising, and soon the entire island will be under water. To make matters worse, the survivors are in the territory of a killer crocodile marking each of them as a food source. The characters must escape from the island before it is too late.

Critique

The killer crocodile film *Rogue* is a curious beast, a pun difficult to avoid. Released in late 2007, *Rogue* was Greg Mclean's second feature following the release of the popular low-budget slasher *Wolf Creek* in 2005. The latter film's extraordinary success had earned Mclean a reputation as an emerging 'hot-shot' director. The most expensive Aussie horror flick ever produced with a budget of A$28 million, and backed by distribution heavyweight Dimension Films, the movie was highly anticipated, following *Wolf Creek's* worldwide success. Yet the movie was by all measures a commercial disaster. *Rogue* was effectively dumped by Dimension Films for its US theatrical release – while *Wolf Creek* opened on 1,749 screens in the United States, *Rogue* opened on just 10 screens – killing its box-office prospects, though its performance at the international box-office up until that point had been poor. The movie earned just US$4.2 million at the global box-office, *Wolf Creek* in comparison grossed US$27 million from a budget of A$1.4 million. However, as the website Thenumbers.com observed, in its list of DVD releases, 5 August 2008, '[*Rogue*] didn't flop because of bad reviews. In fact, it is being called the best killer croc movie ever, and it is certainly better than most horror movies that earn wide releases'. Therefore, a question often asked is 'What went wrong with *Rogue*?' In terms of the marketplace, *Rogue's* performance was handicapped by a major decline in the horror genre's popularity in cinema markets following the exhaustion of the torture porn cycle. In a similar vein to the fate of the slasher sub-genre in the 1980s, audiences tired of an endless stream of formulaic, ultra-violent torture flicks resulting in waning demand. The horror genre dipped to 2.9 per cent of the US box-office in 2008, down from 7.16 per cent in 2007 and between 5-6 per cent since 2005. Consequently, *Rogue* was released into a much tougher marketplace than *Wolf Creek* had been three years earlier. This was compounded further by an influx of dubious creature features – *Primeval* (Michael Katleman, 2007), *Prey* (Darrell Roodt, 2007) *Beyond Loch Ness* (Paul Ziller, 2008) and, to a lesser extent, *The Host* (Bong Joon-ho, 2006) – sapping any remaining interest there may have been for a giant killer crocodile movie. In terms of the film itself, *Rogue's* screenplay was among the first feature films Mclean had written, and was essentially dusted-off and green-lit by Dimension Films based on his success with *Wolf Creek*. While Mclean is a skilled artisan in subverting established horror conventions – he kills off characters that should not die, he subverts audience expectation, and adopts minimalist music scores among others – there is nothing shocking or controversial about the film. *Rogue* is more a thriller than hard-core shock horror, which was disappointing for viewers expecting a 'nasty' film in the vein of *Wolf Creek*. While *Wolf Creek* instilled fear in viewers through disturbingly-realistic depictions of torture and violence, *Rogue* is low on shock value in a marketplace demanding graphic violence and high levels of gore. For Australian viewers, the film was produced for an American audience, and was ironically too Australian – 'mate' and associated clichés felt contrived, Radha Mitchell's Australian accent was 'over the top', and sweeping shots of canyons and picturesque landscapes appeared to come straight from an Australian tourism campaign. To Greg Mclean's credit, the film is divinely shot, and he remains an immense film-making talent. The crocodile is the star of the film, a huge CGI generated killing machine that unfortunately needed more screen time. Though not a classic, *Rogue* is more an enjoyable movie for milder horror audiences than for hardcore horror aficionados. Despite a disappointing commercial performance, *Rogue* is easily among the best creature features of the 2007/08 market cycle and one of the better killer crocodile films of all time.

Mark David Ryan

Storm Warning

Country of Origin:
Australia

Production Company:
Resolution Independent
Storm Warning Productions

Director:
Jamie Blanks

Producer:
Pete Ford
Gary Hamilton

Screenwriter:
Everett De Roche

Cinematographer:
Karl von Moller

Art Director:
Justin Dix

Synopsis

Ignoring a storm warning, city lawyer Rob and his French girlfriend Pia, are forced to land their boat on a remote island. Lost and stumbling upon a ramshackle farmhouse with no one at home, they let themselves in to look for a phone only to discover a clandestine marijuana plantation. Before Robert and Pia can flee, the owners – Poppy and his two sons Brett and Jimmy – return to find their home violated and their secret uncovered. Imprisoned in a barn by a dysfunctional sadistic redneck 'family', Robert and Pia are plunged into a world of violence, torture, sexual and psychological abuse, horse pornography, and dogs with a taste for human flesh. Against overwhelming odds, Pia turns the table on her captors in a desperate struggle for survival with the help of a fish-hook trap, an anti-rape device welded from scrap metal, and a hammer.

Critique

Storm Warning is Australian director Jamie Blanks' first horror film directed down under. After being lured to Hollywood with only a short film under his belt, Blanks became a household name for horror aficionados with his popular US teen slashers *Urban Legend* (1998)

Editors:

Geoff Hitchins

Jamie Blanks

Duration:

83 minutes

Genre:

Horror (backwoods/survival
horror)

Cast:

Nadia Farès

Robert Taylor

David Lyons

Mathew Wilkinson

John Brumpton

Jonathan Oldham

Year:

2007

and *Valentine* (2001). *Urban Legend* grossed over US$70 million at the worldwide box office, while *Valentine* earned over US$36 million (although receiving poor critical reviews). A very different movie from his Hollywood horrors, *Storm Warning* is a typical low-budget independent Australian horror movie in a similar vein to *Wolf Creek* (Greg Mclean, 2005) and *Dying Breed* (Jody Dwyer, 2008). Like these films, *Storm Warning* had a budget between A$1 and A$5 million, it has an ambient and moody aesthetic feel typical of Aussie horror cinema, it explores similar themes of isolation and the dark side of tradition, and revolves around everyday people in an isolated locale where outsiders are not welcome. The movie received strong critical accolades from major horror fanzines (including fangoria.com and bloodydisgusting.com) despite its release straight to DVD rather than the original theatrical release promised to the film-makers by Dimension Films. While critics acknowledge the film brings little new to the 'backwoods' or 'survival' horror sub-genres, they applaud Blanks for a tense, foreboding film driven by an exquisite visual style – particularly masterful digital clouds prevalent throughout the film and constant rainfall generating an ominous mood. The movie was written by veteran Australian horror screenwriter, Everett De Roche – who had written earlier Aussie horror cult titles *Razorback* (1984) and *Patrick* (1978) – and was inspired by the classic children's fable *Goldilocks and the Three Bears*. Based on a screenplay written almost 30 years previously, it is perhaps unsurprising that ordinary people pitted against sadistic killers, and the triumph of strong female characters over their tormentors, have become clichéd themes in horror cinema. Nevertheless, De Roche's story was arguably ahead of its time and sheds light on dark aspects of Australian culture and society still relevant today. *Storm Warning* examines tensions between working-class 'country' folk and upper class 'city-folk'. Poppy, Brett, and Jimmy's violence towards Rob and Pia arises as much from their hatred of Volvo-driving city yuppies as it does from their sadistic nature and need to protect their illegal marijuana trade. Similar to *Wolf Creek*, a deep-seated hatred of foreigners pervades the film. When Jimmy notices Pia's accent he quips, 'you got yourself a frog [French] chick, hey … Hey darling, see this? [Cradling a baby kangaroo under his overcoat] I found him on the side of the road. You like kangaroos darling? Wanna pat him? [When she hesitates] Come on, he won't bite. [As Pia reluctantly reaches forward, Jimmy shouts at her violently, causing her to recoil in fright]. I might though'. Like numerous recent Aussie horror films, Australia is portrayed as a dangerous destination for a holiday. Foreigners, in particular, who stray from the 'beaten track', do so at their own peril. This reoccurring theme, explored in numerous contemporary Australian horror flicks, is perhaps an allegory of underlying racism in Australian culture. Such racism was forged into the popular consciousness in 2005 during the 'Cronulla riots' as mobs of white Australians rampaged through the suburb of Cronulla attacking anyone of ethnic appearance, and made international headlines more recently for a surge in alleged racial violence against Indian university students. Overall, *Storm Warning* is an impressive addition to Blanks' horror resumé, although it paints a bleak picture of aspects of contemporary Australian society.

Mark David Ryan

Undead

Country of Origin:
Australia

Production Company:
Spierigfilm

Directors:
Michael and Peter Spierig

Producers:
Michael and Peter Spierig

Screenwriters:
Michael and Peter Spierig

Cinematographer:
Andrew Strahorn

Production Designer:
Matthew Putland

Art Director:
Jane Culverhouse

Editors:
Michael and Peter Spierig

Duration:
100 minutes

Genre:
Horror (zombie film)

Cast:
Felicity Mason
Mungo McKay
Rob Jenkins
Lisa Cunningham
Emma Randall

Year:
2003

Synopsis

Berkeley is a small peaceful Australian fishing village where locals enjoy a beer and a game of cricket. When local beauty queen Rene's childhood farm is repossessed by the bank, she plans to leave Berkeley for the big city. But upon her departure, the town is bombarded by meteors, transforming the townsfolk into zombies with a hunger for human flesh. On a back road out of town, Rene is rescued by Marion, an outcast gunsmith abducted by aliens months earlier. Taking refuge in Marion's remote farmhouse, they are joined by four other survivors: the charter flight pilot Wayne, his pregnant girlfriend Sallyanne, the overawed police cadet Constable Molly, and the hopeless foul-mouthed Sergeant Harrison. Swarms of ravenous zombies, drawn by the scent of the living, lay siege to the farmhouse. Before long the farmhouse is overrun and, escaping in Marion's van, their only hope is to flee the infected zone. Reaching a towering wall of otherworldly spikes quarantining the town, the survivors discover an alien species – bringing with them acid-rain and rays of light, beaming living organisms into a canopy of ominous clouds – have come to earth to prevent the spread of the virus and to cure the infected.

Critique

Undead has become an indie film-making legend. Michael and Peter Spierig decided to take their film-making careers into their own hands after they were denied public finance and advised by government film agencies to forget popular movie genres. They raised a budget of less than A$1 million from life savings and loans from friends and family. The actual shooting budget ran out during the first day of production and, considering the film-maker's ambitions, this is no surprise. The film comprised Hollywood-esque action sequences, over 300 visual effects, a 41-day film shoot, and 11 interior sets, all of which had to be purpose-built. Materials were scrounged from rubbish bins to build sets, special effects were rendered on a personal laptop (which crashed on a regular basis), and most of the cast and crew were unpaid. But despite the massive challenges, the Spierig Brothers produced an indie film that looks relatively big-budget; the film achieved cinema release in Australia and the United States; and has gone on to become a worldwide cult title. The film is heavily influenced by several popular horror titles. The movie's basic plotline bears similarities to George Romero's *Night of the Living Dead* (1968) – a group of people hide in a farmhouse to survive a zombie rampage – and the film's black comedy and hard-core gore is reminiscent of Peter Jackson's *Brain Dead* (1992). Nevertheless, *Undead* is a highly innovative film and, in a similar vein to Jackson's *Bad Taste* (1987), renews standard conventions by mixing popular movie genres. *Bad Taste* mixes the plotlines of the zombie film with the alien invasion film, spliced with comedy and hard-core splatter (explicit portrayals of blood and guts). Similarly, *Undead* is an action-packed comedy, mixing

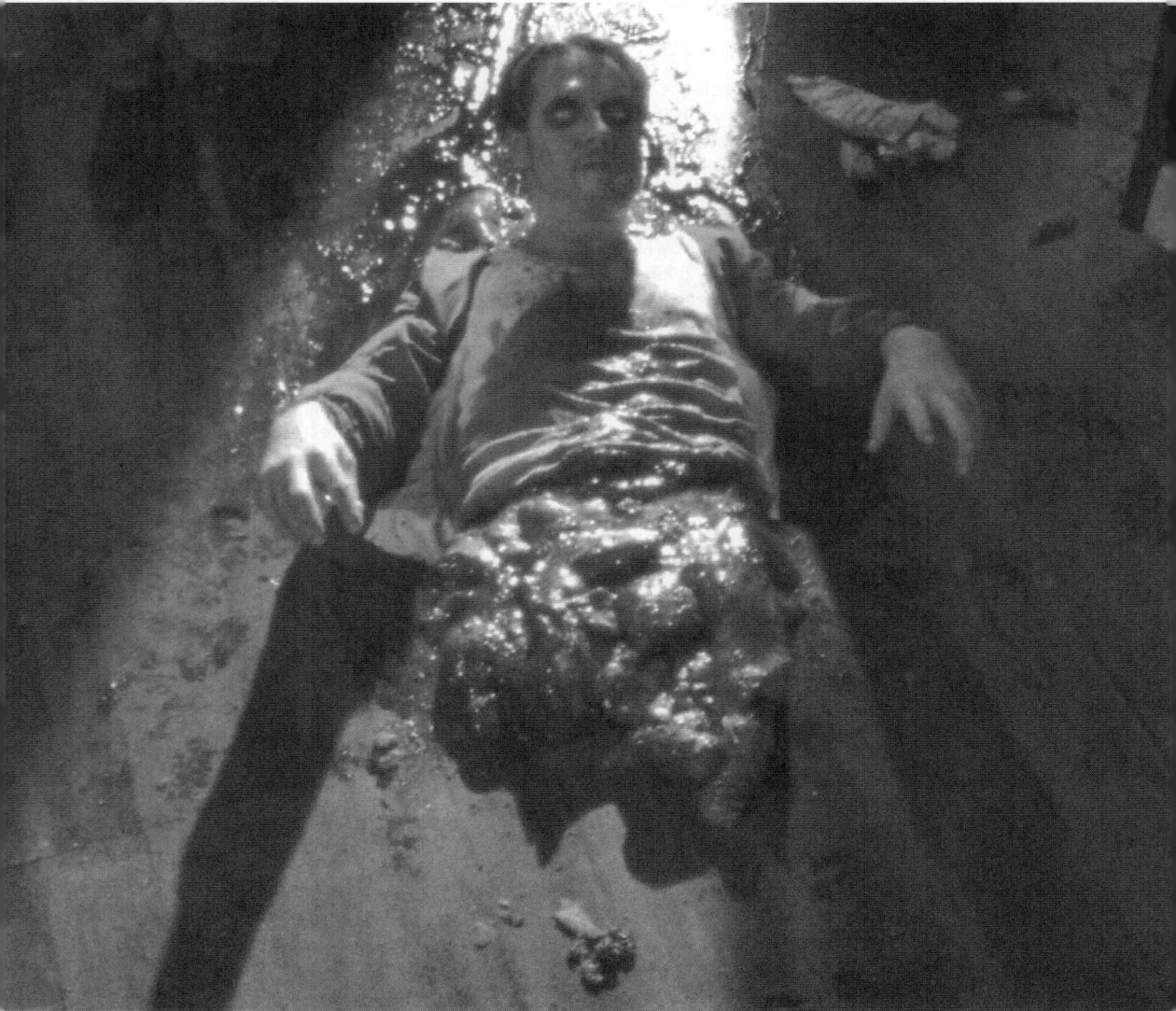

Undead (2003), Spierigfilm.

elements of the western (musical scores and character archetypes such as the lone gunslinger) with a traditional zombie film. While the movie draws upon universal genre conventions, *Undead* has a strong Australian flavour. Like countless Australian movies, the film is set in a stereotypical, dysfunctional rural town populated by beer-loving larrikins and yobbos, the main character is a victim of the tall-poppy syndrome, and the male protagonist is an archetypal laconic Australian male. When unique cultural themes and character types are combined with Aussie humour and ocker accents, the result is a distinctively Australian zombie flick. Standout features of the movie are the originality of characters and hilarious dialogue. Marion, a victim of a previous alien abduction, is a social outcast constantly harassed by police, while Rene is a victim of the tall-poppy syndrome after winning the town's beauty pageant. Both characters are struggling to discover their social identities in a narrow-minded community. But after the outbreak, Marion becomes 'a gun-slinging hero' and Rene, the 'chosen one' who can save Berkeley from destruction. In terms of dialogue, the character sergeant Harrison, in particular delivers some of the most memorable lines of the movie: 'When I was a kid we fucking respected our parents, we didn't fucking eat them!' After bursting into Marion's house pursued by zombies, in arguably the most hilarious line of the movie, Harrison yells: 'It's all those fucking crack marijuana fucking hippie fucking surfie fucking dole-bludging pricks – fuck!' Though the film is an amazing achievement, Undead undeniably has its faults. The movie's beginning is slow and amateurish, and there are pacing problems and script issues, including jarring plot elements such as the bizarre otherworldly wall and the alien twist. Nevertheless, Undead is a movie which deserves to be forgiven for its faults and celebrated as an innovative zombie film with amazing production values and high-octane action sequences, considering its limitations.

Mark David Ryan

Wolf Creek

Country of Origin:
Australia

Production Company:
403 Productions
True Crime Channel
Emu Creek Pictures
Mushroom Pictures (Associated)

Director:
Greg Mclean

Producer:
David Lightfoot
Matt Hearn
Greg Mclean

Screenwriter:
Greg Mclean

Cinematographer:
Will Gibson

Synopsis

Two English backpackers, Liz and Kristy, and their Australian companion, Ben, embark upon a road-trip across Australia from Broome in Western Australia to Cairns on the east coast. Travelling into the outback's dead heart across hundreds of miles of hard asphalt and barren desert, they reach the Wolf Creek meteorite crater, a key destination on their journey. Spending the afternoon at the picturesque site, they return to discover their car has mysteriously broken down, and the skies darkening overhead. When a friendly middle-aged roo-shooter Mick Taylor arrives and offers to tow their car to his camp to get a spare mechanical part, the young backpackers cautiously accept, suspecting Taylor will ask for payment in return for his services. Reaching his camp in an abandoned mining site, miles from nowhere, Liz, Kristy, and Ben have no choice but to stay the night and are assured their car will be fixed by morning. Liz wakes the next afternoon disoriented and reeling at the grim reality she faces – their food was drugged, she is bound and gagged, and Ben and Kristy are missing. Mick Taylor is a serial killer preying on backpackers visiting the Wolf Creek meteor site. First they must escape the clutches of a brutal psychopath, and then somehow navigate their way out of unforgiving desert to reach the safety of civilization ... with no idea of where they are.

Production Designer:

Robert Webb

Editor:

Jason Ballantine

Duration:

94 minutes

Genre:

Horror (slasher)

Cast:

John Jarratt

Cassandra Magrath

Kestie Morassi

Nathan Phillips

Year:

2005

Critique

Wolf Creek is the most popular Australian horror movie of all time. At the time of writing, the movie had earned over A$50 million in worldwide revenue from a budget of A$1.4 million, making it the most commercially-successful Aussie horror movie ever made. On the back of the film's popularity, director Greg Mclean was inducted into the 'Splat-Pack' Hall of Fame – a term denoting directors of prominent ultra-violent 'torture porn' movies in the mid-2000s – alongside *Hostel*'s (2005) Eli Roth, *Saw*'s (2004) James Wan, and *House of a Thousand Corpses*' (2003) Rob Zombie. The film sold to distributors for A$7.8 million making it the first FFC-backed (Film Finance Corporation) film to go substantially into profit before release, and, at the time of writing, was the most successful R-rated film ever at the Australian box-office. The movie is based loosely on two widely-reported true crimes: the murder of British tourist Peter Falconio in the Northern Territory in 1996, and the Ivan Milat Backpacker Murders in the early 1990s. While the movie has developed a notorious reputation as an extremely sadistic and graphically-violent film, it is nowhere near as depraved as this reputation suggests, or as gruesome as *Hostel* (2005), or the *Saw* movies. The 'terror' of the movie arises from disturbingly-realistic onscreen violence – achieved through documentary-style storytelling – forcing viewers to confront the question: What if I were in the same situation?

At the heart of *Wolf Creek*'s popularity is the iconic nature of the movie, elevating it to the status of the quintessential Australian horror movie. Ever since early settlers first confronted the vast and unforgiving expanses of the Australian continent, the landscape has forged itself into popular consciousness. For colonists, this ancient, isolated and mysterious land was alien; many experienced a sense of not belonging. The vast majority of Australians live along the coast and, consequently, the outback has become a mythical place: a dangerous wilderness where the improbable is possible. *Wolf Creek* captures this anxiety towards the outback. In the tradition of the 'monstrous outback', the landscape functions as a fifth character – an ethereal and dangerous entity. Rain falls in a desert; watches mysteriously stop; the landscape seems to oppose the central characters at every turn. Ravines appear from nowhere in the protagonist's dash for freedom; the isolation is oppressive; and, at the end of the movie, Mick Taylor fades into the twilight as though part of the landscape: a 'monster' sent to cleanse it of intruders.

Mick Taylor has become an iconic Australian villain. Like Mick Dundee, the iconic hero of Australia's most famous movie of all time *Crocodile Dundee* (Peter Faiman, 1986), Mick Taylor is a laconic, rugged, larrikin bushman in the mould of the stereotypical Australian male popularized in the work of Banjo Paterson and Henry Lawson, but beneath the surface he is a crazed serial-killer, preying on unsuspecting backpackers. In so doing, the film shatters the stereotypical view of Australianness still held by international audiences around the globe, presenting a negative image of the Australian bushman. As a genre movie, *Wolf Creek* is also an innovative film. On the one hand, *Wolf Creek* follows a typical slasher plotline. Similar plotlines have been used in countless films, from *The Texas Chain Saw Massacre* (Tobe Hooper, 1974) to the *House of Wax* (Jaume Colet-Serra, 2005) remake. But *Wolf Creek's* murderer, Mick Taylor, is not your typical slasher; he is a dark version of Crocodile Dundee. The movie also has a two-act rather than a typical three-act structure; it steers away from spooky music foreshadowing an upcoming bad event; and the main female character, or the 'final girl' to escape in a regular slasher, is the first to die while the 'final boy' – certain to perish – survives the carnage.

Mark David Ryan

ROAD MOVIES

Many of Australia's best known films are road movies: *Walkabout* (Nicolas Roeg, 1971), *The Adventures of Priscilla, Queen of the Desert* (Stephan Elliott, 1994), *The Tracker* (Rolf de Heer, 2002), and *Rabbit-Proof Fence* (Phillip Noyce, 2002), yet these films vary enormously in their tone, their narrative structure and in the kind of audiences they attract. This variety reflects both the hybrid nature of the genre, and the complex and shifting role the Outback plays in the nation's history and cultural imagination.

While classical Hollywood films built around journeys, such as *The Wizard of Oz* (Victor Fleming, 1939) and *Sullivan's Travels* (Preston Sturges, 1941), follow a protagonist who embarks on a 'hero's quest' and returns home wiser and more deeply connected to their community, the American road movie shifted gear radically in the 1960s. According to David Laderman (2002: 1), a cluster of films, including *Bonnie and Clyde* (Arthur Penn, 1967), *Easy Rider* (Dennis Hopper, 1969), *Five Easy Pieces* (Bob Rafelson, 1970), *Two Lane Blacktop* (Monte Hellman, 1971) and *Badlands* (Terrence Malick, 1973), redefined the contemporary genre by embodying 'the fundamental impulse of the road movie: rebellion against conservative social norms.'

These road movies rarely end in redemption for the disaffected outsiders who are escaping their families, the law or other oppressive figures. Plots are episodic and open-ended, with the emphasis on movement as an expression of personal liberty. Stylistically, the travelling camera holds the characters and the ever-receding horizon line in a bond of ecstatic potential, creating a blissful space between decision and consequence, crime and capture, between having and losing ideals. But the price these drifters pay for their transgressive freedom is harsh. The spree is cut short by death, the police or a gradual drift into aimless exile. As Wyatt (Peter Fonda) famously concludes in *Easy Rider* 'We blew it'.

In Australian cinema, this search for a sublime, if transient, release from oppressive norms finds expression in a number of key road moves, mostly from the 1970s. Interestingly, many of them are road movies 'on foot', for, apart from the high octane *Mad Max* trilogy, the identification of cars with freedom in Australian cinema is rarer than one might assume. *Walkabout* (1971), a UK production directed by Nicholas Roeg, explores the Outback as a place of dreamlike reprieve from the city, which is shown at the beginning and ending of the film as a semi-abstract, dehumanizing construction of grids and confined spaces. Two lost English children are guided through the majestic and open landscape by an Indigenous youth (David Gulpilil), who takes his own life after the girl rejects him, an act motivated by the film's vision of the Outback as a kind of Eden that can only ever be lost, rather than by any particular knowledge of Indigenous culture.

Phillip Noyce's *Backroads* (1977) pits two drifters, played by Bill Hunter and Aboriginal activist Gary Foley, together in a stolen car on the backroads of NSW. The largely improvised dialogue that essentially drives the film is a vigorous and at times poignant exchange of ideas about race and identity, cut short when Foley's character is chased and shot like an animal by the police. *In Search of Anna* (1978) presents a moody portrayal of tough guy Tony (Richard Moir), a young Greek-Australian just out of prison, gradually shedding his defensive armour as he hitches north to find his former girlfriend, and escape the expectations of his depressed father and criminal mates. Another 'on foot' road movie, set in colonial Tasmania, is the elegiac *Manganinnie* (1979). As the lone survivor of the brutal massacre of her tribe, Manganinnie (Mawuyul Yanthalawuy) lures a little settler girl away from her father and nurtures her, teaching her to live from the land. When Manganinnie dies from grief at losing her world, the child returns to her family, but, as in *Walkabout*, we sense she will be haunted forever by her journey. *Manganinnie* is one of the few Australian features, along with *Bitter Springs* (Ralph Smart, 1950), to directly address the dispossession of Indigenous Australians of their land. More recently, *Beneath Clouds* (Ivan Sen, 2002) offered the road as a space for two troubled teenagers, Vaughn (Damien Pitt) and Lena (Danielle Hall), who each carry the history of that dispossession in different ways, to form a fragile friendship as they travel towards their uncertain futures.

Beyond these 'cultural critique' (Laderman 2002: 8) road movies, whose restless characters use the road trip as a reprieve from unbearable situations, the Australian road also plays host to more conventionally goal-oriented protagonists, who begin their stories on the outer but are searching for some kind of home. *Rabbit-Proof Fence*, in which three children stolen[1] from their families determine, against terrible odds, to forge a pathway back to their mothers, enacts this story in the most straightforward and redemptive manner. *The Adventures of Priscilla, Queen of the Desert*, and the children's film *Yolngu Boy* (Stephen Johnson, 2000) both feature trios of characters who embark on a journey as a kind of last-ditch attempt to find self-acceptance and the eventual embrace of a supportive community. Two releases from 2009, *Charlie & Boots* (Dean Murphy, 2009) and *Stone Bros.* (Richard Frankland, 2009) continue this tradition, but with a laidback, comic approach, that gently maps their protagonists' personal journeys against the geography of the trip.

Most of these films include sequences where the shifting space and light and colour of the landscape, captured in sweeping aerial shots or by cameras speeding low to the ground, represents a transformative moment: a cinematic dream of emotion and *mise-en-scène* truly in sync; an illustration of the characters' fears and self-doubts dissolving into a rhapsodic glimmer of hope. That this road movie trope has its own 'drag' version in *The Adventures of Priscilla, Queen of the Desert*, with Felicia (Guy Pearce) miming to opera on top of a bus, with silver trail a-billowing, indicates how embedded it is in film-makers' and audiences' understanding of the conventions of the genre.

The road movie/*amour fou* hybrid takes the form of an extended chase: *Kiss or Kill* (Bill Bennett, 1997), *Heaven's Burning* (Craig Lahiff, 1997) and *True Love and Chaos* (Stavros Kazantzicis, 1997) are all driven by a 'lovers on the run' theme, where relationships are forged or tested in the tension of the chase and the enclosed space of a vehicle. Likewise, the suspense thriller *Roadgames* (Richard Franklin, 1981) uses the specific geography of the road trip – crossing the Nullarbor Plain – as a structure on which to hang its story.

The early explorers who ventured inland to bring back news of the 'unknown' interior (which was a rich source of fear and fantasy for the early settlers) figure large in the popular imagination, but surprisingly few films have been made based on their journeys. They do, however, have a road movie counterpart – that of the adventure travelogue. In 1916, Francis Birtles, already famous for long-distance cycling and motoring trips, made his second adventure film, *Across Australia in the Track of Burke and Wills*, in which he retraced the steps of the tragic explorers. Unfortunately, Birtles' films were not widely seen, and no longer survive.[2] In 1956, Keith Adams began touring country halls and cinemas with his self-financed *Northern Safari* (Keith Adams, 1958), a lively and action-packed travelogue made with his wife, sister and their feisty fox terrier, Tiger. The film follows the Adams family driving from Perth to the Gulf, and then back down the West coast. The focus is on Keith's bush skills as he wrangles snakes, crocodiles and scorpions, and joins local Indigenous men on traditional fishing trips. With its catchy theme tune, gorgeous saturated colour, and animal antics (in one memorable scene, Tiger chases and brings down an emu), *Northern Safari* was a big success for Adams, not only in Australia but also in South Africa.

Adams was followed by the Leyland Brothers, who, before their popular TV travel show, honed their skills with *Wheels Across a Wilderness* (Malcolm and Mike Leyland, 1966), a journey from the West coast to the East, which they also toured on the regional cinema circuit. In 1977, Alby Mangels took up the macho mantle, venturing onto the global stage with *World Safari* (Alby Mangels, 1977) and its two sequels. Mangels and his predecessors performed their relentlessly-upbeat, problem-solving, apolitical surface-skimming investigations of distance to an appreciative audience and, in one sense, domesticated the Outback for urban viewers. They, more than earlier cinematic bush heroes like Snowy Baker and Chips Rafferty, were the prototypes for comic characters such as Crocodile Dundee (Paul Hogan) and, thirty years later, in festering-shadow form, *Wolf Creek* (Greg Mclean, 2005)'s serial killer, Mick Taylor (John Jarratt). In 2001, Rachel Lucas re-imagined the independent road movie travelogue with her credit card film *Bondi Tsunami* (Rachel Lucas 2001),[3] in which young Japanese surfers explore the east coast and parts of the Interior in a series of music video-esque sequences that transform landscape and tourist icons into cute accessories for the Japanese girls who have come along for the ride.

I have barely mentioned the *Mad Max* films – arguably they sit more comfortably in the action genre than that of the road movie – but in her fascinating essay, *White Panic*, or *Mad Max* and the Sublime, Meaghan Morris (1998) categorizes *Mad Max* (1979) as one of many 'phobic' narratives in Australian cinema, symptomatic of a paranoid fear that the colonization or 'invasion' of

Australia leaves the country vulnerable to invasion by surrounding, densely populated nations, 'we replay our genocidal past as our apocalyptic future' (Morris 1998: 8). Morris draws particular attention to the scene where Max's wife Jess (Joanne Samuel) is chased from the beach and through the bush by unseen attackers, then run down on the road by a motorcycle gang. There are many other examples of the paranoid, thwarted road movie where the journey begins well but soon leads to entrapment or death in imploding, isolated towns full of vengeful characters.

The recently re-released *Wake in Fright* (Ted Kotcheff, 1971) is a striking example, with its urbane schoolteacher (Gary Bond) drawn into a vortex of debauchery after stopping for one night in the fictional but unforgettable town of Bundanyabba; *The Cars That Ate Paris* (Peter Weir, 1974) presents a community that cannibalizes outsiders and their vehicles; a feminist law student (Deborra-Lee Furness) on a solo road trip becomes embroiled in a subculture of misogyny and rape in *Shame* (Steve Jodrell, 1988); while in *Welcome to Woop Woop* (Stephan Elliott, 1997) an American gets trapped in a town that has been abandoned by the mining company that created it. The town refuses to die and sustains itself on beer and communal singalongs to reruns of Hollywood musicals. Most recently, the horror film *Wolf Creek* (2005), which captures the light-headed pleasures of the road trip so effortlessly in its opening sequences, ends by literally tearing its young travellers apart.Road movies draw on age-old narrative traditions which use the journey as a means to dramatize finding one's place in the world. Australian road movies unfurl across contested country, where the journey can also become a narrative process of investigating and rewriting history.

Notes

1. The Stolen Generations is a term used to describe children of Australian Aboriginal and Torres Strait Islander descent who were removed from their families by government agencies from the mid 1860s to the late 1960s.
2. The National Library of Australia holds stills: Francis Birtles' motor car tour collection, ca. 1899–1928, available to view online. http://nla.gov.au/nla.pic-vn3300502 (accessed 30 September 2009)
3. There is also a tradition of independently-produced and toured Australian surfing films such as *Morning of the Earth* (Albert Falzon, 1972) and *Crystal Voyager* (David Elfick, 1973)

Fiona Trigg

The Overlanders, Ealing.

The Overlanders

Country of Origin:
Australia

Studio:
Ealing Studios

Director:
Harry Watt

Producers:
Michael Balcon
Ralph Smart

Screenwriter:
Harry Watt

Cinematographer:
Osmond Borradaile

Synopsis

During World War II Darwin is under threat of Japanese invasion. A large mob of cattle on the northern coast of WA is due to be destroyed, rather than provide food for the Japanese army. Drover Dan McAlpine decides to take the cattle to safety in Queensland: 'In this war, bullocks are more important that bullets'. He organizes a team to drive the cattle 2000 miles across Australia. The team consists of a couple who set fire to their farm, rather than leave it to the Japanese, and their two daughters Mary and Helen, a sailor nicknamed Sinbad, the comic sidekick Corky, extra horsemen Charlie and Bert, and two Aboriginal stockmen, Jacky and Nipper. The trek takes many arduous months and contains great challenges: crossing crocodile-infested rivers; poisonous grass, capturing and breaking wild horses, water shortages, a dangerous mountain climb and a cattle stampede. Along the way, Sinbad and Mary fall in love, but Sinbad is seriously injured in a fall which requires his rescue by the flying doctor service. Eventually Dan and his gang reach Queensland, where they are met by a government minister who officially thanks them for their effort. They board a plane to fly back to get the next mob.

Editor:

Leslie Norman

Duration:

91 minutes

Genre:

Road Movie

Action Adventure

Cast:

Chips Rafferty

John Nugent Hayward

Daphne Campbell

Jean Blue

Helen Grieve

John Fernside

Peter Pagan

Frank Ransome

Year:

1946

Critique

The journey at the heart of *The Overlanders* is not a personal story but a national one, told through an engaging adventure yarn. The director Harry Watt was an experienced documentary and feature film-maker from Britain, who was brought out to help Australia's war effort in the hearts and minds department. According to Pike and Cooper:

> In 1943 the Australian government approached the British Ministry of Information to see whether the coverage of the Australian war effort could be improved in British propaganda. Watt was seconded from Ealing, although still on their payroll, and sent to Australia as an official war correspondent and a guest of the Australian government. (Pike & Cooper 1998: 205)

Based on extensive research into actual cattle drives, *The Overlanders* is fictional but has a documentary flavour enhanced by Dan's (Chips Rafferty) voiceover commentary, which explains many of the logistical challenges and dangers faced along the way. One of the film's strengths is the way it integrates a detailed overview of the cattle drive and its importance to the war effort with the dramatic action of individual events on the trail.

Chips Rafferty was known to Australian audiences from his work in two Charles Chauvel war dramas, *Forty Thousand Horsemen* (1940) and *The Rats of Tobruk* (1944) and he brings his trademark laconic charm to the part. The 'she'll be right' attitude is evident early on when a manager at the port tries to dissuade Dan from the journey by saying, 'You're trying to drive a mob of half-wild cattle the distance from London to Moscow in a bad season at the wrong time of year', to which Dan replies, 'No wonder they call you old guts-ache. Well, I'll see you in Moscow!'

Apart from the gentle romance which develops between Mary and Sinbad, there are no personal transformations or psychological insights on offer. This is a narrative structured around the step-by-step process of getting the cattle from A to B, but the scenes showing the capture of wild horses, the cattle moving through mountain passes, and the team rounding up the mob in majestic landscapes are lively, suspenseful and often quite beautiful. The film opens with a rather startling image: a map of Australia with a Japanese soldier literally peering over the top of the country, arms outstretched as if to grab it, and the words 'He's Coming South' emblazoned over the top. However, while the war provides the context for the film, the overall tone is positive and concentrates on the good natured way the droving team bring their skills to the service of their country.

The Overlanders was very successful in both Australia and England, and had profitable releases in the USA and parts of Europe. Ealing committed to further local productions and Harry Watt's presence in the country significantly enlivened the local film-making scene.

The Overlanders is a classic example of cinematic mixed messages regarding race, for while the film makes a few deliberate gestures of respect towards Indigenous Australia, the two black stockmen have neither surnames nor backstory, and simply disappear from the film at the end, when the white drovers celebrate their success. Sixty years later, Baz Luhrmann's *Australia* (2008), which borrows heavily from *The Overlanders* in selected events and imagery, if not in tone, attempts (with arguable success) to redress this by having the fate of several Indigenous characters central to its storyline. *Australia* was equally promoted as a 'nation building' film, but this time the government support came from the tourism bodies, who financed a series of commercials linked to the film aimed at the American travel market.

Fiona Trigg

Northern Safari

Country of Origin:
Australia

Director:
Keith Adams

Producer:
Keith Adams

Screenwriter:
Keith Adams

Cinematographers:
Keith Adams
Audrey Adams
Margaret Adams

Editor:
Keith Adams

Duration:
121 minutes

Genre:
Documentary
Road Movie

Cast:
Keith Adams
Audrey Adams
Margaret Adams
Tiger Adams

Year:
1958

Synopsis

Keith Adams, his wife, sister and fox terrier travel from Perth in the south-west of Australia to the Gulf of Carpentaria in the north east of the continent, and back again in a 1948 Buick. Along the way they explore the amazing country and wildlife of central Australia. The accompanying narration fills in details about the landscape and habits of the creatures encountered. Adams catches and handles an array of dangerous animals and reptiles, including crocodiles, snakes and scorpions, and goes fishing with some Indigenous men, joining in their feast of giant turtle. Adams and his family display their excellent camping and bush skills and the lively antics of their fox terrier Tiger.

Critique

It all started when friends would not believe what we had to tell them on our return from numerous safaris through the most difficult and isolated areas of this Continent. To prove our point, we began to bring back photographs. From this we graduated to an 8mm camera, then in 1958, with better equipment, we really set out to put everything on record. The result is *Northern Safari*, a true full-length account of an overland journey …

As the souvenir programme explains, *Northern Safari* began as a home movie, filmed on the trips Keith Adams, his wife Audrey and sister Margaret regularly took together in the north of Australia. Adams worked as an engineer in Perth, but had always loved to fish, hunt and travel in the bush – skills he learned during his childhood in depression-era Tasmania. His DIY ethic carried over to film-making, as a newspaper article from 1964 explains:

Mr Adams' film fever was first fired by barbeque screenings for friends. His kitchen became his film laboratory as he learnt laboriously by trial and error to piece his shots together. His lounge became his recording studio for a sound track of sorts laboriously dubbed on the film. Over this he superimposed a narration he wrote himself. (Flanagan 1964)

Adams toured the film independently, and *Northern Safari* proved a big hit with audiences across the country. A review from the time states:

Three suburban Australians live a searing adventure in the deserts, mountain and rivers, among the world's most primitive relics. They hunt and fish and fossick and encounter. They have adventures which would send most people screaming as in horror from their most awful nightmares. (Penberthy 1966)

Most of the adventures involve Adams and his fox terrier Tiger hunting, handling, killing or cooking wildlife, but the variety of close-ups of wildlife in action, and the brilliant colour of the footage would have been a novelty to Australian audiences who were still seeing their television in black and white. A colleague of mine who recalls seeing the film as a child could immediately remember the theme song, and claims the film had a huge impact on primary school playground activity in the weeks that followed, including the spread of the rather troubling rumour that Tiger had died in a crocodile attack and been replaced by another dog!

While Adams reportedly made a fortune touring the film in Australia and internationally, he never made another film or tried his luck on television. Other adventure travellers who moved on to a career as film-makers or TV programme-makers include Alby Mangels, the Leyland Brothers and Malcolm Douglas.

Fiona Trigg

Backroads

Country of Origin:
Australia

Studio:
Backroads Productions

Director:
Phillip Noyce

Producer:
Phillip Noyce

Screenwriters:
John Emery
Phillip Noyce

Cinematographer:
Russell Boyd

Editor:
David Huggett

Duration:
60 minutes

Synopsis

Gary, a young Aboriginal man at a loss after the breakdown of his marriage, and Jack, an unemployed white drifter, meet by chance and steal a car, some booze and some new clothes. They drive through western New South Wales, drinking and arguing their way to a testy friendship. Stopping briefly at a reserve, Gary visits his son, and Uncle Joe joins their trip. They also pick up Anna, a woman working at a petrol station who is looking for meaning in her life, and Jean-Claude, a French hitch-hiker who Jack taunts with racist remarks. At the coast, Anna drives off in the car, and Uncle Joe drunkenly shoots a stranger. Gary, Jack and Uncle Joe take the dead man's car but, after a brief reprieve at a river hideout, the police catch up with them. Gary tries to run but is hunted down and shot dead. Uncle Joe and Jack are arrested.

Critique

Noyce collaborated on *Backroads* with Aboriginal activist Gary Foley, who, apart from his political actions such as the establishment of the Aboriginal Tent Embassy in Canberra in 1972, had also worked in theatre. As a result, *Backroads* is the first feature in which Aboriginal characters in major roles are neither romanticized nor patronized. Foley and established actor Bill Hunter were encouraged to improvise and the resulting banter has a fresh and rough realism. Noyce's background in documentary is evident in the confidence with which

Genre:
Road Movie

Cast:
Bill Hunter
Gary Foley
Zac Martin
Terry Camilleri
Julie McGregor

Year:
1977

he goes with the flow of the dialogue, capturing the action on the run with a small crew. The sound recordist apparently spent quite some time in the boot.

Backroads balances the frustrated anger of disempowered men carried by both Jack and Gary with easy humour and the dynamic, clean images of cinematographer Russell Boyd. The breezy jazz score effectively enhances the vibrancy of the Pontiac speeding through red dirt country. *Backroads* taps into the zeitgeist of 1970s' Australia, when land rights, the women's movement, and the cultural assimilation of post-war European migrants were hot topics and, for most of the film's length, the dialogue between Gary, Jack, Anna and Jean-Claude carries the drama. The real kick in the story, however, is when Uncle Joe, who has barely said a word throughout, shoots a wealthy fisherman at point-blank range. This act of seemingly-unprovoked violence is quickly answered, and in one sense explained, by the enthusiasm with which the police chase down and shoot Gary dead.

Shot on 16mm, and only 60 minutes in length, *Backroads* had limited commercial exposure in Australia but, after appearing at the Berlin and Cannes festivals, played at London's La Scala cinema for six months. After many years directing in Hollywood, Phillip Noyce returned to Australia to make his second road move, *Rabbit-Proof Fence*.

Fiona Trigg

Wrong Side of the Road

Country of Origin:
Australia

Director:
Ned Lander

Producers:
Ned Lander
Graeme Isaac

Screenwriters:
Ned Lander
Graeme Isaac
The Cast

Cinematographer:
Louis Irving

Art Director:
Jan Mackay

Editor:
John Scott

Synopsis

Wrong Side of the Road is a docudrama set over two days in the lives of actual Indigenous bands *No Fixed Address* and *Us Mob*, with interweaving narratives carried by individual band members. The bands play and drive to a number of gigs in various locations, facing regular harassment by the police and racism from a hotel manager. Pedro is trying to find a job. Les visits his adoptive parents and tries to trace his birth mother. Vonnie visits her boyfriend in jail; flashbacks introduce memories of childhood institutional abuse and walking out on a farm job due to poor conditions. A dramatic confrontation with police on the road lands several musicians in the lock-up, but the film ends with a successful gig in which both bands play to an appreciative audience at a community dance.

Critique

The Indigenous bands *Us Mob* and *No Fixed Address* formed in South Australia in the late 1970s with support from musician Graeme Isaac, who suggested the idea of a film based on their experiences to documentary-maker Ned Lander. Lander and Isaac then developed the narrative material in collaboration with the musicians. The band members, who are all non-actors, play semi-fictionalized versions of themselves, and enact incidents drawn from their own lives or from those of their circle.

Duration:
80 minutes

Genre:
Road Movie
Docudrama
Musical

Cast:
Les Stephens
Chris Jones
Veronica Rankine
Bart Willoughby
John Miller
Ronnie Ansell
Peter Butler
Carroll Karpany
Wally McArthur

Year:
1981

While the narrative does not follow one continuous journey and the film, as such, is not a typical road movie, its loose collection of stories covers familiar generic territory: young restless characters in conflict with oppressive authority, and a search – both explicit and implied – for family, and social acceptance on their own terms. The low key, observational documentary style of the film and the somewhat self-conscious performances do not make for high drama, and we never get particularly close access to any of the characters, but the constant racism faced by the musicians from police and others in the film is an eye-opener for audiences who may not otherwise have had access to this reality, especially as told from an urban Indigenous perspective.

Apart from the film's set pieces, such as *Us Mob* being turned away from playing in a country hotel, and a major punch up with police on the highway, *Wrong side of the Road* also follows the story of Les (Les Stephens) facing an administrative brick wall in an ongoing attempt to trace his birth mother. By the end of the film he learns of her possible location on the 'blackvine', this being one of the many ways that the strength of the community is shown. There are lighter moments, too, that capture the texture of daily life: hanging out and playing music in the kitchen; using a guitar case to hold a lizard caught for a roadside feed; and a determined Auntie laying down the law in relation to an upcoming dance. Tonally, the film sits awkwardly between documentary and drama, however the underlying drama of the situations it describes shines through.

The film opens and closes with strong performance footage, and includes No Fixed Address performing their reggae anthem *We Have Survived*.

Fiona Trigg

Kiss or Kill

Country of Origin:
Australia

Director:
Bill Bennett

Producer:
Jennifer Bennett
Bill Bennett

Screenwriter:
Bill Bennett

Director of Photography:
Malcolm McCulloch

Editor:
Henry Dangar

Synopsis

Nikki, a young woman haunted by her childhood experience of witnessing her mother's murder, seduces, drugs and robs married, travelling businessmen with her partner in crime, Al. When their latest mark dies during the scam in an Adelaide hotel, Nikki and Al set off for Perth with a videotape they find in the businessman's briefcase, showing celebrated former footballer, Zipper Doyle, having sex with a young boy. Before they leave, Nikki phones Doyle's gym and leaves an abusive message. Doyle goes to the hotel to search, in vain, for the tape. He is interviewed by two policemen, Hummer and Crean, whose suspicions are raised when Doyle admits lying to a maid to gain entry to the hotel room. When some of the murdered businessman's credit cards are found by the side of the highway on the way to Perth, the two policemen set off in pursuit. A friendly journalist faxes Doyle a police identikit image of Nikki, and he, too, sets off after the fugitives.

Al and Nikki stay at a motel run by the eccentric Stan. At night, while sleepwalking, Nikki re-enacts part of her childhood memory in which her mother was doused in petrol and set alight. In the morning, Al and Nikki leave in a hurry; later, a cleaner discovers that Stan

Production Designer:

Andrew Plumer

Duration:

96 minutes

Genre:

Crime

Road Movie

Cast:

Frances O'Connor

Matt Day

Chris Haywood

Andrew S Gilbert

John Clarke

Barry Langrishe

Max Cullen

Barry Otto

Year:

1997

has been murdered. Al and Nikki steal a 4WD car from two fishermen, and are almost run off the road by a truck driver. At a truckstop, Nikki overhears two women talking about Stan's murder. She confronts Al, believing he is the murderer. Al admits to stealing money, but denies killing Stan. Al suspects Nikki may have killed Stan while she was sleepwalking. Al fights with the truck driver who tried to run them off the road, watched by Doyle, who somehow has caught up with them.

On the road again, Al realizes that they are being followed, and pulls over. Doyle shoots at them, and they drive off-road into the bush. They discover a man, Adler, hiding in the back of their car. He invites them to take refuge in his home on a former nuclear testing site deep in the desert. The police hire an Aboriginal tracker, Possum Harry, to find the fugitives. He leads them to the locked gates of the nuclear testing site, but they need special permission to enter. At Adler's home, Al and Nikki meet his wife Belle, a jewellery maker. Al pockets a necklace despite Nikki's objections. In the morning Nikki finds Adler and Belle dead in bed with their throats cut. Al punches her, bundles her into the car, and speeds away.

At an isolated shearers' hut he ties her up while he goes to buy supplies. When he returns, Nikki attacks him with a knife but he fights her off, and they come to an uneasy truce. At night, the sleepwalking Nikki pumps petrol into a basin. Al wakes up and confronts her, and she throws the petrol over him but is unable to set it alight. Later, he tenderly nurses her before tying her to the bed. Early the next morning, the police, tipped off by the store clerk, raid the hut and arrest Al and Nikki. In an interview, Nikki confesses to the murders. Possum Harry works out that Adler killed Belle, and then killed himself. A mysterious lawyer arrives at the police station, and forces the police to free Al and Nicki. He takes them to a motel, where Doyle is waiting for them. Despite the police watching the motel, Doyle forces Al and Nikki to drive off with him. The police set up a roadblock, but Nikki deliberately crashes Doyle's car into the police car. Doyle is flung from the car, and killed. In voice-over, Nikki tells how she and Al were acquitted of the businessman's murder and eventually made it to Western Australia where Al works in a vineyard.

One night, Al awakes to find Nikki chopping vegetables in the kitchen. He approaches her, but she pins him to the wall with the knife at his throat before she dissolves into a broad smile and says 'Just kidding'.

Critique

Kiss or Kill was director Bill Bennett's third road movie, after *Backlash* (1986) and *Spider and Rose* (1994). While the latter films were shot in outback New South Wales, this story of young, criminal lovers on the run is set and was shot on the vast, flat Nullarbor Plain that spans much of the distance between Adelaide and Perth. The beautiful strangeness of this unique landscape is strikingly captured by Bennett and cinematographer Malcolm McCulloch. Coincidentally, the same stretch of road with its isolated truckstops and motels was the setting for another Australian road movie made in the same year, Stavros Kazantzidis's *True Love and Chaos* (1997), while one of the stars of

Kiss Or Kill (1998), October Films.

Kazantzidis's film, Miranda Otto, plays opposite one of the stars of Bennett's film, Matt Day, in yet another road movie from 1997, Chris Kennedy's *Doing Time for Patsy Cline*.

The film's title is borrowed from a Dylan Thomas poem, 'Our Eunuch Dreams', first published in 1934, which explores the relationship between cinematic images and real life, and specifically references gangster films ('In this our age, the gunman and his moll/Two one dimensional ghosts, love on a reel/Strange to our solid eye'). An extract from the poem that acts as an introductory title, includes the lines: 'We watch the show of shadows of kiss or kill/ Flavoured of celluloid give love the lie'. Bennett has said in interview that the genesis of the film was the idea that someone you think you know can have a side to their personality that is unfathomable. This idea recurs throughout the film as Al and Nikki question their trust in each other, and it is evident in the two sides of Zipper Doyle: celebrity sportsman, and creepy paedophile. The idea is also the core of a beautifully played scene between the two policemen, in which Crean spins a fantastic tale about his past to his gullible colleague.

Bennett has gestured in interviews to the impact Jean-Luc Godard's *A Bout de Souffle* (1959) had on him in the long gestation of *Kiss or Kill*, and there's also an oblique homage to the final shot of Truffaut's *Les Quatre Cents Coups* (1959) in the penultimate scene in which the two young lovers, Al and Nikki, spin around ecstatically on the white sand of a former nuclear test site, ending on a freeze frame of Al staring directly at the camera. The influence of the French New Wave is clear in the jerky, handheld camerawork and extensive use of jump cuts that punctuate the film, while the repeated transgression of the 180° rule, ever-shifting camera angles and changing focal lengths, and the absence of a musical score mark further departures from the seamless continuity style adopted by most Australian film-makers. Bennett's stylistic choices may have been a reaction to the critical mauling of his previous film, the Hollywood feature *Two If By Sea* (1996).

Kiss or Kill was shot in thirty days and utilizes the semi-improvised style of film-making Bennett had earlier adopted for *Backlash* and for his first feature, *A Street to Die* (1985), as well as for the two drama-documentaries he made for Film Australia in 1989, *Mortgage* and *Malpractice*. For most of the film this works well, although, despite the extensive scene breakdowns provided to the actors, this style runs the risk of leaving holes in the narrative. In truth, it seems to have been a deliberate tactic to leave several threads hanging, but these mysteries are ultimately frustrating rather than endearingly enigmatic. For example, the video of Zipper Doyle seducing a young boy also contains footage of him having sex with a woman. Both Al and Crean identify her as Nikki. To add to the intrigue, when Doyle is sent a photofit of the woman seen with the murdered businessman in the opening scene, his reaction clearly suggests that he recognizes her, but we never discover why. Al's curiosity and suspicion about the identity of the woman in the tape leads to one of the tensest but also most frustrating moments in the film when he confronts Nikki about it one night in bed. At this point it is still unclear whether one or both of the young lovers are murderers. Nikki is shocked by his question, but he then shrugs it off and rolls away from her. She lies stunned, but does not pursue the question further. Is the woman on the tape Nikki? If not, why is she not more outraged at the suggestion that she has had sex with a paedophile, and why does she not deny it? Crean's suspicions are also not satisfactorily resolved. Hummer dismisses the suggestion with the observation, 'No, it's Felicity.' 'How do you know?' asks Crean. 'She's got no teeth,' Hummer cryptically replies. The line gets a cheap laugh, but it does nothing to answer a question that the film has persistently posed, and instead simply creates more confusion. 'Felicity' is never mentioned again. Other unresolved questions and credibility-stretching coincidences remain. How does Zipper manage to catch the couple so quickly? How is he able to follow them to Adler's home? It could be that he is a villain with supernatural powers – he is, after all, treated as something of a deity by those who do not know his seedy side – but this is entirely out of keeping with the rest of the film.

The choice to end the film with Nikki's voice-over summarizing events after the car crash suggests a recognition during post-production that too many narrative threads have been left untied. Unlike the looser, improvised approach to earlier scenes, the film's coda is carefully scripted and perhaps as a result it sits uneasily with the rest of the film. Paradoxically, rather than resolving some of the unanswered questions, this segment unhelpfully creates more, and at the same time makes Nikki even more frustratingly enigmatic. Over the shot of Al dancing with her in the desert, she says 'I thought about all the people we met. Mostly I thought about Al, how well I knew him. How I don't know him at all. Mostly I thought about my secrets. What I kept from him. What I'll always keep from him.' Despite the subtle allusion to *Les Quatre Cents Coups* which suggests that Al may be a grown-up Antoine, it would perhaps have made more sense if this scene had ended with Nikki in freeze frame. She is the emotional centre of the film, and it is her traumatic childhood experience that provides much of the film's energy, but ultimately she remains unknowable. She keeps her secrets not only from Al, but also from the audience.

Ben Goldsmith

Beneath Clouds

Country of Origin:
Australia

Studio:
Autumn Films

Director:
Ivan Sen

Producer:
Teresa-Jayne Hanlon
Douglas Cummings

Screenwriter:
Ivan Sen

Cinematographer:
Allen Collins

Production Designer:
Peter Baxter

Art Director:
Janie Parker

Synopsis

Lena, a light-skinned Indigenous teenager, living unhappily in a small town, leaves home to search for her estranged yet idealized Irish father. Vaughn, an Indigenous youth, escapes from a low security prison farm, intent on visiting his dying mother. They meet on the road. Vaughn helps Lena fend off two men who try to drag her into their car, and the two continue their journey to Sydney together, walking, hitching and gradually gaining each other's trust. Lena challenges Vaughn's choices in life, but does not immediately declare her own Indigenous identity to him. Along the way they encounter a young man who abuses his girlfriend, a wealthy landowner who gives them a lift in his Mercedes and a car load of Vaughn's relatives, who have a violent run-in with the police. Speeding away, they reach the outskirts of Sydney where Lena and Vaughn find his mother's house empty, her bed blood-stained. With the police closing in on Vaughn, Lena boards a train for the city.

Critique

There's a resonant sequence in *Beneath Clouds* which comes just before the final act. Teenagers Lena and Vaughn, tired and hungry from two days of hitchhiking, have a brief, scrappy argument. An elderly gentleman slows his Mercedes to offer a ride; Vaughn gets

Editor:

Karen Johnson

Duration:

87 minutes

Genre:

Road Movie

Drama

Cast:

Dannielle Hall

Damian Pitt

Jenna Lee Connors

Simon Swan

Mundurra Weldon

Athol French

Judy Duncan

Year:

2002

in the front passenger seat, Lena in the back. No one talks. With a knowing half-smile the driver turns the radio to rugby talkback – it is the neutral, equalizing language of sport and Vaughn relaxes. Lena looks out the window. We see her point of view, a luminous vista of mist hanging in the trees. She opens her talismanic photo album to a picture of another misty landscape: Ireland, the birthplace of the father she is trying to find. The radio fades on the soundtrack and music swells. The ever-watchful Lena closes her eyes and sinks into the comfort of the seat. A cop car approaches from behind but does not pull them over. The Mercedes eventually slows and stops by the side of the road. The teenagers get out and watch as the car turns off the highway into a property with impressive gate posts. They continue on foot.

Each scene in *Beneath Clouds* has this same measured quality: a graceful arc that not only moves the characters further along the road, but is so rich in visual *evidence* that the real journey is that of the audience being drawn towards the characters, who are trying so hard to remain inscrutable.

In the driver's 'man-to-man' gesture to Vaughn, we realize how rare it is for him to be treated without suspicion, and what that might do to a young person. In Lena's reverie, when her immediate surrounds momentarily match the idealized image she carries in her head, we feel how exhausting it is for her to be caught between two identities that she is unable to reconcile. When the cop car glides past, but no siren sounds, we understand Vaughn's expectation is that he will be stopped and harassed (we might also remember a scene in *Backroads*, when Gary, driving an expensive car, is similarly surprised not to be pulled over by police). In the general quietude of the scene, we realize what little chance Lena and Vaughn have had just to daydream, without always being on the defensive. In contrast to the wealthy driver, for Lena and Vaughn 'home' is not so clearly signposted.

Ivan Sen's ability to tell emotionally-lucid and effortless allegorical stories with minimal dialogue was clear in the handful of short films he made prior to his first feature, with *Tears* and *Dust* in particular working similar territory to *Beneath Clouds*. Sen is descended from the Gamilaroi and Bigambal language groups of north-west NSW and southern Queensland.

Fiona Trigg

SCIENCE FICTION AND FANTASY

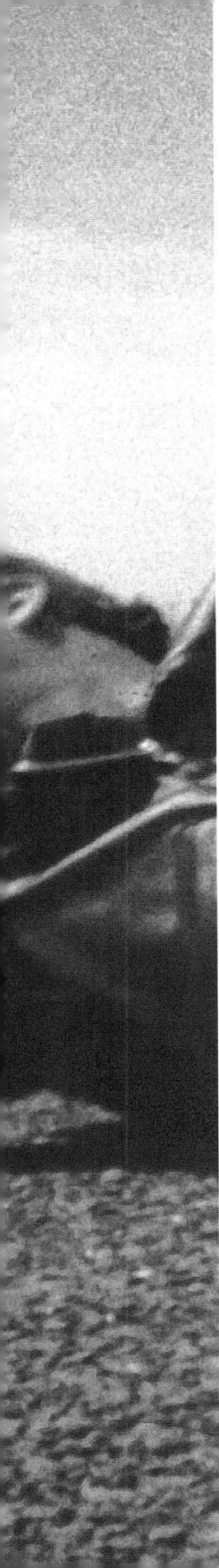

On the Beach was shot in Melbourne in 1959, previewing the
problems of identity that Australian genre cinema would suffer
over the next half century. Director Stanley Kramer headed an
American crew, and the stellar cast included Gregory Peck,
Ava Gardner, Fred Astaire and Anthony Perkins. The production was regarded by Melbournians as bigger than a royal
visit – royal visits were taken a lot more seriously back then.
While the novel on which the film was based had been written
in Australia and was set in Melbourne, the author had recently
migrated from Britain. Could it be called Australia's first science fiction movie? This is a key question, because the answer
depends on how one defines 'Australian', and this in turn
determines whether Australian science fiction cinema is robust
and healthy, or very sick indeed.

In 2004 I was commissioned to write an article on Australian science fiction for the screen by an American editor. My
subsequent research showed that, in the preceding five years,
38 movie-length productions and 35 television series produced in Australia could be classed as science fiction. These
represented over a quarter of Australia's output of movies and
series, but they included films like the *Matrix* trilogy (Andy
and Larry Wachowski, 1999–2003), four seasons of *Farscape*
(1999–2003) and *Star Wars: Episode II – Attack of the Clones*
(George Lucas, 2002). Australians were making a good living
from producing other people's scripts, but this has not always
been the case.

Australian science fiction for the screen began on television
in the 1950s, with series including *The Stranger*, *Wandjinja*,
The Interpretaris, *Vega 4* and *Phoenix 5*. No science fiction
for the cinema was produced locally, but few movies of any
sort were being shot in Australia at that time. *The Cars That*

Left: *Mad Max,* Mad Max.   Science Fiction and Fantasy   225

Ate Paris (Peter Weir, 1974) drew a lot of attention in Australia and internationally in spite of a somewhat unfocused plot. This marginally-genre film was set in a country town where passing motorists and their cars are harvested by local teenagers in heavily modified weapon-cars. Written and produced locally, the film screened at the Cannes Film Festival and helped establish the reputation of director Peter Weir, while its spiked silver Volkswagen became a de facto symbol of the emerging Australian movie industry.

Weir's next film, the atmospheric and unsettling *Picnic at Hanging Rock* (1975), had a lot less action, but a much greater impact and won two international awards. The film takes the form of a retro alien-abduction story. Set in 1900, it chronicles how three schoolgirls and a teacher vanish on an ancient volcano during a St Valentines Day picnic. Although the film was based on Joan Lindsay's 1967 novel, the story intrigued some viewers so much that they began searching contemporary newspapers for reports of an actual incident.

The Last Wave (1977), another Weir film, draws heavily on Aboriginal belief and legend and its impact on Europeans. A Sydney lawyer defends four Aboriginal men accused of a ritual murder and, during his investigations, he discovers a prophecy that a huge tsunami will soon obliterate all life on the continent. Unlike Weir's previous two genre films, *The Last Wave* has a very clear resolution, in the form of the tsunami bearing down on Sydney, and was rewarded with four Australian Film Institute awards out of eleven nominations.

The three *Mad Max* films caused an even bigger sensation than Weir's works, and gave Australian cinema in general an immense boost in self-confidence. *Mad Max* (1979) was directed and co-authored by George Miller, and told a story of lawlessness, social breakdown, atrocity and revenge with quite astonishing energy. It won four local and overseas awards and, because of the strong emphasis on action and car culture, drew a large and diverse audience.

Mad Max 2 (George Miller, 1981) was quite a different film, in fact the Max character was virtually all it had in common with *Mad Max*. It has a post-nuclear war scenario, where Australia has become a scatter of isolated, fortified communities defending their dwindling resources against motorized raiders. Max sides with one such enclave in a series of racing battles against the warlord Humungus. It was also very popular, and won eight awards. The third film, *Mad Max Beyond Thunderdome* (George Miller, 1985), was a lot more lavish and also drew large audiences, but was not as highly rated by viewers and critics. Continuing the post-apocalyptic setting, the story takes place in an enclave that has become a small city, and the centrepiece is a three-dimensional gladiatorial contest.

By the mid-1980s it seemed that Weir and Miller were the Australian equivalents of Spielberg and Lucas, and that genre cinema appeared had a bright future. After its SF-assisted origins, and with the assistance of generous government subsidies and incentives, the Australian film and television industry grew impressively. Along with an outpouring of mainstream films and TV shows, there were several with marginal SF, fantasy or horror themes. Most were not memorable. *Turkey Shoot* (Brian Trenchard-Smith, 1982) features a futuristic prison camp where inmates are set free in bushland to be hunted for sport. *One Night Stand* (John Duigan, 1984) revisits the theme of Armageddon as four Sydney teenagers come to terms with nuclear war breaking out in Europe. In *Razorback* (Russell Mulcahy, 1984), an American tourist seeks revenge on a monstrous feral pig after it eats his girlfriend. The very title of the comedy *Outback Vampires* (Colin Eggleston, 1987) probably says it all.

It was in the late 1980s and early 1990s that international capital and collaboration began to feature more heavily in Australian genre cinema. Overseas producers had realized that Australia was a politically-stable and comfortable place to work in, and costs for highly talented crews, special effects technicians, model builders and actors were around a third of those in Hollywood. The setting for the dystopian *Fortress* (Stuart Gordon, 1992) was actually an American prison of the near future, even though it was shot in Queensland. The novelization was written by an Australian, Rob Gerrand.

Individual Australians were developing an impressive reputation for technical work in genre cinema. For example, in 1987, the Australian cinematographer Don McAlpine worked on *Predator* with director John McTiernan and principal Arnold Schwarzenegger. McAlpine went on to develop his own scene-previewing system for *The Time Machine* (Simon Wells, 2002). At the 2002 Academy Awards, Andrew Lesnie won 'Best Cinematography' for *The Fellowship of the Ring* (Peter Jackson, 2001). This was from a record field of thirteen Australian nominees. 'Best Costume Design' and 'Best Art Direction' went to the mainstream *Moulin Rouge!* (Baz Luhrmann, 2001), to further underscore the Australian presence in international genre cinema production.

Science fiction films written by Australians were few in number in the 1990s. *Dark City* (Alex Proyas, 1998) was a rare exception, being written and directed by an Australian. Much of the A$27 million budget and most of the principal actors came from outside Australia. The setting is a strangely-organic city, administered by shadowy aliens, which exists independently of the wider world. The humans who live there are the subjects of experiments with memory, but occasionally one breaks out of the conditioning and rebels. *Dark City* preceded the *Matrix* films, but had a lot in common with them: all follow the fortunes of a group of humans who discover that they live in a virtual scenario and try to escape. *Dark City* won six Australian and international awards, recouped the cost of production at the box office, and sold well on DVD around the world.

A February 1999 survey of the movies, telemovies, and series in various stages of production in Australia identified ten science fiction or fantasy projects out of a total of 42. These included television series such as *Farscape*, Jonathan Schiff's *Thunderstone*, and Paul Jennings' *Round the Twist 3*. Four years later, when *Star Wars: Episode II – Attack of the Clones* (George Lucas, 2002) was in pre-production in Sydney, it was one of thirteen science fiction or fantasy productions out of 37 projects listed in *Encore* magazine's Production Report. These included *The Matrix Reloaded* (2003) and *The Matrix Revolutions* (2003). Significantly, only *Thunderstone* and *Round the Twist 3* were written by Australians, and these were young adult productions for television. All of the adult shows drew on international funding, and were written by overseas-based screenwriters.

The *Matrix* trilogy is symbolic of the place of science fiction in Australian cinema. The three films were largely shot in Australia, and for a third of what they would have cost in America. They were written and directed by Americans, and drew on international finance. Most of the principal actors were American. On the surface, the films had little to do with Australia in terms of writing, stories or themes, although they provided considerable employment opportunities and experience in the industry for Australians. This was in stark contrast with the situation in television, where Australian science fiction for young adults was both successful and popular, and was largely locally written.

In 2006 *The Mysterious Geographical Adventures of Jasper Morello* (Anthony Lucas, 2005) achieved the unthinkable when it secured an Oscar nomination in its own right in the category 'Best Short Film, Animated'. Made for just A$600,000, and running for only 26 minutes, it tells a story that could easily be expanded into a production four times longer. The highly-innovative silhouette animation technique conjures up a world of highly-advanced steam technology in a Victorian-esque society. Jasper, a disgraced aerial navigator, is given a chance to redeem himself on a quest to find a cure for a plague that is ravaging his country. The film won seven awards, and was nominated for 'Best Screenplay' in the mainstream Australian Film Institute awards for 2005. This was a graphic demonstration that Australians could write innovative science fiction for the screen.

It almost comes as a surprise that Australian science fiction and fantasy literature is flourishing independently of the cinema. Australian authors have been selling science fiction and fantasy novels overseas in record numbers since the late 1990s, and they have achieved considerable acclaim and substantial sales. Greg Egan has won the coveted Hugo Award, Jack Dann the Nebula Award, and Sean McMullen the Polaish Nova Fantastyka Award. It is quite common to find Australian works on the shortlists of most major international awards, and many bestseller lists. In cinema-related literature, John Brosnan wrote *Future Tense* (1978), one of the pioneering studies of genre cinema, Sean Williams and Shane Dix have written spin-off *Star Wars* novels, and Russell Blackford has written *Terminator* spin-off novels. Unfortunately this is largely typical of genre films that are made in Australia. The visions are from overseas, no matter how much of the rest is Australian. Australians can write impressive science fiction, but the cinema is largely unaware of them.

Given the foregoing, is there any chance that distinctly Australian science fiction films will ever become commonplace? Australians can write world-class science fiction, do brilliant special effects work and provide award-winning expertise in cinematography, and international films have made spectacular use of local settings. Australian actors have played such iconic roles as Tolkien's Galadriel and the X-Men's Wolverine, and it is an unusual year when Australians are not among the Oscar nominees. It seems that the only feat Australians seldom manage is selling science fiction scripts intended for adult audiences.

Currently the health of Australian genre cinema depends upon how one identifies it. Apply strict criteria about scripting, settings, funding and stars, and it seems in a very bad state. Merely count the genre movies shot in Australia, and the prospects could not be better. Is there any middle ground? *Dark City* proved that a science fiction script by an Australian can be made into a major and successful production. Even though it was funded from overseas and featured foreign principals, it was nevertheless a vision from Australia. Given how much Australia has going for it in this field, the mystery is that there are not many more films like it.

Sean McMullen

Mad Max

Country of Origin:
Australia

Director:
George Miller

Producer:
Byron Kennedy

Screenwriters:
George Miller
James McCausland

Cinematographer:
David Eggby

Editors:
Cliff Hayes
Tony Paterson

Art Director:
Jon Dowding

Duration:
88 minutes

Genre:
Road Movie
Science Fiction
Fantasy

Cast:
Mel Gibson
Joanne Samuel
Hugh Keays-Byrne
Steve Bisley
Tim Burns
Roger Ward

Year:
1979

Synopsis

Australia, the near future. Law and order on the roads is beginning to break down, and motorcycle gangs are terrorizing outback towns. A quite spectacular early chase between the police and Nightrider flags the incredibly raw energy driving the film. It is here where the iconic smash of the police car through the caravan takes place, and the cycle of revenge between gangs and police begins.

After Nightrider dies, gang leader Toecutter swears revenge on the police. One of traffic policeman Max's colleagues is reduced to a veg-etative state after a gang attack, a girl is gang-raped, and the gang claims an even tighter grip over the rural roads and towns. When Max's wife and child are run down and killed by Toecutter and his gang, Max abandons the rule of law. Armed with a high-performance patrol car, he charges a group of motorcyclists head-on, running most off the road. This is to get Toecutter's attention and draw him into a duel on the roads. Max is subsequently lured out of his car, ambushed and shot in the leg, but he shoots his way out and returns to his car. He pursues the now terrified Toecutter at high speed. His quarry does not see an oncoming truck until it is too late.

With Toecutter embedded in the radiator of the truck, Max now goes after the surviving gang member, who he finds looting a corpse beside a wrecked car. He handcuffs the man to the wreck by his ankle, sets a timer to detonate leaking petrol, then gives him a hacksaw blade. If he wants to live, he can cut his own leg off. A fireball erupts behind Max as he leaves the crash scene. The justice of the outback vigilante has arrived.

Critique

While Peter Weir had introduced the idea of feral motorists terror-izing rural Australia in *The Cars That Ate Paris* (1974), and futuristic road-based violence had already been featured in the American film *Death Race 2000* (Paul Bartel, 1975), it took *Mad Max* to really involve the audience in the action. Ironically, *Mad Max* has less of a futuristic feel than the earlier films, which rely heavily on their exotic vehicles for impact. As science fiction, *Mad Max* merely hints at the idea that something is wrong with society. For example, the police headquarters building is shabby and ill-maintained, suggesting that the force is badly resourced. By contrast, the patrol car that Max uses to annihilate Toecutter and his gang has all the menace of a fighter plane, implying that the authorities are confronting the gangs with open warfare.

In a sense *Mad Max* is the film that *The Cars That Ate Paris* could have been. It has the same type of near-future dystopian setting, with violently-aggressive mobile gangs and law-enforcement breakdown. It differs in having a much tighter plot, characters that really engage audience sympathy, and an ending in which the forces of darkness are annihilated. It is road rage given form; it is the reified revenge fanta-sies of a great many victims of highway bullying.

Both films play upon audience fears of societal breakdown, and those fears are all the more intense because the scenarios are so very close to our own situation. Civil violence, whether in the form of a soccer riot, political demonstration, gang war or drunken brawl outside a party, does give the impression that the authorities have lost control. The temptation is to resort to vigilante tactics, and fight the offenders on their own terms.

In the scene where Max has been forced past the limits of self-restraint and drives his new supercar directly at the oncoming motor-cycle gang, he demonstrates that lawbreakers are only empowered as long as everyone else follows the rules. Traditional heroes followed the rules and set things right. Max tossed the rulebook aside and annihilated those who had been committing atrocities earlier in the film. Quite possibly this awoke a deeply-hidden and very dark empathy with many viewers, and in this it has a lot in common with early Bruce Lee kung fu films.

At a visual level, the film featured spectacular car chases and action scenes, the like of which had never been produced in Australia. Even in America, the idea of a law enforcer giving a criminal the choice between hacking off his own foot and being incinerated left the audience wondering how the resolution would play out until the fireball actually erupted in the distance. Above all, the camera work creates the impression of both speed and danger. The viewer is placed in the position of the character – travelling very fast and not entirely sure if what is on the road ahead can be avoided.

Mad Max may not have had a profound message, but it was certainly an important lesson in what could be achieved in Australia and by Australians. It won four awards, gained an iconic status in Australian popular culture, and proved to the world that Peter Weir's films were not the only significant cinema coming out of Australia. In that sense the achievements of Mad Max were more important than the film itself.

Sean McMullen

Mad Max 2

Alternative Title:
Mad Max 2: The Road Warrior

Country of Origin:
Australia

Director:
George Miller

Producer:
Byron Kennedy

Synopsis

A few years into the future, Australia has been devastated by a nuclear conflict and society has been reduced to fortified villages and marauding gangs. Max, a former police patrolman, has become a wandering survivalist, traveling with his dog in a battered V8 patrol car in an endless search for food, petrol, and ammunition.

After fighting off a gang attack, Max discovers that there is a nearby enclave operating a small oil refinery where he might obtain petrol. He arrives to see that they under siege by a well-armed, motorized gang led by The Humungus and his champion warrior Wez. Max rescues one of the villagers from the gang, then tries to bargain for petrol. He salvages a truck to haul the enclave's petrol tank, but as he tries to leave with his petrol he is stopped by the

Screenwriters:
Terry Hayes
George Miller
Brian Hannant

Cinematographer:
Dean Semler

Editors:
Michael Balson
David Stiven
Tim Wellburn

Art Direction:
Graham 'Grace' Walker

Genre:
Science Fiction

Duration:
95 minutes

Cast:
Mel Gibson
Bruce Spence
Mike Preston
Max Phipps
Vernon Wells
Kjell Nilsson
Emil Minty

Year:
1981

gang. An autogyro pilot rescues the injured Max and flies him back to the enclave.

Max agrees to drive the now-armoured petrol tanker as the villagers try to escape The Humungus and his gang. Max and several of the villagers fight a running battle as they flee the refinery. The Humungus and Wez are killed in the battle for the tanker, but the tanker is now found to be a decoy filled with sand. Some of the gang discover the hard way that the abandoned refinery has been booby-trapped. The villagers escape aboard other vehicles, along with their concealed petrol. The autogyro pilot becomes their leader and takes them east to the coast, but Max chooses to stay in the desert.

Critique

This second film in the Mad Max trilogy has very little in common with its predecessor, apart from the lead character. The background to the action is no longer a society where law and order are breaking down, but a post-nuclear-war Australia in which there is no society at all.

The nuclear war is not especially relevant to the film, however. The classic western movie with settlers fighting running battles against Indians had fallen out of favour by 1981, yet the appeal of speed combined with conflict remained. Substitute motorcycles, cars and trucks for horses and wagons, and many westerns could easily fit into the Mad Max scenario. The punk costumes, brutal rape and graphic murder scenes are not the stuff of classic westerns, yet the often droll characters are not far removed from those of the spaghetti westerns that flourished ten years earlier.

This is not to say that Mad Max 2 is derivative. If it places the *Seven Samurai* (Akira Kurosawa, 1954) plot in Australia's future and adds the western's running battle, is this slavish imitation or brilliant innovation? Some years later I was reminded of Mad Max 2 as I watched *The Terminator* (James Cameron, 1984), with its armed pickup trucks and spectacular chases. There was even a little of Max in the implacable, unstoppable Terminator, yet it was obvious that the film had drawn inspiration from its predecessor rather than copied it.

As science fiction, *Mad Max 2* was no more than a general statement, yet that statement had a powerful impact. In political discussions of the time, people would point out that Australian society might be flawed, but it was still better than a Mad Max Australia. If the film influenced people's opinions about the use of nuclear weapons as a legitimate foreign policy strategy, perhaps it had a greater impact on the general population than highly-academic debates on the morality of mutually-assured destruction.

As in *Mad Max*, the film projects a sense of raw energy and speed by the use of camera work, keeping the viewer very close to the road. One feels that instant annihilation is the price of any tiny lapse of concentration, so it is hard to sit back and be a disinterested observer. The grotesquely-modified fighting cars hark back to Peter Weir's *The Cars that Ate Paris* seven years earlier, but George Miller uses their potential as weapons to the very limit, rather than merely as instruments of vandalism. The characters get little time for development, apart from Max, who had been established by the earlier movie.

Miller appears to have compensated for this by making most of the characters visually distinctive through costuming and makeup. After all, they are highly visible during the many action scenes, even if they say very little.

Mad Max 2 was an unqualified success by most measures. Its box office takings in the US alone were over four times the cost of production, and to this day it has more awards than any other Australian science fiction film. In a 2009 survey of Australian science fiction films available in Melbourne DVD stores, the author found only *Dark City* and *Mad Max 2* on the shelves. This enduring popularity with viewers nearly three decades after its release is probably the strongest evidence that *Mad Max 2* has become a classic of Australian cinema.

Sean McMullen

Dark City

Country of Origin:
Australia

Director:
Alex Proyas

Producers:
Andrew Mason
Alex Proyas

Cinematographer:
Dariusz Wolski

Screenwriters:
Alex Proyas
Lem Dobbs
David S Goyer

Editors:
Dov Hoenig

Production Designers:
George Liddle
Patrick Tatopoulos

Genre:
Science Fiction

Duration:
100 minutes

Synopsis

John Murdoch awakes in a bath in a hotel suite. His forehead is bleeding, he has lost his memory, and there is a murdered, mutilated woman in the bedroom. A stranger rings the phone and warns him to flee before a group of men arrive. From clippings in his pocket he learns that he might have something to do with a recent series of brutal murders of streetwalkers. Murdoch allows a streetwalker to take him home as a type of self-test, but to his relief he finds that he has no urge to harm her. Again alone on the streets, he encounters a group of bizarre strangers in dark, Gothic clothing. They try to exert psychic control over him, and when that fails they try to kill him. Using powers that he neither understands nor properly controls, Murdoch kills one of them, Mr Quick, then flees.

The perspective shifts to that of the strangers, who are aliens. They are studying a group of humans in a huge machine that is the city itself. From time to time they shut the city and its people down and reconfigure it in a process called tuning. They also tamper with the memories of the humans. Murdoch somehow remains awake as the tuning takes place. He looks on in wonder as buildings grow or diminish in seconds. He also realizes that it is always night in the city, and that it is not possible to leave. Slowly Murdoch pieces together what is happening. From the aliens' only human servant, Schreber, he learns that all of their memories are contrived. He is supposed to have become a psychotic murderer after discovering that his wife has slept with another man, but all of that is the result of implanted memories. Murdoch has begun to resist the aliens' conditioning because he has a mutation that confers some of their powers.

The aliens debate what to do with Murdoch. Mr Wall insists that he is a threat to them, but Mr Book thinks he can be the bridge that enables them to become more like humans and so reverse the slow decline of their species. Mr Hand volunteers to be injected with the memories that Murdoch was meant to be given, so that he can better track him down. Murdoch convinces his wife, then a police inspector,

Cast:

Rufus Sewell
William Hurt
Kiefer Sutherland
Jennifer Connelly
Richard O'Brien
Ian Richardson
Bruce Spence
Colin Friels

Year:

1998

that the city is a strange and isolated laboratory. With Schreber and Inspector Bumstead he travels to the edge of the city and smashes a hole in the perimeter. Beyond he finds only deep space. The city is a small artificial world, completely separate from Earth. It is now that Mr Hand catches up with him and takes him prisoner. Mr Book orders Schreber to inject Murdoch with memories that will conclude the experiment, but Schreber substitutes memories of how to control the aliens' machine. After a psychic battle with Mr Book, Murdoch takes control of the city. His intention is to run the city for the benefit of the humans, and he begins by reconfiguring it to have an ocean and daylight

Critique

Dark City was the first major science fiction film since the early 1980s to be written in Australia, and there is a good case to be made for it being the best-written Australian science fiction film of all. Its vision is bold and spectacular, and it has been formally recognized for that vision. It became the first Australian work to win the USA's Academy of Science Fiction, Fantasy & Horror Films Saturn Award for 'Best Film', and among its five other Saturn nominations was 'Best Writer.' It went on to win the Bram Stoker and Film Critics Circle of Australia Awards for 'Best Screenplay.'

The strength of *Dark City* comes from the way that the audience rides with the lead character, who has lost his memory and is also in the process of discovering the city. From the very start there is a sense of Gothic menace amid the Art Deco architecture, and the city itself displays a very disturbing life of its own. Like a computer, it can be reprogrammed but, like a plant, it has parts that can grow or wither.

The alien masters of the city take the very dated position that any problem can be solved if it is broken down sufficiently. Mr Hand volunteers to become a human simulation, in spite of the warnings from Mr Wall. There is never any attempt to cooperate with the humans, who are treated little better than laboratory rats, yet Mr Book makes it clear that the people of his group mind are doomed unless they can understand how to become more like humans. At the most general level this film is an allegory of the relationship of science with our own world, in the sense that a couple of centuries of breaking natural systems down for study has only taught us that most natural systems can only be understood when whole.

In the development of characters, *Dark City* is far in advance of other Australian science fiction films. It is no surprise that Rufus Sewell went on to play Crown Prince Leopold in *The Illusionist* (Neil Burger, 2006): like John Murdoch, the prince is the victim of an elaborate illusion. His character poses any number of questions about identity and reality for the viewer. Does the mere memory of adultery make one's partner an adulteress? Modern medicine is close to being able to remove distressing acts from memory, but does this sponge away the predilection to those acts as well? Will we reach a stage where a person's illusory life as a web avatar becomes more real than their life in the physical world? Should we blot out a criminal's real past and

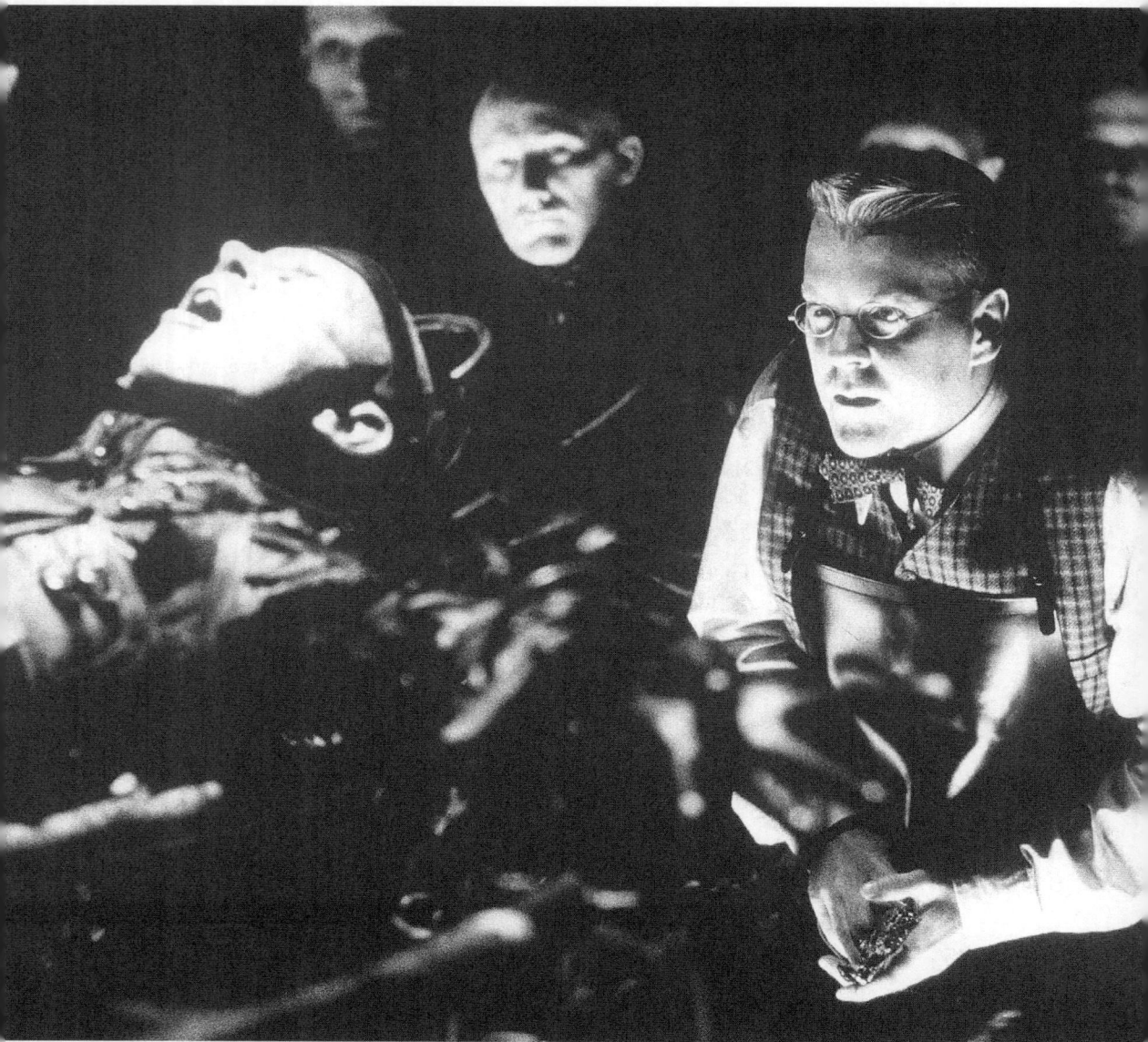

Dark City (1997), New Line. Photographed by Jasin Boland.

allow him to live out his life as a blameless avatar? How much of our present world is already illusory on some levels?

Kiefer Sutherland has the hardest role, playing the fearful and tortured psychiatrist Schreber, but he succeeds in treading the fine line between being a mad scientist or an impassive tool of the aliens. Among the aliens, Richard O'Brien achieves the near-impossible by establishing some sympathy for the ruthless Mr Hand; Ian Richardson is convincingly visionary as the leader, Mr Book; while Bruce Spence dominates all his scenes as the towering and fearsome Mr Wall. After seeing Soence in this minor role, one is left wondering how much more he might have achieved had he not played so many comic characters. Jennifer Connelly is visually splendid as the 1940s' femme fatale, and William Hurt's pragmatic police inspector is almost as tortured as Schreber as he, too, tries to separate illusion from reality.

The main pity of the film is that Alex Proyas did not go on to write more for the cinema. As a director he has achieved very high profile success with *The Crow* and *I, Robot*, but in *Dark City* he demonstrated what original visions he was capable of. Ten years after its release it still features the best science fiction to come out of Australian cinema, while visually it also remains unrivalled.

Sean McMullen

OZPLOI-TATION

Ozploitation is an evocative term that embraces a rather diverse series of Australian genre films produced during the 1970s and 1980s. The term was coined by Australian film-maker, Mark Hartley, in his 2008 feature-length documentary, *Not Quite Hollywood: The Wild Untold Story of Ozploitation*. The documentary, essentially comprising a number of excessive, sensational clips from various genre films of the period, and featuring the enthusiastic endorsement of Ozploitation's most high-profile 'fan', Quentin Tarantino, firmly locates this cycle of films away from their original configuration as commercial genre cinema to the global reaches of exploitation film. In this section I will discuss Ozploitation in the context of a number of key developments and trends within Australian cinema as a whole, and examine the implications of this reframing and rebranding of Australian genre cinema in relation to global shifts in the locus of value attached to exploitation film.

Exploitation films are generally regarded as low-brow, low-budget and mainly independent products aimed at niche audiences (Clark 1995: 3). Often displaying a distinct predilection for the lurid and sensational, their fandom has, historically, been based on the idea of a marginal counter-cinema derived from the notion 'they're so bad they're good'. This also intersects with the minority, 'oppositional' taste cultures encompassed by cult film (Jancovich et al. 2003: 3). Exploitation draws on a series of generic tropes, such as 'sexploitation', 'blaxploitation', teenage exploitation and schlock horror. *Not Quite Hollywood* partly sustains Ozploitation's links to exploitation by utilizing a similar set of tropes. The first of these are the 1970s' sex comedies and ocker films, which constructed a vulgar, hedonistic and predominantly masculine social 'typology of 'Australianness', and included films such as *Stork* (Tim Burstall, 1971), *The Adventures of Barry McKenzie* (Bruce Beresford, 1972) and *Alvin Purple* (Tim Burstall, 1973) (O'Regan 2000). The middle section of the documentary is comprised of low-budget horror flicks and 'creature features' such as *Thirst* (Ron Hardy, 1979) and *Howling III: The Marsupials* (Philippe Mora, 1987), while the final part is devoted to sensational action films, notably the work of Brian Trenchard-Smith (eg. *The Man from Hong Kong*, 1975 and *Turkey Shoot*, 1982). Ozploitation's key directors and writers in addition to Tim Burstall, Brian Trenchard-Smith and Phillippe Mora (who also directed *Mad Dog Morgan* 1976), include Richard Franklin (*The True Story of Eskimo Nell*, 1975; *Patrick*, 1978; *Roadgames*, 1981), Colin Eggleston (*Long Weekend*, 1978; *Outback Vampires*, 1987), and Everett De Roche (writer of many films, including *Harlequin*, 1980; *Roadgames* and *Long Weekend*). However, influential producers such as Anthony Ginnane (eg. *Turkey Shoot*; the *Fantasm* series; *Thirst*), and John Lomond (who specialized in sexploitation, such as *Australia After Dark*, 1974, and *The ABC of Love and Sex: Australia Style*, 1978), also played prominent roles in overseeing the making of these films. Interestingly, the early works of a number of Australia's key 'quality' film-makers such as Bruce Beresford (*The Barry McKenzie* series) and Peter Weir (*The Cars That Ate Paris*) are also categorized by Hartley as Ozploitation.

Ozploitation has to be considered in light of some crucial developments in Australia in the early 1970s that directly impacted on the film industry as a whole, and helped to define the types of features that were able to be made at the time. The most significant of these were changes in arts policy in the late 1960s, which resulted in the introduction of a series of financial incentives by the government to encourage Australia's then-lagging film industry. This included the establishment of film funding bodies in 1970, such as the Australian Film Development Corporation (AFDC which became the Australian Film Commission in 1975) and the Experimental Film Fund, as well as a number of state initiatives, including the Victorian Film Corporation (established 1976) and the South Australian Film Corporation (established 1972) (Verhoeven 2006b: 196) These bodies, initially, were not averse to the production of commercial films. As film scholar, Tom O'Regan has noted, 'the 1969 Arts Council Report advocated the production of low budget, "frankly commercial films" as part of its strategy for Australian film to gain initial success with the Australian public' (O'Regan 2000). A significant number of the films that have been identified as Ozploitation were funded under these initiatives, and produced as part of what is referred to as Australia's 'second wave' of film-making. *The Adventures of Barry McKenzie*, for example, was made on a A$250,000 budget from the AFDC, while *Stork* was partially funded by the Experimental Film Fund (O'Regan 2000).

Another important factor that impacted on the style and content of Ozploitation was the relaxation of Australia's particularly repressive censorship laws and the introduction of the 'R' (18+) rating in 1971. This allowed for a greater (and frequently gratuitous) representation of sex and nudity, which also proved to be a major marketing hook for the films. O'Regan has noted that this trend towards specifically adult-oriented pictures was accompanied by other contributing factors, such as 'the related collapse of the family picture and the development of exhibition venues outside the chains as venues for "unexpected" film successes from "travel" documentaries to soft-core porn' (O'Regan 2000). However, in common with exploitation film, the American, as well as the Australian drive-in market also provided an avenue of release for a number of these genre films, a factor which partly accounts for Tarantino's exposure and hence long-standing admiration of Ozploitation.

The attempt to frame sections of Australian genre cinema within the scope of exploitation cinema is not entirely new. In 1992, Carol Laseur published an article in *Continuum* entitled, 'Australian Exploitation: The Politics of Bad Taste', which argued that films such as *Howling III: The Marsupials* (Philippe Mora, 1987) and *Man of Steel* (Gary Keady, 1989), offered a parodic, counter-cultural resistance that consciously aimed to challenge 'high' cultural values (Laseur 1992). However, her filmography is considerably narrower than that suggested by Hartley in his documentary. In addition to Laseur's work, a number of Ozploitation features, such as the schlock horror film *Thirst*, the biker movie *Stone* (Sandy Harbutt, 1974), and the low-budget *The Cars That Ate Paris* (Peter Weir, 1974) had been situated and consumed within cult cinema's 'realm of difference' (Telotte 1991: 7) for a number of years.

While a number of Ozploitation films conformed to the 'trashy' aesthetics and marginal audience reception that historically characterizes exploitation cinema, a notable handful display production values considerably higher than those connoted by the term itself and also experienced significant box office success, both in Australia and, at times, internationally. These include the sex comedy *Alvin Purple*, panned by critics but a huge hit with Australian audiences, while the profane portrait of the naïve ocker abroad in *The Adventures of Barry McKenzie*, particularly amused both British and Australian moviegoers. Other films are a more direct imitation of mainstream, Hollywood genre offerings and met with critical acclaim upon their release. The Hitchcockian thriller *Roadgames*, for example, was the most expensive Australian production ever undertaken at the time, with a budget of A$1.75 million and, somewhat controversially, starred Hollywood actors Jamie Lee-Curtis and Stacy Keach (Graham 2005).

This raises the question about the extent to which Hartley's conception of Ozploitation conforms to the pulpy 'B'-grade parameters of exploitation cinema. The validity of the term Ozploitation, however, maybe best considered in light of the hegemony that has characterized Australian cinema in the past four decades. During the 1970s, a backlash away from commercial cinema began to emerge in critical and funding sectors in Australia. This was accompanied by distinct shift towards the production of a more 'arty' European style cinema, which also melded with notions of Australian identity and nationalist values. Epitomized by *Picnic at Hanging Rock* (Peter Weir, 1975), these works were deemed to offer a more positive cultural image than that of the apparent vulgarity of the ocker film in particular. As Graeme Turner writes:

> … the version of Australia represented in these films was the kind of place most of the Eurocentric critics and government film assessors wished they did not inhabit … Not surprisingly in a 1975 review of the industry the institutional rhetoric underwent a crucial change. According to the new rubric what Australia needed were 'quality' films which could be the cultural flagships of the nation. (Turner 1989: 103)

As a result, genre production in Australia became increasingly culturally marginalized and divorced from its mainstream contexts, in spite of the fact that it continued to proliferate until the late 1980s. This marginalization provides much of the foundation for Hartley's argument for Ozploitation. As Hartley comments, many Ozploitation films 'were never conceived of as mainstream films in Australia even though they had the bigger budgets and had mainstream subject matter … our sex, our horror, our action, our thrillers were considered "embar-rassments"' (Ryan 2008). In fact, one of the distinct aims of Hartley's project was to create a greater level of cultural recognition of this largely 'overlooked' period of Australian film-making.

In many ways Hartley has achieved this goal. In spite of the fact that *Not Quite Hollywood* did not perform particularly well at the box office, the term 'Ozploi-tation' has achieved critical traction and currency following the documentary's release. Undoubtedly the term's successful migration into the critical lexicon of Australian cinema partly stems from its attachment to a broader pre-determined set of positive cultural values now assigned to exploitation cinema. Film theorist, Jeffrey Sconce (1995) has coined the term 'paracinema' to describe an attitude that inherently resists notions of hierarchies of taste and valorizes 'all forms of cinematic "trash", whether such films have been either explicitly rejected or simply ignored by legitimate film culture'. According to Sconce:

> …the politics of social stratification and taste in paracinema is more complex than a simple high-brow/low-brow split, and the cultural politics of 'trash cul-ture' are becoming ever more ambiguous as this 'aesthetic' grows in influence. In recent years, the paracinematic community has seen both the institution-alization and commercialization of their once-renegade, neo-camp aesthetic. (Sconce 1995: 101)

Hartley's reframing of Australian genre cinema as Ozploitation successfully locates this 'overlooked' period of film-making within contemporary global paracinematic discourses, and these apparent shifts in cultural value attached to exploitation film. This, in turn, has not only assigned Ozploitation cinema a level of cultural legitimacy but has also revealed a series of new marketing opportuni-ties for the films themselves. A series of DVD box sets comprised of various dis-parate films under the label of 'Ozploitation' were released shortly after Hartley's documentary. In addition, retrospectives of the works were shown at various film festivals and cinemas, both within Australia and internationally. This included the Chauvel, a predominantly arthouse venue in Sydney, which advertised a season of Ozploitation films as the '"alternate" masterpieces of the Australian cinema story' (Urban Cinephile 2008). The making of the documentary also succeeded in 'rescuing' a number of prints of films that were deemed lost. Quentin Tarantino, for example, had in his possession the only surviving print of the crocodile movie *Dark Age* (Arch Nicholson, 1987) (Partridge 2008). Ozploitation style films are also experiencing something of a production revival in Australia in recent years. Most of these are horror films, and include Michael and Peter Spierig's *Undead* (2003) and *Daybreakers* (2009), Greg Mclean's *Wolf Creek* (2005) and *Rogue* (2007) and Jamie Blanks' 2008 remake of Colin Egglestone's 1978 film *Long Weekend*.

Overall, the term Ozploitation successfully yokes Australian genre cinema to the global reaches of exploitation film, and hence within contemporary discourses of paracinema, which increasingly assign cultural recognition and legitimacy to the once marginal 'trash' aesthetics of exploitation cinema. This development can also be contextualized within other historical and global shifts in the value and meaning of genre cinema. On perhaps a less grandiose scale, Ozploitation parallels similar critical reconfigurations of genre, such as Hol-lywood 'B' crime pictures into *film noir*, 'women's weepies' into 'classic melo-drama', and the cultural elevation of the Western. The reframing and recognition of Australian genre film-making within global discourses of paracinema also

reveals a more secure cultural position that is less concerned with 'Americaniza-
tion' of Australian culture, and the imperative to construct nationalist notions
of identity and difference. In fact, in an ironic twist, Ozploitation-style films can
sometimes be seen to be championed over so-called AFC genre films which,
as Turner has noted, have increasingly become dogged by intrinsic notions of
cultural elitism and conservatism, and denigrated as mere 'period pieces' (Turner
1989: 104). Whether this is a fair summation of Australian film history is arguable.
However, on a positive note, Hartley's *Not Quite Hollywood*, and the resultant
cultural circulation and critical currency generated by the term 'Ozploitation', has
succeeded in retrieving a prolific period of Australian film-making from obscurity
to create a more holistic archive of national cinema.

Deborah Thomas

The Adventures of Barry McKenzie

Country of Origin:
Australia

Director:
Bruce Beresford

Producer:
Phillip Adams

Screenwriters:
Bruce Beresford
Barry Humphries

Cinematography:
Don McAlpine

Editors:
John Scott

Production Designer:
John Stoddart

Cast:
Barry Crocker
Barry Humphries
Paul Bertram
Spike Milligan
Peter Cook
Mary Ann Severne

Genre:
Ocker Comedy
Ozploitation

Duration:
114 minutes

Year:
1972

Synopsis

At the reading of his late father's will in Sydney, Barry McKenzie is bequeathed A$2000 on the condition he travels immediately to the United Kingdom 'to further the cultural and intellectual traditions of the McKenzie dynasty'. He is accompanied by his Aunt Edna. After a brief interlude in Hong Kong, they arrive at Heathrow where Barry's suitcase of 'personal effects' – dozens of cans of Fosters lager – is confiscated. They are taken for a ride by a taxi driver, travelling to Earl's Court via Stonehenge and Scotland, and eventually arrive at the home of Barry's old mate Curly. Barry takes a room at the run down Kangaroo Court Hotel. At a local pub, Barry is approached by a television director, to star in a commercial for High Camp cigarettes. Edna and Barry travel to Rickmansworth to visit a British family with upper class pretensions who have fallen on hard times.

Mistakenly thinking that her visitors are wealthy, Mrs Gort hopes to marry off her daughter Sarah to Barry. Barry and Sarah go to a Young Conservatives dance; Barry escapes to a back room to join a group of Australian students from a local agricultural college. On the way home, Barry and Sarah fumblingly embrace, while Mrs Gort spies on them with greedy anticipation. Realizing that Barry and Sarah have not 'committed intimacy', Mrs Gort throws Barry out. He hitches a lift back to London with a hippie band, The Disciples, who he regales with his song 'The One-Eyed Trouser Snake'. Believing that this 'authentic Australian folk singer' will make their fortunes, the band convinces Barry to sign a contract to sing at a Leprosy Benefit Night at the Freedom Arts Factory. Barry's rendition of 'Chunder in the Old Pacific Sea' is a sensation, and he is approached by famous impresario Maurie Miller. Miller buys Barry's contract from the Disciples, but an all-in brawl breaks out when Barry misunderstands Miller's intentions.

Barry wakes up in hospital where his colourful vernacular attracts the attention of a psychiatrist, Dr DeLamphrey. Barry vomits on the doctor's head, and is discharged. Edna asks Barry to look for her friend Madge's daughter Gaelene, who now goes by the name of Lesley. Barry is plunged into London's gay scene. He is pursued by a detective who tries to arrest him in a toilet. Lesley and Barry escape, and after a chance meeting with Lesley's former partner Dominic, Barry is invited on to a live television show that Dominic is directing about Australian artists in London. Egged on by Curly and his Australian mates, Barry exposes himself on television. His mates accidentally set fire to the set. They try to douse the flames by urinating on them. Barry again narrowly avoids arrest. Dominic tells him his spontaneous nudity on the live show impressed both the Bishop of Wapping and the Director General of the BBC, who has offered Barry his own series. Edna has her own plans, dragging Barry off to the airport, telling him 'England's not ready for you … you're spoiling our national image'. On the plane on the way back to Australia, Barry confesses to Edna 'In a funny kind of way, I was just starting to like the Poms'.

The Adventures of Barry McKenzie, Longford.

Critique

The Adventures of Barry McKenzie, adapted from a comic strip written by Barry Humphries, is a landmark film in the revival of Australian cinema. It was the first film to be fully funded by the new federal agency, the Australian Film Development Corporation (AFDC), and its unexpected success (in Britain as well as in Australia) both demonstrated that Australian films could be popular, and helped establish the 'ocker comedy' as the first indigenous (sub)genre of the Australian 'new wave'. In common with other ocker comedies including *Stork* (Tim Burstall, 1971), and *Alvin Purple* (Tim Burstall, 1973), *The Adventures of Barry McKenzie* was derided by critics, despite its popular success. But, as Tom O'Regan has argued, these films were vitally important in developing a public profile for Australian films, for encouraging private investment in production, and for convincing exhibitors to screen Australian films.

Much of the comedy in *The Adventures of Barry McKenzie* derives from the gleeful observations of the gulf between Australia and Britain, in particular the contrast between the coarse, vulgar, down-to-earth Australians preoccupied with bodily functions, and the uptight, devious, class-bound and sexually-perverted British. And yet the two nationalities are seen to share some things in common, particularly a casual racism which sits uncomfortably in the background: as Barry and Edna prepare to leave Australia at the start of the film, a caller to a talk-back radio show can be heard in the background asserting 'I think we should keep the colour bar. White Australia to continue', and, after being charged an exorbitant amount of import duty, Barry exclaims 'When it comes to fleecing you, the Poms have got the edge on the gypos'. And, in Britain, a sign outside the Gort's home reads 'No tramps, no hawkers, no coloureds', as a black postman delivers the mail. Mrs Gort then carefully sprays the letters before picking them up.

The film is overtly and aggressively Australian from its opening shot of the Sydney Opera House, framed through the Sydney Harbour Bridge, to the Australian brands and icons that litter the film, including the Qantas flight bag, forever slung across Barry's shoulders, the 'tinnies' of Fosters lager that are the expatriate Australians' favourite tipple, and the lamingtons (an Australian cake) and jars of Vegemite that Edna receives in a care package from Australia. The iconography works both as an act of cultural assertion and as self-parody, as the film explicitly mocks the requirement that films funded by the AFDC demonstrate 'significant Australian content'. Barry and Edna represent the poles of the 'cultural cringe': the Australian attitude to Britain which manifests either as Barry's aggressive and often insulting statements of difference (Barry wears a t-shirt that screams 'Pommy Bastards'), or as Edna's fawning deference and reverence for arcane and anachronistic British traditions. Barry's exaggerated and colourful vernacular is a particularly pointed marker of difference, with the British characters constantly bemused by turns of phrase such as 'I was as dry as a dead dingo's donga' or his memorable insult to an upper class twit at the Young Conservatives' ball: 'I hope all your chooks turn into emus and kick your dunny down', and his almost inexhaustible set of expressions to describe the act of urination: 'point Percy at the porcelain', 'shake hands with the unemployed', 'drain the dragon', 'siphon the python', 'unbutton the mutton'. Edna's obeisance satirizes an attitude common among Australians of British heritage that was often based on exaggerated or erroneous ideas about life in 'the mother country'. Presenting the Gorts with a jar of dripping, Edna proudly tells her hosts that during the Second World War her home was a 'fat for Britain' depot: a neighbourhood collection point for old fat that was 'whisked off to Britain, post haste'. 'Aunty thought you might still be a bit short,' Barry adds.

For all his macho bravado, Barry is in many ways the archetypal Australian abroad. This theme is both universal and quintessentially Australian, and appears in a range of films from Ted Kotcheff's *Wake in Fright* (1971) to Peter Faiman's *Crocodile Dundee* (1986), but by virtue of its London setting, *The Adventures of Barry McKenzie* explicitly and deliberately tackles head-on the special place of Australians in Britain. Several of the film's key creative forces, including Bruce Beresford and Barry Humphries, had migrated to England in the 1960s, and *Barry* clearly engages with the exodus of artists and cultural producers from Australia at this time. In an ironic commentary on the contribution expatriates can make to the imagining of Australia, Barry's mate Curly works fitfully on his 'great Australian novel', 'working out a few of the traditional Australian hang-ups ... exploring the infrastructure of the Lawrentian myth' in his opus entitled *The Blood-Stained Surfboard*.

The film features star turns from comedians and television personalities including Spike Milligan, Peter Cook, Julie Covington and Joan Bakewell, but the real stars are singer Barry Crocker in the title role, and Barry Humphries who plays the roles of Barry's aunt Edna, the leader of the band the Disciples, and the psychiatrist Dr De Lamphrey. The film is based on the comic strip written by Humphries, which was published in the British satirical magazine *Private Eye* in the 1960s. *The Adventures of Barry McKenzie* marked the film debut of Humphries' character Edna Everage, now Dame Edna, a housewife from the Melbourne suburb of Moonee Ponds who would go on to be a global television star with her own series on British, Australian and American networks. The film also marked the debuts of a number of people who would go on to play significant roles in the Australian film revival, including director Bruce Beresford, cinematographer Don McAlpine, and editor John Scott. Producer Phillip Adams had played a key role in convincing Prime Minister John Gorton to invest not only in Australian film production, first through the film board of the Australian Council of the Arts and later through the Experimental Film and Television Fund and the AFDC, but also in film training by setting in motion the process that would lead to the establishment of the Australian Film, Television and Radio School in 1973. Gorton and another Prime Minister who played a key role in the revival of the Australian film industry, Gough Whitlam, Prime Minister between 1972 and 1975, both appeared in the sequel: *Barry McKenzie Holds His Own* (Bruce Beresford, 1974). There is a further political connection: the television programme that Barry exposes himself on at the end of *Adventures* is called 'Midnight Oil', not coincidentally the name of a successful Australian rock band whose lead singer, Peter Garrett, became federal Minister for the Environment and the Arts in 2007.

Ben Goldsmith

The Man from Hong Kong

Country of Origin:
Australia

Director:
Brian Trenchard-Smith

Producers:
Raymond Chow
John Fraser

Screenwriter:
Brian Trenchard-Smith

Director of Photography:
Russell Boyd

Art Directors:
David Copping
Chien Shum

Editor:
Ron Williams

Synopsis

At Uluru in central Australia, a drug deal is foiled by federal policeman Bob Taylor. After a chase up the iconic rock, Taylor captures the courier, Wing Chan. In Hong Kong, Special Branch Inspector Fang Sing Ling's training session is interrupted by the unexpected arrival of a hang-glider, piloted by an Australian woman, Caroline Thorne. After a brief liaison with Caroline, Fang is sent to Australia to extradite Chan. At Sydney airport he is met by Taylor and another policeman, Morrie Grosse, from the Federal Narcotics Branch. Fang interrogates Chan in prison, forcing him to divulge the name of his boss, Jack Wilton, the most powerful gangster in Sydney. On the way to court to formalize the extradition proceedings, Chan is assassinated by a sniper. Fang chases the assassin through the city and into a Chinese restaurant where, after a brutal fight, the assassin is killed. Fang retrieves business cards from the assassin that show he was an instructor at Wilton's Martial Arts Academy. Fang and Taylor visit Wilton's office where his secretary Willard tries to throw them off the scent.

At night in his hotel, Fang is attacked by two of Wilton's henchmen, but manages to fight them off. Fang contacts Caroline who arranges an invitation to a party at Wilton's mansion on Sydney Harbour. Fang confronts Wilton, who provokes a fight. Caroline and Fang escape. At night, Fang scales the outside of the multi-storey building that houses Wilton's Academy, offices, and apartment. Inside, he fights off multiple assailants and is seriously wounded before serendipitously escaping in a passing van driven by Angelica. Angelica takes Fang to her father's

Genre:

Action

Martial Arts

Ozploitation

Duration:

103 minutes

Cast:

Jimmy Wang Yu

George Lazenby

Hugh Keays Byrne

Rebecca Gilling

Frank Thring

Ros Spiers

Roger Ward

Grant Page

Year:

1975

house in the country to recover from his injuries. They fall in love. Some days later they drive back to Sydney, but they are followed by more of Wilton's henchmen. One plants a bomb on the van, which explodes, and Angelica is killed. Fang vows revenge. He flags down a passing motorist and chases down his latest assailants, killing them all. Wilton realizes Fang is coming for him, and barricades himself in his apartment. Fang uses Thorne's hang-glider to fly on to the roof of Wilton's building, and breaks in to the apartment through an unprotected window. Despite his vast array of weaponry and martial arts expertise, Wilton is knocked out by Fang, who tapes a hand grenade into the gangster's mouth and forces him to sign a confession when he comes round. After pulling the pin on the grenade, Fang locks Wilton in his safe, which is filled with munitions and drugs. Fang abseils down the side of the building to hand the confession and evidence to Taylor and Grosse as the grenade explodes, blowing the roof off the building.

Critique

Australia's first martial arts action film was a co-production between Hong Kong production company Golden Harvest and director Brian Trenchard-Smith's Movie Company, with significant investment from BEF Distributors, a subsidiary of the Australian exhibition chain Greater Union. Two years previously, Golden Harvest had co-produced the Bruce Lee smash hit *Enter the Dragon*, with Warner Bros. *The Man from Hong Kong* was its first partnership with an Australian producer, and the first coproduction between Hong Kong- and Australian-based companies. Although the film was almost entirely set in Sydney, much of the production was shot in a Hong Kong studio, where sets including Wilton's gloriously-decorated apartment were built.

The film boasts a magnificent cast, featuring major international stars: Jimmy Wang Yu, a major star in Hong Kong through his films with director Chang Cheh including *One Armed Swordsman* (1967), and one-time James Bond *On Her Majesty's Secret Service*, (Peter R Hunt, 1969) George Lazenby, and scene-stealing supporting actors Frank Thring (an Australian best known internationally for his Hollywood roles in *The Vikings* (Richard Fleischer, 1958); *Ben Hur* (William Wyler, 1959); and *King of Kings* (Nicholas Ray, 1961), whose father, Frank Thring Sr, had been a leading figure in the Australian film industry in the 1920s and 1930s), and Hugh Keays Byrne, a product of the Royal Shakespeare Company. Special mention also must go to perhaps the finest and bravest stuntman Australia has yet produced, Grant Page, who, in addition to a supporting role as the assassin, performed many of the numerous extraordinary stunts which give the film a timeless verve and energy. The unfortunate drug courier Wing Chan is played by (Sammo) Hung Kam Po, already a legendary stuntman and fight choreographer.

British-born director Brian Trenchard-Smith's second feature film (after the semi-documentary *The Love Epidemic*, made earlier in 1975) displays many of the elements that would come to define this prolific director's style: fast-paced action sequences, breathtaking stunts, inventively-staged and energetically-shot chases in cars and on foot, gory and lengthy fights, corny dialogue, and visual jokes, especially in scene transitions such as the shift from a 'groin hit' (another Trenchard-Smith

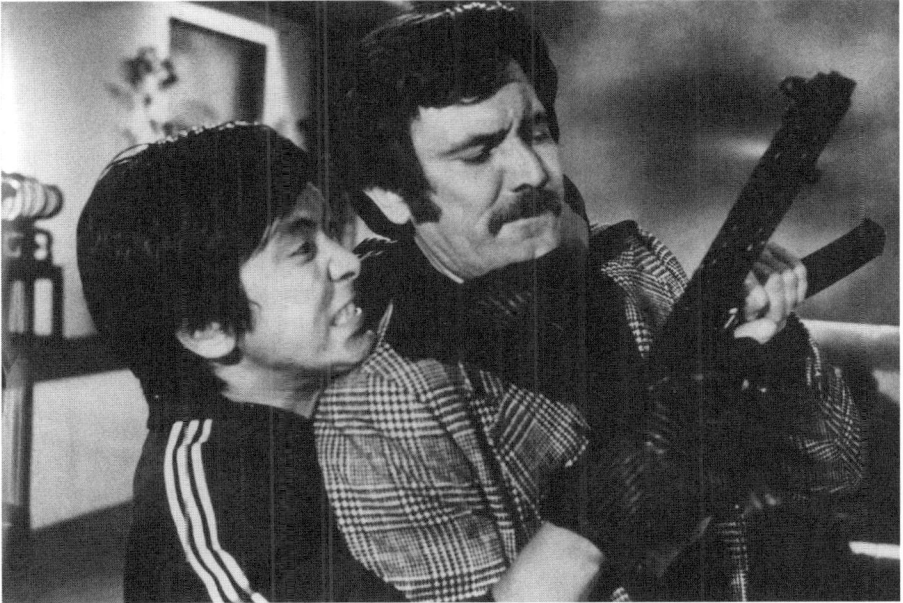

The Man From Hong Kong, Golden Harvest/Movie Co.

trademark to a rack of pool balls breaking apart. While some of the set pieces are overlong, and a romantic getting-to-know-you montage preceding the sex scene between Fang and Angelica is toe-curlingly awful, *The Man From Hong Kong* has deservedly become a cult movie revered by such notable figures as Quentin Tarantino.

Trenchard-Smith's films are not known for their trenchant social commentary, but *The Man from Hong Kong* is also noteworthy for deliberately confronting latent Australian (and cinematic) racism in its ground-breaking love scenes between an Asian man and white women. Fang is repeatedly baited by Wilton and Grosse about his race and, while the film clearly contrasts the methods of the Hong Kong police (the ruthlessly effective Fang tortures his prisoners, deliberately or incidentally kills or maims numerous of Wilton's men, and forces a confession from the underworld boss after taping a hand grenade in his mouth) and their Australian counterparts (comic figures who are efficient, but always one step behind), it is ultimately the Inspector's more direct methods that succeed in bringing down Wilton's crime empire.

Cinematography and production design are two of the film's strongest suits. The use of a hang-glider (claimed by the director as a movie first) permits sweeping aerial views of Sydney and Hong Kong, and the long car chase allows extensive use of the 'rig shot', where the camera is attached to the outside of a vehicle being driven at high speed. The fashions and decor clearly date the film, but many of the sets are exquisitely dressed. In Wilton's apartment, black-and-white tiled floors and antique Chinese ornaments are boldly matched with pumpkin-orange furniture to provide a rich variety of objects to be used and destroyed in the ultimate confrontation between Fang and Wilton.

Ben Goldsmith

Turkey Shoot

Alternative Title:
Blood Camp Thatcher

Country of Origin:
Australia

Director:
Brian Trenchard-Smith

Producer:
William Fayman
Antony I. Ginnane

Screenwriter:
Jon George
Neil D Hicks

Director of Photography:
John R McLean

Production Designer:
Bernard Hides

Editor:
Alan Lake

Genre:
Ozploitation
Prison

Duration:
93 minutes

Cast:
Steve Railsback
Michael Craig
Roger Ward
Lynda Stoner
Olivia Hussey
Noel Ferrier
Carmen Duncan
Michael Petrovich

Year:
1982

Synopsis

In a repressive totalitarian future, in an unspecified time and place, prison camps have been created to 're-educate' people who are deemed to be social deviants. Three new inmates arrive at Camp 47, which is run by the brutal Charles Thatcher, along with a cohort of sadistic prison guards, headed by the gargantuan Ritter. Paul Anders is a dissident escapee from other camps; Rita Daniels has been accused of prostitution; Chris Walters is a shopkeeper suspected of aiding rebels. In a bid to obtain their freedom, these inmates make a deal with Thatcher to participate in a 'Turkey Shoot', where they are to be hunted as unarmed human prey. The shoot is part of the amusement offered by Thatcher for his superiors, Secretary Mallory and other government officials Jennifer and Tito. Thatcher falsely guarantees their freedom if they can outwit and outrun their armed predators until sundown. With the odds against them, the three manage to turn the tables on their pursuers, violently eliminating them one by one. However, at the end of the film everything is destroyed by a government-orchestrated napalm airstrike.

Critique

Turkey Shoot was made in 1982 by the 'kings' of Ozploitation, action director, Brian Trenchard-Smith, and producer, Anthony Ginnane. Encapsulated by its sensational British tagline, 'no film for chickens', *Turkey Shoot*, like Trenchard-Smith's, *Dead End Drive-In* (1986), was one of a number of dystopian, futuristic films that were made after the success of the *Mad Max* films. However, the film displays little of the mainstream, blockbuster aesthetics of *Mad Max II* (George Miller, 1981), or even the grainy, low budget 'realism' of *Mad Max* (George Miller, 1979). *Turkey Shoot*'s production values are undoubtedly located within the realm of exploitation's schlock, 'trash' aesthetics. As such, unlike a number of other films that have been grouped together as 'Ozploitation', *Turkey Shoot* is firmly aligned with the 'B'-grade expectations connoted by the term itself.

Supposedly inspired by George Orwell's novel *1984* (1949), and by the films *The Most Dangerous Game* (Irving Pichel & Ernest B. Schoedsack, 1932), and *The Naked Prey* (Cornel Wilde, 1966), *Turkey Shoot* was denounced by critics on its initial release for its portrayal of graphic violence, and denigrated as 'the low point of Australian cinema.' Noted critic Phillip Adams reputedly walked out of the film claiming it to be the worst he had ever seen, while Geoff Mayer in *Cinema Papers* condemned it for the way it 'relies almost completely on mutilation, torture and killing'. However, such content is the routine stuff of exploitation cinema, and, over the passage of time, *Turkey Shoot* secured itself a cult following. These audiences, rather than perceiving it to be an exercise in disturbing realism, revelled in its hyper-aware, camp excess, quintessentially embodied in the film by the giant, grotesque spectacle of Roger Ward, and such key, bloody moments as the severing of his head entirely from his body; a toe-chomping incident inflicted by Tito's bizarre mutant pet, Alph (Steve

Rackmar and his subsequent bulldozing in half; as well as a host of other assorted gory mutilations.

Conceived under the 10BA tax incentives, *Turkey Shoot* is about as far removed from concerns about constructing a national cinema as is possible. The jungle-like location, futuristic plot and depthless character stereotypes are purely generic. In addition to this, the actors, including those who are Australian, enunciate in perceptible English accents. This peculiarity, evident in other Ozploitation films such as the earlier sex comedy, *Alvin Purple* (Tim Burstall, 1973), can be seen to be emblematic of some of the contradictions and hegemony that characterized public debates about Australian cinema at the time. While, on one hand, there were calls to consolidate a cinema with a sense of national identity and difference (although there was still often a 'cultural cringe' factor associated with broad Australian accents), on the other, there was an imperative for Australian films to appeal to British and American audiences. Of course, Trenchard-Smith, although living and working within Australia at the time, was British in origin, and intent on attracting a commercial, international market for his films. This also appears to be evident in *Turkey Shoot*'s opportunistic attempts to construct a political parable with Margaret Thatcher's Britain via naming the camp commandant 'Thatcher' and releasing the film in Britain on video under the title *Blood Camp Thatcher*. However, any potentially forceful political rhetoric becomes subsumed by the film's commercial and satirical 'B'-grade excesses, evident not only from its gore and assortment of grotesques (including a problematic carnivorous lesbian), but gratuitous nudity, and obvious attempts at sexual titillation and innuendo ('It's less the size of one's gun that counts then the skill with which it is used'). In light of this, *Turkey Shoot*, is perhaps best understood and celebrated for making an authentic, key contribution to the Ozploitation archive of Australian cinema.

Deborah Thomas

Dead End Drive-In

Country of Origin:
Australia

Director:
Brian Trenchard-Smith

Producer:
Andrew Williams

Screenwriter:
Peter Smalley, adapted from the short story 'Crabs' by Peter Carey

Synopsis

A series of titles announce catastrophes around the world: the 'Rocks Riot' in Sydney on Australia Day 1988 leaves 51 dead; a nuclear accident at Mururoa Atoll in December 1988 poisons Pacific fishing grounds, creating food shortages; 103,000 die in 'The Great White Massacre' in Cape Town on 1 April 1989; another Wall Street Crash in June 1990 plunges the capitalist system into chaos and presages the collapse of social order. In an attempt to control rampant unemployment and hyperinflation, the government invokes emergency powers.

Crabs, so named because he once claimed to have a venereal disease to impress his mates, is trying to build himself up in order to become a tow-truck driver like his brother Frank. One day out jogging, Crabs is harassed by the Karboys, a street gang who vie with predatory tow truck drivers for prime pickings from car crashes. To

Cinematography:
Paul Murphy

Editor:
Alan Lake
Lee Smith

Production Designer:
Larry Eastwood

Genre:
Ozploitation
Prison

Duration:
90 minutes

Cast:
Ned Manning
Natalie McCurry
Peter Whitford
Wilbur Wilde
Dave Gibson

Year:
1987

impress his girlfriend Carmen, Crabs borrows Frank's pride and joy, a 1956 Chevy, and takes her to the drive-in cinema, not realizing that the old ozoner has become a detention camp for the young. Two of the car's wheels are stolen and loaded into a police van. Crabs' complaints to the sinister manager of the drive-in, Thompson, bring only an issue of blankets and meal tickets. Thompson explains that Crabs and Carmen have been detained 'until the government decides what to do with you'. Crabs patrols the drive-in, searching for spare parts to fix the car. A consignment of wrecks arrives one day, swiftly followed by cattle trucks containing Asian detainees who will live in the wrecks. With new-found solidarity, the previous inhabitants band together against what they see as an 'Asian invasion'. A White Australia Committee is formed. Crabs takes advantage of the distraction to steal a tow truck and attempt to escape. He is chased around the lot by the police, and crashes the truck. In the ensuing confusion he manages to steal a police van, drive up a conveniently lowered ramp of a car transporter, and leap the wall to freedom.

Critique

Brian Trenchard-Smith's uneven but visually-splendid third feature is based on a Peter Carey short story, 'Crabs'. *Dead End Drive-In* was the second adaptation of Carey's work for the screen after Ray Lawrence's *Bliss* (1985). The short story is a disturbing meditation on inexplicable incarceration and the regulation of social movement, both geographically and generationally. The film expands these themes, adds a pasticcio of generic conventions and stereotypes, and raises a variety of issues intended to act as commentaries on racism and class conflict in Australia. These elements never quite gel, and the issue of racial intolerance is hopelessly-inadequately resolved. The ending of the movie is a significant departure from the short story, in which Crabs decides 'to become a motor vehicle in good health'. He imagines his escape but, out on the highway, he drives for hours without seeing anything or anybody. Finally he turns a corner and sees lights in the distance.

> He turns off the highway and finds himself separated from the lights by a high wire fence. Inside he sees people moving around, laughing, talking. Some are dancing. He drives around the perimeter of the wire, driving over rough unmade roads, through paddocks until, at last, he comes to a large gate. The gate is locked and reinforced with heavy duty steel. Above the gate is a faded sign with peeling paint. It says 'Star Drive-in Theatre. Please turn off your lights'.

Carey's ending is then much bleaker than the film's. Crabs is incarcerated mentally as well as physically, and is ultimately left with no choice but to resign himself to his fate. In offering an alternative to this scenario the film creates multiple problems for itself. The clumsy racial plotline, which could have been a telling commentary on the fate of an underclass that allows itself to be divided and gains spurious solidarity only through the exclusion of others in the same position is like too many other elements, simply left unresolved. Ultimately, the film is quite a let-down. Its storyline and subject matter appear to promise much: a captive population, a sinister government plot, corrupt police, car chases, crashes, and stunning stuntwork. Stunts are a feature of Trenchard-Smith's films, from his prize-winning 1973 television documentary *The Stuntmen*, and feature films *The Man From Hong Kong* (1975), and *Deathcheaters* (1976) which contain some of the best stunt- and camera work yet seen in the Australian cinema. But the acting in *Dead End Drive-In* is largely woeful. Apart from the opening and closing scenes the pacing is far too pedestrian, and the superficial representation of a faceless Asian mob – much like *Romper Stomper* (1992) – is extremely discomfiting.

Ben Goldsmith

Not Quite Hollywood

Country of Origin:
Australia

Director:
Mark Hartley

Producers:
Michael Lynch
Craig Griffin

Cinematographer:
Kurt von Moller

Screenwriter:
Mark Hartley

Editors:
Jamie Blanks
Sarah Edwards
Mark Hartley

Genre:
Documentary
Ozploitation

Duration:
98 minutes

Synopsis

Through interviews with film-makers, actors, cultural commentators and a significant international fan – Quentin Tarantino – and a mountain of clips, Mark Hartley's feature length documentary celebrates Australian genre cinema from the 1970s and 1980s. The film is divided into three sections, showcasing different genres, directors and producers, all united by their marginal status in mainstream histories of Australian cinema. In rough chronological order, the film opens with a section entitled 'Ockers, Knockers, Pubes and Tubes' that concentrates on the ocker comedies beginning with *Stork* (Tim Burstall, 1971) and *The Adventures of Barry McKenzie* (Bruce Beresford, 1972), and the various sex documentaries and pseudo documentaries (for example, *The Naked Bunyip*, John B Murray 1970; *Fantasm*, Richard Franklin [as Richard Bruce], 1976; *The ABC of Love and Sex*, John Lamond 1978) that made the most of the new freedoms afforded by the relaxation of censorship regulations in the early 1970s. The second section, 'Comatose Killers and Outback Chillers', focuses on the thrillers and horror films that made the names of film-makers like screenwriter Everett De Roche (*Patrick*, Richard Franklin, 1978, and *Long Weekend*, Colin Eggleston, 1978), director Terry Bourke (*Night of Fear*, 1972; *Inn of the Damned*, 1975), and producer Antony Ginnane (*Snapshot*, Simon Wincer, 1979; *Thirst*, Rod Hardy, 1979; *Harlequin*, Simon Wincer, 1980). The final section, 'High Octane Disasters and Kung Fu Masters', features the action cinema of Brian Trenchard-Smith (*The Man from Hong Kong*, 1975; *Stunt Rock*, 1978; *Dead End Drive-In*, 1986) and the stunt- and car-chase-driven films that showcased the talents of some of the real unsung heroes of Australian cinema, Grant Page, Peter Armstrong, Guy Norris and their stunt teams.

Cast:
Quentin Tarantino
Brian Trenchard-Smith
Antony I Ginnane
Phillip Adams
Bob Ellis
Richard Franklin

Year:
2008

Critique

Not Quite Hollywood might just as accurately have been titled *Not Quite Australian Cinema*. The film begins from the premise that the films it covers have been unduly overlooked by critics, historians and scholars of the Australian cinema, often despite enormous box office success. Much of the blame for the marginalization of these films is placed at the feet of former Sydney Film Festival director and long-time film critic for *The Australian* newspaper, David Stratton, well-known to Australian audiences as one half of the 'David and Margaret' couple who have dominated film reviewing on Australian television for many years. Stratton's books on the Australian film revival, *The Last New Wave* (1980) and *The Avocado Plantation* (1990), are said to have set the tone for later writers by reviling or simply ignoring many of the films produced in Australia in the 1970s and 1980s in favour of a canon of films and directors deemed more culturally and artistically worthy. Perhaps predictably, *Not Quite Hollywood* swings the other way. The back-slapping, anecdotal, revisionist history told through the many interviews with key figures from the time is only occasionally interrupted by Bob Ellis and Phillip Adams, who are only slightly uncomfortably cast as defenders of the mainstream views. The interviews and clips from the films are interspersed with the fan-boy enthusiasms of Quentin Tarantino, whose geek-chic profile and ency-clopaedic knowledge of exploitation and genre cinema are milked to the full. In sharp contrast, Ellis's scorn for these film-makers and their films is total, but it is his withering and slanderous assessments of the characters, talents and practices of producers like Antony I Ginnane and John Lamond that leavens this sometimes stodgy stew of self-congratulation.

Director Mark Hartley gained access to many of his leading players through his work researching and filming extras for the DVD releases of many of the films that are the subject of *Not Quite Hollywood*. The list of interviewees is impressive, although Tarantino is permitted way too much screen time at the expense of those who were actu-ally there. The cult director's presence appears to have been geared to marketing the documentary, first to investors and subsequently to audiences within and outside Australia, although, given that many of the films celebrated here owe their notoriety to spectacular and opportunistic marketing, perhaps this should be considered a laud-able decision.

The film's colourful, fast-moving style mirrors its subject matter. The many scurrilous, surprising and shocking 'war stories' that comprise the best of the interview grabs are entertaining and informative, while some of the most impressive parts of the film are the titles and original, animated montage sequences that pepper the film. The frenetic editing of sequences from the films blurs together explosions, car crashes, fist fights, dodgy monster animals, naked bodies and fiery stunts into a visceral spectacle that never allows the viewer to think too deeply about what they are seeing. Although this is true to the credo of the exploitation style, it means that the film largely misses an opportunity to engage the films' critics on their own terms by fully demonstrating the skill, artistry and hard work that made these films possible. The main exception is in the last section, in which the work of stuntmen like Grant Page, and the risks that many actors and crew were prepared to take in an era before occupational health and safety guidelines, clearly show the craft, commitment and labour involved in producing spectacular, commercial, genre cinema. Ultimately, the film endorses Tarantino's view – if you do not like this kind of stuff, get out of the cinema – rather than make a case to convince the doubters, many of whom still occupy powerful positions in the Australian film industry, that these films deserve to be rehabilitated.

Ben Goldsmith

NEW
ZEALA

ND

Previous Page: *Whale Rider*, New Zealand Film Comm.

INTRODUCTION: NEW ZEALAND FILM IN 2009 GEOFF LEALAND

The contributors to this first collection on New Zealand cinema provide a wide range of perspectives, from descriptions of New Zealand films past and present, to explorations of particular themes or aspects of New Zealand film-making. Brian McDonnell's reviews of six recent New Zealand films are a good example of the former, and Tony Mitchell's review of local music composition/performance in New Zealand films and Helen Martin's review of the work of local documentary-maker Shirley Horrocks are good examples of the latter.

The general strategy of this particular volume is to firstly privilege a focus on contemporary New Zealand films, especially those films which have been produced since the heady days of the filming of *The Lord of the Rings* trilogy in New Zealand in the opening years of the twenty-first century. A secondary task is to pay attention to the back catalogue of New Zealand films made during the twentieth century – especially those produced in the wake of the renaissance of New Zealand film-making, generally regarded as having its starting point in Roger Donaldson's *Sleeping Dogs* (1977) and the establishment of the New Zealand Film Commission in 1978. This volume has begun to pay attention to the earlier decades of New Zealand film; retrieving older titles such as *Death Warmed Up* (1986) and *Sons For the Return Home* (1979).

Gathering and editing the various entries here has been an interesting and fairly straightforward task, due to the generosity of the contributors. A more daunting task, for me, is writing this introduction, which requires me to provide a broad overview of the state of New Zealand cinema in 2009. This should begin with an adequate definition of 'New Zealand cinema' or, more specifically, a convincing definition of what a 'New Zealand film' might be. The American Film Institute might call the New Zealand film industry 'one of the wonders of the world ... an unparalleled success story',[1] but this is more in the nature of hyperbole than considered analysis. The contention of Film New Zealand is that New Zealand film-makers and films have attracted the world's attention far beyond what might be expected from a small, geographically-isolated country with a modest population (4.2 million citizens).

This may be so but the same can be said of film-makers and films from other countries (Iceland, Romania) which are similarly situated on the periphery of the major production centres of the world. Such films do gain some international traction (*Once Were Warriors* and *Whale Rider* are recent New Zealand-produced examples) but, in general, distribution and exhibition is largely confined to the arthouse cinema, and both box office and critical attention remains miniscule in comparison to the rewards reaped by mainstream cinema.

What is often more difficult and more intellectually demanding is attracting the attention and loyalty of local film-going audiences – that is, to persuade New Zealanders to go to New Zealand-made films, in order to sustain and perpetuate indigenous film-making, and meet the needs of both financial and cultural agendas. More films being produced and more ways of distributing films might seem to assist such agendas but Australian academic Sean Cubitt seems to think otherwise:

> On the one hand, indigenous and migrant cinemas point towards the significance of cultural identities, especially in settler nations like Aotearoa and Australia. On the other, it is in general cultural identity which must bear the brunt of the questions as to why films from one culture are so frequently difficult to export to people of another.
>
> Sadly, it appears that increasing levels of communication – in terms of both access and sheer numbers of images – enabled by the growth of internet communications and digital film equipment have not made our cultural diets more varied. (Cubitt 2009)

Certainly, in respect of New Zealand, the general range of film titles available at local cinemas has not greatly varied from a long-established dependence on Hollywood releases, despite the growth of an arthouse sector and continuing popularity of annual international film festivals. By international standards, New Zealanders remain keen film-goers (with per-capita cinema-going figures of 8.6 in 2007 and 9.4 in 2008[2] and a local box office dominated by mainstream titles.[3]

Obviously, the struggle to find local audiences for local film is not peculiar to New Zealand, especially where there is not a long tradition of film-making or where film-making is regarded as an integral part of state cultural policy. The opportunity to see locally-made films is a fairly recent phenomenon for New Zealanders (even though the novelty has now worn off), and even though structures for government support for New Zealand film-makers remain (primarily through the New Zealand Film Commission), they are also under renewed scrutiny.

According to the New Zealand Film Commission Act (1978), for any production to qualify as 'a New Zealand film' it needs to meet criteria of local subject material, locations, creative and acting talent, funding sources, and local ownership of equipment and technical facilities. In 2009, the National Government initiated a review of the NZFC, arguing that the requirements of the 1978 Act no longer reflected the screen-production realities of the twenty-first century. This intervention (not the first since the NZFC was set up) was motivated by continuing complaints that the Commission was failing in respect of the commercial potential of locally-made films, where the great majority of state-subsidized film-making never returns on its costs ('a rule of thumb is that one feature film in ten makes a profit and one in eight breaks even on production costs)'.[4]

The 2009 Review of the NZFC was also a reflection of the change of government in November 2008, when the three-term and very arts-friendly Labour administration was replaced by a coalition of right-leaning National, Act and the Maori Party and the re-emergence of a market-oriented approach to cultural production in New Zealand.

The difficulty of achieving a consensus of what a 'New Zealand film' might entail in 2009 has been further complicated by shifts in global film-making patterns over the past decade or two. This is exemplified in New Zealand-based director Peter Jackson, the figure who led the 2009 review of the NZFC (together with David Court, Head of Screen Business at the Australian Film, Television and Radio School). If Mexican film director Guillermo del Toro truly believes that New Zealand cinema is 'Hollywood the way God intended it', then Peter Jackson (now Sir Peter Jackson) is the godlike colossus who straddles and overshadows the local industry. Jackson can be best described as a New Zealand-born and New Zealand-based *global* film-maker.

A number of Jackson's earliest films (*Bad Taste*, *Heavenly Creatures*) have elements of New Zealand in them (locations in *Bad Taste*; *Heavenly Creatures* based on a notorious murder in Christchurch) but in no way can his later efforts be described as 'New Zealand films', especially four of the highest-global-grossing films of all time (*The Lord of the Rings* trilogy and the 2005 re-make of *King Kong*). Indeed, Tim Wong describes *King Kong* as 'possibly the least New Zealand film ever made' (Wong 2006). These films are produced in New Zealand (and officially described as 'US/New Zealand' productions) and draw on local creative talent (directing, editing, SFX, support actors and extras) and New Zealand locations (often digitally altered beyond recognition).

Many might regard such distinctions as mere pedantry, for popular sentiment (aided and abetted by various branches of the New Zealand media) frequently claims such films as 'New Zealand films', and Peter Jackson as New Zealand film-maker *par excellence* and worthy of unmitigated praise and a knighthood. In many ways, Jackson's position as global film-maker living and producing in New Zealand highlights the continuing tension between the vital role off-shore (or 'foreign') film production plays in New Zealand (in terms of sustaining an infrastructure for the industry), and the desire to create films which are clearly grounded in New Zealand history and culture (between commerce and culture, if such an argument is to be simplified). In the wake of the New Zealand premiere of his 2009 adaptation of *The Lovely Bones*, Jackson explains,

We wanted it to be not a simplistic Hollywood film, nor an esoteric film either. So we tried to balance it.(Baillie 2009)

The jury is still out on whether he has succeeded for reviews of *The Lovely Bones* have been rather diffident for a film designated as 'USA/UK/New Zealand'. Jackson has certainly brought great benefits to New Zealand (employment opportunities, growth of production facilities, a spur to other off-shore productions from a variety of sources, including Bollywood, incentives for destination tourism)[5] but he has also made it difficult to think of New Zealand film in a clear and uncomplicated fashion.

It is, thus, the role of this particular contribution to the Directory of World Cinema to make the road to an understanding of New Zealand film a little clearer. The contributors to this collection have focused on films (feature films, documentaries, short film, experimental film) which are both *from* New Zealand and *of* New Zealand. My expectation is that they will lead readers to an appreciation of the film output of a small South Pacific nation, both in terms of the experiences shared with film-makers in other small countries, but also the factors which have enabled New Zealand to achieve a surprising presence in world cinema.

Notes

1. Highlighted on the industry-suppport site Film New Zealand. http://www.filmnz.com/introducing-nz/film-industry-history.html. Accessed 16 December 2009.
2. Figures from European Audiovisual Laboratory/Nation statistics (Uerominitor International) 2009.
3. Of the 258 films released in NZ in 2008, only one local film (*Second-Hand Wedding*, with $NZ1.9 million) challenged the continuing domination by imported titles. Films such as *Mamma Mia* ($NZ7.6m), *The Dark Knight* ($NZ6.8m) and *Quantum of Solace* ($NZ4.8m) took of the largest share of the $NZ156.5m New Zealand box office in 2008. In 2009, five NZ films (plus some festival-only releases) were included in the 273 films released, earning $NZ3.54m or 2.1% of the total NZ box office.
4. From a Discussion Paper for Review of Government Screen Funding Arrangements, Wellington Ministry of Culture and Heritage, 2009.
5. Examples include Jackson as producer of the 2009 scifi global hit *District 9*, the 800 Wellington-based Weta Workshop experts who worked on special effects for James Cameron's global success *Avatar*. By 2008, there were 2,223 businesses operating in the screen industry in NZ, with 95% of these active in screen production. Revenue from the industry reached $NZ2.743 billion in 2008 (Statistics New Zealand: Screen Industry Statistics, 2009).

Death Warmed Up, Tucker/Nz Film Corp.

Death Warmed Up

Studio/Distributor:
The Tucker Production
Company

Director:
David Blyth

Screenwriters:
Michael Heath
David Blyth

Producer:
Murray Newey

Cinematographer:
James Bartle

Art Direction:
Robert Pearson

Synopsis

Schoolboy Michael decides to visit his scientist father at the medical research facility on the outskirts of their local town. He witnesses his father having a heated argument with a colleague, Dr Archer Howell, over their experiments into 'life elongation' and the dangers that mutant genes may hold.

Dr. Howell follows Michael and subjects him to mind-altering processes, leaving him prone to Howell's commands. Howell drives Michael to his home, where he proceeds to murder his parents. He is committed to an insane asylum and the path is clear for the doctor to continue his dangerous experiments without interference.

Seven years later Michael is released from the asylum and with three friends, Sandy, Lucas and Jeannie, catches a ferry to a remote island on the proviso of a holiday but with the intent of getting revenge on Dr Howell, who has a research facility there. After an alter-cation on the ferry with two sleazy characters, Spider and Tex, Jeannie voices her concerns over their trip. Whilst exploring the island's tunnel system the friends make a gruesome discovery, and the situation takes a turn for the worse.

With an alienated Spider releasing the mutant psychos from the facility the entire island is under threat, with Michael still determined to confront Dr Howell.

Bad Taste, Wingnut Films.

Composer:
Mark Nicholas

Editor:
David Huggett

Duration:
85 minutes

Genre:
Horror

Cast:
Michael Hurst
Margaret Umbers
William Upjohn
Norelle Scott

Year:
1986

Critique

Death Warmed Up was the first of many subsequent horror movies to be funded by the New Zealand Film Commission and predates Peter Jackson's *Bad Taste* (1989) and *Braindead* (1992). It is easy to see that fellow Kiwi Jackson must have been influenced to a degree by David Blyth's movie as it is a gloriously over-the-top splatter movie which unashamedly wears its no-budget B-movie status as a badge of honour. Employing many of the traits familiar to both the archetypal horror movie – mad scientists, friends in peril, hideous creatures – and the modern gore movies – extreme graphic violence, electronic soundtrack and a DIY punk aesthetic – it carves itself out a niche as something of a cult curiosity. Those wishing for a refined, glossy affair would be well advised to look elsewhere, but for those that can appreciate the often demented joys of head explosions, disembowelments, copious amounts of oozing blood and cheesy one-liners, then this is an enjoyable if somewhat minor movie in the canon of 80s' horror films.

The acting is a little broad in places, which is no great surprise given its budgetary constraints and genre standing, with Gary Day giving a particularly hammy performance as Dr Howell – his character being yet another in the long line of mad scientists to be portrayed onscreen as a comedic cross between Dr Moreau and Herbert West, the re-animator. The rudimentary plot allows for a number of surprisingly well-executed set pieces that belie the movie's humble origins, with the director certainly making good use of what is at hand for these scenes. The World War II tunnel sequence, for example, looks fantastic; claustrophobic, tense and smartly lit, it is arguably the highlight of the movie. A siege situation involving the gang of friends and the marauding mutant psychos later in the film also works well, creating moments of genuine tension. The island itself looks beautiful and it is hard not to see why so many filmmakers have made use of the country's scenery in recent years, for it makes an interesting contrast to the chaotic bloodletting that dominates the film's final half hour.

The plot itself disintegrates into a wildly grimy, messy and semi-coherent climax, as the creatures released by Spider (David Letch) lay waste to anyone that they can get their hands on. Michael's encounter with Dr Howell is almost sedate compared to the carnage going on around them, but it does set up a satisfyingly bleak if slightly confusing climax. There could easily have been a sequel spawned by the film's ending but it has never materialized; something which may be surprising considering the success of later horror movies from the Antipodes and the increasing trend towards franchises and remakes that dominate contemporary cinema.

All in all, *Death Warmed Up* is certainly rough around the edges and perhaps one for B-movie lovers only, but it deserves to be recognized in the lineage of New Zealand films and for low budget film-makers of all genres. For the viewer jaded by much of contemporary horror cinema's generic fodder and in need of a healthy dose of nostalgia, they could do a lot worse than seek out this often overlooked oddity.

Neil Mitchell

Fracture

Production Company:
Crime Story Limited

Distributor:
Polyphony Entertainment

Director:
Larry Parr

Producer:
Charlie McClellan

Screenwriter:
Larry Parr (from the novel Crime Story by Maurice Gee)

Cinematographer:
Fred Renata

Synopsis

Fracture is an ensemble piece, its complicated narrative tracing the intricate interplay of contacts among a disparate group of Wellingtonians. One uniting factor is Leeanne Rosser, a young solo mother. Her brother Brent triggers off events by his burgling upmarket houses. When the occupant of one (Ulla) returns home unexpectedly, Brent attacks her and causes her to strike her head as she topples down the stairs. The injury paralyses her. This crime serves to link the lives of two disparate families: an affluent family named Peet (Ulla's in-laws), and Brent and Leeanne's working-class family. While Leeanne displays pluck, resourcefulness and determination in attempting to find accommodation and security for herself and her baby, Brent begins to deteriorate mentally as the consequences of his violent action sink in. Displaying a psychopathic lack of remorse and a disintegrating identity, he takes his fear of arrest to extreme lengths by severing his fingers to destroy his fingerprints and by murdering a fence who threatens to expose him. Meanwhile Leeanne tries unsuccessfully to reconcile with her hostile mother and attempts to help Brent. Ulla's accident brings out her family's compassionate side while Leeanne's father finds the strength to invite her to live with him.

Art Director:

John Harding

Editor:

Jonathan Woodford-Robinson

Duration:

107 minutes

Genre:

Drama

Cast:

Kate Elliot
Jared Turner
Tim Lee
Miranda Harcourt
John Noble
Liddy Holloway
Jennifer Ward-Lealand
Michael Hurst

Year:

2004

Critique

Fracture's director Larry Parr has been better known during his long career in film and television (dating back to *Sleeping Dogs* in 1977) as a producer rather than for directing. He has been particularly known for his energetic participation in projects reflecting the Maori part of his heritage. Wittily, he has all *Fracture*'s senior professionals (judge, police detectives, hospital doctor) played by Maori actors, subverting social statistics by having brown authority figures mete out justice to white criminals. Parr produced many films in the 1980s but his company Mirage Films folded after the 1987 stock market crash. The company he owned when he began making *Fracture*, Kahukura Productions, also suffered financial collapse. He now works in Maori television.

Fracture is a relatively little-known film, especially compared to *In My Father's Den*, released in the same year and, like *Fracture*, adapted from a novel by Maurice Gee. It had little critical attention, which is a shame because it is an ambitious and interesting, if flawed, piece of work. Unusually for a New Zealand film, it belongs to the same narrative mode exemplified by such American films as *Grand Canyon* (Lawrence Kasdan, 1991), *Short Cuts* (Robert Altman, 1993), *Magnolia* (Paul Thomas Anderson, 1999) and *Crash* (Paul Haggis, 2005), i.e. a panoramic, ensemble film having a large number of characters and multiple storylines rather than a unified plot following one or two protagonists.

As a portrait of Wellington, *Fracture* could be termed Dickensian. Like that author, both Gee (an admirer of Dickens) and Parr examine the issue of the need for families and communities to take personal and social responsibility for each other in an increasingly self-centred culture (especially during the property/share market boom of the 1980s). The film favours social cohesion rather than the social fracture indicated by its title. As in the American film *Crash*, lives collide in *Fracture*: those of Ulla and Brent most tragically. They both become casualties of Brent's crime.

Through its two main groups of characters, the film explores the theme of family. Leeanne becomes a Madonna figure, giving help and inspiration as she wanders the city with her baby, even feeding her brother Brent like a child. The normally aloof Howie Peet (played by John Noble of the TV series *Fringe*) gives the paralysed Ulla whisky through a straw and his ex-wife Gwen is ready to help Ulla with euthanasia. Howie even shows paternal care for his errant son Gordie, in jail for fraud and incarcerated among tough gang members. Howie is a rather clichéd Dickensian rich man whose drive and ruthless ambition must be softened by a change of heart.

Leeanne's outwardly pious mother Irene proves not to be a true Christian (her religiosity is judgmental rather than nurturing); in contrast, her father Clyde is more the true Christian in terms of helping and showing the compassion encapsulated in Matthew 25:40: 'In as much as ye have done it to one of the least of these my children, ye have done it to me.' Clyde bashes a violent slob, knocking him cold, much to the audience's satisfaction. He also takes Leeanne and her part-Polynesian child back to form a new family unit. The accident to

Ulla thus brings family members together, creating a more tightly-knit community rather than letting them persist in their atomized lives. Even Brent seeks a replacement mother figure in Mrs Ponder, the fence, although his bizarre fantasy proves futile and murderous. This pattern of family self-reliance is summarized near the end by Leeanne who, when offered a ride home from police station, states what is almost the film's motto: 'We'll make our own way.'

Brian McDonnell

In My Father's Den

Production Company:
Fathers Den Productions Limited/IMFD Limited

Distributor:
Icon Film Distribution (NZ)
Optimum Releasing (UK)

Director:
Brad McGann

Producers:
Trevor Haysom
Dixie Linder

Screenwriter:
Brad McGann (from the novel by Maurice Gee)

Cinematographer:
Stuart Dryburgh

Art Director:
Phil Ivey

Editor:
Chris Plummer

Duration:
127 minutes

Genre:
Mystery
Drama

Synopsis

Expatriate war journalist/photographer Paul Prior returns from Europe to his childhood home in the Central Otago region of New Zealand for the funeral of his father Jeff. He meets his embittered brother Andrew, Andrew's repressed wife Penny and their son Jonathon who, like Paul, is interested in photography. He also meets a 16-year-old teenage girl called Celia, daughter of his ex-girlfriend Jackie. The film's first half mixes these present-day events with flashbacks to Paul's childhood and adolescence when he discovered his father's den, and Paul's family suffered a tragedy involving his religiously-inclined mother. Halfway through the film, Celia, after befriending Paul who has become her English teacher, disappears, and a mystery grows concerning her fate. Paul becomes a prime police suspect because of their closeness and the audience is encouraged to speculate on whether they also have a blood relationship. The film's second half juggles the 'present' of the investigation with flashbacks to the recent, growing friendship between Paul and Celia. Audience curiosity about what has actually happened intensifies, as do conflicts between Paul and other relatives and community members. In the film's final scenes the various mysteries of the plot are explained and family secrets resurface.

Critique

In My Father's Den is one of the most accomplished films ever made in New Zealand, ranking with *The Piano*, *Heavenly Creatures* and *Once Were Warriors*. As both scriptwriter and director, Brad McGann shows extraordinary skills in what was first feature film. Sadly, it was also his last as he died from cancer at just 43, before he could work on another film. Adapting Maurice Gee's 1972 novel, McGann made radical revisions to the plot as he reconceptualized its core messages. Among these changes were two notable ones: McGann changed the identity of a killer from the novel's perpetrator to another character, and he also made Paul Prior and Celia blood relatives whereas in the novel they were completely unrelated.

The novel's themes had been the venomous effects of Puritanism, conformity and repression and the stifling effects of provincialism. McGann replaced these issues with an emphasis on the links between actual warfare and the battlegrounds of family life, lack of

In My Father's Den (2004), IFMB/Little Bird.

Cast:

Matthew Macfadyen
Emily Barclay
Colin Moy
Miranda Otto
Jodie Rimmer
Jimmy Keen

Year:

2004

communication leading to damaging secrets, and the intergenerational continuity of creative impulses. At the film's heart is the mystery of Paul Prior: who he is now and what has made him this way – his enigmatic nature eventually shown as originating in traumas he suffered from breaches of trust by those closest to him, including his mother and his father.

Misunderstandings and their consequences are also foregrounded: Penny thinks Celia is Andrew's mistress; Penny misinterprets Jonathon's photos; Celia reacts to Paul's photograph of her as a baby; Jackie interrupts the birthday party at the den (the film's most crucial and poignant scene); Andrew and Jonathon see Paul and Celia running in from the rain. These confusions are exacerbated by conflicting feelings of constraint and hope and by families becoming war zones instead of sites of forgiveness.

Shifts in sexual politics from the 1970s to the twenty-first century help explain McGann's making Paul and Celia blood relatives. He wanted to desexualize Paul's relationship with Celia, while sexualizing that of another key pair of characters. This shift in tone means that almost all the film's men are seen negatively in terms of their sexual dysfunctions: Andrew's mother fixation; Paul's asphyxiation fetish; Jeff's adultery; Gareth's harassment of Celia; Jonathon's stalking and voyeurism. In contrast, the film applies positive discrimination to its women characters: they are mostly professionals in what might be seen as principally male occupations (religious minister, principal of a co-educational school, senior police detective).

Paul is probably the most complex fictional character ever presented in a New Zealand feature film, given many flaws such as drug-taking and sexual fetishes that balance his virtues of honesty and creative temperament. For much of the film his strengths as a protagonist are matched by the equally creative Celia, who is really the story's saving grace. Overlaying several key scenes is Celia's voice-over reading of a short story she has submitted to a creative writing contest and this provides an effective coded commentary on plot events.

McGann shuffles time in a particularly complex way with 21 flashbacks. There is a big narrative jump halfway through the film, with an abrupt change in tone and a different use of recent and distant flashbacks. This interplay of past and present is taken from such models as Dennis Potter's TV series *The Singing Detective* and the Canadian film *The Sweet Hereafter*. *In My Father's Den* has a double ending juxtaposing fateful family sins and dishonesty with the happier possibility shown by Paul and Celia amicably resolving their relationship. This suggests the potential for a contemporary family formation which does not need to be based on conventional or hierarchical generations.

Brian McDonnell

No. 2

Alternative Title:
Naming Number Two (US)

Production Company:
Colonial Encounters & Southern Light Films

Director:
Toa Fraser

Producers:
Tim Bevan
Philippa Campbell

Screenwriter:
Toa Fraser (from his stage play)

Cinematographer:
Leon Narbey

Art Director:
Phil Ivey (Production Designer)

Editor:
Chris Plummer

Duration:
94 minutes

Synopsis

Nanny Maria, the elderly matriarch of a Fijian family living in the Auckland suburb of Mt Roskill, plans a feast in celebration of her family and to announce the name of her successor (or 'No. 2') as leader of the group. Almost all the film's events take place at her house on a single day as the family helps her prepare for the banquet. Grandchildren Erasmus and Charlene offer the steadiest and most practical assistance in preparation for the meal, while another grandson, Soul, is groomed by Nanny Maria as her successor. Nanny Maria gets on with her grandchildren far better than she does with her own sons and daughters because, in varying degrees, she finds these children either obstructive or distant or lacking in fidelity to family values and the mores of their Fijian heritage. Finally the feast takes place, attended by the whole extended family along with friends, and it becomes a big success and a warm, loving occasion. Nanny Maria is delighted at this celebration of life but when, after the meal, she slips away to the quiet of her own room, she dies peacefully, dreaming of the past.

Critique

Toa Fraser first wrote *No. 2* as a one-person stage play starring Madeleine Sami. When adapted into film form and released in 2006, it was praised (along with *Sione's Wedding*, released at much the same time) as marking a step towards greater maturity in the representation in New Zealand's film culture of Pacific Island stories and characters. Many of the observations made about the cultural impact

Genre:

Drama (family drama)

Cast:

Ruby Dee
Mia Blake
Rene Naufahu
Miriama McDowell
Taungaroa Emile
Xavier Horan

Year:

2006

of *Sione s Wedding* could also be applied to *No. 2*. The latter film made only a fraction of the box-office income of *Sione's Wedding* ($NZ700 000 vs. $4.1M) but that is largely explained by *No. 2*'s genre status as a relatively-serious arthouse drama in contrast to the broad comic appeal of the other film.

Fraser adapted his own stage drama into a screenplay designed for a conventional cast of actors and then directed the film as well. He based it on the Fijian part of his background and centred it on the figure of an old woman, Nanny Maria, who is the matriarch of a large, disunited family. Sad that her own children seem to have drifted away from both her and their Fijian heritage (and feeling her advancing tears weighing heavily on her), Nanny Maria becomes determined to hold an old-style family feast that will bring the disparate parts of her family together and allow her to announce her choice of new family leader.

Through this storyline, which adheres to the classical unities of time and place, Fraser is able to explore several themes. These include generational conflicts and tensions along with family dynamics. Attention to tradition and ceremony are very important, as is reconciliation. Much of the film has a warm emotional tone, which is often conveyed by music, especially the song 'Bathe in the River' sung at the climax of the feast. It could be argued that Fraser perhaps squeezes in too many themes: one instance is the rather obscure curse that is associated with the sealed-up front door of the house, a curse whose significance remains cryptic.

At the centre of the film is the dominant figure of the bossy Nanny Maria, who cajoles and scolds to achieve her goal of the short-notice party, but who has a great sense both of occasion and humour. As played by African-American actress Ruby Dee, she emerges as one of the warmest, most charismatic protagonists in recent New Zealand film. Some predicted Dee's casting would be controversial because Fraser brought in an ethnic outsider to play a Fijian character, but no such debate ever eventuated and all found her contribution to the film admirable. With great dedication, she even returned to New Zealand to complete *No. 2* after her husband Ossie Davis died suddenly during production and she flew back to New York for his funeral.

The couple had appeared together in Spike Lee's 1989 film *Do the Right Thing*. Fraser has acknowledged his debt to that film in his conceptualization of *No. 2*, which is a paean to the suburb of Mt Roskill similar to Lee's treatment of Bedford-Styvesant in *Do the Right Thing*. Mt Roskill becomes a virtual character in *No. 2*, a languid paradise and ethnic melting pot markedly different from the hellish wilderness of South Auckland in such films as *Once Were Warriors*. The characters of *No. 2* clearly like living in New Zealand and the film bears no resemblance to the stereotypical 'cinema of unease', where characters are tortured figures in an alienating landscape. Some of its performances may be uneven, but *No. 2* remains a funny, emotional ensemble piece and an impressive debut by Toa Fraser.

Brian McDonnell

Once Were Warriors

Studio/Distributor:
Communicado

Director:
Lee Tamahori

Producer:
Robin Scholes

Screenwriters:
Riwia Brown
Alan Duff

Cinematographer:
Stuart Dryburgh

Art Director:
Shayne Radford

Production Designer:
Michael Kane

Editor:
Michael Horton

Duration:
90 minutes

Genre:
Drama

Cast:
Rena Owen
Temuera Morrison

Year:
1994

Synopsis

The Heke family live in a harsh, urban world of gangs, poverty and alcohol-fuelled domestic violence. Beth's complicity with her husband Jake's habitual drunkenness alienates her older children, who variously turn to crime, gang subculture and Maori heritage for a sense of identity. The tragedy that follows an all-night party in their home precipitates a crisis which ultimately brings most of the family back together in a positive new way, albeit via widely-varying routes. While showing the devastating effects of alcoholism and poverty in this slice of life, the film also celebrates the vibrancy and style of urban Maori culture, transforming Alan Duff's bleak novel into a hopeful, if at times shocking film.

Critique

Announcing loudly that this will not be a depiction of the postcard-green New Zealand seen in tourist brochures, the opening shot pulls back from one such advertising hoarding to reveal a grimy urban backdrop of highways, fumes, cyclone fences and drug deals. Green has been expunged from the film, which concentrates on traditional Maori blacks and reds, and filtered brown skin tones. Director Lee Tamahori even covered grass with dirt to maintain the look. His direction produces a tight, convincing portrait of a family caught in a pattern of poverty and alcohol abuse, and features some of the most confronting depictions of domestic violence, and its consequences, seen on film.

Though devastating in its tale of family breakdown, the film nonetheless offers hope in its unpromising setting. This is principally achieved by the journey several characters take toward incorporating their *Maoritanga* (Maori heritage) into urban life. Boogie, Nig and Beth their mother all grow into quite disparate yet effective responses to what it might mean to be a warrior in modern New Zealand. Only Jake's understanding of what it means to be a warrior is rejected; drunken pub brawls and wife-beating have no role in life of a modern Maori warrior, the film seems to suggest. In bringing an accommodation of *Maoritanga* into everyday urban life, the film resists romanticizing Maori heritage and the dehistoricization that often goes with it. Maori are not projected back into a timeless past, but rather shown to be part of a developing, adapting and surviving culture.

The film's soundtrack and *mise-en-scène* celebrate the special stylistic fusion that can be found in modern Maori/Pasifika life, especially in South Auckland: the so-called capital of Polynesia. This, and the more positive narrative of Riwia Brown's screenplay highlighting Beth's story, transforms Duff's dark novel into a film of enormous resonance that has found great popularity in New Zealand.

Criticisms have been levelled at the film for decontextualizing the circumstances of the family. There is no reference to colonial depredation, other than the fact that the only *Pakeha* (non-Maori New Zealanders) roles in the film are as agents of the law. The Maori in the film are also concentrated in the working class, unlike the few *Pakeha*

Once Were Warriors, New Zealand Film Comm.

shown. With no exploration of these contexts, the family circumstances could be seen to be all of their own making, unconnected to
loss of land, culture and sovereignty associated with colonialism. In
keeping with Duff's overall, deeply conservative vision, salvation only
comes from within. No change in colonial relations will deliver the
Heke family from self-destruction; they must do it themselves, and in
the film's final hopeful turn, most of them do.

Duff was the sole screenwriter for the less successful 1999 sequel
What Becomes of the Broken Hearted? directed by Ian Mune.

Mandy Treagus

Out of the Blue

Production Company:
Condor Films Limited

Director:
Robert Sarkies

Producers:
Steven O'Meagher
Tim White

Screenwriters:
Graeme Tetley
Robert Sarkies (from book by
Bill O'Brien)

Cinematographer:
Greig Fraser

Art Directors:
David Kolff
Ken Turner

Editor:
Annie Collins

Duration:
103 minutes

Genre:
Drama

Cast:
Karl Urban
Matthew Sutherland
Lois Lawn
Tandi Wright
William Kircher

Year:
2006

Synopsis

Out of the Blue is based on historical events which took place in the far south of New Zealand in Aramoana, a Dunedin seaside suburb. The film opens on a montage depicting a typical early summer's morning as the small community wakes and begins its regular routines of preparing for work and getting children off to school. Unfortunately for many in this mixed group of workers, pensioners and alternative lifestylers, this is the day when the fragile mental stability of disturbed Aramoana loner David Gray cracks apart violently and tragically. Gray's annoyance at children crossing his land quickly escalates into his killing twelve members of the tiny community, along with a local police officer responding to calls for assistance. The death toll is increased by Gray's arsenal of assault rifles and his readiness to use them. During his rampage, Gray indiscriminately shoots adult men, women and children. The film follows the fates of these victims and other people either wounded or trapped in their homes awaiting help. Local cop Nick Harvey leads attempts to rescue casualties and to restrict Gray's movements and further threat. The next morning Gray confronts special tactics police and they shoot him fatally.

Critique

On the 13 November 1990, 33-year-old David Gray shot and killed 13 people (including police officer Stu Guthrie) in the tiny seaside settle-ment of Aramoana. This event was the biggest mass murder in New Zealand's history. The film's storyline is compressed into approximately 24 hours, beginning with one sunrise and ending on the morning of the following day. Apart from a couple of brief flashbacks to earlier police visits to Gray's crib (small beach cottage), the plot is entirely chronological.

Aramoana is an untidy, sloppy, hippie-style community. Coastal landscapes and limpid, placid scenes are stressed early on to indicate the peace before the storm. There is a deliberate low-key tone and a restrained, semi-documentary feel to the whole film. A lack of clear photographic focus and shallow depth of field are used to simulate the eccentric and socially-awkward Gray's eyesight problems and his being cut off from world. His subjective world is one of intrusive noise such as radio static and paranoid delusions.

The tragedy itself begins at the end of the school day, which is quickly evoked in poignant vignettes. A neighbour is shot first because his kids cut through Gray's yard, which he protects with boundary stones, but other people remain oblivious to what has hap-pened. Now Gray is on a rampage: an old man and people passing in a truck are shot dead. In line with the film's spirit of realism, no one seems to think to phone the police and an old lady named Helen is the only help to any of the wounded, despite being effectively semi-crippled. Gray puts on camouflage-style blackface paint below his woollen beanie.

Around dusk, Sgt Guthrie from the Port Chalmers police station and a younger officer named Nick attend. Nick serves as the film's normal'

Out of the Blue (2006), Condor Films.

person (a surrogate for the audience) who shows human reactions to horrific events. After nightfall, Nick hesitates to shoot Gray, even though he sees him with Stu Guthrie's pistol and knows Gray must have killed him. The film methodically follows the police procedures without any attempt at sensationalism. They search Gray's crib while night seascapes show the besieged hamlet, as phones ring in empty houses. Nick, finally able to go home, cries after watching his own child Jordan sleeping. All these scenes are effectively understated.

It is morning again. Similar long shots to the opening show another ironically-brilliant, beautiful day. Gray hides in another crib and sets up mattresses as defences. He wipes his face clean as he stares in a mirror and the audience realizes for the first time that under his beanie he is bald. The climactic gun battle comes as a shock and Gray is mown down by unemotional and nonchalant armed police. He struggles as they handcuff him and writhes as they smoke cigarettes. No help is given and he dies like an animal. An epilogue returns the Aramoana community to something resembling normality. But a few days later, people burn down Gray's crib in a kind of exorcism, a strangely common superstitious act in New Zealand after homicides.

Director Robert Sarkies, after making only one other feature (a comedy drama about university students, called *Scarfies*), has succeeded masterfully in bringing potentially-controversial material to the screen with understatement, respect and restraint.

Brian McDonnell

River Queen

Studio/Distributor:
Silverscreen Films/The Film Consortium

Director:
Vincent Ward

Producers:
Don Reynolds
Chris Auty
Tainui Stephens

Screenwriters:
Vincent Ward
Toa Fraser

Cinematographer:
Alun Bollinger

Art Direction:
Shayne Radford

Production Designer:
Rick Kofoed

Editor:
Ewa J Lind

Duration:
114 minutes

Genre:
Historical Drama

Cast:
Samantha Morton
Keifer Sutherland
Cliff Curtis
Temuera Morrison

Year:
2005

Synopsis

As the abandoned daughter of a military medical officer, Irish-born Sarah finds herself in the midst of the New Zealand Maori Wars of the 1860s. While still a teenager, she has born a son to a Maori boy who has since died. Her son is kidnapped at the age of seven by his grandfather, and seven years of searching elapse before Sarah is brought into contact with him again, by which time he has fully identified with his Maori family against the Crown forces. Loyalty is not a simple affair; not only do Maori fight on both sides, but Sarah herself moves between two lives, two potential lovers and two military forces. Ultimately she must choose between them, and in so doing identify who she will be in her adopted land.

Critique

After films exploring cross-cultural relationships in other contexts, Vincent Ward returns to his home country in *River Queen* to explore this theme in its past. Any film by Ward is worthy of notice, and while *River Queen* promises much, it mostly fails to deliver. Filmed in magnificent locations on the Whanganui River, the grandeur of the landscape is unfortunately never matched by any sense of epic in character or story. Stunning cinematography by Alun Bollinger, and the locations captured by him, are almost enough to redeem the film from its incoherence and lack of emotional engagement, but not quite. There seems to be no way into the character of Sarah for the audience, with Samantha Morton strangely limited in the role.

Stories about trouble on the set have become legendary. Ward was certainly sacked and the direction given to Bollinger at one point, with Ward brought back in for post-production. Some sources blamed Morton. Whatever the case, there is a measure of dislocation about her performance that keeps the viewer at bay, unable to really care about her dilemmas. Other performances are variable. Doyle's (Keifer Sutherland) breathless Irish accent fails to convince, and the Crown Commander remains a cardboard cut-out. Wiremu (Cliff Curtis), Te Kai Po (Temuera Morrison) and the young Boy (Rawiri Pene), on the other hand, make the best of their material, confusing as it is at times.

Ward seems to fall victim to his historical sources. By attempting to blend a range of real figures from the past – Ann Evans, Titokowaru and Caroline Perrett – Ward loses sight of a coherent narrative and

River Queen, Silverscreen Films.

convincing symbolism. In the attempt to include elements from all of these disparate lives, the script overplays its hand. One of the results of this is that the film actually includes several rebirth scenes for Sarah, where it can really only sustain one with any credibility. Immersion in the river, affecting once or even twice, is too often evoked to be able maintain any meaning.

The film is about being torn, and about constructing identity in new and changing circumstances, but Morton's performance shuts the audience out from feeling this with her. There are also several blatant allusions to *The Piano*, which serve no explicable purpose. The voiceover narration immediately evokes the narrative style of the earlier film, and in this context, what purpose is served when Wiremu lose his finger?

Too much remains inexplicable in this film. It sets out to explore identity in a deeply- yet unevenly-divided world, and while Sarah makes her choice, it is hard see what contributed to it. Te Kai Po also seems to betray his own forces, yet the reasons for this are not fully explored, either. The setting remains, its significance felt in every shot, and seen around every bend of the magnificent river. Despite failing to live up to its ambitions, *River Queen* remains intriguing by almost being a brilliant film.

Mandy Treagus

Sione's Wedding

Alternative Title:
Samoan Wedding (US)

Production Company/ Distributor:
South Pacific Pictures Limited

Director:
Chris Graham

Producers:
John Barnett
Chloe Smith

Screenwriters:
James Griffin
Oscar Kightley

Cinematographer:
Aaron Morton

Art Director:
Iain Aitkin (Production Designer)

Editor:
Paul Maxwell

Duration:
97 minutes

Genre:
Comedy

Cast:
Oscar Kightley
Iaheto Ah Hi
Shimpal Lelisi Robbie Magasiva
Teuila Blakely
Madeleine Sami

Year:
2006

Synopsis

Four young male Samoan friends living in Auckland (Stanley, Sefa, Michael, Albert) get into trouble with their pastor and local elders because of their perceived irresponsibility and lack of maturity. They are told that unless they get serious girlfriends they will not be welcome at the upcoming wedding of Michael's brother Sione. The film follows the comical attempts by the group either to find new female companions or to patch up relations with live-in girlfriends. Albert becomes besotted with a beautiful cousin dubbed Princess, who is visiting from Samoa, but slowly learns that his true soulmate is his co-worker Tania. Sefa has become rather indifferent towards his long-time love Leilani but recommits to her when she becomes pregnant. Stanley pursues a glamorous fantasy figure but finally opts for a more realistic and suitable partner. Only Michael does not change his ways, admitting he is an out-and-out womanizer with a reciprocated penchant for *Palagi* (European) women. The film climaxes with Sione's actual wedding, which the four companions attend and where they reassert their friendship.

Critique

The release of both *Sione's Wedding* and *No.2* within a few months during 2006 made that a key year for New Zealand films whose stories were about Pacific Islanders. *Sione's Wedding* quickly became a major hit, earning more than $NZ4 million at the box-office, which made it the highest-earning comedy film ever made in New Zealand (surpassing even 1981's *Goodbye Pork Pie*). This performance was even more remarkable because it was estimated at the time that more than $1 million in takings was probably lost because pirated DVD versions of the film were sold illegally in the months before and after its release. *Sione's Wedding* obviously struck a chord with viewers and commentators attributed much of this success to its positivity and benign representation of contemporary Polynesian life in Auckland.

The movie's producer John Barnett and his company South Pacific Pictures had played an important role in making the shift away from grim negativity in film depictions of Polynesian life. Perhaps the key transitional film for his company in this regard was *Whale Rider* (2002), which moved away from the largely dystopian vision of Maori life seen in *Once Were Warriors* eight years before. *Whale Rider*, a hugely popular film, presented a Hollywood-type triumphalist heroine in young female protagonist Paikea rather than the tragically-violent figure of *Warrior*'s Jake ('the Muss') Heke. Further ground work in celebrating specifically Pacific Island culture was laid by stage comedy troupe the Naked Samoans (several of whose members played leading roles in *Sione's Wedding*) and by the cult animated television show *bro'town* whose characters were voiced by many of the same actors.

Evidence of the immediate impact of *Sione's Wedding* can be seen in the comments of reviewers and other journalists. Editorial writer Pamela Stirling in the *NZ Listener* said the film's writers had 'captured a new confidence and optimism about the browning of New Zealand' and pointed out that *Sione's Wedding*'s characters were plainly very comfortable about being themselves. Reviewer Graham Adams

No.2, Silverscreen Films.

(*Auckland Metro*) said the film depicted a 'lush-looking inner-city Auckland where everybody is either brown, wants to be brown or wants to sleep with someone brown'. Most of the film's events take place in an idealized version of the inner-city suburb of Grey Lynn with its verdant parks and *umu* (earth oven) parties held in sunny back-yards full of sub-tropical trees and shrubs. Other reviewers noted that *Sione's Wedding* was so unselfconsciously Poly-centric that the viewer could easily accept seldom seeing any white characters at all.

The film also cleverly added to its commercial appeal by appropriating narrative conventions from recent Hollywood romantic comedies (e.g. *Knocked Up*, *The Ugly Truth*, *The Wedding Crashers*) that feature men who have trouble growing up and settling into mature relationships. It then added subtle nuances that helped such conventions tie in neatly with the values of Polynesian New Zealand life. For instance, Samoan culture provided an inflection on this 'adultescence' genre because it features many adult men still living at home with their parents, on whom they might be financially dependent, attending church regularly, and being cowed by authority figures, especially their mothers.

Thus *Sione's Wedding* broke no new ground in its subject matter (youthful male high jinks) or in its storytelling mode (conventional, even formulaic, Classical Hollywood narrative). However, much of its social impact and commercial success resulted from its refreshing take on city life via the viewpoint of members of a newly confident ethnic minority in the new Auckland, and the comic panache and energetic attractiveness of its Pasifika cast.

Brian McDonnell

Sons for the Return Home

Production Company:
Pacific Films Productions
Limited

Distributor:
Kerridge Odeon (original
distributor)

Director:
Paul Maunder

Executive Producer:
Don Blakeney

Screenwriter:
Paul Maunder (from the novel
by Albert Wendt)

Cinematographer:
Alun Bollinger

Art Director:
Vincent Ward

Editor:
Christine Lancaster

Duration:
117 minutes

Genre:
Drama

Cast:
Uelese Petaia
Fiona Lindsay
Moira Walker
Lani John Tupu
Anne Flannery
Alan Jervis

Year:
1979

Synopsis

Sione, a young Samoan man studying at university in Wellington, meets and falls in love with Sarah, a young *Palagi* (European) woman also studying there. The film's plot follows the troubled evolution of their relationship. It also traces the previous life history of Sione from his arrival in New Zealand as a small child accompanying his parents who have migrated from Samoa. All these events in New Zealand are remembered in flashback by the adult Sione who has reluctantly returned with his parents to Samoa after breaking up with Sarah. He recalls meeting her, their relationship blossoming, and the rather fraught occasions when they meet each other's parents and experience prejudice and closed-mindedness. The young couple embark on a road trip through the North Island of New Zealand where they encounter Maori culture and also quarrel. Pressures mount on them and they split up before Sione's return to Samoa. He discovers that he feels just as out of place and alienated in the Samoan environment as he had in Wellington and, after having a bitter confrontation with his mother, he flies back to New Zealand from Apia. Sarah is last seen looking wistful while visiting London.

Critique

Sons for the Return Home is unique in being the first feature film to take as its subject matter the experience of Pacific Islanders in New Zealand. Now, 30 years later, it is fascinating to compare its depiction of this topic with more current releases such as *Sione's Wedding* or *No.2*. The young couple at the foreground of *Sons for the Return Home* would now be the age of the parents of the young people of the latter two films. In effect, the new films show a new generation of Pacific Island New Zealanders who have progressed beyond the bleak situation of Sione and Sarah. The 1979 film dramatizes troubled race relations personified in a tale of a doomed romance whereas the more recent films are able to have their conflicts take place entirely within the Polynesian segment of the New Zealand population. Sione in *Sons for the Return Home* feels out of place and alienated in both Samoa and New Zealand while the Pasifika characters in the twenty-first-century films feel comfortable, confident and very much at home in their adopted country.

The novel *Sons for the Return Home* was the first ever published in English by a Samoan, and Albert Wendt was the first fiction writer to look at New Zealand life from the perspective of a Pacific Islander. The film had a mixed Samoan and New Zealand cast but all members of the principal crew were *Palagis* (white New Zealanders). Wendt's book was thus filtered through the sensibilities of scriptwriter/director Paul Maunder and others so that it became a Samoan-New Zealand story told by Europeans. Maunder did, however, try to construct the film so that a strong post-colonial message came through, one which would compare the experience of Samoan migrants to New Zealand with that of Maoris since white settlement.

He also rearranged the novel's order so that Sione's adult experiences in Samoa now follow his relationship with Sarah (both characters are unnamed in the book) to bring in the Samoan sections much earlier, partly for their exotic nature. Therefore, in the film we first see Sione in Apia or his parents' village and he then remembers earlier events in New Zealand. This results in a tremendous number of flashbacks and of time-shuffling that eventually becomes confusing. The infamous police dawn raids of the 1970s, aimed at catching Island overstayers, were added as plot items by Maunder – an appropriate and successful piece of updating. These scenes, along with those showing Sarah in a London pub, make the film more understandable to an international, particularly British, audience as a universal story of oppression.

Maunder and his collaborators, such as art director Vincent Ward, create a clever visual contrast between the film's two settings: Wellington dominated by cold blues and greys which make even the love scenes seem passionless, while Samoa's warm colours in vegetation, sky, ocean, islets, flowers and firelight speak of a more welcoming land.

Maunder claimed that he had cut out the sociological strand of the novel's Apia sequences in favour of the personal story. Nonetheless, what was described as the didactic, Marxist side of his aesthetic upset veteran producer John O'Shea and he had his name taken off the film's credits, saying that the heart and warmth had been cut from the story.

The resulting film combines a personal love story with a political film depicting the deleterious effects of colonialism and this causes an awkward mix of tone, despite generally fine performances. In 1990 another of Wendt's Samoan fictions *Flying Fox in a Freedom Tree* was made into a film by Martyn Sanderson.

Brian McDonnell

Whale Rider

Title:
Whale Rider

Studio/Distributor:
South Pacific Films
Apollomedia
Pandora Films

Director:
Niki Caro

Producers:
John Barnett
Tim Sanders
Frank Hubner

Synopsis

Shot in the remote coastal village of Whangara on the east coast of New Zealand's North Island, *Whale Rider* tells the story of a Maori family dominated by an embittered old chief burdened with the knowledge that there is no male heir to carry on his role. Rejecting his baby granddaughter after the death of her twin brother, the hoped-for male chiefly heir Koro, nevertheless comes to accommodate her in his life, while she clearly adores her grandfather and longs for his affection and recognition. Their relationship and its development, imbued as it is with ancestral significance, is the primary focus of the film. Named by her father for their chiefly ancestor, the original whale rider, Paikea is a keen student of traditional arts, even those forbidden to girls, such as using the *taiaha* (fighting stick). This tale of female empowerment is intertwined with the village's movement from listlessness to purpose, and its simple yet picturesque setting adds to the poignancy of the film's resolution.

Screenwriter:
Niki Caro

Cinematographer:
Leon Narbey

Production Designer:
Grant Major

Editor:
David Coulson

Duration:
101 minutes

Genre:
Children's

Cast:
Keisha Castle-Hughes
Rawiri Paretene
Vicky Houghton
Cliff Curtis

Year:
2002

Critique

Whale Rider has been received rapturously on the world stage, winning numerous awards across a range of countries and festivals. While depicting an exclusively Maori community, the film has resonated with universal concerns such as generational family tension, small town decline and, most notably, the aspirations and talents of a young girl in an unsupportive environment. That these issues are all resolved by the film's end, and also imbued with ancestral and mythic significance, would seem to make this the most hopeful of recent films concentrating primarily on Maori communities. Caro's writing and directing are assured, the cast admirable, and the setting beautifully spare and striking.

Though it is an adaptation of the novel of the same name by Witi Ihimaera, the film differs from the book in telling ways. The process of adaptation from novel to film is necessarily one of reduction and simplification, but the differences here are significant, and contribute to criticisms of the film. While the book tells essentially the same story, it is told in the context of a wider world in which Maori strive for rights in the national context. Paikea's grandfather Koro does not just cycle her to school or work on his outboard motor; in the novel he is a prime mover in political activism, travelling the country to represent his people, his tiredness as much the result of political fatigue as despair over finding a suitable chiefly heir.

Whale Rider, New Zealand Film Comm.

In removing politics from the film and isolating the community from the wider world, the film enhances the mythic qualities inherent in ancestral stories while removing them from their actual colonial context. It also concentrates the source of the community's problems squarely on the intransigence of the old man, rather than on any external circumstances. All of this contributes to a romanticization of Maori culture, moving it into the timeless, ahistorical mythic realm in which the impact of colonialism can be ignored.

While *Whale Rider* is a highly successful New Zealand film, it may not serve the Maori pursuit of sovereignity as well as it at first appears to.

Mandy Treagus

EXPERIMENTAL FILM
MARTIN RUMSBY

Although the greatest work of visual art made by a New Zealander, Len Lye's *Free Radicals* (1958), is an experimental film and despite the fact that New Zealand has a burgeoning experimental film scene with a continuous history stretching back to the early 1970s, Kiwi film artists are the most neglected practitioners within the New Zealand cultural and media arts milieu.

There are five dominant trends in New Zealand experimental film-making:

1. Identity politics:
Emerged in the 1970s and early 1980s around gay, women's, and Maori issues in the work of Peter Wells, Lisa Reihana, Brent Hayward, Joanna Margaret Paul, and Chris Kraus. Such concerns have continued in recent work by artists such as Campbell Farquhar and Rachel Rakena.

2. Landscape:
Both Joanna Margaret Paul and Philip Dadson began addressing landscape in experimental film in the early 1970s and it is, today, a sub-genre of experimental film that is on the critical ascendant and is yet to reach its peak. Contemporary film artists addressing landscape include Philip Dadson, Peter Wareing, Martin Rumsby, and Lissa Mitchell.

3. Psychodramatic and poetic:
The historic psycho-dramatic form of experimental film-making appeared in the work of David Blyth – *Circadian Rhythms* (1976) and George Rose – *The Sadness of the Post Intellectual Art Critic* (1979) and was continued in the work of artists

such as Kathryn Dudding in the 1980s. Psychodramatic and poetic forms of experimental film-making are currently being revitalized by practitioners such as Emit Snake-Beings and Richard von Sturmer.

4. Visual music:
This tradition is the one that has come from from Len Lye and, more recently, Michael Nicholson, Nova Paul, Jed Town as well as in the work of Video VJs such as Naomi Lamb.

5. Installation and expanded cinema:
In a purely visual-arts sense, some of the historic concerns of experimental film-makers have found their way into art installation, performance-based work, and expanded cinema events. Starting with Leon Narbey's installation environment *Real Time* (Govett-Brewster Art Gallery, New Plymouth, 1970) and continuing today in the work of Janine Randerson, Eve Gordon and Sam Hamilton's *Parasitic Fantasy Band*, Rachel Rakena, and Jed Town.

Aerial Farm

Philip Dadson

Duration:
20 minutes

Year:
2003

Following a residency in Antarctica in 2003 intermedia artist Philip Dadson produced a series of sonic digital cinema works collectively exhibited as an installation titled Polar Projects. *Aerial Farm* was part of this series.

For *Aerial Farm* Dadson manipulated a few short camera pans up and down an array of transmission aerials at Scott Base in Antarctica. The central aerial has a large tubular ring suspended around it, over which various wires stretch down to a base plate. The black outline of the aerial against the white background makes it appear almost as a sketch on paper, but a sketch that moves. In this way, Dadson is able to emphasize the relationship between cinema and the visual, rather than literary arts. As the weather deteriorates to white-out conditions (like a blank cinema screen) the aerial forms are enveloped by snow; they seem to advance and recede in two- and three dimensions, creating visual ambiguities for the viewer, who may then find themselves beginning to question the nature of appearances and relationships between individual perceptions, cultural constructions, and nature. One is reminded of the Russian Constructivist artist Vladimir Tatlin's design for a revolutionary tower, Marcel Duchamp's sketchlike *Chocolate Grinder* and even the sketches of Leonardo da Vinci. Somehow, the revolutionary history of visual art has found its way into utilitarian design, which is then reinterpreted by an artist as art. Even further than this, the sound of the wind blowing through the wires creates various harmonics, almost as nature playing or playing with technology – as our human endeavours and constructions remain subject to the influence of and modification by nature.

Martin Rumsby

Aucklantis

Gabriel White

Duration:
25 minutes

Year:
2008

Gabriel White encapsulated his Auckland in *Aucklantis* one of a series of digital videos that he shot in Korea, China, and Mexico in the early twenty-first century.

Aucklantis opens on a shot of a man, Gabriel White, getting out of a car and attempting to push it backwards. As soon as he relaxes, the car begins to roll back from whence it came: a fitting metaphor for Auckland, a city that favours the private motor car over public transport. White then takes us on a pedestrian tour of his city, making a series of wry observations along his way past streams of anonymous automobiles. As White engages us, we ask: Who are these drivers, what are they doing, and where are they going in such a hurry? How do they interact with their drive-through locality as a community? What awaits them at their destination? His low-tech hand-held camera sways across supermarket shelves as White tells us that he always confuses the terms Eveready (batteries) with Everyday (low prices). He dreams that he is sleepwalking in the supermarket as a captain of an industry that specializes in sleep ware – pyjamas, sheets, slippers, hot water bottles, beds, lullabies, sleeping pills. White tells us that he aims to become the master of the sleeping universe and making everything (everyday and Eveready) as tiring as possible, reducing people to a state of inertia. As he trails his camera on foot through inner city Auckland, from Freemans Bay to downtown, White muses on time, classification and other puzzles facing a cinematic literati. His narration does not simply illustrate or reinforce what we are seeing but actually modifies how we look at what we are seeing, and extends our understanding of, and relationship to, the images. He becomes confused by the signs and meanings of society, misreading words to create whole new associations, almost as the deeper meanings that may underlie surface appearances. He becomes lost in society to such an extent that he loses his shadow.

White's work presents a refreshing and humorous urbanity in its lively engagement of wit with locality.

Martin Rumsby

Meet Me At The Horizon

Parasitic Fantasy Band – Eve Gordon and Sam Hamilton

Duration:

16 minutes

Year:

2007

Eve Gordon and Sam Hamilton have created a series of films, film/performance and expanded cinema events that address processes of cinema, employing antique technologies refigured in new and vibrant form, often as silent cinema with live music and performers. Gordon and Hamilton assert an interest in cinema,

> As it once was in its fragile yet ecstatic beginning, an explorative realm for bold new ideas and experimental modes of experience. (41st Auckland International Film Festival Catalogue, 2009: 45)

Meet Me At The Horizon (approximately 16 minutes) opened on an image of a Hindu statuette which was subjected to a variety of live image manipulations. These included the diffuse beam of a backwards-facing film projector being played back across the screen as a diaphanous floating abstraction. The image split as Gordon wielded a hand-held lens in front of the projector lens. This effect caused the projected image to fragment, distort and repeat itself in echoes across the screen.

A text then played across various parts of a split screen, made up of images from up to three projectors, sometimes playing one at a time, or two in unison, or all three together. The printed text, like surrealistic silent movie inter-titles, repeatedly played across the screen, shifting from frame to frame as a disembodied electronic voice laboured to pronounce the text over and over again.

The unique nature of cinema was further highlighted by the simultaneous projection of strips of dirtied and scratched coloured film leader as flicker films (one black frame alternating with one white frame phased together in oscillating patterns) from one, two, and/or three projectors, whose beams merged, extended, and contracted through various aspect ratios from 4.3 to wide-screen formats.

Twentieth-century painters and sculptors revealed process in the visual arts, showing them to be more than illustrative narratives. Composers from Edgar Varèse to Terry Riley and Charlemagne Palestine showed that there is more to music than melody. Writers such as James Joyce and Gertrude Stein highlighted language over story. So Gordon and Hamilton address the photo-mechanical nature of cinema, at times almost as alchemists, in medium-specific work that reveals both how cinematic images are constructed as well as how we may see the world anew through cinema, if we are willing to look at the processes through which cinematic images and meaning arrive on the screen.

Martin Rumsby

Tanka

Richard von Sturmer

Duration:
24 minutes

Year:
2007

The personal is rendered poetic in *Twenty-Six Tanka Films* by Richard von Sturmer, a 24-minute-long cycle which was made between 2004 and 2007. Taking his lead from the Japanese Tanka form of unrhymed Japanese verse of five lines, von Sturmer presents semi-descriptive poetic paradoxes in films made up of two or three shots accompanied by equally brief poetic statements.

Generally, Tanka contain two poetic images. The first is taken from nature; the second is a kind of meditative complement to the nature image. Tanka look simultaneously at nature and the observer of nature.

Like visions on a crystalline reflecting pool, von Sturmer's quiet, assured films muse on the transitory nature of experience. Seeing a moth on a razor stem, the artist decides to remain unshaven. Following a shadow down a street of one-eyed cats, past a scoria mound, he sees himself walking on another planet. Von Sturmer evokes a depth and reality behind surface appearances in what may be the terrain between life and death; an escalator from which no one arrives or departs.

As von Sturmer recites in one of his Tanka: 'The machines of darkness are working all the time while in remote areas small defenders hold the ground.'

Von Sturmer, a practitioner of Auckland street theatre in the mid-1970s, later collaborated with David Blyth in writing the surrealistic psychodrama *Circadian Rhythms* (1976) as well as contributing dialogue for Blyth's *Angel Mine* (1978) – the first film ever funded by the interim New Zealand Film Commission. Besides writing the New Zealand hit song 'There Is No Depression In New Zealand' in the 1980s, von Sturmer was also a member of the rock group The Plague and the performance art duo The Human Animals. Von Sturmer acted in the film *One of those B's*, about the Hawera based writer Ronald Hugh Morrieson, as well as in the first Polynesian existentialist film, Martyn Sanderson's *Flying Fox In A Freedom Tree* (1989). In addition to his activities as a film artist, von Sturmer writes and publishes poetry; his books include *We Xerox Your Zebras*, *Network of Dissolving Threads* and *Suchness: Zen Poetry and Prose*.

Martin Rumsby

DIRECTORS
SHIRLEY HORROCKS,
DOCUMENTARY
FILM-MAKER

Since the 1990s, director/producer Shirley Horrocks, working out of her company, Point of View Productions, has undertaken the important cultural work of documenting New Zealand's arts, culture and history in painstakingly-researched, in-depth films that record, educate and celebrate. In addition, Horrocks' particular interest in social issues has led her to accruing a considerable body of work on challenges faced by such groups as women, Maori and Pacific Island people, and people with disabilities.

Horrocks has experience in all aspects of documentary production, and often includes dramatized segments in her work. She has filmed on local and international shoots with large and small crews, in a variety of film and video formats. Excellent production values are a signature of Horrocks' stylish films, assisted by careful collaboration with leading practitioners, such as cinematographer Leon Narbey, editor Bill Toepfer, actor Miranda Harcourt, sound recordist Richard Flynn, researcher Roger Horrocks and co-producer Robin Laing.

Her work has a very wide audience, winning a number of prestigious awards and screenings in festivals around the world, in addition to television screenings in New Zealand and Australia. Her ambitious commissioned dramas are widely used by community groups and throughout the NZ school system. All Point of

View's documentaries are receiving long-term use in settings as diverse as public libraries, art galleries, literary festivals, New Zealand embassies, universities and schools.

Where New Zealand's leading artists and art forms are her subjects, Horrocks focuses on those whose work has been obscured by New Zealand's marginal position in the world and who, in her opinion, deserve to be much better known internationally. Exemplifying this are: *Questions for Mr Reynolds* (2007), exploring the richness, diversity and spirit of the work of distinctive artist John Reynolds; *The Comics Show* (2007), an entertaining and visually-inventive film revealing the highly-creative NZ subculture of writing and drawing comics and graphic novels, showing many scenes of artists at work and illustrating a rich array of approaches to the genre; *The New Oceania: Albert Wendt, Writer* (2005), profiling the life, work and influence of a dedicated writer who has helped pave the way for many Pacific artists; *Marti: The Passionate Eye* (2004), celebrating the work of photographer Marti Friedlander in a tribute that has con-tributed substantially to public recognition of her importance as an artist while at the same time giving photography a higher profile as art in New Zealand; *Early Days Yet* (2001), an important tribute to the life and work of Allen Curnow, the first, and, to date, only film to be made about the poet; and *Flip and Two Twist-ers* (1995), made with the purpose of giving wider currency to the life and work of the great New Zealand-born kinetic artist Len Lye. The narrative shows Lye's sculptures being kept in working order by a team led by Evan Webb of the Len Lye Foundation and building massively-scaled sculptures, for which Lye left plans but could not achieve in his lifetime. As shown through Leon Narbey's camera and lighting, the installed sculptures dance, glide, twist and slither: beautiful 'figures of motion' (to use Lye's own words), gleaming and shimmering as if with a life of their own. In the words of Shirley Horrocks, 'Leon shot Len's sculpture better than it's ever been shot before.'

To delve into the complexity of her subjects by immersing the viewer in their worlds and minds, Horrocks establishes a relationship of trust which provides ample space for them to tell their own stories in their own style. This involves a meticulous and thorough process of quiet observation and dialogue. She avoids voice-over commentary and as an interviewer stays off camera, seeking to function as a catalyst rather than a participant. This method is exemplified well in *Early Days Yet*. Allen Curnow, a private man who shunned publicity, was almost 90 when the film was finished, and it is testament to Horrocks' skills as an interviewer that we hear him so warmly and openly talking about ideas, people, places and poetry. Speaking with wit and insight about his influences, Curnow canvases territory that tells as much about 90 years of New Zealand's cultural history as about the man himself. Shot by Leon Narbey, clever visual representa-tions, which Horrocks calls 'poem videos', illustrate Curnow's poetry readings and demonstrate the film-maker's skill in manipulating footage of a diverse nature into a satisfying whole.

Horrocks is fascinated by process, showing both the artists' finished products and their prior planning and experimentation. She also focuses on the contexts within which the artists work. While many New Zealand art documentaries are based on a single, intensive shoot, Horrocks likes to extend filming over as long a period as possible, with the aim of capturing the depth and breadth of her sub-jects. The filming of *Questions for Mr Reynolds*, for example, began with the art-ist's trip to the Hokianga in March 2006 and ended in his studio in April 2007, with footage captured over the year, including Reynolds' production of Cloud for the Sydney Biennale, three landscape works, the painting of a room at the Auckland

City Gallery, architectural projects, Swanndri (iconic New Zealand clothing brand) designs and an exhibition of paintings and objects at Sue Crockford Gallery. Locations included Sydney, the Kaipara, and gold mine country near Macraes Flat in Otago.

Alongside her interest in specific artists, Horrocks delves into arts and cultural events and into historical moments, in documentaries which provoke thought and provide a rich cultural record. Films falling into this category include: *Dance of the Instant: The New Dance Group (2008),* lifting the veil on a little-known, radical group pioneering modern dance in New Zealand in 1945–1947, an inspiring example of the power of creative thinking and sheer determination; *The Real New Zealand* (2000), a droll look at the experience of tourists in New Zealand homestays; *Sweet As* (1999), celebrating the Sweetwaters Music Festival; *Kiwi As* (1998), on New Zealand colloquial English and other aspects of local culture; *Transformers* (1996), capturing an intriguing exhibition of art-in-motion at the Auckland City Art Gallery; *For Love or Money* (1996), profiling the passions of prominent New Zealanders who collect art; *Kiwiana* (1996): the first documentary to bring the idea of 'kiwiana' to the television audience and one of the top-rating documentaries of 1996, the film triggered off a number of other documentaries about 'the way we were' and has had considerable influence culturally; and *Putting Our Town on the Map* (1994), a documentary with Miranda Harcourt that reveals imaginative and quirky ways in which small New Zealand towns are attempting to attract attention.

To enrich and texture her documentaries, Horrocks searches out news footage, home movies and other archival material. To name some examples: *Questions for Mr Reynolds* includes footage of John's Diner, shot by George Rose in the 1980s, and of Reynolds' wedding (shot by Simon Raby and directed by Niki Caro); *Flip and Two Twisters* includes hitherto-unseen footage of Len Lye's work shot by an American television producer in the 1960s in New York; *Dance of the Instant: The New Dance Group* has a wealth of archival information – original film footage, photographic evidence, reviews and articles – that, added to present day interviews with the dancers, brings the story of an important phase of New Zealand dance history to life.

Always interested in film's potential for advocacy, Horrocks began her documentary-making career in 1984 with *Patterns for the Future*, a widely distributed film in which a number of women, from a variety of industries, talked about the struggles they faced in advancing their careers. She made *Pleasures and Dangers: Artists for the 90s,* in 1990, the year of New Zealand's centennial celebrations, giving a voice to six emerging women artists – mixed-media artist Merilyn Tweedie (also known as 'et al'), film-maker Alison Maclean, painter Julia Morrison, photographer Christine Webster, painter Alexis Hunter and mixed media artist Lisa Reihana – all of whom have gone on to establish international careers. Along with a book of the same name, the film is a rich resource, used as a reference in art galleries, schools and tertiary institutions.

Actor Miranda Harcourt's tour of prisons with *Verbatim* (a play she developed from interviews she and William Brandt conducted with convicted murderers, their families and their victims' families) was the subject of Horrocks' 1993 documentary *Act of Murder.* Along with footage of *Verbatim* performances, the film's record of responses from prison audiences provides a fascinating extra dimension, bringing home to the viewer the complexities and difficulties faced by all the parties. It also provides a very interesting glimpse into the inspirational off-stage work of one of New Zealand's leading actors.

In the commissioned training drama *Managing Diversity* (1999), managers are encouraged to understand and promote cultural diversity. More recently, Horrocks was commissioned by Maori Television to write, produce and direct *He Wawata Whaea, The Dream of an Elder*. Screening on Maori Television in 2009, the documentary vividly tells the story of a remarkable life. Merimeri Penfold is a great champion of Maori language and culture, a leading activist in many campaigns and organizations, and a composer of haka and waiata. The documentary, much of it in Te Reo (with English subtitles), provides profound insights into the evolution of a society's thinking and practices over the last 80 years.

While many of her documentaries focus on the life and work of inspirational individuals, Horrocks also has an impressive body of commissioned work advocating health (topics include healthy eating and dealing with drug addiction) and giving a voice to those who, through a health issue, may find themselves on the fringes of society (the diabetic, the schizophrenic, the hearing impaired). Between 1998 and 2004, Horrocks made approximately fifty half-hour documentaries for television's Inside Out series, several of which won awards, covering many aspects of disability.

An important part of New Zealand's cultural infrastructure, Horrocks' films often have the added dimension of an accompanying book or study guide. The works commissioned for school health programmes, *Shop for Your Life, Stay in Touch* and *Sophie's Story*, etc., come with comprehensive study guides targeting the school health curriculum. Associated with *Questions for Mr Reynolds*, *Certain Words Drawn*, a book edited by Laurence Simmons, was a finalist in the national book awards in 2008. *Pleasures and Dangers: Artists for the 90s*, was the basis for an eponymous book.

Art that Moves: The World of Len Lye, is an 18-minute dramatized film about how the young kinetic artist Len Lye came up with his idea of an art of motion. Screened at the New Zealand International Film Festival and at Melbourne's Museum of the Moving Image in 2009, the film is distributed as a DVD with Roger Horrocks' book *Art that Moves* (Auckland University Press, 2009).

Helen Martin

DIRECTORS SHUCHI KOTHARI AND MULTICULTURALIST NEW ZEALAND FILMS

Although the Treaty of Waitangi – a formal agreement between indigenous Maori and British colonialists (whose descendants, along with other European New Zealanders, are known as Pakeha) – established Aotearoa/New Zealand officially as a bicultural nation in 1840, Asians displaced Pacific Islanders as the third largest ethnic group in the mid-1990s, and refugees from various continents have been visible presences in urban areas for over a decade. Chinese immigrants arrived with the nineteenth-century gold rush, and Indian immigrants came not so much later. One would not know about this multiculturalism, though, from New Zealand films made prior to this century.

Only two features, cinematographer-turned-director Leon Narbey's *Illustrious Energy* (1988) and Gregor Nicholas' *Broken English* (1997), provided pre-millennial images that suggested New Zealand's national stories might include people other than Maori, Islanders, and Pakeha. *Illustrious Energy*, an aesthetically-pleasing film that led Maori actress Tungia Baker (*The Piano*, Jane Campion, 1993) to ask whether it was about the Chinese or about the camera's love affair with the land,[1] has, until recently, been unavailable for screening because of its production company's financial difficulties in the wake of the 1987 stock market crash. *Broken English*, a story of immigrants intermingling in Auckland, was hardly more successful, perhaps because it relied on unrefined ethnic stereotypes.

In this decade, however, new voices are being heard, such as directors Sima Urale and Roseanne Liang, whose parents immigrated from Samoa and China, respectively. Urale, the first Samoan woman film director, trained as an actor in New Zealand's national drama school, realized the limitations being Samoan would put on her access to roles then available, and went to Australia to train as a film-maker. In 1996, her first post-student work appeared: an award-winning short film called *O Tamaiti* (*The Children*).[2] She shot *O Tamaiti* in black and white to 'shed the stereotypical images of Pacific Islanders as the kitsch culture with colorful paraphernalia too often depicted in contemporary films,' according to press kit and interview quotations of the time. Her second film was a documentary on velvet paintings, *Velvet Dreams* (1997), made on commission for New Zealand television, with a male voice-over narration and a playful imitation of film noir narrative and other stylistic elements. All the colour and kitsch missing from *O Tamaiti* fill *Velvet Dreams*' images, until at the end the narrator admits, 'It dawned on me that she was never gonna be a reality. The velvet woman was a dream of a bygone generation, a romantic vision of the past.' *Velvet Dreams* also sets a more direct challenge to viewers when several Polynesian women, posed as topless images from velvet paintings, turn out to be live, postmodern, and more than capable of returning our gaze. Since then, Urale has directed commercials, music videos, short films, and her first feature, *Apron Strings* (2008), which screened at the 2008 Toronto International Film Festival (TIFF).

Liang began with a documentary, *Banana in a Nutshell* (2005),[3] that was a success at the New Zealand International Film Festivals and when it aired on national television. Her humorous look at life as a Chinese New Zealander focuses on her own family, especially the obstacles her father set for her Pakeha fiancé before agreeing to their marriage. Liang's first Film Commission-funded short *Take 3* had its premiere at the 2008 New Zealand International Film Festivals (NZIFF). *Take 3* follows three young women of different Asian origins, but all born in New Zealand, as they audition for parts in films and commercials. The Pakeha auditioning them are clueless about cultural differences, and the auditions ring the changes of stereotypes about Asians: emotionally reserved, sex workers, academic overachievers – and inferior. *Take 3* preceded screenings of Urale's *Apron Strings* at the NZIFF, which brings us back to Shuchi Kothari.

Kothari, an Indian immigrant who has lived in New Zealand since 1997, may ultimately be seen as the single most influential voice of multiculturalism in New Zealand cinema for her work as writer and producer of short and feature films directed by, among others, Urale and Liang, including *Take 3* and *Apron Strings*. Kothari's scripts have so far been optioned and produced in the United States, New Zealand, and India. With Sarina Pearson, in 1999 Kothari set up Nomadz Unlimited, 'a small production company dedicated to fostering provocative projects that resonate with the nomadic experience of the company's founders.'[4] Both Pearson and Kothari have studied for degrees in the United States, although Pearson finished her PhD at the University of Auckland, where both hold senior lectureships in the Department of Film, Television, and Media Studies.

Nomadz was nominated as one of the New Zealand Film Commission's Short Film Executive Producer Groups for 2006/2008 (NZFC 2007). As part of its support for film production within New Zealand, the Commission has devolved funding to different executive producers each year or so, who then choose from applications for funding with the goal of mentoring completed films within the space of a year or two. Among the films that Nomadz has executive-produced are *The Six Dollar Fifty Man* (Mark Albiston and Louis Sutherland, writers and directors, 2009), *Bridge* (Jochen FitzHerbert, writer and director, 2008), *Patu Ihu* (Summer Agnew, director; Summer Agnew and Warren Beazley, writers, 2008), and *Take 3* (Roseanne Liang, writer and director, 2008). The films Nomadz has produced with Kothari as the writer, include *Clean Linen* (Zia Mandviwalla, director, 2007), *Coffee & Allah* (Sima Urale, director, 2007), and *Fleeting Beauty* (Virginia Pitts, director, 2004). Many of these films have won awards, with *The Six Dollar Fifty Man* receiving a Special Distinction award at Cannes in 2009.

Whereas *Apron Strings* (co-written by Kothari and Dianne Taylor) looks at cross-cultural and cross-generational relations in which Polynesians, Asians, and Pakeha learn to trust each other enough to begin a dialogue, *Coffee and Allah* considers the African-immigrant experience. As producers Kothari and Pearson describe *Coffee & Allah*, it is a reminder of the politics of exclusion experienced by immigrants in general and Muslim women in particular. In it, Abeba Moham-med, a recent refugee in New Zealand, leads a quiet life, strictly veiled, ventur-ing out of her home only for coffee beans, which allows a Samoan barrista to grow interested in her.[5] "The beauty of this script is that it begins with isolation and alienation, but as it progresses, subtle connections are slowly but surely made with Abeba and her new surroundings. For me, this is a gentle film with a strong message about acceptance,' says director Sima Urale. Producer Sarina Pearson adds, 'We were lucky to find Zahara Abbawaajji, an Oromo Ethiopian living in New Zealand. She has no acting experience at all but she really brought the character of Abeba to life' (NZFC 2007).

Apron Strings, which Kothari also coproduced, is the first product of a funding initiative begun in the fiscal year 2004/2005, involving the New Zealand Film Com-mission, New Zealand On Air, and Television New Zealand, to produce relatively short features intended to be broadcast on prime time television (NZFC 2005). Set in Auckland, on a street where a traditional Pakeha cake shop is struggling to survive while a small Indian restaurant nearby is doing well, along with other Asian businesses, *Apron Strings* explores troubled relations between mothers and sons, including issues of responsibility, bitter regrets, and forgiveness, all mixed in with the friction caused by multicultural conflicts over loyalty and money. One of the more influential local reviews damned Urale's direction with faint praise, but kept its strongest criticism for the script, arguing that the writers 'seem to lack faith in their audience's intelligence' (Larsen 2008: 43). The film's problems primarily origi-nate in the fact that the film was always intended for a television audience, and it is not the weakest of low-budget films produced by Auckland film-makers working within the restrictions of their means. Seen within the context of Kothari's work, *Apron Strings* demonstrates two of her most obvious auteurist characteristics: the importance of food, the omnipresence of intercultural contact, and the role that food often plays in mediating intercultural contact.[6]

Kothari's first short film in New Zealand also employed food as a metaphor to explore the Indian subcontinent's colonial history. Despite its strong New Zealand connections, *Fleeting Beauty* met with rejections from both the Film Commission and Creative New Zealand for its lack of 'New Zealand content.' Determined to make *Fleeting Beauty* in New Zealand as a New Zealand film, Kothari phoned Nandita Das, knowing the Indian actress only through the latter's films. Das, who has worked with such directors as Mrinal Sen and Mani Ratnam, is best known to the Western world for her appearance in her second feature, Deepa Mehta's *Fire* (1996).[7] To Kothari's relief, Das agreed to come to New Zealand and participate in the film. From that, a friendship was forged, leading to Das' directorial feature debut, *Firaaq* (2008), from a script co-written by Kothari and Das. *Firaaq* presents the impact on people, regardless of their social class, age, or religion, of the 2002 attacks in Gujarat of Hindus against Muslims, as the film's characters find them-selves interacting with each other, sometimes aware of each other's identity, but often not, during the course of twenty-four hours. *Firaaq* is, as Kothari acknowl-edges, 'a hard film' to watch (TV3 2009) but its intensity is matched by an integrity that itself offers hope despite its story of hopelessly violent events.

Kothari told a New Zealand television interviewer that, in a conversation with British director Gurinder Chadha (*Bhaji on the Beach*, 1993; *Bend It Like Beckham*, 2002; etc.), Chadha said that the more specific a story is to its cultural context, the more universal a film's appeal can be – an opinion often expressed by key figures among New Zealand film-makers and funders, most notably by Gaylene Preston. Kothari says that 'One of the things … that makes [Firaaq] universal is that ultimately we've looked at the nature of violence but how it impacts on people's relationships, and that's something that I feel translates quite easily' (ibid). Indeed, Firaaq has been successful around the world, including screenings at Telluride as well as at TIFF during the same year that Apron Strings appeared there.

A Hindu, Kothari is married to Nabeel Zuberi, a Muslim, so she knows what it is to worry about his physical safety. She feels at home anywhere, she says, and while there are some New Zealand stories she would be comfortable writing, she also knows that she does not have the knowledge to write other New Zealand stories. She is currently working on a project about an Indian family in New Zealand in the 1970s, funded in part by the NZ Film Commission's Writer's Award for 2009. She jokes that she writes best about India while living away from it, and that she will work on her New Zealand project while living in India (TV3 2009).

In addition to her films, Kothari, along with Pearson, has ventured into television work, producing a comic series called A Thousand Apologies, 'springing from the A Thousand Apologies Collective formed by Kothari in early 2002. Its members were students of Auckland University's Postgraduate production programme . . . [whc] shared something else . . .; they were of various Asian extractions and all felt the need to make a TV show that represented their experiences as Asian New Zealanders.'[8]

Kothari sees herself as having one foot in India and one in New Zealand. In an essay entitled 'Television and Multiculturalism in Aotearoa New Zealand,' Kothari, Pearson, and Zuberi write that '"multiculturalism" is a descriptive term for ethnic diversity as well as a range of different philosophies, political positions, and cultural arguments about how a society organises this diversity' (Horrocks & Perry 2004: 137). Herself embodying multiculturalism, Kothari's contribution to screen representations of New Zealand's multiculturalist reality is already substantial, with more obviously yet to come.

Notes

1. Conversation with author, Wellington, 27 September 1995.
2. It received the Silver Lion for Best Short Film at Venice in 1996 and screened at Sundance and Telluride (from the Film Commission's Newsletter: http://www.nzfilm.co.nz/NewsAndMedia/NZFilmNewsletter/Complete_Newsletter.aspx?nodeAliasPath=/NewsAndMedia/NZFilmNewsletter/Newsletters/NZ_Film_News_October_2007; accessed 22 September 2009).
3. Which, according to the New Zealand Film Commission's August 2009 newsletter, is being developed into a feature film by John Barnett's South Pacific Pictures (http://www.nzfilm.co.nz/NewsAndMedia/NZFilmNewsletter/Complete_Newsletter.aspx?nodeAliasPath=/NewsAndMedia/NZFilmNewsletter/Newsletters/NZFC_News_August_2009; accessed 23 September 2009).
4. Http://www.nomadzunlimted.com/about.html; accessed 9 September 2009.
5. Http://www.nomadzunlimted.com/allah_home.html. Accessed 23 September 2009.
6. In 2001, Pearson produced and Kothari wrote and presented a documentary, directed by Susan Pointon called A Taste of Place: Stories of Food and Longing, about various immigrants to New Zealand, about what is means to them to prepare the food typical of their mother countries in their adopted country, using ingredients which often only approximate the original materials, see Shuchi Kothari & Sarina Pearson (2004) Film Excerpts: A Taste of Place: Stories of food and Longing,' in Michael Hanne (ed.) Creativity in Exile, Amsterdam, New York: Rodopi, p. 227.
7. Http://www.nanditadas.com/film.htm; accessed 24 September 2009.
8. Http://www.scoop.co.nz/stories/PO0809/S00337.htm; accessed 22 September 2009.

Harriet Margolis

DIRECTORS
VINCENT WARD

Films by New Zealand director Vincent Ward first beguile their viewers through their haunting, evocative imagery. This has marked his international work from *Vigil* (1984) onwards: from the child, Toss, clambering across paddocks in tutu and gumboots, to old Niki in *Rain of the Children* (2008) lying naked in a bare, dark, main street nuzzled by a ghostly white stallion.

Such images articulate themes, tensions and contradictions inherent in Ward's vision as a director. This vision, across a whole body of work has seen him described as an auteur director. Coupled to his renowned doggedness and intensity, it has also significantly shaped his difficult relationship with Hollywood and commercial cinema, whether through projects he did not complete himself (*Alien 3*) or those he did, in advertising work for Singapore Airlines and others.

His recent films continue to reflect all these issues, sometimes in new and unanticipated ways. *River Queen* (2005) saw him dismissed from the set and later rehired after disagreements and disasters. It saw him attempt to marry CGI and conventional cinematography; to create an epic that, itself, incorporated Maori and European histories in a story of the 1860 Maori wars set on the Whanganui river. Like his two preceding features, *Map of the Human Heart* (1993) and *What Dreams May Come* (1998), it met mixed critical reception, attacked for sentimentalism but praised for an extraordinary visuality.

Yet *River Queen* and *Rain of the Children* highlight Ward's capacity to compress and integrate opposites: naturalism and CGI effects; the rational and irrational; documentary and drama; western and non-western cultures; childhood wonder and adult brutalities; primitive worlds with technological innovation.

Rain of the Children not only accomplishes this but incorporates elements new to Ward's work. This enables him to resolve or recuperate some of the personal, bicultural and cinematic tensions that have always accompanied his films.

It is a film of redemption: a deeply-felt meditation on personal and cultural history that seeks to resolve each, but in different ways. Within cinema, redemption evokes German expressionist film and Sigmund Kracauer's theories on the creation of spiritual, filmic moments. Ward has long acknowledged his expressionist debt. Here, though, it is fused with new elements.

Principally, this is through autobiography. With *Rain of the Children*, Ward returns to the scene of his first, student documentary, *In Spring One Plants Alone* (1981). For the first time, he faces the camera as a character in his own work. In the original film he lived with, and recorded, the simple, difficult lives of 80-year-old Puhi and her schizophrenic son, Niki, in their dishevelled Urewera farmhouse. His return, long after their deaths, is to their history and his own, and to a larger, darker history of the Tuhoe people. The suffering of Puhi and Niki echoes the suffering inflicted on the separatist spiritual community of the Maori prophet Rua Kenana.

This followed their ejection from it, and the community's ensuing destruction by a government bent on land sales. Puhi believed herself cursed and Ward's later film illuminates the contradictory meaning of this legacy by tracing the complex beliefs and practices he could not comprehend 27 years earlier. It amounts to a redemption of the past, dramatized through a vivid reproduction of the Kenana community and documented in Ward's interviews and self-revelations, approached with humility, awkwardness and grace.

Such grace echoes and recuperates Ward's own filmography, from the isolation of his first film, *State of Seige* (1978) to the bewildered medieval travellers confronting contemporary Auckland in *The Navigator* (1988). It resonates through his work as mesmerizing, luminous images: moments that persistently attempt to marry polarities and to glimpse the ineffable on screen.

John Farnsworth

FROM COMIC-GOTHIC TO 'SPLATSTICK': BLACK HUMOUR IN NEW ZEALAND CINEMA
ALFIO LEOTTA

New Zealand cinema has gained international recognition for conjuring up serious and dramatic images with films such as *The Piano* (1993), *Once Were Warriors* (1994) and *Whale Rider* (2003) that mainly targeted the audiences of art and essay cinema. Film scholars have emphasized the uniqueness of New Zealand cinema, allegedly characterized, on the one hand, by a dark, gloomy and edgy look, on the other by the centrality of beautiful and haunted landscapes (Horrocks 1989; Neill & Rymer 1995). To describe the distinctive stylistic features of the cinema of Aotearoa, commentators have often resorted to the notion of the 'Kiwi Gothic' (Tincknell 2000). The Kiwi Gothic constructs New Zealand not as a place of some pastoral idyll but rather as an environment where danger and horror lurk everywhere. The Antipodean gothic is generally considered to be an expression of the settler anxiety that derived from the confrontation with a hostile and alien environment, such as the native New Zealand bush. Unlike the European gothic, which often tells ghost stories set in old castles, the Kiwi version of the gothic often deals with alienation, family traumas and uncanny experiences in very familiar places. According to William J Schafer, the creation of haunted landscapes in New Zealand film is an instrument, however paradoxical, intended to create a sense of belonging to the land (Schafer 1998). In Freudian terms, the experience of the uncanny (*unheimlich*) as ghostly, horrific and terrifying is a necessary component of the transition from a sense of alienation from the land to a sense of being rooted in it (*heimlich*). The importance of the problem of estrangement from the land in settler societies such as New Zealand could possibly explain the popularity of dramatic and gothic narratives at the expense of the comedic genre.

Until recently, comedy as a genre has never flourished in New Zealand cinema, and yet shades of humour have featured in various forms in films that are generically classified as 'dramas'. Unexpected comic undertones characterize films such as Roger Donaldson's *Sleeping Dogs* (1977) and *Smash Palace* (1981), *The Scarecrow* (Sam Pilsbury, 1982) or *The Quiet Earth* (Geoff Murphy, 1985). In *Sleeping Dogs* the protagonist's final gesture of defiance, before he is gunned down by the army, subverts the dramatic tone of the film. In the final sequence of *Smash Palace*, the protagonist Al kidnaps his rival Ray by putting a noose around his neck and attaching it to his shotgun using a No. 8 wire, a humorous reference to Kiwi ingenuity. Al then forces Ray to drive onto a railway line and wait for a lethal crash with an approaching train. As the train passes behind them on another track, Al bursts into laughter enjoying his own dark humour. Similarly, in *The Scarecrow* and *The Quiet Earth*, 'serious' themes such as rape and apocalyptic catastrophes are punctuated by moments of subversive black humour.

According to John Clarke the creator of the iconic Kiwi comic character Fred Dagg, humour identifiable as coming from New Zealand emerged during World War II as a means of dealing with the carnage, tragedy and death caused by the conflict (Clarke 2009). Since the outset, therefore, Kiwi humour has been characterized by dark undertones. This is particularly true in New Zealand film comedies, which often feature tragic elements, such as the death of the protagonist, Jerry, in *Goodbye Pork Pie* (Geoff Murphy, 1980) or murder and crime in *Came a Hot Friday* (Ian Mune, 1984).

The paradoxical overlap of gothic and comic elements, which seems to be a prominent feature of New Zealand cinema, was pushed to the extreme by one of the most influential film-makers of this country, Peter Jackson. Jackson's first film feature, *Bad Taste* (1998), combines all his film influences: the slapstick gags of Buster Keaton and the absurdist tendencies of Monty Python; the special effects of zombie and horror B-movies; the style of fantasy epics such as *King Kong* (1933). The result is a revolutionary blend of traditional film genres such as comedy, science fiction and splatter/horror that has been defined as 'splatstick' (Grant 2007). *Bad Taste* tells the story of a New Zealand government special force ('The Boys') that attempts to stop an unlikely alien invasion. The aliens, who are able to mutate their physical form and appear as normal humans, have exterminated the inhabitants of a small town in rural New Zealand (Kaihoro, population 75) in order to supply meat for their intergalactic fast-food chain. The aliens also capture charity worker/con man Giles, who is marinated by the aliens in preparation for their departure feast. The retribution of the boys, aka AIDS (Astro Investigation and Defence Service), is merciless as they attack the aliens and free Giles. During the battle, one of the 'Boys', Derek, played by Peter Jackson himself, falls from a cliff, breaking his skull. However, Derek soon regains consciousness and, after securing his loose brains into his skull with a belt, he sadistically slaughters the remaining aliens with a chainsaw. In the surreal final sequence, the heritage house, which is both the headquarters and the spaceship of the aliens, is launched into orbit. Derek, who has been trapped inside the house/spaceship, confronts and butchers the leader of the aliens, announcing further revenge to the aliens' planet.

Intertextual references and parody are important elements of Jackson's films and his extensive knowledge of cinema is particularly apparent in his first film: the opening sequence of the government official smoking a cigarette with a prosthetic finger is a humorous homage to *The Godfather* (Coppola, 1972); the scene that features Derek chasing the aliens with a chainsaw is a clear hint to Kubrick's *The Shining* (1980); the theme of an invasion by carnivorous aliens able to disguise themselves as human beings is a common trope of much sci-fi literature and in particular draws upon the 1980s' popular American TV show *V: The Series* (1984–1985). The numerous references that the film makes to Hollywood productions reflect the impact of American popular culture on New Zealand cultural identity. Cinema, particularly Hollywood, played a crucial role in the formation of a 'New Zealand culture'. In 1945, Gordon Mirams defined New Zealanders as 'a nation of film fans'. He calculated that whereas in the US there is one movie theatre for every 8700 people, in New Zealand there is one for approximately every 3000 (Mirams 1945). The absence of any form of protection of the national film industry, and the consequent virtual lack of local production until the 1970s, led to the invasion of the New Zealand market by British and American cultural products. In Lealand's words, the final outcome of this process was that 'the mythologies of Hollywood became "naturalised" in the absence of any more powerful propositions, integral to the ways of "reading" the world for New Zealanders' (Lealand 1988: 90).

New Zealand film-makers have extensively drawn upon Hollywood genre conventions, adapting them to the cultural specificity of the country. Jackson is probably the most successful New Zealand artist in this enterprise of cultural bricolage. Jackson's works are typically postmodern, as his use of existing film conventions leads to creative and playful outcomes such as the invention of the splatstick genre. According to Lawrence McDonald (1993), the comic power of Jackson's films derives by their relation of second degree to the splatter sub-genre. For McDonald, what makes possible the amalgam of slapstick comedy and splatter is 'the fortuitous fact that both derive from a physical, body based focus, rooted in a "low-cultural" comedic mode and a "low-cultural" sub-genre' (McDonald 1993: 11). Jackson's production is located within the domain of low culture and consciously positioned in opposition to the accepted and recognized film tradition. The obsession with the absurd and the comically grotesque in splatstick films is a deliberate attack on both the dominant Hollywood industry and the 'serious', high-brow tone of the national film production. The cultural tensions between high culture and low culture generated by the splatstick became apparent when Jackson's third film *Braindead* (1992) was selected as 'Best Film' of the year at the 1993 New Zealand Film and Television Awards. After the celebration, juror John Cranna, publicly criticized the rest of the jury's decision by defining *Braindead* as 'a crude horror that makes a mockery of serious film-making in New Zealand' (Cranna cited in Wu 2003: 91).

The critical power of Jackson's films is a consequence of their economic marginality. *Bad Taste* was funded by Jackson's salary as photo engraver at a Wellington's newspaper, and shot with the help of friends during weekends over a period of three years. A grant offered by the New Zealand Film Commission provided finance that was mainly invested in the post-production stage. Paradoxically, the extremely low budget of *Bad Taste* and the lack of financial pressure deriving from the need to recoup investors' money allowed Jackson great creative freedom and the possibility of experimenting with genres. The combination of comedy and horror and the consequent transgression of genre boundaries appealed to an active spectator rather than a passive one. *Bad Taste* targeted the niche market of cult fans by explicitly attacking the norms, values and standards of mainstream cinema. According to Harmony Wu: 'By doggedly pursuing the niche cult market by pushing the limits of taste ..., Peter Jackson's gross out films, it might be argued, afforded him the capital both (economic and cinematic) to transcend the limitations of working in a tiny national cinema' (Wu 2003: 92). *Bad Taste* achieved global recognition in cult cinema circuits and this paradoxically contributed to reinforcing the international perception of New Zealand cinema as unconventional and characterized by strange and dark obsessions.

Jackson's second film *Meet the Feebles* (1990) is also a low-budget, low-culture production that exploits the pleasures derived by the mixing of genres. The film, originally conceived for Japanese television, is another splatstick (or rather 'spluppet', for the protagonists of the films are puppets) that makes extensive use of parody and intertextual references. The obvious source of inspiration of the film is the famous Henson's *Muppet Show* (1976–1979): the Feebles are, in fact, a troupe of animal-figured puppets who are rehearsing for a live television show. The hippo singer, Heidi, is in love with the show's producer, Bletch, who cheats on her with the cat, Samantha. Meanwhile Harry the Hare, the MC of the troupe, has a threesome with two female bunnies and contracts a disfiguring disease diagnosed by the doctor as the 'big one'. The Fly, a press reporter who assumes that Harry contracted a sexually-transmitted disease, wants to publish the scandal in a local tabloid. Bletch is not only the show's producer, he is also a drug dealer who provides drugs to the rest of the troupe. After a failed drug deal with gangster Cedric, Bletch and his friends confront Cedric's crab crewmen and defeat them. Bletch successfully returns to the theatre, but the live show is a disaster: Harry the Hare vomits endlessly; the Indian contortionist is unable to free his head that is stuck in his rectum; Heidi accidentally destroys the set. In the grotesque climatic sequence, Heidi, rejected by Bletch and taunted by Samantha, takes revenge on the two lovers and most of the troupe by killing them with a machine gun. The film mixes slapstick comedy, violence and explicit sexual violence with satire of the entertainment industry and human nature in general.

Meet the Feebles reinforced Jackson's status as king of splatstick, and convinced investors of his talent. Jackson's third feature film, *Braindead*, benefited from a relatively large budget (NZ$3,000,000) and carried no traces of the amateurish style that characterized *Bad Taste*. *Braindead* inflects the tradition of the zombie film with Jackson's peculiar splatstick style. The story starts in Sumatra (a tribute to Jackson's favourite film *King Kong*), where a New Zealand zoo official, despite the warnings of local tribes, has captured a rare rat-monkey (the obscene result of the rape of local monkeys by plague rats). After the zoo official is bitten by the monkey, he is dismembered and killed by his guides, who then send the rat-monkey to the Wellington zoo. Meanwhile, in the New Zealand capital city, hapless Lionel starts a romantic relation with Spanish shopkeeper Paquita. Lionel's domineering mother is opposed to the liaison and follows the couple on a date to the local zoo, where she is bitten by the rat-monkey. Mother's health deteriorates quickly as she develops an uncanny craving for raw meat. Shortly after Mother dies, she comes back to life as a zombie and bites her nurse. The zombie epidemic quickly spreads and Lionel attempts to conceal the scandal by hiding the living dead in the house's cellar. Lionel's uncle Les discovers the corpses and blackmails his nephew, who is obliged to give Les the house in exchange for silence. Uncle Les throws a housewarming party to celebrate his newly-acquired house, but the zombies escape from the cellar and contaminate the guests. During the last 35 minutes of the film Lionel, Paquita and Uncle Les fight the zombies in a gory battle that features mutilated limbs, severed heads and animated intestines. During the battle Lionel discovers that his irrational fear of water is connected to a childhood trauma: he was the witness of the murder of his father and his mistress, who were drowned by Lionel's revengeful mother. In the final sequence of the film Lionel confronts his mother, who, meanwhile, has become a gargantuan monster. She literally sucks him back into her womb but, in a Freudian re-birth, the protagonist cuts his way out of her monstrous body.

While *Meet the Feebles* did not feature any precise reference to New Zealand, *Braindead* represents a return to the local content that featured prominently in *Bad Taste*. Jackson's third film is filled with references to New Zealand history and culture: from the theme of meat processing and the New Zealand cult of the chainsaw in *Bad Taste*, to the iconic Flymo lawnmower used by Lionel to exterminate the zombies in *Braindead*. Both *Bad Taste* and *Braindead* are set in rural or suburban New Zealand and open with images of a young Queen Elizabeth, a reference to the lingering influence of the British Empire on New Zealand life (Creed 2000). Furthermore, the narrative of both films revolves around the destruction of symbols of 'Britishness': good taste, heritage homes and the suburban surrogate of the Queen – the Mother (who significantly in *Braindead* speaks with a strong British accent). As Barbara Creed aptly puts it: in Jackson's films 'the comedy lies in the disjuncture between the way in which these islands' suburbs see themselves as bastions of British civilisation and the barbaric events that actually unfold on the streets and the homes' (Creed 2000: 63).

Jackson's subsequent project, *Heavenly Creatures* (1994), the true story of a matricide that shocked 1950s' New Zealand, also evokes the tropes of the colonial experience, distance and motherhood, but it is a clear move away from the splatstick of his first three films. *Heavenly Creatures* marks Jackson's debut into art cinema and, although it retains elements of fantasy and horror, it lacks the grotesque humour that characterizes his earlier works.

Jackson returns to combine horror and comedy in the Hollywood production *The Frighteners* (1996), which starred Michael J Fox as a psychic who uses his abilities to befriend ghosts, convincing them to haunt rich suburban houses that he will then free for a fee. Troubles arise when Bannister has to confront the ghost of a vicious mass murderer who has promised to kill him. The film was a partial flop in the targeted mainstream American market, as the audience was confused by the blend of comedy and horror. At the same time, it did not please the old splatstick fans, as the grotesque comic and splatter elements were restrained by the American production more concerned with appealing to family audiences.

Braindead effectively represented Jackson's last splatstick movie, and his influence on other New Zealand film-makers during the 1990s was limited. The only other film that explored the combination of horror and comic elements is David Blith's *Grampire* (aka *Moonrise*, 1991) a Disneyesque story for children about an American boy visiting his New Zealand grandfather, who turns out to be a vampire.

The mid-1990s represented a period of new renaissance for New Zealand cinema, with films such as *The Piano*, *Once Were Warriors* and *Heavenly Creatures* achieving huge success, both among the critics and the public of the world arthouses. It seemed that New Zealand cinema had started taking itself seriously again, leaving no room for the low-culture triviality of the splatstick. However, New Zealand black humour is a prominent feature of films of the late 1990s and early 2000s, such as *Topless Women Talk About Their Lives* (1997), *Scarfies* (1999) and the *Price of Milk* (2001), where comedy blends with serious issues such as suicide, crime, death and colonial guilt.

The production of *The Lord of the Rings* trilogy (2001–2003) had a dramatic impact on the New Zealand film industry by raising the profile of local film-makers and leaving long-lasting legacies such as studios and other film infrastructures. Even though the film production was concerned with guaranteeing fidelity to the original Tolkien text, Jackson's splatstick style is apparent in the films, particularly in the battle scenes and in the representation of the villains: the Orcs, Goblins and Uruk-hais. In a scene from the *The Two Towers* (2002), Saruman's Uuruk-hais are confronted by their allies, the Orcs, who grow hungry and tired as they are chased by Aragorn. One of the Orcs suggests eating prisoners Merry and Pipino, but he is killed instead by the Uruk-hai's leader, who then humorously announces, 'Dinner is ready!' The corpse of the Orc is subsequently dismembered and cannibalized by the hungry monsters in a sequence that is clearly reminiscent of Jackson's early splatstick.

The legacy of Peter Jackson is also particularly evident in the work of young New Zealand film-makers such as Jonathan King, who, in 2006, revived the tradition of the Kiwi splatter-comedy in his debut film *Black Sheep*. King's collaboration with Weta Workshop (Academy Award winner for *The Lord of the Rings*' special effects) lies at the heart of the film, which combines a defining image of New Zealand, such as the sheep, with buckets of gore. *Black Sheep* is the elaboration of a simple idea: what if sheep revolted by feasting on human flesh and turning their victims into huge were-sheep? The tagline of the film encapsulates the essence of the narrative: 'There are 40 million sheep in New Zealand and they are pissed off!'

The protagonist of the film is Henry Odfield, who returns to the family farm in rural New Zealand looking for a buy-out from estranged brother and ambitious farmer Angus, who is carrying out a reckless genetic engineering programme. Because of a childhood trauma, Henry suffers from a paralyzing sheep-phobia and his nightmare comes to life when a couple of inept environmental activists release a mutant lamb onto the farm, causing thousands of sheep to turn into bloodthirsty predators. Along with farm manager Tucker and animal rights activist Experience, Henry is stranded at the farm and forced to confront both the murderous flock and Angus, who refuses to stop the genetic engineering experiment. Soon Henry discovers that a bite from an infected sheep causes humans to transform into dangerous ovine-mutants. The carnivorous sheep attack a delegation of international investors who are gathered at the homestead for Angus' presentation of his new genetically engineered breed, killing, mutilating and creating more monstrous sheep-zombies. In the climactic finale Henry confronts and defeats his brother Angus, who has meanwhile turned into a gigantic sheep-monster. In the closing sequence, Henry, who has finally overcome his sheep-phobia, ponders the idea of starting an organic farming business with Tucker and Experience.

The film plays upon the contemporary fear of genetic manipulation and the guilt of meat-processing, one of New Zealand's main exports and sources of wealth. The narrative conveys an obvious critique of the new generation of New Zealand farmers who put greed above respect for nature: the main source of conflict between the two brothers is their relation to the memory and values of their father, who embodied the 'old-school farming tradition'. Much of the humour derives from the reference to New Zealand culture: the opposition between the urban and the rural; New Zealanders attitude towards sheep; the subversion of the national cliché of the beautiful scenery, which in the film is associated with horror and death.

As we already mentioned, however, an important stylistic feature of the film is its relation to the Kiwi splatstick tradition. References to Peter Jackson's early films are so numerous that Black Sheep could be considered a tribute to the Wellington 'splattermeister'. One of the main assets of Black Sheep was the involvement of Weta Workshop, which in turn is closely associated with Jackson himself. From the stylistic and narrative point of view, director Jonathan King often quotes specific scenes from Jackson's early works: the mutant lamb that is the origin of all the troubles in Black Sheep is obviously reminiscent of the mutant Rat-Monkey in Braindead; the scene in which a brutally-mutilated investor throws a severed arm to an approaching sheep is a precise reference to a sequence of Bad Taste, in which a dying alien ineffectively tries to stop Derek's lethal chainsaw by throwing a pine cone at him; the finale of King's film, where the protagonist is confronted with the monstrous persona of an estranged member of the family, echoes the conclusive sequence of Braindead. More significantly, perhaps, both Braindead and Black Sheep deal with the process of overcoming the childhood trauma of the father's death. In both cases, trauma is linked to the colonial experience and alienation from the land. In Braindead, Lionel's father is murdered by Mother, who, in turn, is a metaphor of the oppressive legacy of the British Empire. In Black Sheep, Henry's father is literally swallowed by the land as he falls from a cliff to save a sheep. In both cases the trauma is overcome by facing an excess of horror that is so radical and extreme that it becomes comic. An interesting parallel can be found in New Zealand literature and particularly in Bruce Mason's play The End of the Golden Weather (1959), in which the dramatic performance of the father's protagonist as Jack the Ripper anticipates the tones of splatstick film:

> The victim struggles to sit up: the doctor flattens him with an imperious gesture. He saws furiously, making a ghastly, ticking scratching sound. Now that didn't hurt, did it? Stop laughing! Pin back the flaps ... that's the way ... Now we have to dig. Get at the root of the trouble. Where's my garden trowel? (Mason 1981: 10–11)

Comic and horror blend in the world of New Zealand writers such as Mason or Morrieson; a world of childhood reading and theatrics that involve safe adventures and vicarious experiences with death and dissolution (Schafer 1998).

Similarly, in the cinematic Kiwi splatstick, the excess of horror and splatter is part of a maturation process in which alienation and fear are literally slashed and cut to pieces within the safe boundaries of the comic. Gothic or splatter comedy is therefore a means to bridge and reconnect the *unheimlich* to the *heimlich*: by exposing the horror in all its physicality and confining it to the domain of the comic, splatstick counters the settler anxiety derived from alienation from the land. Kiwi splatstick has the therapeutic and liberating power of a carnival midway as, in Peter Jackson's words, 'there is a laugh with every drop of blood'.

FILM MUSIC IN AOTEAROA/ NEW ZEALAND
TONY MITCHELL

Actor Sam Neill's highly subjective 1995 documentary on New Zealand cinema for the British Film Institute's A Century of Cinema series, *Cinema of Unease*, emphasizes a 'uniquely dark and strange film industry' and focuses on the brooding, desolate and often threatening 'psychological interiors' that he regarded many of the country's films as embodying. Neill goes so far as to characterize the history of New Zealand film as a 'lonely road through this indifferent landscape, this isolated space' (Neill & Rymer, 1995). Instrumental music for Neill's documentary was provided by composer/songwriter Don McGlashan and his rock group the Muttonbirds, who have specialized in producing a number of edgy, gothic songs about the New Zealand landscape, and the film theme became part of the group's repertoire, which suggests the idea of 'cinema of unease' has had a particular purchase, while it can also be applied to a number of major subsequent New Zealand films. Although Neill revoked his label on NZ National radio in 2007, favouring the phrase 'cinema at ease' instead – surely a far more troubling expression – arguably, it still has a certain aptitude, connecting with a prevailing strand of 'New Zealand gothic' which is often strongly expressed through film music, and which Conrich and Davy (1997) describe as frequently located in places of isolation, remote or distinctly rural environments where there exists delayed industrialism. Here, individuals are trapped within a landscape that appears 'alive'. Dwarfed by the power of the land, the Kiwi Gothic presents its characters as fragile, eccentric or disturbed (Conrich and Davy 1997: 7).

Neill's view has been hotly disputed by Horrocks (1999) among others (see Babington 2007: 19–21), and criticized for providing a narrow, complacent and distorted view of New Zealand film. But, arguably, this 'lonely road' of psychological interiors is often expressed distinctively and evocatively through the atmospheric music which has accompanied particular sequences in many of the country's major films. McGlashan's film music is a particularly salient example: in Jane Campion's An Angel at My Table (1990) his hauntingly Celtic combination of descant recorder, harmonica and melodica provides one of the most distinctive themes in New Zealand film music, and one that provides suitably evocative accompaniment for the striking opening image of the film's red-headed protagonist, the novelist Janet Frame, as a young child walking along a lonely country road. Campion's more internationally-known film The Piano (1993) with its well-known theme music and score by British composer Michael Nyman, is arguably the most widely represented and analysed example of film music in New Zealand cinema (see Gorbman 1999; Van Leeuwen 1998). However, Campion herself regards herself and the film as Australian and many New Zealanders are highly critical of the film's representation of the subservient, colourful and rather naïve, folksy Maori characters in the film, which tends to support the interpretation that the film and its music provide a very colonialist and unrealistic portrayal of nineteenth-century New Zealand (see Pihama 1999).

Schopenhauer once claimed, 'suitable music played to any scene, action, event or surrounding seems to disclose to us its most secret meaning, and appears as the most accurate and distinct commentary on it' (in Lanza 1994: 11) This statement can be applied effectively to the music of a significant number of New Zealand feature films, where it often provides 'psychogeographical' sonic readings of New Zealand's urban and rural landscapes, which tend to play a dominant role in many films where the relationship between people and landscape is explored. Silent films shown in New Zealand cities in the pre-talkie period were sometimes accompanied by live Wurlitzer organs, such as the one in the grand Civic Theatre in Auckland, and the Auckland Wurlitzer Organ Trust still occasionally holds screenings in the art deco Hollywood Cinema in Avondale of old silent films such as Chaplin's Modern Times with live accompaniment. Alfred Hill is generally considered the first composer of film music in New Zealand, contributing orchestral music often dealing with Maori themes: Hei Tiki in 1935, and the sound remake of major New Zealand film-maker Rudall Hayward's Rewi's Last Stand in 1940. Although discredited in the late twentieth century for what were perceived as rather exotic orchestral attempts to represent Maori music and themes, Hill's music is now being re-evaluated as a sincere and serious early attempt by a composer to engage with Maori musical culture.

The decades preceding the 1960s were a lean period in New Zealand cinema, with only the Tourist Board making promotional films about the country's flora, fauna, landscape and topography, often accompanied by grandiose orchestral music. John O'Shea, the director of Pacific Films, was the most important figure of this decade, producing and directing the black and white feature film *Runaway* in 1964, influenced by European film-makers such as Michelangelo Antonioni, and combining the road trip of its playboy protagonist on the run from the law with a visual showcase of the country's landscapes from north to south. The film starred Maori soprano Kiri Te Kanawa as one of the protagonist's conquests, and archetypal 'Kiwi bloke', popular author Barry Crump, also played a role. Incidental jazz-styled music, with clarinet, piano and even organ was provided by composer Robin Maconie, and described by one contemporary reviewer at the time as 'always apt but never intrusive' (*NZ Listener*, 6 November 1964), The title song was sung diegetically by Maori popular balladeer Rim D Paul, backed by Maori showband the Quin Tikis, and released as a single on local label Zodiac. *Runaway* has a strong iconic value, representing New Zealand's rather gauche attempt to become a sophisticated European culture, while its music expresses more Indigenous cultural concerns. O'Shea followed this existential drama with a light-hearted comic road movie, again in black and white, and arguably the country's first Indigenous musical, *Don't Let it Get You* (1966). Filmed in Rotorua and Sydney, the film deals with events surrounding a summer music festival featuring Australian singer Normie Rowe and an impressive line-up of Maori musical talent. Kiri Te Kanawa appears as 'guest artist' singing a Rossini aria to children in a Maori marae, along with Rim D Paul, Maori showband members Herma and Eliza Keil and the Quin Tikis, while Maori musical icon Howard Morrison plays himself as a character in the film. Patrick Flynn is credited with incidental music, with Robin Maconie contributing one of the songs. An LP of songs from the film, featuring Howard Morrison and others, was the first New Zealand film soundtrack recording to be released in 1966, and Babington has suggested, perhaps controversially, that the film provides evidence of how the local popular music scene of the mid 1960s was 'dominated by Maori and Polynesian performers, whose talent the film showcases' (Babington 2007: 104).

Roger Donaldson's *Sleeping Dogs* (1977), with music by former Underdogs blues-rock guitarist Murray Grindlay, Maori disco crooner Mark Williams and the group Ariel Railway, was also released as a soundtrack LP, and signalled that the 'New Zealand film renaissance' of the late 1970s and 1980s was on the way. Grindlay went on to provide some of the highly distinctive and dramatic music, including the Maori *taonga puoro* reconstructed and performed by Hirini Melbourne and Richard Nunns, featuring the *purerehua*, the whirring bull roarer, for Lee Tamahori's international success about violence and redemption in a South Auckland Maori family, *Once Were Warriors* (1994). This film also included important songs by Maori groups, Southside of Bombay and Upper Hutt Posse, and guitarist Tama Renata (see Mitchell 1996). Melbourne and Nunns have provided *taonga puoro* and advice on Maori music for a number of feature films, including Merata Mita's *Mauri* (1988), *The Maori Merchant of Venice* and Peter Jackson's *Lord of the Rings* trilogy. Barry Barclay's important Maori identity drama *Ngati* (1987) had powerful traditional Maori *waiata* arranged by singer and performer Dalvanius. Grindlay and Murray McNabb also provided music for Gregor Nicholas' flawed but important Maori-Serbian inter-racial drama, *Broken English* (1996).The music for trumpeter Geoff Murphy's road movie *Goodbye Pork Pie* (1980), with music by prominent NZ film composer John Charles, as well as blues singer Hammond Gamble and guitarist Mike Caen of rock group Street Talk, also had a vinyl release. Charles also provided the music for Murphy's important *Utu* (1982) a powerful story of

Maori revenge in colonial times, which also included Maori chants and musical motifs (see Mitchell 1984a). He also scored Murphy's science fiction film *The Quiet Earth* (1983).

Donaldson's domestic drama *Smash Palace* (1982) occasioned an EP release of the title track from the film, by singer Sharon O'Neill, while internationally-renowned, NZ-born jazz pianist Mike Nock's highly evocative solo piano and percussion recording for Geoff Steven's plane crash drama *Strata* (1984), which includes a rearrangement of a theme by Erik Satie, is now sadly a rare vinyl collector's item on Kiwi Pacific Records. Jazz also provided an evocative period soundtrack for Sam Pillsbury's *The Scarecrow* (1981), the best of a number of film adaptations of 'small town gothic' novels written in the 1960s by Ronald Hugh Morrieson, where pianist Phil Broadhurst, along with Hong Kong-based songwriter duo Andrew Hagen and Morton Wilson, formerly of the rock group Schtung, provided often janty period jazz settings, with the occasional quote from George Gershwin. As Geoff Chapple noted in the *NZ Listener* (17 April 1982), 'The music … adds nicely to the film's spooky moods. I think Morrieson, a musician himself, would have approved.' In 1986 Murray Ball's animated film *Footrot Flats*, from his comic strip of the same name, became the most popular New Zealand film of its time. The theme song from the film, 'Slice of Heaven' by Polynesian reggae group Herbs and Dave Dobbyn, released two months in advance of the film, reached number one on the NZ music charts and was named Song of the Year at the 1986 New Zealand Music Awards. It has since become something of an 'unofficial New Zealand national anthem' and was used extensively to promote the country in advertisements in Australia and elsewhere by the NZ Tourist Board. The soundtrack album to the film also included Herbs' rather more militant song 'Nuclear Waste'.

Vincent Ward is probably the prime specialist in New Zealand gothic: his 1984 film *Vigil*, about a young girl's coming of age in a rural backwater, featured highly evocative, dramatic music on piano, violin and percussion by prominent composer Jack Body. Body also scored Ward's documentary study of a bewitched Maori woman, *Rain of the Children*, (2008). Victoria Kelly has composed scores for a wide range of films, from the Hitchcock-Herrmann-like orchestral scores for horror films *The Ugly* (Scott Reynolds, 1997) and *The Locals* (Greg Page, 2003), and the splatter sheep-clone *Black Sheep* (Jonathan King, 2006), to the country-and-western comedy *Magik and Rose* (1999), and Robert Sarkies' powerful study of the 2000 Aramoana massacre *Out of the Blue* (2006) – which also featured an important song by Don McGlashan: 'Don't Let Me Down'. *Under the Mountain* (2009), Jonathan King's adaptation of Maurice Gee's children's gothic science fiction-horror novel set in the volcanic underworld of Auckland, also had an orchestral score by Kelly. Gee's novel *In My Father's Den* was made into a distinctively 'southern gothic' homecoming drama set in the Otago countryside by Brad McGann in 2004, with music by British composer Simon Boswell, a sometimes associate of Italian cult horror-director Dario Argento. The film also made highly effective use of Patti Smith's song 'Horses' in representing the state of mind of its female protagonist. Pop and jazz musician Peter Dasent had a productive role in the early films of Peter Jackson, providing often quirky, unconventional music for the splatter-horror film *Braindead* (1992), the puppet-porn *Meet the Feebles* (1989), and Jackson's extremely effective dramatization of the 1954 Christchurch Parker-Hume murders, *Heavenly Creatures* (1994), working in the two girls' highly-evolved fantasy world based on the songs of Mario Lanza. David Long provided music for Jackson's *Lord of the Rings* trilogy, which included 'cultural music' and 'the sound of the ring' composed with ambient-electronic trio Plan 9, whose other work has included music for Gaylene Preston's psychological thriller *Perfect Strangers* (2003), the spoof kung-fu movie *Tongan Ninja* (2002) – which also featured songs written by Flight of the Conchords' Jermaine Clement and Bret McKenzie – and Jackson's and Costa Bote's highly effective mockumentary about a fictitious New Zealand silent film-maker, *Forgotten Silver* (1995). Stewart Main and Peter Wells' operatic, high camp melodrama *Desperate Remedies* (1993) represents a highly idiosyncratic departure in New Zealand cinema, especially in its lush music by Robin Scholes, played by the Auckland Philharmonic Orchestra, which Mark Tierney in *The Listener* (11 September 1993) described as the film's 'high point … The best music ever composed for a New Zealand film, no question'. Australian ambient musician and prominent Hollywood film soundtrack composer Lisa Gerrard scored Niki Caro's highly successful 2002 film *Whale Rider*, which introduced Keisha Castle-Hughes in an extraordinary performance as the young Maori protagonist. *Mojo* magazine noted (September 2003): 'Gerrard couples her muezzin-like glossolalia with the rich Polynesian traditions of vocal music to paint an evocative picture of a culture in uneasy liaison with the 21st century.'

Rock musicians have been important in lending urban soundscapes and atmospheres to new Zealand film; apart from McGlashan, whose idiosyncratic and distinctive work for Anthony McCarten's *Show of Hands* and Toa Fraser's 2008 British-made comedy *Dean Spanley* have complemented his early work, Neil Finn composed piano music and songs for Christine Jeffs' breakthrough film *Rain* (2001), set in Scandretts Bay, a small seaside holiday location in the 1960s. Dave McArtney provided the driving but rather inappropriate rock score with members of his group Hello Sailor in *Queen City Rocker (1986)*, a largely forgotten but eminently-recuperable film about the conflict between punk street kids and gangsters promoting massage parlours and rock gigs in Auckland, with its final scene partly based on the Queen Street riots which occurred after a rock concert in Aotea Square in 1984. A number of bands associated with the Flying Nun label have provided music for films such as *Scarfies* (1999), the Sarkies brothers' gothic comedy about students in Dunedin, and Harry Sinclair's quirky comedy *Topless Women Talk About Their Lives* (1997). The JPS Experience provided evocatively-jangling songs for Alison McLean's Rotorua-based psychological drama *Crush* (1992), and Shayne Carter provided moody, dark rock music for Stuart McKenzie's 2003 film *For Good*. Warren Maxwell, the part-Maori leader of the highly-distinctive successful Wellington reggae groups Trinity Roots, Fat Freddy's Drop, and Little Bushman, contributed haunting guitar-based music with words in Maori to Armagan Ballantyne's highly evocative drama about a Maori family in the Hokianga, *The Strength of Water* (2009).

That New Zealand film music is beginning to be valued in its own right, at least in educational contexts, was demonstrated by a concert which took place in the Auckland Town Hall on 27 May 2009, entitled 'Discover NZ Film Music', performed by the Auckland Philharmonia Orchestra, and including a study guide and extensive programme notes for secondary schools. Pieces performed include John Charles' 'Sunrise from *The Quiet Earth*', Don McGlashan's song 'Bathe in the River' from Toa Fraser's 2006 Fijian family drama *No. 2*, Victoria Kelly's *Black Sheep* Suite, Clive Cockburn's *Pirihana o Arakona* from *The Maori Merchant of Venice*, arrangements of exerpts by Wellington rock group the

Phoenix Foundation from the 2007 comedy *Eagle vs. Shark*, and an arrangement of Murray Grindley's *Once Were Warriors* Theme. A season of films was also screened in Wellington in February 2009 showcasing New Zealand music in New Zealand films. Sample sound clips and CD information of the music from some 160 New Zealand films from *Rewi's Last Stand* to *Dean Spanley* can be accessed on nzvideos.org/soundtracks. Film and audio clips from some films scored by New Zealand composers are also contained in a promotional DVD-CD set *New Zealand Composers on Screen* (2005), released by New Zealand Trade and Enterprise and Investment New Zealand.

HORROR IN NEW ZEALAND: A QUIVERING OF BORDERS
BEVIN YEATMAN

The tradition of the horror genre is not strong with the audiovisual media in New Zealand but elements of horror, or the energies often signalled as part of a 'Kiwi gothic', are evident in many works. If gothic can be understood as a 'fascination with the borders between categories –life/death, sanity/madness, domesticity/monstrosity – a shifting warp of the familiar' (Lawn 2006) then a focus on horror resonates with this boundary-crossing and suggests that there is an underlying fascination in capture and escape, both metaphorical and literal, as well as an accompanying fear of bodies being ripped open and dispersed – an ultimate trauma of the experience of death or, at the very least, anxiety over the vulnerability of the body.

A faint trace of three different approaches to horror can be found in works more evidently marketed as being part of a horror genre. These include the Jacksonian line of splatter horror with its strong emphasis on comedy as a driving force, with a low budget as its constriction, and the works that follow this line after *Braindead* (Jackson, 1992) and *Bad Taste* (Jackson, 1987) would include *Black Sheep* (King, 2006) and *The Locals* (Page, 2003). A second line, recently, beginning with Glen Stranding, is work with a stronger budget and an appeal to a more serious conception, dealing in issues involving contamination by the irrational – *The Truth About Demons* (Standring, 2000) – and the contamination of the body – as is explored in *Perfect Creature* (Standring, 2006). A further strand is reflected in the television series *Mataku* (Bennett and Berger, 2002–05), which is translated from the Maori as a 'quivering', again suggesting the crossing or vibration of boundaries and, in this series, it is that of the ancestors and the imbrication of traditional space-time with that of the contemporary.

Black Sheep wraps three different strands of gothic interest into a comedic horror that reflects typical themes mentioned above. The process of boundary-crossing, or the quivering, are here reflected in the capture and desire to escape the land and, similarly, the dreadful potency of familial relationships and, finally, the contamination of the body – in this case, contamination caused through unfortunate genetic experiments. The protagonist Henry returns to the family farm to give it all to his tormenting brother, only to find that this same person has been conducting a genetic programme on sheep that have turned them into monsters whose bite can also mutate the human body. A positive outcome can only be achieved when Henry accepts that he must manage the farm and, therefore, undermine the extremism of both his brother, with his total investment in a scientific experimentation, and Grant the 'environmentalist', who would see a 'back to nature' abandonment of any farming management as the only solution. The capture of these 'solutions' is escaped through the balanced management of more traditional practices. The power dynamics of the family is realigned and the mutation of the bodies remains solely with Angus, Henry's brother, and Grant, while the rest of those infected escape being sheep. The film is hilarious in parts, especially with images of marauding sheep ravenous for human flesh, and works more on a stereotyping of characters to play out the horror scenarios that it offers than developing in-depth characterization.

The Locals has a stronger interest in examining a rural past that has been sidestepped by most contemporary urbanites who seek comfort in the city and experience an uneasy relationship with the land and its historical implications. Two young men, Grant and Paul, cross over a bridge (a zone to another space/time) after meeting two young women dressed in clothes reminiscent of a past. In this place they are terrorized by locals who are all, it turns out, dead, captured here in this place by the past owner of the land, also dead, but who cannot give up control. The locals, then, are symptoms and images of a past heritage – a time that has been forgotten by the urban dwellers Grant and Paul, but a time that they must acknowledge and help to release from the control of the patriarchal landowner before being able to escape again across the bridge back to the contemporary. Again, death and the fear of death play their own cards in the dramatics of the story, with murder and the threat of death major energies that drive the narrative. This film has less emphasis on humour as an undercurrent and is a genuine attempt to create affects of fear and trauma through the suspense of the narrative, lighting effects and the rhythms of the editing and audio.

The Truth About Demons is a more stylish and serious approach to the quivering of boundaries. In this film, the main protagonist, Dr Harry Ballard, an anthropologist who spends time amongst the categorizing processes of his profession, signified by the myriad boxes in his archives, is toyed with by Le Valiant, the leader of an occult group, who plays a game the object of which is the slow destruction of Ballard. This, then, is the rational and irrational quivering together with the rational scientist discovering that darker forces are playing with him, creating an intersection of reality and unrealities that he is captured by and needs to escape. The final escape, it seems, is a refuge in a psychiatric hospital – another entrapment. This is a dark film, sustained by a lighting regime that expresses these dark forces with limited but highly expressive light, and delves into the trauma of the body and its own borders through a series of special effects that have bodies physically penetrated and ripped apart by the dark forces that are encountered. Again, the thematic emphasis is on capture and escape and the fear of a vulnerable body but, in this case, the ambivalence of the sense of reality and the process of the game-playing builds an intense sense of horror which no longer has comedic effects but is a sustained experience.

Standring's second film *Perfect Creature* continues to develop a sophisticated style with a focus now on contamination of the body; in this instance through the experimentation of genetics and also as a secondary fear that of the invasive qualities of influenza. The story is developed around two brothers, both of The Brotherhood, a highly evolved mutation of human beings, with Sirus seeking his brother Edgar, who has infected himself with a toxic virus in an effort to develop a further evolutionary trigger for the survival of his kind. Sirus has become engulfed in murderous rage, and needs to be contained, but has escaped and is endeavouring to destroy the humans by forcing them to ingest the poisonous toxin he has himself been infected with while, at the same time, playing a game of hide and seek with his brother. This work cannot be easily categorized as solely a horror film as it suggests different generic categories, as they intersect and contaminate each other, but the power of the story, and the fears that it deals with, as well as the special effects – including the swiftness and grace of movement and the heightened soundscape – all enhance a horror dimension. The fear of body intrusion; the fear of death, not only of an individual but of a species; the fear of an uncontrollable regime of scientific experimentation; and the affective energies conjured by the construction of the film, all offer a strong sense of the characteristics of horror.

Finally, the third force that inflects the strands of horror in New Zealand audio-visual work is that represented by the series *Makatu*. These works have been based on traditional Maori stories and explore the potency of the ancestors as they quiver between the boundaries of past and present and redress wrongs or grievances that have incurred. The contemporary is captured again by the past and must work out another relationship, or be killed in the process. The power of the horror is not so much placed on an emphasis of body terror, although death is a common outcome, but for these works the terror comes because of the all-encompassing power of the ancestral past: a power that remains emphatically in the present and a power that cannot be repressed.

The experience of horror, then, is embedded in numerous audiovisual works and has been registered as a part of a Kiwi gothic: a crossing of boundaries that works to make the familiar unfamiliar, but an unfamiliar that registers, often, in dark and strange forces. The genre of horror does manifest itself in particular films and there are three strands that seem to be emerging from the traditions of film-making. These are not entirely separate categories as they all seem to be focusing on underlying themes, registered here as that of a quivering between boundaries or borders and structured as processes of capture and escape. There is a strong focus on family relations, on the heritage of the past, especially as it is expressed through the politics of land, as well as a fascination with the shadow of science and its playing with seemingly-uncontrollable forces, and, finally, a fascination with the body and its vulnerabilities. The future for this type of work is strong, as it is a potent means of exploring the undercurrents of a nation exposed both to the forces of a powerful past and those unknown, of the future, that shape the complexities of the present.

SCIENCE FICTION CINEMA IN NEW ZEALAND
SCOTT WILSON

Science fiction remains a difficult genre to place within the cinema of New Zealand. Considering the genre's long international history, the extensive list of canonical texts and immediately-identifiable iconographies, the absence of numbers of science fiction feature films in New Zealand could lead one to assume that science fiction, for whatever reason, remains predominantly a genre of the metropolitan centres and not of the global (and especially post-colonial) peripheries. Yet it is possible to argue that a version of Antipodean science fiction exists and, furthermore, that it is one that demonstrates an awareness of (if not an adherence to) the tropes of the genre, as well as a willingness to bend those generic markers in ways that appear to be entirely in keeping with this country's cinema history.

The obvious starting point for this discussion must therefore be Geoff Murphy's magisterial *The Quiet Earth* (1985). While not the first New Zealand film to include elements of the genre, *The Quiet Earth* is the first local feature film to be identified and marketed as a science fiction text. Yet this film, despite its adherence to the genre's various demands, also demonstrates the deep ambivalence that seems to run through the centre of many New Zealand genre films and, for this reason, *The Quiet Earth* functions both as a starting point and as a perfect exemplar for this discussion. *The Quiet Earth*'s narrative – based on a novel of the same name – concerns a scientist who awakens to discover he is seemingly the last man on Earth, the result of some secret experiment gone horribly awry (a scenario which is echoed in the 2007 Will Smith-vehicle *I Am Legend*). As the narrative progresses, our protagonist – the iconic Bruno Lawrence as scientist Zac Hobson – discovers that he shares this denuded landscape with two others – a European/Pakeha woman (Alison Routledge as Joanne) and a Maori man (Pete Smith as Api). At this moment the film alters its trajectory to become a terse exploration of different kinds of tensions, with the mounting pressure of the original crisis as a background against which these more familiar (to a New Zealand audience) issues play out.

Herein lies the ambivalence mentioned above; this film, as a genre text, seeks to adhere to its generic requirements and we see this with the framing narrative, the plot devices that move the narrative forward and, especially, the film's still-shocking conclusion. But, in a manner that appears to be typical for New Zealand cinema, other elements intrude, extending the film beyond science fiction. Necessarily, as Rick Altman (1999) and others have theorized, it is impossible for any film to adhere to a single genre, meaning that narrative and iconographic hybridity are the order of the day and science fiction has proved to be especially prone to this. Yet it is worth exploring the fact that those extra-generic elements that intrude into *The Quiet Earth* and demonstrate its ambivalence and hybridity are the same kinds of elements that led Sam Neill to suggest that what defines New Zealand cinema is the presence of these moments of 'unease'. Thus Zac's role as a singular protagonist for much of *The Quiet Earth*'s length provides us with yet another example of 'the man alone' – that singular figure of the New Zealand arts who emerges out of, and speaks to, a particular kind of European post-settlement anxiety concerning masculinity, ethnicity and geo-location. Similarly, the love-triangle that develops between Zac, Joanne and Api has less to do with the science fictional overtones of the framing narrative, and much more to do with the specific kinds of unstated, but very present, tensions surrounding ethnicity, gender and sexuality – exactly the same kinds of issues present in Murphy's earlier *Utu* (1983). Similar tensions are present in Roger Donaldson's *Sleeping Dogs* (1979), a film whose only qualifying generic factor is the fact that it is set in an alternate present and details a dystopic society crumbling under its own parliamentary corruption.

Thus we can posit the fact that what typifies the presence of elements of science fiction in New Zealand cinema is the notion that they will have been, always already, hybridized in such a way as to provide room for local genre films to continue the ostensible project of this country's national cinema at large: exploring issues and themes of identity. This might go some way to explain the absence of what we might refer to as 'pure' science fiction on our screens. Instead, this notion encourages us to widen our search beyond the classical iconographies identified by Vivian Sobchack in her article 'Images of Wonder: The Look of Science Fiction' (1987) and, instead, search for elements of SF as occurring within other genres. In this fashion, Peter Jackson's first feature *Bad Taste* and Vincent Ward's *The Navigator: A Medieval Odyssey* (both 1988) offer a sense of how Science fiction elements can be included in films that are more obviously aligned with other modes of representation.

Bad Taste, the film that launched the horror-splatter-comedy-gore sub-genre, is ostensibly concerned with an alien invasion of small-town New Zealand, with our only line of defence being the brave men of the Astro-Investigation and Defence Service (AIDS). Such is the level of the humour present in *Bad Taste*, a film that, nevertheless, remains both a vital document in Jackson's oeuvre and a pivotal text for New Zealand cinema, given its international popularity and success. In complete contrast is Ward's *The Navigator*. Set in plague-ravaged fourteenth-century England, a young boy leads a group of pilgrims through the earth to twentieth-century Auckland on a quest to end the devastation in their home land and time. Whilst the allegorical possibilities of these films lie beyond this brief entry, both work to adhere to, and extend, their respective versions of their genres (*Bad Taste* can be seen as SF-inflected horror/comedy, whilst *The Navigator* refers to SF in the same art-cinema way as Tarkovsky's *Stalker*, 1979) in order to produce films that are both recognizably *of* their genres, whilst at the same time, are more than that.

Outside the putative mainstream represented by these early examples, other elements of science fiction can be seen, most clearly in the films of David Blythe. His early features, *Angel Mine* (1978) and *Death Warmed Up* (1984), both include SF elements in their plots: *Angel Mine* features leather-clad dopple-gangers and pre-Viagra performance enhancement, whilst *Death Warmed Up* explores genetic manipulation and mutant assassins. Despite the fact that *Death Warmed Up* gained some international success as a SF-horror, both films remain on the periphery of this country's cinematic memory. Indeed, *Angel Mine*, an exploration of suburban lethargy and ennui, was both the first film to be funded by the newly-formed New Zealand Film Commission, and the first (and only) to be issued with the now-hysterical R18 warning 'Caution: Contains Punk Cult Material'.

What is worth noting is the manner with which the landscape of this country, long a feature of the 'cinema of unease' alluded to above, functions also as an ubiquitous 'every-space' (a characteristic of the New Zealand cinema industry that reaches its ostensible apotheosis with Jackson's *Lord of the Rings* trilogy), meaning that more international genre films are made here than are produced locally. Harley Cokliss' *Battletruck*, (1982, re-released internationally as *Warlords of the Twenty First Century*) is one of the few identifiably science fiction films to use this location which, perhaps in keeping with Neill's statements, seems to attract many more Horror productions than any other genre. So it is that *30 Days of Night* (David Slade, 2007) and *Underworld III: Rise of the Lycans* (Patrick Tatopolos, 2009) make use of local landscapes and personnel to produce SF/Horror films that are not set here. In contrast to this is the visually-fascinating (and locally-produced) *Perfect Creature* (Glenn Standring, 2005) which offers a distinct variation on the vampire/horror theme. This film is, arguably, more interesting than the international examples mentioned above due to it being set in an alternate 1960s' New Zealand, making it a 'steampunk'/horror hybrid, as well as geographically locating it specifically on these shores.

Because cinematic science fiction is both so clearly established in the popular imagination, and so oriented around the production of spectacle as the means to realize its particular cinematic visions, this genre seems to require far larger budgets of its individual texts if they are to satisfy audience expectations and compete in an international market – the only real avenue for local texts to make substantial profits. This may go some way to explaining the absence of indig-enous science fiction feature films beyond the few examples discussed above. Indeed it may be worth suggesting that local examples of cinematic magical realism provide a greater indication of an Antipodean response to the thematic demands of science fiction, whilst permitting the realizing of a fantastic vision within the constraints of a small indigenous industry. Thus whilst Harry Sinclair's *The Price of Milk* (2000) is clearly a rural idyll, Florian Habicht's *Woodenhead*

(2003) is a far more troubling affair and, at times, suggests that it be read as a post-apocalyptic text more than the re-told fairy tale it was marketed as.

Therefore, if magical realism necessitates a particular representation of the world – one more obviously realist – against which the magical elements can be highlighted, it would seem that this sub-genre might offer a greater chance for our local industry to explore the fantastic content of science fiction without having to compete with those films and industries with greater access to resources. Further to this, the narrative strengths of magical-realist texts lie in their ability to absorb and utilize indigenous story types – an ability that can only be copied by the science fiction text with some difficulty (at least in the West). Again, one may posit that this difficulty has much more to do with audience expectation than the restrictions of the genre itself and, indeed, Asian science fiction proves how well local myths and stories can be adapted to a technologically-inflected cinematic vision. So we are left considering the relative dearth of local science fiction and, although this is not a uniquely Antipodean phenomenon, it is one that speaks volumes about the relationship of science fiction (and, especially, audience expectations of the SF text) to those smaller industries that are unable to raise the budgets necessary to produce texts that might visibly share in the genre's iconography.

RECOMME READING

Altman, Rick (1999) *Film/Genre*, London: British Film Institute.

Australian Film Commission (2007) *Dreaming in Motion: Celebrating Australia's Indigenous Filmmakers*, Sydney: Australian Film Commission.

Australian Film Commission (2002) *Foreign Film and Television Production in Australia: A Research Report*, Sydney: Australian Film Commission.

Babington, Bruce (2007) *A History of the New Zealand Fiction Feature Film*, Manchester: Manchester University Press

Baillie, Russell (2009) 'Showtime and funtime', *New Zealand Herald* 18 December.

Barbour, Dennis H (1999) 'Heroism and Redemption in the Mad Max Trilogy' *Journal of Popular Film and Television*, 27:3, pp. 28–34.

Barclay, Barry (1990) *Our Own Image*, Auckland: Longman Paul.

Baxter, John (1986) *Filmstruck: Australia at the Movies*, Sydney: ABC,

Baxter, John (1970) *The Australian Cinema*, Sydney: Pacific Books.

Bertram, Dean (2009) *The Underground Australian Movie Renaissance*, Institute of Public Affairs, Melbourne. Available: http://www.ipa.org.au/publications/ 1697/the-underground-australian-movie-renaissance. Accessed: 24 September 2009.

Bertrand, Ina (2004) ''Good Taste at Hanging Rock'? Historical Nostalgia in the Films of the Australian Revival' *Metro* 140, pp. 42–7.

Bertrand, Ina (1999) 'The Anzac and *The Sentimental Bloke*: Australian Culture and Screen Representations of World War One' in M. Paris (ed.) *The First World War and Popular Cinema: 1914 to the Present*, Edinburgh: Edinburgh University Press, pp. 74–95.

Bertrand, Ina (ed.) (1989) *Cinema in Australia: A Documentary History*, Kensington, NSW: University of New South Wales Press.

Bertrand, Ina (1978) *Film Censorship in Australia*, St Lucia: University of Queensland Press.

Bertrand, Ina & Routt, William D (2007) *'The Picture That Will Live Forever': The Story of the Kelly Gang*. St. Kilda, Melbourne: ATOM.

Blackwood, Gemma (2007) '*Wolf Creek*: An unAustralian story?' *Continuum: Journal of Media & Cultural Studies*, 21:4, December, pp. 489–97.

Blythe, Martin (1994) *Naming the Other: Images of the Maori in New Zealand Film and Television*, Metuchen, NJ: The Scarecrow Press.

Bourne, Christopher (2005) '*Age of Consent*' *Senses of Cinema* 36, http:// archive.sensesofcinema.com/contents/cteq/05/36/age_of_consent.html. Accessed 30 January 2010.

IDED

Boym, Svetlana (2001) *The Future of Nostalgia*, New York: Basic Books.

Brodie, Ian (2006) *A Journey Through New Zealand Film,* Auckland: HarperCollins.

Brown, David Michael (2007) 'Turkey Shoot: The Cheap Thrill of the Hunt', *Metro*, 162: 94–6.

Buckley, Anthony (2009) *Beyond a Velvet Light Trap: A Filmmaker's Journey from Cinesound to Cannes*, Prahan, Vic: Hardie Grant.

Bunney, Andrew (2001) 'From *Wogboy* to *Mallboy*: The Good, the Bad, and the Lovely' *Senses of Cinema*, 12 http://archive.sensesofcinema.com/contents/01/12/australian.html Accessed 30 January 2010.

Burton, Geoff & Caputo, Raffaele (eds.) (1999) *Second Take: Australian Film-Makers Talk*, St Leonards NSW: Allen & Unwin.

Buscombe, Ed (1988) 'The Western: A Short History' in E. Buscombe (ed.) *The BFI Companion to the Western*, London: Andre Deutsch/BFI Publishing.

Cairns, Barbara & Martin, Helen (1994) *Shadows on the Wall: A Study of Seven New Zealand Feature Films*, Auckland: Longman Paul.

Churchman, Geoffrey B (ed.) (1997) *Celluloid Dreams: A Century of Film in New Zealand*, Wellington: IPL Books.

Clarke, J. (2009) Wit & Humour. *New Zealand Listener*, 1 August 2009: 18–20.

Clark, Randall (1995) *At a Drive-in or Theater Near You: The History, Culture and Politics of the American Exploitation Film*, New York: Garland Press Inc.

Cohan, Steven (ed.) (2002) *Hollywood Musicals: The Film Reader*, London and New York: Routledge.

Collins, Felicity (2009) 'Wogboy Comedies and the Australian National Type' in C. Simpson, R. Murawske & A. Lambert (eds.) *Diasporas of Australian Cinema*, Bristol: Intellect Books, pp. 73–82.

Collins, Felicity (2008) 'Historical Fiction and the Allegorical Truth of Colonial Violence in *The Proposition*' *Cultural Studies Review*, 14:1, pp. 55–71.

Collins, Felicity (2006) 'The Hedonistic Modernity of Sydney in *They're a Weird Mob*' *Senses of Cinema* 40, http://archive.sensesofcinema.com/contents/06/40/theyre-a-weird-mob.html. Accessed 30 January 2010.

Collins, Felicity (2002) 'Brazen Brides, Grotesque Daughters, Treacherous Mothers: Women's Funny Business in Australian Cinema from *Sweetie* to *Holy Smoke*' *Senses of Cinema* 23, http://archive.sensesofcinema.com/contents/02/23/women_funny_oz.html Accessed 30 January 2010.

Collins, Felicity & Davis, Therese (2004) *Australian Cinema after Mabo*, Cambridge & New York: Cambridge University Press.

Cook, Pam (2007) 'Researcher's Tales', as presented at the BFI National Library, 10 December 2007, http://www.bfi.org.uk/filmtvinfo/researchers/tales/pam-cook.pdf. Accessed 16 October 2009.

Conomos, John (1992) 'Cultural Difference and Ethnicity in Australian Cinema' *Cinema Papers* 90, pp. 10–15.

Conrich, I & Davy, S (1997) *Views from the Edge of the World: New Zealand Film. Studies in New Zealand Culture, vol. 1*, London: Kakapo Books.

Conrich, Ian & Murray, Stuart (2008) *Contemporary New Zealand Cinema: From New Wave to Blockbuster*, London: IB Taurus.

Conrich, Ian & Murray, Stuart (eds.) (2007) *New Zealand Filmmakers*, Detroit: Wayne State University Press.

Corrigan, Timothy (1998) 'Auteurs and the New Hollywood' in J. Lewis (ed.) *The New American Cinema*, Durham, London: Duke University Press, pp. 38–63.

Coyle, Rebecca (ed.) (2005) *Reel Tracks: Australian Feature Film Music and Cultural Identities*, Eastleigh: John Libbey.

Coyle, Rebecca (2000) 'Speaking Strine: Locating "Australia" in Film Dialogue' in Philip Brophy (ed.) *Cinesonic: Experiencing the Soundtrack*, Sydney: AFTRS.

Craven, Ian (ed.) (2001) *Australian Cinema in the 1990s*, London: Frank Cass.

Creed, B (2000) '*Bad Taste* and antipodal inversion: Peter Jackson's colonial suburbs', *Postcolonial Studies*, 3(1): 61–68.

Crimmings, Emma, & Graham, Rhys (eds.), *Short Site: Recent Australian Short Film*, Melbourne: ACMI, 2004.

Cubitt, Sean (nd) 'Cultural identity', blog. http://seancubitt.blogspot.com. Accessed 18 December 2009.

Cunningham, Stuart (2008) *In the Vernacular: A Generation of Australian Culture and Controversy*, St Lucia: University of Queensland Press.

Cunningham, Stuart (1990) 'The Big Picture on Short Films.' *Filmnews* 20.5, p.8.

Cunningham, Stuart (1989) 'The Decades of Survival: Australian Film 1930–1970'. In Albert Moran & Tom O'Regan (eds.) *The Australian Screen*, Ringwood: Penguin, pp.53–74.

Cunningham, Stuart (1985) 'Hollywood Genres, Australian Movies', in A Moran & T O'Regan (eds.) *An Australian Film Reader*, Sydney: Currency Press, pp. 235–41.

Dalziell, Tanya (2009) 'Gunpowder and Gardens: Reading Women in *The Proposition*,' *Studies in Australasian Cinema* 3:1.

Davis, Erik (2009) 'Cinematical Interview: *Australia* Director Baz Luhrmann', *Cinematical*, 4 March, http://www.cinematical.com/2009/03/04/cinematical-interview-australia-director-baz-luhrmann/. Accessed 8 October 2009.

Dawson, Jonathan (2001) 'The Fourth Wall Returns: *Moulin Rouge* and the Imminent Death of Cinema' *Senses of Cinema* 14 http://archive.sensesofcinema.com/contents/01/14/moulin_rouge.html. Accessed 30 January 2010.

Dennis, Jonathan & Bieringa, Jan (eds.) (1996) *Film in Aotearoa New Zealand*, Wellington: Victoria University Press.

Dermody, Susan & Jacka, Elizabeth (1988a) *The Screening of Australia: Anatomy of a National Cinema*, Paddington: Currency.

Dermody, Susan & Jacka, Elizabeth (1988b) *The Imaginary Industry: Australian Film in the Late 1980s*, North Ryde, NSW: Australian Film, Television and Radio School.

Dermody, Susan & Jacka, Elizabeth (1987) *The Screening of Australia: Anatomy of a Film Industry*, Paddington: Currency.

Duncan, Kath, Goggin, Gerard & Newell, Christopher (2005) 'Don't Talk About Me… Like I'm Not Here: Disability in Australian National Cinema', *Metro*, 146/147, pp. 152–9.

Dyer, Richard (2002) 'Entertainment and Utopia' in S Cohan (ed.) *Hollywood Musicals: The Film Reader* London & New York: Routledge, pp. 19–30.

Dzenis Anna (1999) 'Short Film.' in Ina Bertrand, Brian McFarlane & Geoff Mayer (eds.) *The Oxford Companion to Australian Film*, Melbourne: Oxford UP, pp. 447–50.

Edwards, Sam & Martin, Helen (1997), *New Zealand Film 1912–1996*, Auckland: Oxford University Press.

Ellis, Katie (2008) *Disabling Diversity: The Social Construction of Disability in 1990s Australian National Cinema*, Saarbrücken: VDM Verlag.

Ellis, Katie (2007) 'Disability as Visual Shorthand: Theme and Style in 1990s' Australian National Cinema', *Metro*, 152, pp. 135–9.

Ellis, Katie (2006) 'Rehabilitating 1990s Australian National Cinema: *The Sum of Us*' *Senses of Cinema*, 39. http://www.sensesofcinema.com/contents/06/39/rehab_australian_cinema_1990s.html. Accessed 30 January 2010.

Fielding, Raymond (1965) *The Technique of Special Effects Cinematography*, London: Focal Press.

Flanagan, Keith (1964) 'Outback Film Proved a Point', *The West Australian*, 2 November.

Freebury, J. (1987) 'Screening Australia: *Gallipoli*: A Study of Nationalism on Film' *Media Information Australia* 43, pp. 5–8.

Freiberg, Freda (1994) 'Lost in Oz? Jews in the Australian Cinema', *Continuum: the Australian Journal of Media & Culture* 8:2 pp. 196–205.

French, Lisa (2009) 'Poetry In Motion: The Short Film Form In Australia' in Amit Sarwal and Reema Sarwal, (eds.), *Creative Nation: Australian Cinema and Cultural Studies Reader*, SSS Publications: New Delhi, 2009: 83–98.

French, Lisa (ed.) (2003) *Womenvision, Women and the Moving Image In Australia*, Melbourne: Damned Publishing.

French, Lisa & Mark Poole (2009) *Shining a Light: 50 Years of the Australian Film Institute*, The Moving Image no. 9, St Kilda: Australian Teachers of Media.

Gardner, Anthony (2006) 'Monstrous Nationalism: *Wolf Creek* and the UnAustralian', paper presented at Monsters and the Monstrous: Myths and Metaphors of Enduring Evil 4th Global Conference, Mansfield College, Oxford, United Kingdom, 18–21 September. Available: http://www.wickedness.net/Monsters/M4/gardner%20paper.pdf [Accessed 27 March 2008].

Gibson, Ross (1992) *South of the West: Postcolonialism and the Narrative Construction of Australia*, Bloomington: Indiana University Press.

Gibson, Ross (1988) 'Formative Landscapes' in Scott Murray (ed.) *Back of Beyond : Discovering Australian Film and Television* Sydney : Australian Film Commission.

Gillard, Garry & Achimovich, Lois (2003) 'The Representation of Madness in Some Australian Films', *Journal of Critical Psychology Counselling and Psychotherapy* 3:1, pp. 5–19.

Gillespie, Pat (1995) 'Strictly Ballroom', in S. Murray (ed.) *Australian Film 1978–1994: A Survey of Theatrical Features*, Melbourne: Oxford University Press, p. 349.

Goggin, Gerard & Newell. Christopher. 'Imagining Diversity: Disability and Australian Film.' Proceedings of the Australian and New Zealand Communications Association (ANZCA) *Designing Communication for Diversity* conference. Queensland University of Technology, 9–11 July 2003.

Goldsmith, Ben (2009) 'Settings, Subjects and Stories: Creating Australian Cinema' in Amit Sarwal and Reema Sarwal (eds.) *Creative Nation: Australian Cinema and Cultural Studies*, New Delhi: SSS Publications, pp. 13–26.

Goldsmith, Ben (1997) 'Government, Film and the National Image: Reappraising the Australian Film Development Corporation' *Australian Studies* 12:1, pp. 98–114.

Gorbman, Claudia (1999), 'Music in *The Piano*', in Harriet Margolis (ed) *Jane Campion's The Piano*, Cambridge University Press, pp. 42–58.

Graham, Aaron W (2005) 'Great Directors: Richard Franklin', *Senses of Cinema*, May 2005, http://archive.sensesofcinema.com/contents/directors/05/franklin.html, accessed 27 October 2008.

Grant, B K (2007) 'Bringing It All Back Home – The Films of Peter Jackson', in Ian Conrich and Stuart Murray (eds.) *New Zealand Film-makers*, Detroit: Wayne State University Press, pp. 88–102.

Greer, Germaine (2008) 'Once upon a time in a land far, far, away', *The Guardian*, 16 December http://www.guardian.co.uk/film/2008/dec/16/baz-luhrmann-australia. Accessed 8 October, 2009.

Hall, Ken G (1977) *Directed by Ken G. Hall: Autobiography of an Australian Film Maker*. Melbourne: Lansdowne.

Hall, Sandra (1985) *Critical Business: The New Australian Cinema in Review*, Adelaide: Rigby.

Haltof, Marek (1993) 'In Quest of Self-Identity: Gallipoli, Mateship and the Construction of Australian National Identity' *Journal of Popular Film and Television* 21:1, pp. 27–38.

Hamilton, Peter & Mathews, Sue (1986) *American Dreams, Australian Movies*, Sydney: Currency.

Hardy, Ann (2006) 'The Accidental Author: Collaborative and Sequential Authorship in New Zealand Film Production', *Media Magazine* 148.

Harris, Richard (2007) *Film in the Age of Digital Distribution: The Challenge for Australian Content*, Strawberry Hills: Currency House.

Hart, Carol (2006) 'Portraits of Settler History in *The Proposition*' *Senses of Cinema* 38. http://archive.sensesofcinema.com/contents/06/38/proposition.html. Accessed 30 January 2010.

Harrison, Tony (2005) *Australian Film and TV Companion*, 2nd ed. Broadway, NSW: Citrus Press.

Hawker, Philippa ([1993]2008), '*Dead End Drive-In*', *Senses of Cinema* 48, http://archive.sensesofcinema.com/contents/08/48/dead-end-drive-in.html. Accessed 30 January 2010.

Herd, Nick (2004) *Chasing the Runaways: Foreign Film Production and Film Studio Development in Australia 1988–2002*, Strawberry Hills: Currency House.

Hergenhan, Laurie (1993) *Unnatural Lives: Studies in Australian Convict Fiction*, Revised ed. St Lucia: University of Queensland Press.

Hocking, Scott (ed.) (2006) *100 Greatest Films of Australian Cinema*, Richmond, Victoria: Scribal Publishing.

Hodsdon, Barrett (2001) *Straight Roads and Crossed Lines: The Quest for Film Culture in Australia from the 1960s*, Shenton Park, WA: Bernt Porridge Group.

Hoorn, Jeanette (2005) 'Comedy and Eros: Powell's Australian Films *They're a Weird Mob* and *Age of Consent*' *Screen* 46:1 pp. 73–84.

Horrocks, Roger (2009) *Art that Moves: the work of Len Lye*, Auckland: Auckland University Press.

Horrocks, Roger (1999) 'New Zealand Cinema: Cultures, Policies, Films', in Deb Verhoeven (ed), *Twin Peeks: Australian and New Zealand Feature Films*. Melbourne: Damned Publishing.

Horrocks, R. 1989. The creation of a film feature industry, in Stefano Toffetti & Jonathan Dennis (eds.) *Te Ao Marama*, Torino: Le Nuove Muse, pp. 100–3.

Horrocks, Roger & Perry, Nick (eds.) (2004) *Television in New Zealand: Programming the Nation*, Melbourne: Oxford University Press.

House of Representatives Standing Committee on Communication, Information Technology and the Arts (2004) *From Reel to Unreal: Future Opportunities for Australia's Film, Animation, Special Effects and Electronic Games Industries*, Canberra: The Committee.

Jancovich, Mark, Reboll, Antonio Lazaro, Stringer, Julian & Willis, Andy (eds.) (2003) *Defining Cult Movies: The Cultural Politics of Oppositional Taste*, Manchester & New York: Manchester University Press.

Jeffrey, Tom (ed.) (2006) *Film Business: A Handbook for Producers*, revised ed., Crows Nest, NSW: Allen & Unwin in association with the Australian Film, Television and Radio School.

Jennings, Karen (1993) *Sites of Difference: Cinematic Representations of Aboriginality and Gender*, Melbourne: Australian Film Commission.

Jones, Dorothy (1985) 'Winning and Losing: Australian Humour', in Pavel Petr, David Roberts & Philip Thomson (eds.) *Comic Relations: Studies in the Comic, Satire and Parody*, Frankfurt am Main: Verlag Peter Lang.

Jones, Stan (2006), 'Go, Ape! The Identity of New Zealand Filmmaking Post-*Rings*' *Metro Magazine* 148.

Kirkby, Diane (2007) ' "Ocker Sheilahs" and "Bloody Barmaids": *Caddie*, Biography and Gender History in 1970s Australian Historical Film' *Australian Historical Studies* 38, pp. 279–95.

Kitson, M (2003) 'The Great Aussie Car Smash at the End of the World' *Australian Screen Education* 31, pp. 64–9.

Kothari, Shuchi & Pearson, Sarina (2004) 'Film Excerpts: *A Taste of Place: Stories of food and Longing*,' in Michael Hanne (ed.) *Creativity in Exile*, Amsterdam: Rodopi.

Kroenert, Tim (2007), 'Reign of Terror', *Inside Film*,101, pp. 28–9.

Kuna, F & Strohmaier, P (2002) 'Australian Film: Policy, Text and Criticism' in Xavier Pons (ed.) *Departures: How Australia Reinvents Itself*, Melbourne: Melbourne University Press, pp. 112–25.

Laderman, David (2002) *Driving Vision: Exploring the Road Movie*, Austin, TX: University of Texas Press

Landman, Jane (2006) *The Tread of a White Man's Foot: Australian Pacific Colonialism and the Cinema, 1925–62*, Canberra: Pandanus Books.

Langton, Marcia (2008a) 'Faraway Downs Fantasy Resonates Close To Home', *The Age*, 23 November. http://www.theage.com.au/national/faraway-downs-fantasy-resonates-close-to-home-20081122-6eie.html. Accessed 8 October 2009.

Langton, Marcia (2008b) 'Why Greer is Wrong on *Australia*', *The Age*, 23 December, http://www.theage.com.au/opinion/why-greer-is-wrong-on-australia-20081222-73kk.html. Accessed 8 October 2009.

Langton, Marcia (2003) 'Grounded and Gendered: Aboriginal Women Australian Cinema', in Lisa French (ed.) *Womenvision: Women and the Moving Image in Australia*, Melbourne: Damned Publishing.

Langton, Marcia (1993) *Well, I Heard It On the Radio and I Saw It On the Television…: An Essay for the Australian Film Commission on the Politics and Aesthetics of Filmmaking By and About Aboriginal People and Things*, Sydney: Australian Film Commission.

Lanza Joseph (1994) *Elevator Music*, London: Quartet, p.11.

Larsen, David (2008) 'A Hint of Spices,' *Listener* 16 August: 43.

Laseur, Carol (1992) 'Australian Exploitation: the Politics of Bad Taste', *Continuum: The Australian Journal of Media and Culture*, vol. 5, no. 2, http://wwwmcc.murdoch.edu.au/ReadingRoom/5.2/Laseur.html. Accessed 27 October 2008.

Lawn, Jennifer (2006) 'Warping the familiar', in Misha Kavka, Jennifer Lawn and Mary Paul (eds.) *Gothic NZ: The darker side of kiwi culture* (pp. 11–21). Dunedin: Otago University Press.

Lawson, Sylvia ([1969]1985) 'Australian Film, 1969', republished in Albert Moran & Tom O'Regan (eds.) *An Australian Film Reader*, Sydney: Currency Press, pp.175–83.

Lealand, Geoff (1988) *A Foreign Egg in Our Nest?: American Popular Culture in New Zealand. Wellington: Victoria University Press.*

Lealand, Geoff & Martin, Helen (2005) 'The National Cinema of Aotearoa/New Zealand', *Screen Education* 39.

Levy, Wayne (1995) *The Book of the Film, and the Film of the Book: A Bibliography of Australian Cinema and TV*, Melbourne: Academia Press.

Lindley, Arthur (2003) 'Translations of the Flesh: International Relations as Romantic Comedy in Recent Australian and British Film' *Senses of Cinema* 28, http://archive.sensesofcinema.com/contents/03/28/oz_brit_romantic_comedy.html Accessed 30 January 2010.

Lohrey, Amanda (1982) 'Australian Mythologies – Gallipoli: Male Innocence as Marketable Commodity' *Island Magazine* 9:10, pp. 29–34.

Long, Chris. (1995a), 'Australia's First Films: Part Fifteen – *Under Southern Skies* (1902)', *Cinema Papers* 106 (October), pp.38–41, 54–5.

Long, Chris (1995b) 'Australia's First Films: New Light on the Limelight Department', *Cinema Papers* 107 (December), pp.34–7.

Long, Chris & Sowry, Clive (1994) 'Australia's First Films: Facts and Fables, Part Eight: *Soldiers of the Cross*: Milestones and Myths' *Cinema Papers* no. 99, pp. 60–67, 82–3.

Longmore, Paul (1987). 'Screening Stereotypes: Images of Disabled People in Television and Motion Pictures' in Alan Gartner & Tom Joe (eds.) *Images of the Disabled, Disabling Images,* New York: Praeger, pp. 65–78.

Lucas, Rose (1998) 'Dragging it Out: Tales of Masculinity in Australian Cinema, from *Crocodile Dundee* to *The Adventures of Priscilla, Queen of the Desert*' *Journal of Australian Studies* 22:56, pp. 138–46.

Luhrmann, Baz (2002) 'Welcome to a Garden of Earthly Delights…', DVD Booklet, *Moulin Rouge!* DVD, Twentieth Century Fox Home Entertainment, region 4.

McDonald, Lawrence (1993) A Critique of the Judgement of Bad Taste or Beyond Braindead Criticism: The Films of Peter Jackson. *Illusions*, 21–22 (Winter): 9–15.

McDonnell, Brian (2007) *On Reflection: New Zealand film reviews from North & South, 1986–1993*, London: Kakapo Press.

McDouall, Hamish (2009), *100 Essential New Zealand Films*, Wellington: Awa Press.

McFarlane, Brian (2008) 'There's a Lot Going on in *Australia*', *Metro Magazine* no. 159: 10–15.

McFarlane, Brian (1987) *Australian Cinema 1970–85*, Melbourne: William Heinemann Australia.

McFarlane, Brian (1987) *Australian Cinema*, New York: Columbia University Press.

McFarlane, Brian & Mayer, Geoff (1992) *New Australian Cinema: Sources and Parallels in American and British Film*, Cambridge: Cambridge University Press.

McFarlane, Brian, Mayer, Geoff & Bertrand, Ina (eds.) (1999) *The Oxford Companion to Australian Film*, Melbourne and New York: Oxford University Press.

McGilligan, Pat (1986) 'Under Weir... and Theroux' *Film Comment* 22:6, pp. 23–32.

Maher, Sean (2004) *The Internationalisation of Australian Film and Television through the 1990s*, Sydney: Australian Film Commission.

Malone, Peter (ed.) (2001) *Myth & Meaning: Australian Film Directors In Their Own Words*, Strawberry Hills: Currency.

Malone, Peter (1977) 'Baz on the Bard', *Eureka Street*, March: 44–6.

Margolis, Harriet, Cubitt, Sean, King, Barry & Jutel, Thierry (eds.) (2008) *Studying the Event Film: The Lord of the Rings*, Manchester: Manchester University Press.

Martin, Adrian (2003) *The Mad Max Movies*, Sydney: Currency Press.

Mason, B (1981) *Bruce Mason Solo*. Wellington: Price Milburn.

Matthews, Philip (2008) 'No miracles, only curses: Rain of the Children'. Available at: http://secondstogo.b ogspot.com/2008/08/im-stranger-here-myself-vincent-ward.html. Accessed 18 March 2010.

Mathijs, Ernest (ed.) (2006) *The Lord of the Rings: Popular Culture in Global Context*, London: Wallflower Press.

Mayer, Geoff (1983) 'Turkey Shoot' *Cinema Papers* 42, 69–71.

Mayer, Geoff & Beattie, Keith (eds.) (2007) *The Cinema of Australia and New Zealand*, London and New York: Wallflower Press.

Mills, Jane (2001) *The Money Shot: Cinema, Sin and Censorship*, Annandale, NSW: Pluto Press.

Mirams, Gordon (1945) *Speaking Candidly: Films and People in New Zealand*, Hamilton: Pauls Book Arcade.

Mitchell, Tony (1996) *Popular Music and Local Identity: Pop, Rock and Rap in Europe and Oceania*, London: University of Leicester Press.

Mitchell, Tony (1984a) '*Utu*: A New Zealand Revenge Tragedy.' *Film Criticism* 8(3): 47–53.

Mitchell, Tony (1984b) 'Vincent Ward: The eloquence of isolation' *Art New Zealand* 30, Autumn: 36–39.

Molloy, Bruce (1990) *Before the Interval: Australian Mythology and Feature Films, 1930–1960*, St Lucia: University of Queensland Press.

Moore, Tony (2005) *The Barry McKenzie Films*, Sydney: Currency Press.

Moran, Albert (ed.) (1993) *Film Policy: An Australian Reader*, Brisbane: Institute for Cultural Policy Studies.

Moran, Albert (1991) *Projecting Australia: Government Film since 1945*, Sydney: Currency Press.

Moran, Albert & O'Regan, Tom (eds.) (1985) *An Australian Film Reader*, Sydney: Currency Press.

Moran, Albert & O'Regan, Tom (eds.) (1989) *The Australian Screen*, Ringwood, Vic: Penguin.

Moran, Albert & Vieth, Errol (2005) *Historical Dictionary of Australian and New Zealand Cinema*, Lanham, MD: Scarecrow.

Moran, Albert & Vieth, Errol (2006) *Film in Australia: An introduction*, Cambridge University Press: Cambridge.

Morris, Jenny (1997) 'A Feminist Perspective.' in Ann Pointon and Chris Davies (eds.) *Framed*. London: British Film Institute, pp. 21–30.

Morris, Meaghan (1998) 'White Panic or *Mad Max* and the Sublime', in Kuan-Hsing Chen (ed.) *Trajectories: Inter-Asia Cultural Studies*, London: Routledge, pp. 239–62.

Mudie, Peter (1997) *Ubu Films: Sydney Underground Movies 1965–1970*, Kensington, NSW: University of New South Wales Press.

Murray, Scott (ed.) (1995) *Australian Film 1978–1994: A Survey of Theatrical Features*, Melbourne: Oxford University Press in association with the Australian Film Commission.

Murray, Scott (ed.) (1994) *Australian Cinema*, St Leonards, NSW: Allen & Unwin in association with the Australian Film Commission.

Murray, Scott (ed.) (1980) *The New Australian Cinema*, West Melbourne: Nelson.

Neale, Steve (2000) *Genre and Hollywood*, London: Routledge.

Neill, Sam & Rymer,Judy (directors) (1995) *Cinema of Unease* [video recording], London: British Film Institute.

New Zealand Film Commission (NZFC) (2007) Newsletter, October, http://www.nzfilm.co.nz/NewsAndMedia/NZFilmNewsletter/Complete_Newsletter.aspx?nodeAliasPath=/NewsAndMedia/NZFilmNewsletter/Newsletters/NZ_Film_News_October_2007. Accessed 22 September 2009.

New Zealand Film Commission (NZFC) (2005) *Annual Report*, http://www.parliament.nz/NR/rdonlyres/FBC53B84-B656-4784-8782-9F345183B2B9/19379/DBHOH_PAP_12891_9092.pdf. Accessed 23 September 2009.

Nicoll, Fiona (2001) *From Diggers to Drag Queens: Configurations of Australian National Identity*, Sydney: Pluto Press.

Nikro, S (2001) 'The Self as Stranger: Re-viewing *The Cars That Ate Paris*' *Southerly* 61:1, pp. 13–17.

O'Donoghue, Darragh (2008) '*Strictly Ballroom* (Baz Luhrmann, 1992)', Iconic Moments in Cinema: Australia, Part 1, *Senses of Cinema*, issue 49, http://archive.sensesofcinema.com/contents/08/49/iconic-moments-australian-cinema.html. Accessed 9 October, 2009.

O'Regan, Tom (2000) 'Australian Film in the 1970s: The Ocker and the Quality Film', Murdoch University, , http://wwwmcc.murdoch.edu.au/ReadingRoom/film/1970s/html. Accessed 22 July 2008.

O'Regan, Tom (1996) *Australian National Cinema*, London, New York: Routledge.

O'Regan, Tom (1989) 'Cinema Oz: the ocker films', in Albert Moran &Tom O'Regan (eds.) *The Australian Screen*, Ringwood: Penguin, 1989, pp. 75–98.

O'Shea, John (1999) *Don't Let It Get You: Memories—Documents*, Wellington: Victoria University Press.

Parsons, Fred. (1973) *A Man Called Mo*. Melbourne: Heinemann.

Partridge, Des (2008) 'Quentin Tarantino Backs Mark Hartley's Ozploitation Doco', *The Courier Mail*, 31 July, http://www.news.com.au/couriermail/story/0,,24101258-5003420,00.html

Pearlman, Karen (2009) 'Genre is not a Dirty Word', *Limina* no. 1, p. 83.

Penberthy, James (1966) '*The Genius in a battered Buick*', *The Sunday Times*, 24 July. Accessed 20 October 2008.

Pender, Anne (2005) 'The Mythical Australian: Barry Humphries, Gough Whitlam and the 'New Nationalism'' *Australian Journal of Politics and History* 51:1, pp. 67–78.

Petrie, Duncan (2007) *Shot in New Zealand: The Art and Craft of the New Zealand Cinematographer*, Auckland: Random House.

Petrie, Duncan & Stuart, Duncan (2008) *A Coming of Age: 30 Years of New Zealand Cinema*, Auckland: Random House.

Pihama, Leonie (1999) 'Constructions of Maori in *The Piano*', in Harriet Margolis, *Jane Campion's* The Piano, New York: Cambridge University Press, pp. 114–234.

Pike, Andrew & Cooper, Ross (1998) *Australian Film, 1900–1977. A Guide to Feature Film Production*, revised edition, Melbourne: Oxford University Press.

Porter, Dorothy (2000) 'It's too hard to write good – I'd rather write bad', *Australian Humanities Review*, http://www.australianhumanitiesreview.org/archive/Issue-March-2000/porter.html. Accessed 18 March 2010.

Prescott, Nick (2005) 'All We See and All We Seem…' Australian Cinema and National Landscape' Flinders University eprint, http://dspace.flinders.edu.au/dspace/bitstream/2328/1565/1/N_Prescott.pdf. Accessed 18 March 2010.

Radnor, Hilary, Fox, Alistair & Bessiere, Irene (eds.) (2009) *Jane Campion: Cinema, Nation, Identity*, Detroit: Wayne State University.

Rains, Stephanie (2007) 'Journeys through the unfamiliar in the films of Vincent Ward', in Ian Conrich & Stuart Murray (eds.) *New Zealand film-makers*, Detroit, MI: Wayne State University Press, pp. 273–88.

Rattigan, Neil (1991) *Images of Australia: 100 Films of the New Australian Cinema*, Dallas: Southern Methodist University Press.

Rattigan, Neil (1938) '*Crocodile Dundee*: Apotheosis of the Ocker' *Journal of Popular Film & Television*, 15:4 pp. 148–55.

Rayner, Jonathan (2005) 'Terror Australis': Areas of Horror in the Australian Cinema', in Steven Jay Schneider & Tony Williams (eds.) *Horror international*, Detroit, IO: Wayne State University Press.

Rayner, Jonathan (2000) *Contemporary Australian Cinema: An Introduction*, Manchester: Manchester University Press.

Read, Lynette (2006) 'New Zealand Film: National Identity and the Films of Vincent Ward', *Metro Magazine* 148.

Read, Lynette (2004) *Vincent Ward: The Emergence of an Aesthetic*, PhD Thesis. Available at: http://researchspace.auckland.ac.nz. Accessed 1 March 2010.

Reade, Eric (1979) *History and Heartburn: The Saga of Australian Film 1896–1978*, Sydney: Harper and Row.

Rekhari, Suneeti (2008) 'The "Other" in Film: Exclusions of Aboriginal Identity from Australian Cinema' *Visual Anthropology* 21:2 pp. 125–35

Reid, Mary-Anne (1999) *More Long Shots: Australian Cinema Successes in the 1990s*, Sydney and Brisbane: Australian Film Commission and Australian Key Centre for Cultural and Media Policy.

Reid, Mary-Anne (1993) *Long Shots to Favourites: Australian Cinema Successes in the 1990s*, North Sydney: Australian Film Commission.

Reid, Nicholas (1986) *A Decade of New Zealand Film: 'Sleeping Dogs' to 'Came A Hot Friday'*, Dunedin: John McIndoe.

Rene, Roy (1945) *Mo's Memoirs*, Melbourne: Reed and Harris.

Reynaud, Daniel (2007) *Celluloid ANZACs: The Great War Through Australian Cinema*, Melbourne: Australian Scholarly Publishing.

Reynaud, Daniel (2005) *The Hero of the Dardanelles and Other World War I Silent Dramas* Canberra: Research and Academic Outreach National Film and Sound Archive Monographs.

Reynaud, Daniel (1999) 'Convention and Contradiction: Representations of Women in Australian War Films 1914–1918', *Australian Historical Studies*, 29:113, pp. 215–30.

Routt, William D. (2001) 'More Australian than Aristotelian: The Australian Bushranger Film 1904–1914.' *Senses of Cinema* 18 (January-February 2001) http://www.sensesofcinema.com/contents/01/18/oz_western.html. Accessed 13 November 2009.

Rustin, Emily (2001) 'Romance and Sensation in The "Glitter" Cycle', in Ian Craven (ed.) *Australian Cinema in the 1990s*, Oxford: Frank Cass, pp. 133–48.

Ryan, Mark David (2009) 'Whither Culture? Australian Horror Films And The Limitations Of Cultural Policy', *Media International Australia: Incorporating Culture and Policy*, 133, pp. 43–55.

Ryan, Mark David (2008a) *A Dark New World: Anatomy Of Australian Horror Films*, PhD Dissertation, Queensland University of Technology. Available: http://eprints.qut.edu.au/18351/1/Thesis.pdf . Accessed 18 March 2010.

Ryan, Mark David (2008b), 'Writing Aussie horror: an interview with Shayne Armstrong and Shane Krause', *Metro*, 159, pp.46–8.

Ryan, Tom (2008) 'Tom Ryan in Conversation with Mark Hartley', *The Monthly Online: Australian Politics, Society and Culture*, Slow TV, transcript http://www.themonthly.com.au/tm/node/1164. Accessed 3 December 2008.

Ryan, Tom (1999) 'The State of Australian Cinema Since *Shine*' *Positif* 458, pp. 82–5.

Sabine, James (ed.) (1995) *A Century of Australian Cinema*, Port Melbourne: Mandarin Australia.

Sarwal, Amit & Sarwal, Reema (eds.) (2009) *Creative Nation: Australian Cinema and Cultural Studies Reader*, New Delhi: SSS Publications.

Schafer, William J (1998) *Mapping the Godzone: A Primer on New Zealand Literature and Culture*. Honolulu: University of Hawai'i Press.

Shuchi Kothari & Sarina Pearson (2004) 'Film Excerpts: *A Taste of Place: Stories of food and Longing*,' in Michael Hanne (ed.) *Creativity in Exile*, Amsterdam, New York: Rodopi.

Sconce, Jeffrey (1995) 'Trashing' the Academy: Taste, Excess and Emerging Politics of Cinematic Style', in Ernest Mathijs & Xavier Mendik (eds.) *The Cult Film Reader*, Maidenhead, UK: Open University Press.

Seidman, Steve (1981) *Comedian Comedy: A Tradition in Hollywood Film*. Ann Arbor, MI: UMI Research.

Shakespeare, Tom (1999) 'Arts and Lies' in Marian Corker & Sally French (eds.) *Disability Discourse*, Buckingham: Open University Press, pp. 164–72.

Sheckels, Theodore F. (2002) *Celluloid Heroes Down Under: Australian Film 1970–2000*, Westport, CT: Praeger.

Shelton, Lindsay (2005) *The Selling of New Zealand Movies*, Wellington: Awa Press.

Sheppard, Deborah (2000) *Reframing: A History of New Zealand Film Women*, Auckland: HarperCollins.

Shirley, Graham & Adams, Brian (1989) *Australian Cinema: The First Eighty Years*, Sydney: Currency.

Sibley, Brian (2006) *Peter Jackson: A Film-Maker's Journey*, London: HaperCollins.

Simpson, Catherine, Murawska, Renata & Lambert, Anthony (eds.) (2009) *Diasporas of Australian Cinema*, Bristol and Chicago: Intellect.

Sobchack, Vivian (1987) *Images of Wonder: The Look of Science Fiction*, New York: Unger.

Sowry, Clive (1984) *Film Making in New Zealand: A Brief Historical Survey*, Wellington: New Zealand Film Archive.

Speed, Lesley (2008) 'The Comedian Comedies: George Wallace's 1930s Comedies, Australian Cinema and Hollywood' *Metro* 158 pp. 76–82.

Speed, Lesley (2005) 'Life as a Pizza: The Comic Traditions of the Wogsploitation Films' *Metro Magazine* nos. 146–47, pp. 136–44.

Starrs, D Bruno (2008) 'Enabling the Auteurial Voice in *Dance Me to My Song*' *M/C Journal*, 11:3 http://journal.media-culture.org.au/index.php/mcjournal/article/viewArticle/49. Accessed 30 January 2010.

Stratton, David (1990) *The Avocado Plantation: Boom and Bust in the Australian Film Industry*, Chippendale, NSW: Pan Macmillan.

Stratton, David (1980) *The Last New Wave: The Australian Film Revival*, London, Sydney: Angus & Robertson.

Sutherland, Romy (2005) 'Peter Weir' *Senses of Cinema* http://archive.sensesof cinema.com/contents/directors/05/weir.html. Accessed 30 January 2010.

Telotte, J P (1991) 'Beyond All Reason: The Nature of the Cult', in J P Telotte (ed.) *The Cult Film Experience*, Austin, Texas: University of Texas Press.

Teo, Stephen (2001) 'Australia's Role in the Global Kung-Fu Trend: *The Man from Hong Kong*' *Senses of Cinema* 16 http://archive.sensesofcinema.com/contents/cteq/01/16/man_hk.html. Accessed 30 January 2010

Thomas, Deborah (2009) 'Tarantino's Two-Thumbs Up: Ozploitation and the Reframing of the Aussie Genre Film' *Metro* 161, pp. 90–5.

Thoms, Albie (2000) *Surfmovies: The History of the Surf Film in Australia*, Noosa Heads, Qld: Shore Thing.

Thoms, Albie (1978) *Polemics for a New Cinema*, Sydney: Wild & Woolley.

Thornley, Davinia (2009) 'Talking Film, Talking Identity', *European Journal of Cultural Studies* 12:1.

Tincknell, Estella (2000) 'New Zealand Gothic? Jane Campion's *The Piano*', in Ian Conrich & David Woods (eds.) *New Zealand: A Pastoral Paradise?* Notthingam: Kakapo Books, pp. 107–19.

Totaro, Paola (2008) 'Now Baz Feels the Wrath of Greer', *The Sydney Morning Herald*, 17 December, http://www.smh.com.au/news/entertainment/film/now-baz-feels-the-wrath-of-greer/2008/12/16/1229189620786.html. Accessed 8 October, 2009.

Tsiolkas, Christos (2002) 'Through Clouds: A Discussion of *Kandahar* and *Beneath Clouds*' *Senses of Cinema* 20 http://archive.sensesofcinema.com/contents/02/20/kandahar.html. Accessed 30 January 2010.

Tulloch, John (1982) *Australian Cinema: Industry, Narrative and Meaning*, Sydney: George Allen & Unwin.

Tulloch, John (1981) *Legends on the Screen: The Australian Narrative Cinema 1919–29*, Sydney: Currency Press.

Turnbull, Sue (2008) 'Mapping the vast suburban tundra: Australian comedy from Dame Edna to Kath and Kim', *International Journal of Cultural Studies* 11.1: 15–32.

Turner Graeme (1997) 'Australian Film and National Identity in the 1990s' in Geoffrey Stokes (ed.) *The Politics of Identity in Australia*, Melbourne: Cambridge University Press, pp. 185–92.

Turner Graeme (1989) 'Art Directing History: The Australian Period Film', in Albert Moran & Tom O'Regan (eds.) *The Australian Screen*. Melbourne: Penguin, 1989.

Turner, Graeme (1986) *National Fictions: Literature, Film, and the Construction of Australian Narrative*, Sydney: Allen & Unwin.

Turnour, Quentin (2005) 'Contexts in Which to Place *They're a Weird Mob* and Into Which You Might Never Have Placed It Before' *Senses of Cinema* 36, http://archive.sensesofcinema.com/contents/cteq/05/36/weird_mob.html. Accessed 30 January 2010.

TV3 (2009) *Full interview with Firaaq writer Suchi Kothari*, http://www.3news.co.nz/Full-interview-with-Firaaq-writer-Shuchi-Kothari/tabid/337/articleID/111568/cat/101/Default.aspx; accessed 9 September 2009

Urban, Andrew et al. (1998) *Dance Me to My Song*. Urbancinefile. Available: http://www.urbancinefile.com.au/home/view.asp?Article_ID=1656. July 2004.

Urban Cinephile (2009) 'Australia Beats Babe Box Office', News, *Urban Cinefile*, 26 February, http://www.urbancinefile.com.au/home/view.asp?a=15443&s=News_Files_Archives. Accessed 16 October 2009.

Urban Cinephile (nd)'Ozploitation Season at the Chauvel', Urban Cinefile, http://www.urbancinefile.com.au/home/view.asp?a=14628&s=News_Files_Archives . Accessed 17 February 2010.

Vanderbent, Saskia (2006) *Australian Film*, Harpenden: Pocket Essentials.

Van Leeuwen, Theo (1998) 'Emotional times: the music of *The Piano*,' in Rebecca Coyle (ed) *Screen scores: studies in contemporary Australian film music*, Sydney: AFTRS/Allen & Unwin, 1998, pp. 39–48.

Verhoeven, Deb (2009) *Jane Campion* London: Routledge.

Verhoeven, Deb (2006a) *Sheep and the Australian Cinema*, Carlton: Melbourne University Press.

Verhoeven, Deb (2006b) 'Film and Video', in Stuart Cunningham and Graeme Turner (eds.), *The Media and Communications in Australia*, (2nd Ed), Sydney: Allen & Unwin.

Verhoeven, Deb (ed.) (1999a) *Twin Peeks: Australian and New Zealand Feature Films*, Melbourne: Damned Publishing.

Verhoeven, Deb (1999b). 'When Familiarity Breeds... Ken G.Hall, Disability and National Cinema', in Deb Verhoeven (ed.) *Twin Peaks*. Melbourne: Damned Publishing, pp. 51–68.

Verhoeven, Deb (1995) 'The Film I Would Like to Make: In Search of a Cinema (1927–1970)', in J. Sabine (ed.) *A Century of Australian Cinema*, Port Melbourne: Mandarin Australia, pp. 130–153.

Walton, Storry (2005) *Shooting Through: Australian Film and the Brain Drain*, Strawberry Hills: Currency House.

Williams, Deane (2008) *Australian Post-War Documentary Film: An Arc of Mirrors*, Bristol & Chicago: Intellect Books.

Wilson, Jake (2003) 'Unpopular Populism or The Decline and Fall of the Little Aussie Battler: Notes on Australian Film Comedy in 2003' *Senses of Cinema* 29 http://archive.sensesofcinema.com/contents/03/29/australian_comedy.html. Accessed 30 January 2010.

Wong, Tim (2006) 'Out of the mist', *Landfall* 211, Autumn.

Wu, Harmony H (2003) 'Trading in horror, cult and matricide: Peter Jackson phenomenal bad taste and New Zealand fantasies of inter/national cinematic success', in by Mark Janchovich et al. (eds.) *Defining Cult Movies*, Manchester: Manchester University Press, pp. 84–108.

Wright, Robin (1995) *Developing Our Own Space: Place and Identity in Recent Australian Cinema*, London: Sir Robert Menzies Centre for Australian Studies.

AUSTRALIA & NEW ZEALAND CINEMA ONLINE

Australian Cinema Online

Australian Centre for the Moving Image
http://www.acmi.net.au/default.aspx
ACMI evolved from the Victorian State Film Centre to become a major cultural venue in Melbourne dedicated to the moving image – cinema, television and digital culture. The Centre hosts exhibitions, film festivals, live events, educational programmes, and creative workshops. ACMI is also a major archive, with substantial holdings of film prints and related materials.

Australian Cinematographers' Society
http://www.cinematographer.org.au/home
The ACS is the professional association for Australian cinematographers. The website contains information about the society, technological developments, and discussion of the past and present of Australian cinema from a cinematographer's perspective.

Australian Directors' Guild
http://www.adg.org.au
The ADG (formerly the Australian Screen Directors' Association) is the professional association for film, television and digital media directors, documentary makers, animators, assistant directors and independent producers. The website contains information about events of interest to members including the guild's annual conference, news, and resources for directors.

Australian Film Institute
http://www.afi.org.au
Founded in 1958, the AFI is Australia's foremost screen culture organization. The website contains information about the annual AFI Awards, Australian films currently screening in cinemas, and a collection of short films available for viewing by members.

Australian Film Institute Research Collection
http://www.afiresearch.rmit.edu.au/
The Australian Film Institute Research Collection is a non-lending, specialist film and television industry archive. The Collection is open to the public and housed at RMIT University in Melbourne. The website contains information about the collection, and a searchable catalogue.

Australian Film, Television and Radio School
http://www.aftrs.edu.au
The AFTRS is the national centre for professional education and advanced training in film, broadcasting and interactive media for Australian citizens and permanent residents. The school's main campus is at Moore Park in Sydney, adjacent to the Fox Studios Australia site. The school also has offices in each Australian state. The website contains information about current courses, research, and events, news about the achievements of alumni, and video and audio content, and the search-able catalogue of the Jerzy Toeplitz library, which contains a large collection of scripts, books, magazines and journals on Australian and international cinema.

Australian Screen
http://aso.gov.au/
Australian Screen is an outreach program of the National Film and Sound Archive. The site provides access to information and educational resources about Australian film and television, including excerpts from a broad range of feature films, documentaries, television programmes, newsreels, short films, animations and home movies. Many of the entries are accompanied by teachers' notes to enable their use in secondary and tertiary programmes.

Culture and Communication Reading Room
http://wwwmcc.murdoch.edu.au/ReadingRoom/
This website, developed by students at Murdoch University, is no longer updated, but is still a valuable archive of writing, reviews and analyses of Australian film, radio and television, cultural policy and cultural studies.

Directory of World Cinema
http://worldcinemadirectory.org/
The website for the Directory of World Cinema series featuring film reviews and biographies of directors. An ideal starting point for students of World Cinema.

Inside Film
http://www.if.com.au
Inside Film is a monthly magazine which covers the production, distribution and exhibition of Australian films, as well as technological developments. The website contains news stories, employment information, video content and information about Australian films currently in production.

National Film and Sound Archive
http://www.nfsa.gov.au/
The NFSA is Australia's principal audiovisual archive, based in Canberra. The website contains information about the Archive's national screening and access programmes, information about preservation activities, educational and online learning resources, and searchable catalogue of the Archive's collection of over 1.3 million items.

Screen Australia
http://www.screenaustralia.gov.au/
Screen Australia is the principal federal government agency assisting the
production, promotion, development and distribution of Australian films,
documentaries and television programmes. The agency was formed in 2008
following the merger of the former agencies: the Australian Film Commission,
the Film Finance Corporation, and Film Australia. The agency also conducts
research and collects statistics on aspects of Australian film and television, with
much of this work published online via the annual National Production Survey,
and the regularly updated service Get the Picture.

Screen Hub
http://www.screenhub.com.au
Screen Hub is a subscription-based service for industry professionals and
researchers. The site provides news about the industry in Australia and New
Zealand, and regular jobs and events bulletins.

Screening the Past
http://www.latrobe.edu.au/screeningthepast/
Screening the Past is an international refereed online journal of screen history.
The journal publishes articles on all aspects of world cinema history, with a
particular interest in Australian cinema and screen culture.

Senses of Cinema
http://www.sensesofcinema.com
Senses of Cinema is an Australian-based online journal of cinema. The journal
includes articles on all aspects of world cinema, though it has a particular interest
in Australian cinema past and present. The journal also focuses on particular
films or bodies of work (through articles and regular sections 'Cteq Annotations'
and 'Great Directors'), as well as on film theory and philosophy, and reports on
film festivals.

Urban Cinefile
http://www.urbancinefile.com.au
Website covering world cinema, from an Australian perspective. The site is
edited by Australian critic and film writer Andrew Urban, and contains news and
reviews of films and DVDs released in Australia (including over 400 reviews of
Australian films), interviews with filmmakers, and competitions.

Women in Film and Television
http://www.wift.org/index.html
WIFT was founded in 1982 to support women working in the screen industries
in Australia. The website contains information about membership, the annual
WOW Festival, a calendar of events, and information about the Mentor Scheme,
a programme established to provide opportunities for women entering the
screen industries to gain professional mentoring, with the aim of redressing the
gender imbalance in Australian film and television.

New Zealand Cinema Online

New Zealand On Screen
www.nzonscreen.com/
A site which offers access to the back catalogue of the best of New Zealand-produced film and television, for both local and overseas users. Content is arranged under themes, or you can troll through full episodes of older TV programmes, or part or full films, or read interviews and profiles. An initiative from the funding agency New Zealand On Air.

New Zealand Film Commission
www.nzfilm.co.nz
The site for the New Zealand film-funding agency (established 1978). A source for news of locally-made film, funding decisions, box office statistics, and teaching resources. Most recently, there will news of the 2009 review of the Commission, led by Peter Jackson. One particularly useful resource on the site is *New Zealand Film Commission: Teacher's Guide*, written by Geoff Lealand and Sandra Chesterman.

Film New Zealand
www.filmnz.com/
Information on New Zealand film locations and infrastructure. A featured story on the site, in January 2010, explored the reasons why James Cameron chose to create much of his blockbuster *Avatar* in New Zealand.

The New Zealand Film Archive
www.filmarchive.org.nz
Collects, protects and projects New Zealand's film and television history. Based in Wellington, New Zealand. Runs exhibitions and screenings, and offers support to researchers and students.

New Zealand On Air
www.nzonair.govt.nz
Government-funded agency which funds local television programming, public service radio and New Zealand-made music. Often invests in local film-making, in the expectation that such films will get television screenings.

Maori Television Service
www.maoritelevision.com/
State-funded channel (now two channels) established in 2003, to sustain and promote Maori language and Maori interests. Generally regarded as a essential part of the New Zealand mediascape.

The Moving Image Centre
http://mic.org.nz/
Auckland-based centre for the celebration of media and interdisciplinary arts.

Screen Production and Development Association (SPADA)
www.spada.co.nz
The professional body of the New Zealand screen industry. Offers structural, legal and moral support for New Zealand film and television producers, as well as running its annual industry conference.

Onfilm
www.onfim.co.nz
A long-established, monthly print magazine for the New Zealand screen industry, with features, profies and full in-production details. The website offers additional material: a January 2010 article featured an interview with Peter Jackson about the making of his *The Lovely Bones*.

The Lumiere Reader
www.lumiere.net.nz/reader
A New Zealand online journal dedicated to film criticism and review of the arts. Includes commentary and editorials, features, interviews, reviews and essays – on cinema in New Zealand and abroad.

Mediascape
www.mediascape.ac.nz
A site rich in resources on the New Zealand screen industry. Features a detailed bibliography of New Zealand film resources. The site is a venture of the New Zealand Broadcasting School (Christchurch).

Illusions
www.illusions.org.nz
Access to the New Zealand print journal, which features scholarly articles on New Zealand film and the performing arts. Published three times per year.

New Zealand Film
www.zeroland.co.nz/new_zealand_film.html
A site for accessing a wide range of New Zealand film resources.

Screen Directors Guild of New Zealand
www.sdgnz.co.nz
Resources and information on the screen industry in New Zealand. Includes material from the SDGNZ print journal *Take*.

TEST YOUR
KNOWLED

Questions

1. With which film-making organisation did Cecil Holmes begin his career?
2. Who wrote the novel on which Michael Powell's 1969 film *Age of Consent* was based?
3. What is the name of the feature film of which Peter Weir's short film *Michael* forms part?
4. Name the actor who won an Oscar for their role in *The Year of Living Dangerously*?
5. Which three films make up Baz Luhrmann's 'Red Curtain Trilogy'?
6. Which celebrated editor cut Baz Luhrmann's first three films, and was nominated for an Oscar for her work on *Moulin Rouge!*?
7. What is the name of Hugh Jackman's character in *Australia*?
8. Who was the co-writer and star of *Dance Me to My Song*?
9. Name the two actors who play David Helfgott in *Shine*?
10. Who directed *Peel: An Exercise in Self Discipline*, which won the Palme D'Or for Best Short Film at the Cannes Film Festival in 1986?
11. In which year was the Australian Film, Television and Radio School founded?
12. Which Academy Award-nominated Australian film is set during the Korean War?
13. Which Australian film, made in 1906, has been entered on UNESCO's Memory of the World register?
14. Name the director and star of the 1970 film *Ned Kelly*?
15. How many cinematographers did Charles Chauvel employ in making *Forty Thousand Horsemen*?
16. What is the title of the short story on which Ray Lawrence's film *Jindabyne* is based, and who was the author?
17. Who plays the title role in Geoffrey Wright's *Macbeth*?
18. What is the name of the visual effects technique invented by the director of *For the Term of His Natural Life*, Norman Dawn?
19. What unfortunate record was set by the prison film *Stir* at the 1980 AFI Awards?
20. Who or what was the Heidelberg School?
21. On which day do the girls disappear in *Picnic at Hanging Rock*?
22. Who produced Gillian Armstrong's film *My Brilliant Career*?
23. *Strike Me Lucky* starred which hugely popular comedian in his first and only feature film?
24. How many feature films starring vaudeville comedian George Wallace did FW Thring direct?
25. The Production Designer of *Crocodile Dundee* was also the Art Director of *Mad Max 2*. Who is he?
26. In *Muriel's Wedding*, where does Muriel's husband David come from, and why does he want to marry her?

GE

27. What is the name of the character played by Noah Taylor in *The Year My Voice Broke*, and what was the title of the sequel?
28. Name the director and cinematographer of *Somersault*?
29. Which two monster crocodile films were released in 2007?
30. The horror film *Cut* features a cameo by which Australian actor and musician?
31. What are the first names of the Spierig brothers, directors of *Undead*?
32. What is the name of Keith Adams' faithful fox terrier and star of *Northern Safari*?
33. The docudrama *Wrong Side of the Road* features which two Indigenous bands?
34. What are the names of the leaders of the outlaw gangs in *Mad Max* and *Mad Max 2*?
35. Why does Barry go to London in *The Adventures of Barry McKenzie*?
36. Which Australian director of photography, nicknamed the 'Heidelberg cinematographer', shot *Picnic at Hanging Rock*, *The Man from Hong Kong*, *Crocodile Dundee* and *Backroads*, among many others?
37. Which 1977 film is widely regarded as initiating the renaissance in New Zealand cinema?
38. Who was the writer-director of *In My Father's Den*?
39. Name the two lead actors and the characters they play in *Once Were Warriors*?
40. *Sons for the Return Home* (1979) and *River Queen* (2005) were shot by which celebrated New Zealand cinematographer?
41. What is the name of the lead character and the actor who plays her in Niki Caro's film *Whale Rider*?
42. What are the five dominant trends in New Zealand experimental filmmaking identified by Martin Rumsby?
43. Poet Allen Curnow is the subject of which documentary by Shirley Horrocks?
44. What is the name of the production company set up by Shuchi Kothari and Sarina Pearson in 1999?
45. Why do aliens take over the town of Kaihoro in Peter Jackson's first film *Bad Taste*?
46. What term was coined to describe Peter Jackson's early genre-bending films *Bad Taste*, *Meet the Feebles*, and *Braindead*?
47. What was the title of Sam Neill's 1995 documentary about New Zealand cinema for the BFI's A Century of Cinema project?
48. Described as 'New Zealand's unofficial national anthem', the song 'Slice of Heaven' was the theme song of which animated film?
49. Which composer and songwriter has written music for films including *An Angel at My Table*, *Out of the Blue*, *Show of Hands* and *No. 2*?
50. Who plays the scientist Zac Hobson in Geoff Murphy's *The Quiet Earth* (1985)?

Answers

1. The National Film Unit of New Zealand.
2. Norman Lindsay.
3. *Three to Go.*
4. Linda Hunt.
5. *Strictly Ballroom, William Shakespeare's Romeo + Juliet,* and *Moulin Rouge!*
6. Jill Bilcock.
7. The Drover.
8. Heather Rose.
9. Noah Taylor and Geoffrey Rush.
10. Jane Campion.
11. 1973.
12. *Birthday Boy.*
13. *The Story of the Kelly Gang.*
14. Tony Richardson and Mick Jagger.
15. Five (George Heath, Frank Hurley, Tasman Higgins, Bert Nicholas, John Heyer).
16. 'So Much Water So Close to Home', by Raymond Chandler.
17. Sam Worthington.
18. The glass shot.
19. The film received 11 nominations, but did not win a single award.
20. A group of late nineteenth century Australian painters including Tom Roberts, Frederick McCubbin and Arthur Streeton, whose subjects and characteristic use of light influenced the look of the AFC genre or period films of the 1970s and early 1980s.
21. Valentine's day, 14 February 1900.
22. Margaret Fink.
23. Roy 'Mo' Rene.
24. Three: *His Royal Highness; Harmony Row; A Ticket in Tatts.*
25. Graham 'Grace' Walker.
26. South Africa. He wants to marry Muriel to enable him to qualify for an Australian passport and thus be eligible to swim in the Olympics.
27. Danny Embling. *Flirting.*
28. Cate Shortland and Robert Humphreys.
29. *Black Water* and *Rogue.*
30. Kylie Minogue.
31. Michael and Peter.
32. Tiger.
33. No Fixed Address and Us Mob.
34. Toecutter and The Humungus.
35. A bequest in his father's will is conditional on him travelling to London to "further the cultural and intellectual traditions of the McKenzie dynasty".
36. Russell Boyd.
37. *Sleeping Dogs,* directed by Roger Donaldson.
38. Brad McGann.
39. Rena Owen (Beth Heke) and Temeura Morrison (Jake Heke).
40. Alun Bollinger.
41. Paikea, played by Keisha Castle-Hughes
42. Identity Politics; Landscape; Psychodramatic and Poetic; Visual Music; Installation and Expanded Cinema.

43. *Early Days Yet.*
44. Nomadz Productions.
45. To use the res dents as raw material for an inter-galactic fast food chain.
46. Splatstick.
47. *Cinema of Unease.*
48. *Footrot Flats.*
49. Don McGlashan.
50. Bruno Lawrence.

NOTES ON CONTRIBUTORS

Felicity Collins teaches Cinema Studies at La Trobe University and is the Chief Investigator of an Australian Research Council project on Australian Screen Comedy with Sue Turnbull and Susan Bye.

Adrian Danks is Senior Lecturer and Head of Cinema Studies in the School of Applied Communication, Royal Melbourne Institute of Technology (University). He is co-curator of the Melbourne Cinémathèque, and Cteq: Annotations on Film, and Australian Content editor for *Senses of Cinema*. He is currently writing several books, including one on the history and practice of home moviemaking in Australia.

Bonnie Elliott is an award-winning cinematographer. In 2008 she shot her debut feature film in Iran, for producers Julie Ryan and Kate Croser. *My Tehran for Sale* premiered at the 2009 Adelaide Film Festival.

Katie Ellis is a lecturer in the School of Media, Communication and Culture at Murdoch University in Western Australia, and the author of *Disabling Diversity* and *Disability & Web 2.0*. Her main areas of research focus on disability, cinema, and digital and networked media.

John Farnsworth teaches at the New Zealand Broadcasting School (Christchurch, NZ). He has written extensively on a wide variety of media and film areas. He also has continuing links with media industries.

Lisa French is Associate Professor in Cinema Studies, Media and Communication at RMIT University. She is the co-author of the books *Shining a Light: 50 Years of the Australian Film Institute* (2009) and *Womenvision: Women and the Moving Image in Australia* (2003).

Stephen Gaunson recently completed his PhD thesis on the Ned Kelly Movies in the School of Media & Communication at RMIT University. His work has been published in various cultural studies and film studies journals including *Screen Education*, *Metro*, and *Colloquy*.

Ben Goldsmith is a research fellow in the Centre for Critical and Cultural Studies, University of Queensland. He has published widely on Australian cinema and international film production. His latest book *Local Hollywood: Global Film Production and the Gold Coast* (with Susan Ward and Tom O'Regan) was published by University of Queensland Press in 2010.

Kristina Gottschall is a full-time PhD student at Charles Sturt University, Australia. Her doctoral research mobilizes theories on post-structuralism and pedagogy to (re)conceptualize Australian film culture as social practice geared towards the production of youth subjectivities. Kristina sees her work crossing the domains of education, cultural studies, film studies, gender studies, and cultural history. Her interests include film and popular culture, representations of gender and sexuality, and the politics of subjectivity. Kristina is currently the post-graduate representative of the Australian Association for Research in Education.

Fincina Hopgood is the Book Reviews Editor for *Senses of Cinema* (www.sensesofcinema.com) and a Fellow in the School of Culture and Communication at the University of Melbourne. She is writing a book, based on her PhD research, on the portrayal of mental illness in recent films from Australia and New Zealand.

Geoff Lealand is an Associate Professor, Screen and Media Studies, University of Waikato. He writes about, teaches, thinks about, and promotes television studies, media literacy, blogging and journalism, world cinema, New Zealand film, popular music, children and media--and composting.

Alfio Leotta is a PhD candidate in the Department of Film, Television and Media Studies at the University of Auckland. His primary research interests focus on the relationship between film and landscape, history of New Zealand cinema, and New Italian Cinema. His PhD is a study of film and tourism in New Zealand.

Ramon Lobato is a postdoctoral fellow with the ARC Centre of Excellence in Creative Industries and Innovation at the Institute for Social Research, Swinburne University of Technology. His research interests include film distribution and informal media economies

Harriet Margolis has published on New Zealand cinema, feminist film, Jane Austen adaptations, and women's romance novels. An editorial board member for *Screening the Past*, she has edited an anthology on *The Piano* for Cambridge University Press (2000), co-edited one on *The Lord of the Rings* phenomenon for Manchester University Press (2008), and is currently co-editing with Alexis Krasilovsky an anthology of interviews with international camerawomen.

Helen Martin has written extensively on New Zealand film since the 1980s. Her books include the award-winning *Shadows on the Wall: a study of seven New Zealand feature films*, co-written with Barbara Cairns, and *New Zealand Film, 1912–1996*, co-written with Sam Edwards.

Brian McDonnell is a Senior Lecturer in Media Studies at Massey University (Albany, New Zealand). He authored *Fresh Approaches to Film* and co-authored (with Geoff Mayer) the *Encyclopedia of Film Noir*.

Brian McFarlane is an Adjunct Associate Professor at Monash University. He has written widely on Australian and British film and is the co-editor of the *Oxford*

Companion to Australian Film (1999) and compiler, editor and chief author of *The Encyclopedia of British Film* (Methuen/BFI, 3rd edition 2008).

Neil Mitchell manages an independent videostore in Brighton, UK. He has a BA in Visual Culture and writes freelance on film. He has contributed reviews for the Cambridge film festival and essays and reviews in various volumes of the Intellect World Cinema Directory series.

Tony Mitchell is a Senior Lecturer in cultural studies and popular music at the University of Technology, Sydney. He is the author and editor of several books and has co-edited journals such *Perfect Beat*. He is currently editing a book on New Zealand music and has a website, Local Noise, on Australasian hip hop. www.localnoise.net.au

Martyna Olszowska is a PhD student in the Institute of Audiovisual Art, Jagiellonian University, Krakow, Poland. Her thesis focuses on contemporary Australian cinema. She is currently working on a book about Peter Weir.

Daniel Reynaud is an Associate Professor and Dean of the Faculty of Arts at Avondale College. He has published articles and books on Australian cinema's treatment of the Great War, and has worked with the National Film and Sound Archive of Australia in locating, identifying and partially reconstructing early silent war films.

Martin Rumsby is a film artist and writer from Auckland. Over the past decade he has been working on a cycle of landscape films. He has written extensively on his notions of film as art in *Millennium Film Journal*, *The Independent Eye* and *Illusions*.

Mark David Ryan is a research associate for the Queensland University of Technology, and a leading expert on Australian horror movies. Outside of academia, he is currently a researcher for John Jarratt's production company, Winnah Films, working on a feature film screenplay about 1960s' politics and Australia's involvement in the Vietnam War.

Lesley Speed is a lecturer at the University of Ballarat, Australia. Her research about comedy and youth film in Australia, the US and Britain has been published widely, and her current research centres on 1930s' Australian comedy films.

Deborah J Thomas has a PhD in Film, Media and Cultural Studies from the University of Queensland. She teaches at the University of Queensland and Queensland University of Technology, and has previously published on Ozploitation cinema.

Mandy Treagus is a Senior Lecturer in the School of Humanities at the University of Adelaide, where she teaches Pacific literature and film, and Victorian literature and culture. She is currently writing a cultural history of colonial displays of Pacific Islanders.

Fiona Trigg is Exhibitions Curator at the Australian Centre for the Moving Image, Melbourne.

Scott Wilson teaches film theory and history at the Unitec Department of Performing and Screen Arts (Auckland). His interests range widely across issues of hermeneutics, reception theories, fan cultures and object relations in a contemporary Western setting. He is currently writing a book on the cinema of David Cronenberg.

Bevin Yeatman is a Senior Lecturer in the Department of Screen and Media Studies, University of Waikato, where he teaches production, digital cinema and critical theory, with a particular interest in innovative approaches to teaching.

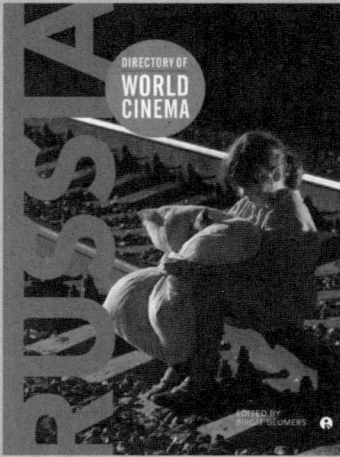

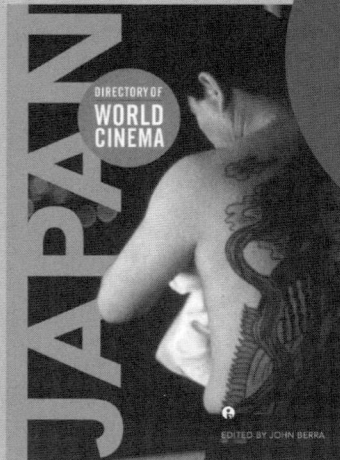

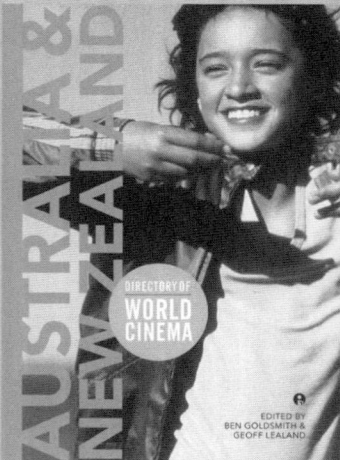